Grammar between Norm and Variation

VARIOLINGUA
NONSTANDARD - STANDARD - SUBSTANDARD

Herausgegeben von

Jörn Albrecht
Nelson Cartagena
Beat Glauser
Beate Henn-Memmesheimer
Jens Lüdtke
Klaus J. Mattheier
Baldur Panzer
Hubert Petersmann †
Edgar Radtke

Band 40

PETER LANG

Frankfurt am Main · Berlin · Bern · Bruxelles · New York · Oxford · Wien

Alexandra N. Lenz
Albrecht Plewnia
(eds.)

Grammar between
Norm and Variation

PETER LANG
Internationaler Verlag der Wissenschaften

Bibliographic Information published by the Deutsche Nationalbibliothek
The Deutsche Nationalbibliothek lists this publication in the Deutsche Nationalbibliografie; detailed bibliographic data is available in the internet at http://dnb.d-nb.de.

ISSN 1430-6778
ISBN 978-3-631-61004-6
© Peter Lang GmbH
Internationaler Verlag der Wissenschaften
Frankfurt am Main 2010
All rights reserved.

All parts of this publication are protected by copyright. Any utilisation outside the strict limits of the copyright law, without the permission of the publisher, is forbidden and liable to prosecution. This applies in particular to reproductions, translations, microfilming, and storage and processing in electronic retrieval systems.

www.peterlang.de

Contents

Alexandra N. Lenz & Albrecht Plewnia:
On Grammar between Norm and Variation 7

Markus Hundt:
New norms – How new grammatical constructions emerge 27

Beate Henn-Memmesheimer:
Ephemera and Tradition-Founding Grammatical Constructions:
Staging and Acceptance 59

Ulrich Busse & Anne Schröder:
Problem areas of English grammar between usage, norm, and variation 87

Renata Szczepaniak:
Während des Flug(e)s/des Ausflug(e)s? German Short and Long Genitive
Endings between Norm and Variation 103

Stephan Elspaß:
Regional Standard Variation in and out of Grammarian's Focus 127

Jürg Fleischer:
Norm and variation in the relative order of accusative and dative personal
pronouns in German: Evidence from corpora (18th–21st century) 145

Christa Dürscheid & Nadio Giger:
Variation in the case system of German – linguistic analysis and
optimality theory 167

Petra Campe:
Syntactic variation in German adnominal constructions: An application
to the alternatives 'genitive', 'apposition' and 'compound' 193

Joybrato Mukherjee:
Corpus-based Insights into Verb-complementational Innovations in Indian
English: Cases of Nativised Semantico-structural Analogy 219

Reinhard Goltz:
Norms and Variation in the Process of Modernizing and Vitalizing
the Low German Regional Language 243

Claudia Maria Riehl:
Norm and variation in language minority settings 275

Alexandra N. Lenz (Wien) & Albrecht Plewnia (Mannheim)

On Grammar between Norm and Variation

1. Introduction

Already thirteen years ago, the publishing company Peter Lang Verlag published a (German) volume with the title "Norm und Variation" ('Norm and Variation') (Mattheier (ed.) 1997). Klaus Mattheier, editor at that time, deliberately stuck to the order of the concepts 'norm' and 'variation' although, as he pointed out, that order is misleading:

> "Schon die Reihenfolge [...] suggeriert eine bestimmte strukturelle bzw. genetische Reihenfolge der Phänomene, die mit den Verhältnissen in der Sprachwirklichkeit nicht völlig übereinstimmt. Man wird zu der Vorstellung geführt, daß in einer Einzelsprache bzw. in der Sprache allgemein zuerst eine Sprachnorm gegeben ist und die Variation dieser nachgeordnet ist. Der Begriff 'Variation' suggeriert darüber hinaus, daß es eine Norm, einen Gebrauch, einen Usus in der Sprache geben muß, zu dem in der Sprachwirklichkeit beobachtbare sprachliche bzw. sprachsozioloigsche Phänomene 'eine Variation' bilden." (Mattheier 1997: 7) 'The order alone [...] suggests a certain order of the concepts in structure or their generation, which does not correctly correspond with the reality of language. It suggests that, in any given language or even in language in general, a given linguistic norm exists to which a variation is then subordinated. The concept of 'variation' further suggests that there must be a norm, a convention, a custom in this language to which some phenomena, linguistic or linguistic-sociological, are 'a variation'.'

We should, however, in fact turn the order around: It should rather be: 'variation and norm', or even better: 'diversity and norm', as it is primarily variation which is expressed in speech production and reception, and this variation "[wird] erst in einem zweiten Schritt durch die Alterität, den Bezug auf das soziale Gegenüber, in einem Usus bzw. in Normen ‚eingefangen'." (Mattheier 1997: 7).[1] Regardless of this fact, the pair of concepts 'norm and variation' has been established in exactly this order as a collocation,[2] and can therefore be found in the title of this volume.

Although the titles correspond, the volumes are quite different, particularly because our volume focuses on the systematic level of grammar. The volume

---

[1] 'Only in a second step is it 'caught' by alterity, by reference to the social counterpart, in a custom, i.e. a norm.'

[2] With regard to German, the preference is clear: A Google search (14th April 2010) returned 12,600 results for the German sequence of terms "Norm und Variation" in this order, while only 201 results for "Variation und Norm" came up. The English term "norm and variation" mirrors this preference with 60,600 results, outnumbering "variation and norm" which achieved 41,300 hits.

published in 1997 contains – in addition to a larger number of theoretical contributions – empiric investigations dealing almost exclusively with phonetico-phonological phenomena of norm and variation. Only very marginally are other systematic levels discussed. Syntax is a neglected field within the study of linguistic variation, which certainly is partly based on the belief (appearing in literature again and again) that „Syntax ist prinzipiell weniger variabel als Phonetik und Morphologie und daher auch weniger funktionell einsetzbar." (Henn-Memmesheimer 1997: 55)[3] One of the declared objectives of this volume is to empirically tackle the thesis that syntax offers few possibilities of variation.

Analysing the relationships between norm, variation and grammar, we have taken on a field of study which emerged only recently: While the potentially conflicting concepts of norm and variation have often been the focus of many sociolinguistic and other variation studies, such studies are rarely based on the linguistic level of grammar, and even less rarely on syntax. A look into grammar-oriented research literature demonstrates that an interest in variation has only emerged over the previous decades and significantly increased only today. As it is socioculturally determined, a discussion of norms always has to take existing sociocultural backgrounds into consideration. Taking this into account, the discussion and the examples used below – just as the other contributions to the volume – limit themselves to two large modern European languages, mainly German and secondly also English. There is an abundant number of sociolinguistic studies on these languages which may be woven into the discussion.

The present contribution consists of two main parts: The first main part (section 2) focuses first on the concept of norm in general and then on language norms in particular (section 2.1). The objective of our discussion is to sketch, in consideration of the background of current research literature, some crucial elements of (language) norms which are relevant to the context as a whole. Subsequently, we give attention to the phenomenon of grammatical variation which turns out to have become increasingly often a subject of linguistic research and even of public language awareness (section 2.2). The second main part (section 3) deals with fundamental research questions which are also examined by the other contributions to the volume. In theoretical discussions as well as specific empirical analyses on English and German, they epitomise the complex relationship between norm and variation.

---

[3] 'Syntax is principally less variable than phonetics and morphology, and it is therefore more difficult to use it functionally.'

2. Norm and Variation

2.1 On Language Norms and their Characteristics

The first contribution to this volume (by Markus Hundt) deals with some very fundamental questions on the topic of language norms and their characteristics. At this point, we will only mention some selected aspects of this field which contribute to the theoretical classification of the complete volume.

As language norms constitute norms whose reference object is language – defined in simplified terms – basic features of norms also apply to the discussed concept of language norms.[4] Thinking about norms and their nature regularly leads to their social conditional factors and value as their main characteristics,[5] in a very basic manner, as Takahashi puts it:

> "The term 'norm' [...] generally stands for a measure or criterion for something which gives guidelines for people's acts and forbearances [...]. Out of technical or social necessities, common values come into existence, which are shared and diffused among the community members. When they are internalised and on the whole observed by the members, they are described as „norms", some of which might be officially or unofficially codified in order to clarify the contents and meet the needs of inquiry and promulgation." (Takahashi 2004: 172)

Gloy represents a similar approach. He focuses on obligation as the key element through which norms function:

> "Eine Norm *i. e. S.* ist der intentionale Sachverhalt einer Verpflichtung (Obligation). Das konstitutive Merkmal 'Obligation' bedeutet: eine Norm verkörpert zwar häufig, aber keineswegs ausschliesslich ein Richtigkeits- bzw. Korrektheitsurteil; ihr Verpflichtungscharakter kann z.B. auch das Zweckmässige, das Angemessene, das Legale o. a. betreffen. Das Merkmal 'Intentionalität' bedeutet u.a.: für die Existenz einer Norm ist ihre Formuliertheit (oder gar Statuiertheit) nicht ausschlaggebend. – Normen sind inhaltlich bestimmte Regulative, die sich auf die Ausführung oder Unterlassung bestimmter Handlungen und Handlungssequenzen beziehen können ('Handlungs- und Verfahrens-Normen'), auf die Auswahl und Verwendung bestimmter Mittel, die eine Handlung erst konstituieren bzw. ihren Vollzug ermöglichen ('Instrumental-Normen'), auf die Beschaffenheit eines Handlungsergebnisses ('technische oder Produkt-Normen'), schliesslich auf die Inhalte des Denkens, Wünschens, Bewertens und Interpretierens sowie die Form ihrer Entäusserung." (Gloy 2004, 392) 'A norm in the narrower sense is the intentional circumstance of an obligation. The constitutive element of 'obligation' means that a norm often, but not always, typifies a judgement on accuracy or correctness; its obligation element may however also concern the appropriate, adequate, legal or similar. The element of 'in-

---

[4] Alternative, norm-related concepts are not discussed here; in this respect cf. Gloy 2004: 392 et seq. and Takahashi 2004: 172 et seq.

[5] Dovalil (2006: 12-36) provides an extensive overview of other norm definitions. Markus Hundt's article gives a theoretical discussion of the concept of norm (in this volume).

tentionality' means, inter alia, that it is not decisive for a norm's existence that it has been expressed (possibly even as a statute). Norms are regulative principles, defined by their content, which can relate to the execution or failure of actions or sequences of actions ('norms of actions and procedures'), to the selection and use of certain measures constituting an action or enabling their execution ('instrumental norms'), to the state of a result of an action ('technical norm or product norm'), and finally to the contents of thinking, wishing, evaluating and interpreting, as well as the form expressing them.'

In order to assess language norms, it is further significant to consider that they are acquired as social facts (cf. also Labov 2001: 427-429).

"Social life, including language usage, is governed by norms – socially shared concepts of appropriate and expected behaviour. The most basic of these concepts are acquired in early childhood through socialisation. In the case of language norms this means that the first language norms adopted are the ones of everyday spoken language. Compared to the prescriptive norms of the standardised language, these uncodified norms are perhaps less conscious yet more natural […] in every sense of the word: they are more numerous, acquired earlier in life and mastered by all native speakers. […] Norms are inherently social." (Kauhanen 2006: 34)

Language norms can thus be described as a specific type of social norms:

"Unter die […] *sozialen* Normen fallen als Teilmenge die *Sprachnormen*. Letztere sind Erwartungen […] und/oder explizite Setzungen deontischer Sachverhalte, die ihrem Inhalt zufolge die Bildung, Verwendungsabsicht, Anwendung und Evaluation sprachlicher Einheiten der verschiedensten Komplexitätsgrade regulieren (sollen)." (Gloy 20004: 394) '*Language norms* are a subset of *social norms*. They are expectations […] and/or explicit settings of deontic circumstances which (intend to) regulate, according to their content, establishment, purpose of usage, application, or evaluation of linguistic elements at numerous levels of complexity.'

As a consequence, as rules, they have to reach a certain level of abstractness, and violations may be socially sanctioned:

"Eine Sprachnorm ist eine historisch veränderliche und aufgrund der Reflexion sozialer Phänomene intersubjektiv existierende Bewusstseinskomponente, die als Regulator sprachlicher Erwartungen und Handlungen funktioniert und die sich auf gleichartige und zahlenmäßig nicht näher bestimmbare Kommunikationssituationen bezieht. Die Verletzung der Sprachnorm beschert dem Sprachbenutzer gewisse (negative) Folgen." (Dovalil 2006: 26) 'A language norm is an awareness component that changes historically and exists, due to the reflection of social phenomena, intersubjectively. Its function is to regulate linguistic expectations and actions, and it relates to communication situations equal in type but indeterminable in number. A violation of a language norm leads to (negative) consequences for the language user.'

The decisive element that distinguishes language norms from other norms is their reference object: Language norms codify language and language behaviour. They may refer to an entire language system (e.g. German), to one part of an entire language (e.g. standard language(s) or non-standard varieties, such as dialects, sociolects or technical languages), or even to individual phenomena.

They refer to aspects such as phrasing, adequacy of situation and evaluation of language. Norms are negotiated behaviour regularities of social groups. In case of language norms, speaker communities constitute such social groups. Language norms fulfil numerous functions: They function as aids to orientation, behaviour guidelines and evaluation standards, both for the speaking individual or for its speaker community, and for norm authorities who check, evaluate and sanction the respective social actions. As the foreword of the renowned German dictionary Duden shows in its first edition, language norms are further assigned forces of language cultivation and even language maintenance:

> "Die Sprache unserer Zeit bedarf in der Schule, noch mehr im Leben, wenn jeder äußere Zwang gefallen zu sein scheint, sorgsamer Pflege und treuer Hut, um vor Willkür, Verwahrlosung und Verflachung geschützt zu sein. [...] Es geht um das Bestehen der deutschen Sprache überhaupt." (Duden-Grammatik [1]1935: Foreword)
> 'The language of our time requires in school, even more so in life, when all exterior constraints seem to have fallen away, careful cultivation and devoted guard in order to be protected from caprice, neglect and growing shallowness. [...] The continued existence of the German language itself is at issue.'

Just as norms in general, language norms show various levels of validity which may or may not correlate with different types of codifications and sanctions. Language norms – as social norms – exist in an articulated and non-articulated form. Among articulated norms, codified norms constitute a specific type. They are not only expressed but also fixed in writing, for example "in legalising files of authorised organisations ('stated norms') or in non-legalising files of other exercising authorities ('informal norms'). Dictionaries play an outstanding role here." (Gloy 2004: 394).[6] In general, modern European languages have developed codes for the linguistic core areas of their standard languages (pronunciation, grammar, lexis, in particular orthography). The status of a language does, however, not depend on the codification of a language, as, for example, Lower German (cf. Goltz [in this volume]) or Luxemburgian (Letzebuergesch) proof. The language norms of Luxemburgian have been negotiated and put into writing only over the last decades (cf. Gilles/Moulin 2003).

While varieties of standard languages are generally based on codified norms, the norms of non-standard varieties are frequently "subsistent": "The underlying rules do not exist in writing, so that speakers cannot draw back on them to correct their own norms. [...] Standard varieties, on the other hand, have an abundance of rule sets [...]. The codes are used as correctives in countless situations and are binding on official institutions." (Huesmann 1998: 19) The validity of subsistent norms (or „covert norms", Labov 2001: 215-222) is not determined and supported by official institutions but by (partially unconsciously) inherited

---

[6] On the various types of norms also cf. v. Polenz 1999: 229 et seq. and Hundt (in this volume).

conventions, values and expectations of the social group who considers the subsistent norms binding.

How valid a norm is can, inter alia, be expressed by the sanctions applied in case of a norm violation. For example, if the grammaticality of a sentence is violated, it is clearly marked as "mistake" in a school essay, influencing the grade. On the other hand, if, due to context, a standard language version is used rather than the local dialect, this choice might be interpreted as disloyalty towards local communities, even leading to an exclusion of the group which is loyal to its dialect (cf. Lenz 2003). Existence and validity of norms become apparent when they are violated. Violations of norms and the sanctions accompanying them therefore essentially influence the constitution of norms. The complex functions of violations of norms in the network of grammaticality, acceptability and the setting up of language norms are dealt with in Markus Hundt's contribution (in this volume). A decisive fact in the discussion of language norms is that the question of norm-compliant or norm-violating language usage can in general only be answered in consideration of the specific situation. What is sanctioned as a marked mistake in a written essay does not have to constitute a violation of a norm in a text message or family conversation. In such contexts, it might not be punished by sanctions and, on the contrary, might be assessed as perfectly adequate communication. Compliance with norms and consequences of norm violations are further controlled by aspects of attitude. If, for example, a language or variety carries a positive evaluative-attitudinal charge, its use can be tolerated or even looked upon favourably, even though the norm stipulates a different language behaviour for just these situations or contexts. The "Covert Prestige" (Trudgill 1983) of non-standard language elements can decisively contribute to the enforcement of destandardisation processes (cf. Auer 1997, Mattheier/Radtke (eds.) 1997, Deumert/Vandenbussche (eds.) 2003, Daneš 2006, Mattheier 1997, Spiekermann 2005). For example, Daneš (1968/1982) states a decreasing competence in and prestige of the standard among the Czech younger generation. Extralingual factors such as increasing social mobility, and growing norm scepticism contribute to the questioning of the validity and legitimisation of standard varieties and to the popularisation and deliteralisation that accompany a loosening of language norms.

At first glance, norm and variation may seem to be opposite terms. *Variation* (see section 2.2) means the existence of the possibility to choose; it means dynamics, while *norm* stands (rather) for the opposite, for stability and statics, as it is highlighted by Hermann Paul (1970: 404):

> "[Eine i]deale Norm [...] gibt an, wie gesprochen werden soll. Sie verhält sich zu der wirklichen Sprechtätigkeit etwa wie ein Gesetzbuch zu der Gesamtheit des Rechtlebens in dem Gebiete, für welches das Rechtbuch gilt, oder wie ein Glaubensbekenntnis, ein dogmatisches Lehrbuch zu der Gesamtheit der religiösen Anschauungen und Empfindungen. Als eine solche Norm ist die Gemeinsprache wie ein Gesetzbuch oder ein Dogma an sich unerveränderlich. Veränderlichkeit würde

ihrem Wesen schnurstracks zuwider laufen. Wo eine Veränderung vorgenommen wird, kann sie nur durch eine ausserhalb der Norm stehende Gewalt aufgedrängt werden." '[An i]deal norm [...] determines how one should speak. It is to real speech activities what a code of law is to the entirety of legal life in the area where the code of law applies, or what a creed, a dogmatic textbook is to the entirety of religious beliefs and sentiments. As such a norm, standard language itself is unchangeable, just as a code of law or a dogma. Changeability would straightway run contrary to its essence. Wherever a change is applied, it can only be imposed by a force outside the norm.'

Language can be such a force, or more exactly: the potential dynamic that is inherent to language, which is also mentioned in the foreword of the 1959 edition of the Duden-Grammatik (The editor's foreword [i.e. Paul Grebe]):

"Wer Tag für die Tag die zahlreichen Anfragen überprüfen kann, die aus allen Kreisen der Sprachgemeinschaft bei uns eingehen, erfährt am besten die Wahrheit des Humboldt Wortes, daß die Sprache kein Ergon (Werk, statisches Gebilde), sondern eine Energeia (wirkende Kraft) ist, die das 'Worten der Welt' (Weisgerber) täglich neu vollzieht." (Duden-Grammatik ²1959: 7) 'Who reviews the numerous queries we receive from all parts of the language community every day, experiences the truth of Humboldt's saying best: that language is not an ergon (work, static structure) but energeia (acting force), performing the "wording of the world" (Weisgerber) anew every day.'

If language norms want to "keep up" with their reference objects, they will have to adjust to their continuously changing objects or even precede them – promptly, with delay or anticipating.[7] They are thus only limitedly static and, just as their reference object language indeed "historically changeable" (Dovalil 2006: 26). This applies to norms of both general language and technical language. Research literature leads a controversial discussion about what exactly happens when norms change and new norms emerge, and about their trigger moments and driving factors (cf. also Hundt [in this volume]). According to Gloy (2004: 397), "[w]hat was first made usable for the change of language (Keller 1990), [...]" can be "extended to the genesis of norms. Their derivation from undiscovered habitual processes [...] could be an opportunity to incorporate pre-normative normalities ("regularities") and a subsequently conscious normalisation into a uniform concept of norms, and to account for the dialectic of standardised and standardising processes."

2.2 Grammatical Variation as an Increasing Research Laboratory and Topic of "Laymen"

In the context of current sociopragmatic research results, Peter von Polenz (2000: 28) finds that variation is – in addition to economics, evolution and inno-

---

[7] Please refer to Gloy 2004: 396 et seq. for a critical discussion of the emergence and change of norms.

vation – one of the main factors that cause changes of language and any associated dynamics of linguistic norms. Subject to conditions and goals of communication, language users chose, knowingly or unknowingly, available linguistic means which serve – more or less successfully – to fulfill their sociopragmatic, communicative or other demands. In the field of linguistics, it is mainly due to William Labov (see especially 1966, 1972, and more recently 1994 and 2001) that variability and variation have been recognised to be inherent characteristics of language, or speech, through which they moved into the focus of linguistic research (cf. Milroy/Milroy 1997). While variability refers to the general coexistence of alternative language units in a heterogeneous system and in its varieties, variation means the concrete realisation of variability in concrete language use.

Variation and norm are both constants of human existence: the search for the other possibility, being as a variation comprised in every system including grammar, on the one hand; norms as a social fact on the other hand, making reactions to linguistic acts predictable and thereby making linguistic acts themselves calculable. As we have seen above, the term *norm*, being used as a social (and not primarily linguistic) concept, not only covers directive norms aiming at a codified standard enforced by strong social obligations. It expressively also includes subsistent norms which support every variety, every system; norms to which speakers adhere, more or less consciously. In this meaning, variation not only comprises varying forms or, respectively, cognitive semantic concepts side by side, but also a complex and dynamic system of coexistent and possibly clashing norms with a different status and a different (a.o. local, social) range each, one of which often but not necessarily comes with high social prestige, being the standard norm.

A review of current linguistic research shows that grammar and especially syntax of non-standard varieties is a young but increasingly important research field. In linguistic subdisciplines like syntactic theory and typology, we can observe a growing interest in language (micro-)variation and empirical data (see for example, Barbiers [et al.] (eds.) 2008). The fact that areal varieties, and among them especially dialects are a rich source of data is likewise increasingly recognised and promotes the inclusion of especially syntax into areas of linguistic inquiry that traditionally focused more on other linguistic levels, notably phonetics/phonology, morphology, and the lexicon. With regard to the dialect syntax of West Continental Germanic languages, only few completed or ongoing projects exist. These include the *Syntactische Atlas van de Nederlandse Dialecten (SAND)*, which started from an explicitly theoretical interest in microvariation but which also addressed the dialectological need for data from areal variation. The SAND project also implemented standards for the electronic acquisition and availability of data via databases and online language maps (see Barbiers/Cornips/Kunst 2007). Concerning the German language area, only three syntax projects covering smaller dialect areas can be mentioned up to now. Among them, the *Syntaktischer Atlas der Deutschen Schweiz (SADS)* definitely ranks first (see Bucheli/Glaser 2002). Besides SADS, the *Sprachatlas von Niederbayern (SNiB)*, a subproject of the *Bayerischer Sprachatlas*, included a limited number of syntactic phenomena (cf. Eroms [et al.] 2006). Thirdly, the project on "Syntax hessischer Dialekte (SyHD)" may be noted whose work started in summer 2010 (under the direction of Jürg Fleischer (Marburg), Alexandra N. Lenz (Vienna), Helmut Weiß (Frankfurt)). Aside from these atlas projects for Dutch and German dialects, other syntax projects on European languages are currently underway (http://www.dialectsyntax.org/). Most of these projects are part of the research network "EdiSyn (European Dialect Syntax)" established by Sjef Barbiers (Meertens Instituut, Amsterdam). Apart from the European atlas projects, a number of smaller dialect syntactic studies from various perspectives have been carried out during the last decades, including: Abraham/Bayer (eds.) 1993, Penner (eds.) 1995, Weiß 1998, Ledgeway 2000, Barbiers/Cornips/van der Kleij (eds.) 2002, Cornips/Corrigan 2005, Fleischer 2002, Seiler 2003, Dubenion-Smith 2007. In these works, linguists from very different disciplines (syntacticians, dialectologists, typologists, variationist linguists, sociolinguists and historical linguists) collaborate because dialects offer a unique empirical basis for the analysis of syntactic phenomena.

What was outlined with regard to dialects also applies to the registers in close-to-standard areas. For example, research into the variation of German everyday language or colloquial German has almost completely been limited to lexis and pronunciation. "Variation in grammar, however, has gone almost unnoticed." (Elspaß [in this volume]). One of the first approaches aiming at closing this gap in research is the *"Atlas zur deutschen Alltagssprache (AdA)"* (atlas on German everyday language), available online under <http://www.uni-augsburg.de/alltagssprache>. Stephan Elspaß presents the abundance of its productive data and mapped results (in this volume).

Also variation on the level of grammar in standard language, or at least close-to-standard language registers, attracts growing interest. The Institut für Deutsche Sprache in Mannheim, Germany, provides a good example: It currently carries out a project on "Grammatische Variation im standardnahen Deutsch (Vorstudien zu einer 'Korpusgrammatik')" ('Grammar Variation in close-to-standard German [Preliminary Studies for a 'Corpus Grammar']'):

> "Ziel des Projekts ist die korpusgestützte Erforschung der Variation im standardnahen Deutsch (einschließlich der Variation im Standard selbst), die längerfristig eine Grundlage für die Erstellung einer Grammatik des Deutschen bilden soll, in der – entgegen der bisher in der Grammatikographie gängigen Praxis – die Variation im Sprachgebrauch gezielt fokussiert und umfassend aufgearbeitet wird."[8] 'The goal of the project is to use corpora to study variation as expressed in close-to-standard lan-

---

[8] http://www.ids-mannheim.de/gra/korpusgrammatik.html (14th April 2010)

guage (including the variation in standard German itself). In the long run, the study will form a basis for the composition of a German grammar which – contrary to the common method in grammaticography – will focus on and comprehensively investigate variation in language use.'

Just as the articles of the present volume, the mentioned projects are evidence of how productive comprehensive corpus analyses on grammatical variation are in synchrony and diachrony. As the goal of the above mentioned project to create a "grammar of language use" shows, the results of the study of grammar focusing on variation increasingly influence even the codification of linguistic norms themselves. The intention to link codified norms to the reality of language is also expressed in the foreword of the most recent Duden Grammar:

"Die Dudengrammatik *beschreibt* die geschriebene und die gesprochene Standardsprache der Gegenwart. Dabei fußt sie auf dem aktuellen Forschungsstand. [...] Besonderes Gewicht haben Autoren und Redaktion außerdem auf die Analyse *aktueller Sprachbelege* und die entsprechende Auswahl an Beispielen gelegt. Durch das Dudenkorpus und modernste elektronische Suchmöglichkeiten konnten große Mengen aktueller Texte, besonders aus der Presse und dem Internet, ausgewertet werden." (Duden-Grammatik [8]2009: Foreword, highlighted by A. N. L./A. P.) 'The Duden-Grammatik *describes* written and spoken contemporary standard language. It is based on the status of current research. [...] Authors and editors attached particular importance to the analysis of *current linguistic evidence* and a respective selection of examples. By means of the Duden Corpus and state-of-the-art search technologies, large amounts of current texts, in particular from media and the Internet, could be analysed.'

However, an increasing interest in grammatical (micro-)variations and empirical data on grammar is not only found within linguistic research. Also laymen, the speakers themselves and the non-linguistic public, exhibit an increasing interest in grammatical questions, as the popularity of popular science 'guidebooks' or other descriptions of grammatical 'oddities' reflects. Books and series of books such as "*Der Dativ ist dem Genitiv sein Tod*" by Bastian Sick (2004 et seq.) as regards German, and "Shoots and Leaves. The Zero Tolerance Approach to Punctuation" by Lynne Truss (2005) as regards English bring phenomena and, at the same time, (supposedly?) valid norms and their violations to the attention of individuals and the community.[9] As regards standard language, "those seeking advice" may also directly consult legitimate norm authorities or draw upon their written codes (normative dictionaries and grammars) in cases of doubt. A large number of reference books and guidebooks exists for standard contemporary German and English, all of them more or less legitimate and well-known. The broad range is completed by institutionalised contact points dealing with written and oral enquiries. The *Gesellschaft für deutsche Sprache* and the editorial de-

---

[9] Among linguistic experts, popular scientific guidebooks often provoke criticism, cf. for example the discussion on Bastian Sick's collection of columns at Maitz/Elspaß (2007), or, even more pronounced, Meinunger (2008).

partment of Duden offer their help with all questions on standard German. It is clearly more difficult for consulters to find assistance with a minority language, linguistic enclave or an institutionalised second-language variety (cf. Goltz [in this volume], Riehl [in this volume] and Mukherjee [in this volume]). Written sets of rules on grammar are in general neither available for dialects and colloquial languages. Exceptions to the rule are areal varieties with supra-regional popularity which – in the age of the Internet – frequently have online platforms, providing them with a more or less official character.[10]

3. Current Research Questions (on this Volume)

The present volume aims at giving an insight on the complex interaction between language norms on the one hand and grammatical variation on the other hand, using two closely related modern European languages, German (High German and Low German) and English as examples. We intend to trace out more clearly the multi-dimensional area of conflict in its diverse possibilities resulting from the existence of varying forms and differing norms. Eleven articles in total are intended to show exemplary and from different perspectives with fittingly selected issues from morphology, morpho-syntax, morpho-phonology, and syntax of especially German (with 9 articles) and secondly also English (with 2 articles) with their respective varieties what different types of constellation can be formed, how norm and variation influence each other, and finally, how this interaction can promote processes of linguistic change. The articles of the volume cover different approaches to the matter. We set value in a proper balance of the subject matters morphology, morpho-syntax, syntax in an embracement of historic perspectives along with the description of processes of linguistic changes, as well as that analyses and reflections referring to single phenomena are accompanied by corpus analyses with statistic value, and finally in a continuous representation of the object languages German and English (with their respective varieties).

Mainly four central topic areas are examined. They are outlined below, explicitly referring to the articles of this volume: firstly, emergence and change of norms and grammatical constructions; secondly, the question of the relationship between codes of norms on the one hand and real language usage on the other hand; thirdly, the competition or co-existence of standard and non-standard language norms; and finally, fourthly, the special situation of subsistent norms in minority languages (regional languages, linguistic enclaves) and "institutionalised second-language varieties".

---

[10] An example is the online appearance of the "Akademie för uns kölsche Sproch" (Acadamy of the dialect Kölsch) where it is possible to graduate with *Kölsch-Abitur* and even *Kölsch-Examen* (http://koelschakademie.finbot.com/).

(1) On Emergence and Change of Norms and Grammatical Constructions

The main questions arising here are: How do new norms emerge? What roles do factors of acceptability and frequency of a linguistic unit play? Which "new" grammatical phenomena have the stamina to become a norm? What do these phenomena have what linguistic "flashes in the pan" don't have? What do violations of norms contribute to the emergence of new norms and change of existing norms? What factors motivate, support and control violations of norms?

In his article, **Markus Hundt** argues that in the end, violations of norms substantially contribute to the fact that speakers become at all aware of the existence and validity of norms. Violations of norms and the accompanying sanctions thus also influence the constitution of norms. Accordingly, the speakers themselves have a decisive influence on emergence, stabilisation and change of norms. An analysis of norms thus has to include this "linguistic sovereign" (Ammon 1995) as a central moment. With regard to German and its standard variety (varieties)[11], fixed and prescriptive norms only exist fully for orthography and partially for orthoepy. However, descriptive norms can also be found for other system levels, for example lexis or grammar. In general, more than giving strict behaviour instructions, they intend to be of "practical aid" (Duden ^{8}2009: Foreword) in cases of doubt.

An essential difference between codified, prescriptive and authorised norms on the one hand and descriptive norms offering guidance on the other hand is, according to Hundt, how explicit the norm is expressed, rather than the claim for validity of both norm types. As he illustrates on the basis of "weird", that is relatively young and not fully accepted syntactic German constructions, syntax, syntactic variation and syntactic norms are a fruitful field of study for the emergence and change of language norms.

In her study, **Beate Henn-Memmesheimer** shows that it is possible that certain phenomena which do not comply with norms are not really "violations of norms". Her contribution is concerned with grammatical innovations whose semantic/constructional patterns correspond to existing non-conforming patterns of standard German. Growing acceptance, increasing frequency of use and situational contexts of the innovations she analyses are explained by processes of grammaticalisation and exaptation.

(2) On the Relationship of Codes of Norms and 'Real' Language Usage

The second topic area focuses on the relationship between codified norms on the one hand and real language usage by speakers and writers on the other hand. In what relationship are language norms, and how do they correlate? Do codes of norms allow for statements and conclusions on real language usage? How does

---

[11] On the question if any and if so, how many standard varieties exist in German, cf. Ammon (1995), Schmidt (2005).

real language usage influence emergence and change of language norms? What kind of influence would be helpful? How can "long-term variabilities" in standard language registers be explained, although codified norms of the standard language provide for binding rules supporting one version?

Ulrich Busse and **Anne Schröder** concentrate on the question to what extent codes of norms reflect actual language usage. On the basis of several usage guides and grammar books, they examine whether a change with regard to norms and the acceptability of language variation has taken place over the last century in these publications. Then they compare the results of their studies to 'real language' by looking at real usage in the framework of an extensive corpus analysis. It turns out that the English reference works they used for selected "cases of doubt" provide data that are surprisingly close to the actual language usage.

At times, it is not only reasonable but necessary to consider empirical material when determining norms, as **Renata Szczepaniak**'s contribution (among others) illustrates. In her study on the variation of genitive forms of nouns, Szczepaniak inquires preferences of morphological form alterations within flexion classes which have risen themselves from a long lasting modification process in the phonological system. The variation of the genitives *-es* and *-s*, still present in contemporary German, is a phenomenon which remains insufficiently described in contemporary grammar books, making it hard to follow particularly for non-native speakers. Only comprehensive empirical analyses, as Szczepaniak provides them, disclose precise (phonological) control factors for both versions, which are essential to explain the variation and to formulate any rules or norms.

(3) On the Competition of Standard and Non-standard Language Norms

The co-existence and competition of codified norms in standard language on the one hand and usage norms on the other hand are the focus of the third topic area. How do norms of standard language relate to the in general subsistent norms of non-standard varieties (particularly dialects and regiolects)? What role does areal variation play in this competitive situation, also in the awareness of speakers? Where do reflections of areal variations appear in close-to-standard language? Where do subsistent and codified norms overlap? How can we approach subsistent norms empirically? Are there any deviations from standard which can be explained as systematic grammatical options?

It has been generally accepted that standard language and close-to-standard everyday language allows areal variation (cf. Milroy/Milroy 1985); the details, however, are widely unknown. In his contribution, **Stephan Elpaß** uses several case studies to examine the areal variation of standard German and close-to-standard everyday language, in the framework of his investigation of the "Atlas zur deutschen Alltagssprache". He shows that the data he collected empirically frequently do not correspond with the regionality markers in grammar books.

Jürg Fleischer deals with similar questions in his contribution on the relative order of accusative and dative personal pronouns in German. While the codified standard is relatively clear, data on real language usage are not. Taking various corpora into account, among them historical data, Fleischer is able to show that the factually existing variation is connected with the dialect structure of German.

The dynamic processes of language change are also examined by **Christa Dürscheid** and **Nadio Giger**. The system of case markers in the German flexion of nouns is relatively clearly determined by norms; although real language usage shows a certain degree of variation. In particular, Dürscheid and Giger show that many deviations from standard forms in the area of German noun flexions, which are evidenced in their data collection, can be justified in the framework of optimality theory.

Petra Campe is concerned with a completely different level of competing norms. In German, there are several ways to encode adnominal relations, e.g. by means of the case (mostly genitive), by prepositions or by paraphrasing constructions, such as compounds. However, these patterns are not completely equivalent. Campe illustrates their restrictions at individual cases and how their variations need to be modified.

(4) On Subsistent Norms of Minority Languages (Regional Languages, Linguistic Enclaves) and "Institutionalised Second-language Varieties"

The fourth large topic area focuses on the special situation of multilingualism. What are unique norm constellations and conflicts arising in multilingual communities? How are external and internal standards balanced in institutionalised second-language varieties, how in language minority settings? What do speakers of minority languages and speakers of their varieties use as orientation? What roles do umbrella standard languages play with regard to minority languages?

Joybrato Mukherjee shows in his contribution on verb-complementational innovations in Indian English how new regional standard forms establish. He puts into perspective innovative forms in standard Indian English in the area of verb complementation, including 'new' prepositional verbs, 'new' ditransitive verbs and 'new' light-verb constructions. These innovations indicate a certain degree of autonomy on the part of Indian users of English. Specifically, the new forms can be explained as exponents of rationally motivated analogies that Indian English speakers draw between existing formal and semantic templates in British English and the emerging new forms and structures in Indian English. The processes can be described as cases of nativised semantico-structural analogy. As the innovative forms discussed are low-frequency phenomena which are used alongside the standard 'native' variants, large corpora are needed to find authentic instances.

Another case which is extraordinarily interesting from a sociolinguistic point of view are languages which have no or only partially fixed norms, despite their official status as a language. One of those languages is Low German, discussed by **Reinhard Goltz** in his article. Numerous speakers of Low German think this language has no grammar. In fact, Low German has not developed any kind of standard. High German has, for several centuries, assumed the role of a standard language. The immediate neighbourhood of High and Low German in Northern Germany has led to a history of contact over centuries. Generally, structures of the prestigious High German influence elements of the regional language and their interaction. Considering sinking numbers of speakers and decreasing communications in Low German, the process is currently accelerating, i.e. the readiness of the speakers to take over such structural elements taken or derived from High German rises. On the one hand, the expected processes of convergences to New High German could be demonstrated in this structurally asymmetric constellation of Low German. On the other hand, there are multiple cases in which speakers choose hyper forms of Low German. Such hyper forms can be interpreted as a conscious rejection of and distance marker to High German. They also show, however, that speakers are (no longer) aware of the (subsistent) norms of Low German.

The relationship between Low German and High German is very insightful because both languages are historically closely related. Obviously, situations where varieties or languages are umbrellaed by a non-related standard language are also extremely interesting. Linguistic enclaves constitute such special cases, examined by **Claudia Maria Riehl** in her article. For the language learning process of speakers of linguistic enclave varieties, codified norms of the standard language of the country of origin usually play no or only a marginal role. Linguistic enclave communities develop their own subsistent norms. Quite frequently, language usage and the respective subsistent norms deviate significantly from the norms of the home country. As Riehl is able to show, several factors influence how close or distant norms of linguistic enclaves are to the norms of the home country. One of those factors is the language that serves as written language in the respective linguistic enclave.

The eleven articles collected in this volume thus offer the most various access to the discussed questions on norm and variation. In their entirety, they reflect the current discussion of the topic. Focusing on the object languages German and English ensures a high level of topical consistency. On the other hand, the four large topic areas (Emergence and Change of Norms and Grammatical Constructions; Relationship of Codes of Norms and 'Real' Language Usage; Competition of Standard and Non-standard Language Norms; and subsistent Norms of Minority Languages and "Institutionalised Second-language Varieties") cover a large range of relevant issues, thereby certainly giving an impetus to new and further investigations.

The contributions to this volume are based on selected lectures held during the 2007 annual conference of the Deutsche Gesellschaft für Sprachwissenschaft (DGfS) in Siegen, Germany, in the thematic session "Grammar Between Norm and Variation". Thanks are given to all participants of the thematic session who contributed to productive discussions and thereby to the success of this volume. We are obliged to Elke Joseph for critical comments (language and otherwise) and corrections. Thirdly and finally, our many thanks go to the editors of the serial VarioLingua for including this volume.

4. References

Abraham, Werner & Josef Bayer, eds. 1993. *Dialektsyntax* (Linguistische Berichte, Sonderheft 5). Opladen: Westdeutscher Verlag.

Ammon, Ulrich. 1995. *Die deutsche Sprache in Deutschland, Österreich und der Schweiz. Das Problem der nationalen Varietäten*. Berlin & New York: de Gruyter.

Auer, Peter. 1997. "Führt Dialektabbau zur Stärkung oder Schwächung der Standardvarietät? Zwei phonologische Fallstudien". *Standardisierung und Destandardisierung europäischer Nationalsprachen* ed. by K. J. Mattheier & E. Radtke, 129-162. Frankfurt/M.: Lang.

Barbiers, S., O. N. C. J. Koeneman, M. Lekakou & M. H. van der Ham. 2008. *Microvariation in Syntactic Doubling*. Amsterdam: Meertens Institute.

Barbiers, S., L. Cornips & J. P. Kunst. 2007. "The Syntactic Atlas of the Dutch Dialects (SAND): A corpus of elicited speech and text as an on-line Dynamic Atlas". *Creating and Digitizing Language Corpora: Vol. 1, Synchronic Databases* ed. by J. Beal, K. Corrigan & H. Moisl. Palgrave-Macmillan: Hampshire.

Barbiers, S., L. Cornips & S. van der Kleij, eds. 2002. *Syntactic Microvariation*. Amsterdam: Meertens Institute Electronic Publications in Linguistics, vol. II.

Bucheli, Claudia & Elvira Glaser. 2002. "The Syntactic Atlas of Swiss German Dialects: empirical and methodological problems". *Syntactic Microvariation* ed. by S. Barbiers, L. Cornips & S. van der Kleij, 41-74. Amsterdam: Meertens Institute Electronic Publications in Linguistics, vol. II.

Cornips, Leonie & K.P. Corrigan. 2005. *Syntax and Variation. Reconciling the Biological with the Social* (Current Issues in Linguistic Theory 265). Amsterdam & Philadelphia: John Benjamins.

Daneš, František. 1968/1982. "Dialektische Tendenzen in der Entwicklung der Literatursprachen". *Grundlagen der Sprachkultur, Teil 2* ed. by J. Scharnhorst & E. Ising, 92-113. Berlin: de Gruyter.

Daneš, František. 2006. "Herausbildung und Reform von Standardsprachen und Destandardisierung – Development and Reform of Standard Languages and Destandardization". *Sociolinguistics/Soziolinguistik. An International Handbool of the Science of Language and Society / Ein internationales Handbuch zur Wissenschaft von Sprache und Gesellschaft. Band 3, Teil 1. 2., vollständig neu bearbeitete und erweiterte Auflage* ed. by U. Ammon, N. Dittmar, K. J. Mattheier & P. Trudgill, 2197-2209. Berlin/New York: de Gruyter.

Deumert, Anna & Wim Vandenbussche, eds. 2003. *Germanic standardizations. Past to present.* Amsterdam & Philadelphia: John Benjamins.

Dovalil, Vít. 2006. *Sprachnormenwandel im geschriebenen Deutsch an der Schwelle zum 21. Jahrhundert. Die Entwicklung in ausgesuchten Bereichen der Grammatik* (Duisburger Arbeiten zur Sprach- und Kulturwissenschaft 63). Frankfurt/M.: Lang.

Dubenion-Smith, Shannon Andrew. 2007. *Verbal Complex Phenomena in the West Central German Dialects.* Dissertation, University of Wisconsin–Madison.

Duden-Grammatik. [1]1935. *Der große Duden. Grammatik der deutschen Sprache.* Bearb. von Otto Basler. Leipzig: Bibliographisches Institut.

Duden-Grammatik. [2]1959. *Grammatik der deutschen Gegenwartssprache* ed. by Dudenredaktion & P. Grebe (Der große Duden 4). Mannheim: Bibliographisches Institut.

Duden. [7]2005. *Die Grammatik. Unentbehrlich für richtiges Deutsch. Duden Band 4.* Mannheim & Leipzig & Wien & Zürich: Dudenverlag.

Duden. [8]2009. *Die Grammatik. Unentbehrlich für richtiges Deutsch. Duden Band 4.* Mannheim & Leipzig & Wien & Zürich: Dudenverlag.

Eroms, H. W., B. Röder & R. Spannbauer-Pollmann. 2006. *Bayerischer Sprachatlas. Sprachatlas von Niederbayern. Band 1: Einführung mit Syntaxauswertung.* Heidelberg: Winter.

Fleischer, Jürg. 2002. *Die Syntax von Pronominaladverbien in den Dialekten des Deutschen: eine Untersuchung zu Preposition Stranding und verwandten Phänomenen* (Zeitschrift für Dialektologie und Linguistik, Beihefte 123). Stuttgart & Wiesbaden: Steiner.

Gilles, Peter & Claudine Moulin. 2003. "Luxembourgish". *Germanic standardizations. Past to present* ed. by A. Deumert & W. Vandenbussche, 303-329. Amsterdam & Philadelphia: John Benjamins.

Gloy, Klaus. 2004. "Norm/Norm". *Sociolinguistics/Soziolinguistik. An International Handbool of the Science of Language and Society / Ein internationales Handbuch zur Wissenschaft von Sprache und Gesellschaft. Band 3, Teil 1. 2., vollständig neu bearbeitete und erweiterte Auflage* ed. by U. Ammon, N. Dittmar, K. J. Mattheier & P. Trudgill, 392-399. Berlin & New York: de Gruyter.

Henn-Memmesheimer, Beate. 1997. "Verwendung von Elementen des Standard-Nonstandard-Kontinuums als Ergebnis funktionaler Handlungswahl". *Norm und Variation* ed. by K. J. Mattheier, 53-68. Frankfurt/M.: Lang.

Huesmann, Anette. 1998. *Zwischen Dialekt und Stand: Empirische Untersuchung zur Soziolinguistik des Varietätenspektrums im Deutschen* (Reihe germanistische Linguistik 199). Tübingen: Niemeyer.

Kauhanen, Irina. 2006. "Norms and Sociolinguistic Description". *A Man of Measure. Festschrift in Honour of Fred Karlsson on his 60th Birthday* ed. by M. Sumoninen et al. 34-46. Turku: The Linguistic Association of Finland, Special Supplement to SKY Journal of Linguistics 19.

Keller, Rudi. 1990. *Sprachwandel: Von der unsichtbaren Hand in der Sprache*. Tübingen: Francke.

Labov, William. 1966. *The Social Stratification of English in New York City*. Washington, DC: Center or Applied Linguistics.

Labov, William. 1972. *Language in the Inner City: Studies in the Black Vernacular*. Philadelphia: University of Pennsylvania Press.

Labov, William. 1994. *Principles of Linguistic Change. Volume 1: Internal Factors*. Oxford: Blackwell.

Labov, William. 2001. *Principles of Linguistic Change. Volume 2: Social Factors*. Oxford: Blackwell.

Ledgeway Adam. 2000. *A Comparative Syntax of the Dialects of Southern Italy: A Minimalist Approach*. Oxford: Blackwell.

Lenz, Alexandra. 2003. *Struktur und Dynamik des Substandards. Eine Studie zum Westmitteldeutschen (Wittlich/Eifel)* (Zeitschrift für Dialektologie und Linguistik. Beihefte 125). Stuttgart: Steiner.

Maitz, Péter & Stephan Elspaß. 2007. "Warum der 'Zwiebelfisch' nicht in den Deutschunterricht gehört". *Informationen Deutsch als Fremdsprache* 34(5). 515-526.

Mattheier, Klaus J., ed. 1997. *Norm und Variation* (Forum Angewandte Linguistik 32). Frankfurt/M.: Lang.

Mattheier, Klaus & Edgar Radtke, eds. 1997. *Standardisierung und Destandardisierung europäischer Nationalsprachen* (VarioLingua 1). Frankfurt/M.: Lang.

Meinunger, André. 2008. *Sick of Sick? Ein Streifzug durch die Sprache als Antwort auf den "Zwiebelfisch"*. Berlin: Kadmos.

Milroy, James & Lesley Milroy. 1985. *Authority in Language. Investigating Language Prescription and Standardisation*. London & New York: Routledge & Kegan Paul.

Milroy, James & Lesley Milroy. 1997. "Varieties and Variation". *The Handbook of Sociolinguistics*. ed. by F. Coulmas, 47-64. Oxford: Blackwell.

Paul, Hermann. 1970. *Prinzipien der Sprachgeschichte*. Tübingen: Niemeyer.

Penner, Zvi, ed. 1995. *Topics in Swiss German Syntax*. Bern: Lang.

von Polenz, Peter. 1999. *Deutsche Sprachgeschichte. Vom Spätmittelalter bis zur Gegenwart. Band 3: 19. und 20. Jahrhundert.* Berlin: de Gruyter.

von Polenz, Peter. 2000. *Deutsche Sprachgeschichte. Vom Spätmittelalter bis zur Gegenwart. Band 1: Einführung. Grundbegriffe, Deutsch in der frühbürgerlichen Zeit.* Berlin: de Gruyter.

Schmidt, Jürgen Erich. 2005. "Die deutsche Standardsprache: Eine Varietät – drei Oralisierungsnormen". *Standardvariation – Wie viel Variation verträgt die deutsche Sprache?* (Jahrbuch des Instituts für Deutsche Sprache 2004) ed. by L. M. Eichinger & W. Kallmeyer, 278-305 Berlin: de Gruyter.

Seiler, Guido. 2003. *Präpositionale Dativmarkierung im Oberdeutschen* (Zeitschrift für Dialektologie und Linguistik. Beihefte 124). Stuttgart: Steiner.

Sick, Bastian. 2004. *Der Genitiv ist dem Dativ sein Tod. Ein Wegweiser durch den Irrgarten der deutschen Sprache.* Köln: Kiepenheuer & Witsch [and further volumes].

Spiekermann, Helmut. 2005. "Regionale Standardisierung, nationale Destandardisierung". *Wie viel Variation verträgt die deutsche Sprache?* (Jahrbuch des Instituts für Deutsche Sprache 2004) ed. by L. M. Eichinger & W. Kallmeyer, 100-125. Berlin: de Gruyter.

Takahashi, Hideaki. 2004. Language Norms/Sprachnorms. *Sociolinguistics/Soziolinguistik. An International Handbool of the Science of Language and Society / Ein internationales Handbuch zur Wissenschaft von Sprache und Gesellschaft. Band 3, Teil 1. 2., vollständig neu bearbeitete und erweiterte Auflage* ed. by U. Ammon, N. Dittmar, K. J. Mattheier & P. Trudgill, 172-179. Berlin & New York: de Gruyter.

Trudgill, Peter. 1983. *On Dialect. Social and Geographical Perspectives.* Oxford: Blackwell.

Truss, Lynne. 2005. *Eats, shoots & leaves: the zero tolerance approach to punctuation.* London: Profile Books.

Weiß, Helmut. 1998. *Syntax des Bairischen* (Linguistische Arbeiten 391). Tübingen: Niemeyer.

Wurzel, Wolfgang U. 1984. *Flexionsmorphologie und Natürlichkeit. Ein Beitrag zur morphologischen Theoriebildung* (Studia Grammatica 21). Berlin: Akademie-Verlag.

Markus Hundt (Kiel)

New norms –
How new grammatical constructions emerge

1. Types of language norms

How can we define what a language norm is? Previous literature on this subject shows clearly that there is no clearcut definition of language norm which is accepted uncontroversially by the linguistic community. On the other hand we have some aspects of language norms which are common sense and which are prominent in nearly every attempt to define language norms.

- *Obligation:* This is the deontic character of a language norm. Norms commit the speaker/writer to a specific language use. The language norm prescribes what is or is not permitted in language use.
- *The claim of validity and the application of the language norm:* Both are essential. Whether language norms are applied or not, it is crucial that the rules inherent in a norm are obligatory, i.e. that the language norms hold for the variety which is under control of the norm. Furthermore it is obvious – especially with respect to language norms – that the application of the norm is an essential part of the norm itself. That language users stick to the norms and that they expect this from the other language users creates what is called in language norm discussions the anticipation of an expected action ('Erwartungserwartung').
- *Sanctions* are also part of language norms. Part of their function is to maintain the norm, to force the subjects under the norm, and also to establish the norm as such. For example, violations of language norms are sanctioned in orthography, morphology, syntax, semantics and stylistics in school (by good or bad grades) or in professional contexts (e.g. by getting a job or not).
- *Associated values:* Language norms are closely associated with certain social values. Norms are not only constituted by rules of actions which emerge from frequent language use, norms are also associated with values, i.e. statements about the well-formedness (*langue*), the adequacy of language use in specific communicative situations ('Situationsangemessenheit') and therefore about legitimate (and illegitimate?) actions.
- *Explicitness of the norm:* Norms don't have to be put down in codices to claim validity or even to be applied. The codification of the norm is not an essential part of the norm itself. Language norms in particular are to some extent independent of their own codification. Of course there are codifications of language norms, e.g. the *Duden* for the German language. But – despite

the fact that the *Duden* is a descriptive grammar and therefore doesn't state or prescribe norms – language norms are applied even without codification. In addition to this we must take into account that there are various sections of the language system that aren't normed by acts of prescription. Only the German orthography and (partially) the orthoepy is under the control of a (more or less) fixed and prescriptive norm.

This list of common sense features of language norms isn't exhaustive. An acceptable definition of language norms has to be more specific in some respects. Therefore we want to discuss two attempts at modelling the area of (language) norms in more detail. First, an approach from language philosophy will be discussed (Georg Henrik von Wright). Second, we will look at a model which is focussed on the interrelation/interaction of the language system (langue) on the one hand and language use (parole) on the other ('System-Norm-Rede-Modell'). The first model has its advantages in defining all kinds of norm (a more general perspective). The second model focuses on three features of language norms specifically: the frequency of the constructions, the acceptability and the well-formedness with respect to the language system.

Features of norms and of language norms in the approach of Georg Henrik von Wright (1963/1979):

In his book *Norm and Action* G.H. von Wright discusses in minute detail the various aspects of norms. What he proposes is an analysis of the concept 'norm' and of its neighbours. Three related concepts are important for the notion of a norm (see Fig. 1).

related concept	maingroup of norms	subgroup of norms

law
- laws of nature: descriptive
- laws of the state: prescriptive
- laws of logic: a priori
(neither descriptive nor prescriptive)

moral principle

directive
= technical norm
- means of attaining a certain end
- neither descriptive nor prescriptive

norm ↔ **ideal rule**

prescription ← similar → **custom** ← similar → **rule**

- norm giver
- norm subjects
- norm promulgation
- sanction

- similar to norms
- normative pressure
- the norm isn't given to the norm subjects by a person/instituion etc.
→ **anonymous norms**
- don't have to be codified
→ **implicit prescriptions**

- rules of grammar → more flexible than the rules of a game

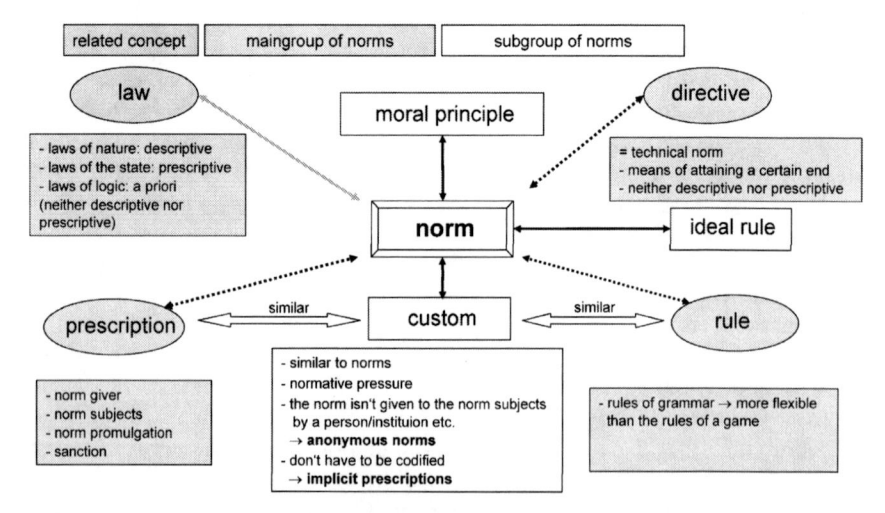

Figure 1: Types of norms: the meanings of "norm" (following von Wright 1963/1979)

The starting point is the concept LAW. Von Wright doesn't analyse this concept in detail at this point, but LAW is important for the discussion of the concept of NORM as a neighbouring or superordinate concept. He specifies three types of law: the laws of nature, the laws of the state, and the laws of logic. The laws of nature are of a descriptive kind, the laws of the state are of a prescriptive kind. The laws of logic are neither prescriptive nor descriptive, i.e. they are both only in some respects. The laws of logic determine the area in which logical reasoning is possible. The "rules of logic determine which inferences and affirmations are 'possible' (correct, legitimate, permitted) in thinking."[1] This is similar to following the rules of a game: If somebody doesn't follow the rules of a game, they are not playing the game at all. Maybe they are playing another game. The rules of games can be changed by the players. This is a difference to the laws of logic. Neglecting the laws of logic means being in conflict with truth, i.e. no reasonable thinking/arguing is possible at all. To norms laws are superordinate concepts. This puts the focus on the question of description and prescription in establishing norms. There are three types of norms, following von Wright: directives, rules and prescriptions.

Directives are technical norms. They function as "*means* to be used for the sake of attaining a certain *end*".[2] They are neither descriptive nor prescriptive. The prototypes of rules on the other hand are the rules of games. When we look at language norms and ask what they share with rules of games, we can see that the rules of language are less stable than the rules of (some) games, e.g. chess. Even if we don't agree with this statement, since we can observe that the rules of chess have changed over time, it is no doubt true that the rules in a language constantly change over time.

> "But the rules of grammar have a much greater flexibility and mutability than the rules of a game. They are in a constant process of growth. What the rules *are* at any given moment in the history of a language may not be possible to tell with absolute completeness and precision."[3]

Prescriptions have four defining elements: the norm giver/norm authority, the norm subjects, the promulgation of the norm, and the sanctions associated with the norm. In all these respects prescriptions differ from rules. In my view this holds true also for the rules of language. We can say that language norms are associated with a norm giver, the norm subjects, the promulgation of the language norm and sanctions, but I think this is only true for some of the language norms in the German language. Only in orthography is there a concrete norm giver, the Kultusministerkonferenz der Länder. The norm subjects which must fear to be sanctioned are in this case schools and administrative institutions.

---

[1] Von Wright (1963: 5).
[2] Von Wright (1963: 9).
[3] Von Wright (1963: 7).

They can be sanctioned if they neglect orthographical norms. But for other parts of the language system there is no imposed norm of this kind. Here we have emergent norms where we cannot name a concrete norm giver. The language users aren't subjected to the norm in the way they are to prescriptions. Thirdly, the sanctions of language norms are of a different kind than the sanctions of prescriptions. If you are socialised within a certain German dialect, it is more than likely that you will have problems in some areas of profession. If you aren't able to switch between the codes of standard German and your own dialect, you will be (directly or indirectly) sanctioned if you want to work in a university. But even in this case the sanction isn't imposed with respect to an explicit norm manifested in a codex. It is imposed with recourse to emergent norms (stylistics, the choice between different varieties and so on).

Following von Wright, there are three types of subgroups of norms: moral principles,[4] ideal rules and customs (see Fig. 1). They resemble the main types of norms in some respects; in others, they differ substantially. Von Wright concludes that "they fall, so to speak, 'between' the major groups".[5] In this paper only the customs are of further interest. They are relevant for defining language norms. Customs are kinds of social habits, kinds of "patterns of behaviour for the members of a community."[6] They are similar to norms in so far as they guide the actions of people in a specific way. The members of a language community are put under a normative pressure by the common usages.

> "We can characterize this difference between customs and laws of nature by saying that the former present a genuinely normative or prescriptive aspect which the latter lack. Customs are 'normlike' in the sense that they *influence* conduct; they exert a 'normative pressure' on the individual members of the community whose customs they are. The existence of this pressure is reflected in the various punitive measures whereby the community reacts to those of its members who do not conform to its customs. In this respect customs are entirely unlike laws of nature, and resemble, not so much norms which are rules, as norms which are prescriptions."[7]

In my opinion this is the crucial point. Language norms as rules of the common language usage (customs) are like prescriptions. This holds true as neglecting language norms leads to sanctions for those who break the norms. We saw that language norms usually don't have a concrete norm giver. In this respect they are anonymous norms following von Wright. They are valid even without codification, as the codification of the norm comes after the establishment of the norm. This is a wide view of norm. Some researchers propose that we should

---

[4] Von Wright uses *moral norm, moral principle, moral rule* synonymously (1963: 11). To emphasize the difference from the neighbouring and partly superordinate concept of NORM I will choose the label *moral principle* here.
[5] Von Wright (1963: 16).
[6] Von Wright (1963: 8).
[7] Von Wright (1963: 9).

only talk of language norms when they are codified e.g. by the Kultusministerkonferenz der Länder or by codices like the Duden. In my opinion it is reasonable to take a wider definition of language norm. Even before codification the norm is active. The codification of language norms can help to spread them, to carry them forward to the following generations etc. When we accept that language norms are in existence even before codification, we can see them as implicit prescriptions.

As a second step von Wright looks at different parts of norms.[8] Where the first step was a kind of analysis of the conceptual domain of NORM (Begriffsfeldanalyse), this second step is an attempt to find the essential semantic features of the concept (see Fig. 2).

norm-kernel	character: obligation-norms vs. permissive norms content: "that which ought to or may or must not be or be done" (1963: 71) condition of application: categorical vs. hypothetical norms
special features of prescriptions	norm giver: authority orders, permits, prohibits... norm subject: "agents, to whom the prescription is addressed or given" (1963: 77) situation: localisation in time
further factors	promulgation: norm-formulation and „making known to the norm subjects" (1963: 125) sanction: "threat of punishment for disobedience" (1963: 125)

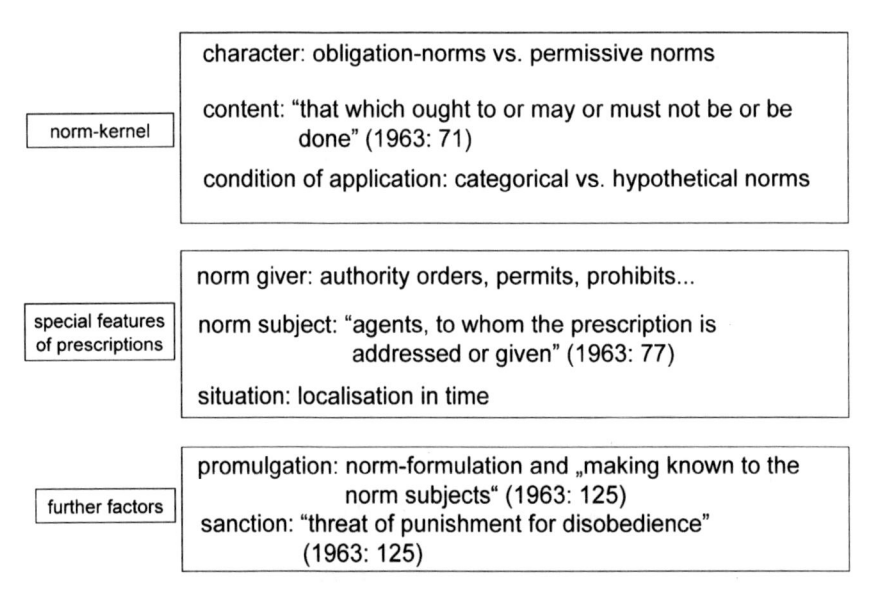

Figure 2: Types of norms: Features of norms (following von Wright 1963/1979)

Part of the core meaning of norm is its 'character', – whether it is a obligation norm or a permissive norm. The content of the norm describes what is to be done or what shouldn't be done. The condition of application divides between categorical and hypothetical norms, i.e. here the question is whether the norm subjects have to follow the norm at all times or only in specific situations. The parts of the norm which are similar to prescriptions do have a norm giver, a norm subject and a localisation in time (when/how long does the norm apply).

---

[8] Von Wright (1963: 70ff.)

As further factors von Wright claims the promulgation of the norm and the feature 'sanction' mentioned previously.[9] Norm promulgation focuses on the explicit formulation and on spreading the norm to the norm subjects. These three aspects of the meaning of NORM (core meaning, special features, further factors) are reminiscent of a prototype approach to analysing the semantic content of concepts. There is a semantic core (character, content, condition of application) and a field of features which can apply in some cases but do not have to do so necessarily. The boundaries of the concept of norm are therefore fuzzy. But despite all the possible fuzziness in the definition of norm, it is also true for language norms that we can usually tell whether they are violated or not. What language norms are, is usually not seen until these norms are violated in some ways. Therefore the violation of language norms draws a line between two areas. On the one hand language norms make statements about what is allowed in a language, i.e. which language uses are inside the norm. On the other hand norms can tell what isn't permitted, i.e. which language uses aren't covered by the norm. This distinction is relevant when we look at the 'System-Norm-Rede-Modell'. In this model those types of language usages which show high frequencies, which are accepted by the speakers/writers and which are covered by the language system (*langue*), constitute the area within the language norm.

In von Wright's approach it is possible to define language norm in a more specific way than with the help of those common-sense features mentioned above (obligation, claim of validity, application of the norm, sanctions, associated values, explicitness of the norm). Von Wright's model structures these meaning features and makes their interrelations clear.

The model of system, norm, and parole:

As a second approach to the problem how to define a language norm I want discuss a model which goes back to Eugenio Coseriu (1970). This model was later modified and amplified by Eroms (2000) and Hundt (2005). I think it is a useful complement to the approach of von Wright. In the 'System-Norm-Rede-Modell' three factors are relevant: the language system (*langue*), language usage (*parole*) and the intersection of these both areas. Language usage which is located in this intersection is actually produced as part of parole on the one hand, and is covered by the language system on the other hand, i.e. it is grammatically well-formed. Language usage which isn't in this intersection doesn't belong to the norm as it is not well-formed, i.e. it is not covered by the language system. (see Fig. 3)

---

[9] Von Wright (1963: 125ff.)

Types of language norms:
Norm as usage covered by the language system

system | **norm** usage covered by the system | **parole**

- possible utterances which actually are not producet
- actually produced utterances
- covered by the system
- high frequency
- acceptable
- actually produced utterances which aren't covered by the system
- low frequency

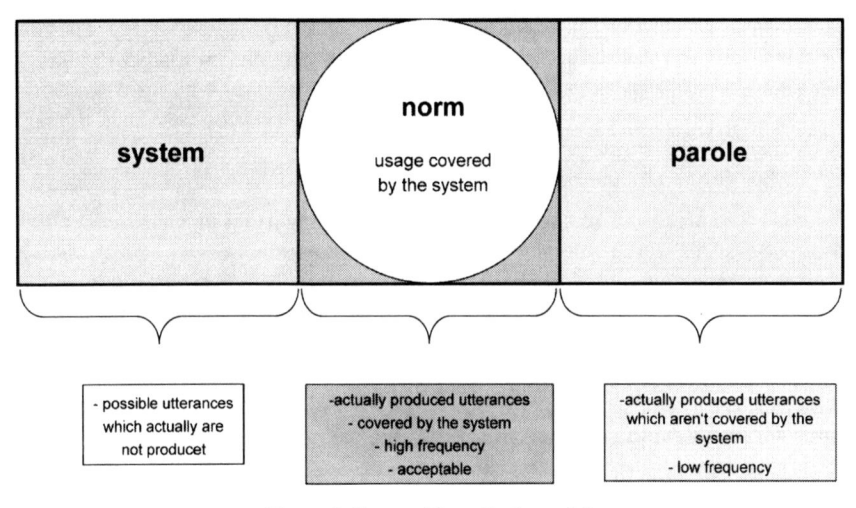

Figure 3: System-Norm-Rede model

This model also explains why a lot of possible language forms aren't covered by the norm despite the fact that they are well-formed. So if you produce e.g. fivefold embedded relative clauses they are covered by the language system but surely not by the norm as these kind of constructions wouldn't be acceptable for the language users (due to the difficulties in decodability). It is clear that the 'System-Norm-Rede-Modell' is only a tentative approach to solve the problem of language norms. There are a lot of further problems when we take a closer look at the model. For example, the question arises what to do with utterances which are commonly accepted by the language user, but which are not (or at least not yet) covered by the language system. In this case either we have to accept that the language system has to be changed and that acceptability is in those cases a clear sign of the fact that the underlying rules have changed. Or we have to accept that acceptability alone isn't a sufficient condition for putting an utterance under the roof of the norm. I think the truth lies in between. Acceptability on the one hand is an indicator of the fact that the underlying system has changed already. But there have to be clear-cut underlying language rules, i.e. rules which divide the grammatical from the ungrammatical utterances. The existence of these rules are a precondition for acceptability. Therefore in my opinion there are no constructions which are highly accepted on the one hand and not covered by the language system on the other.

In summary I thus propose an operational definition of language norms. Language norms are:

a) related to the levels of the language system.
b) related to the varieties of a language (social, functional, historical varieties).
c) defined by the criteria following von Wright.
d) only manifest in actually produced utterances. We can only see that language norms exist in language usage.
e) further defined by the concept of ACCEPTABILITY.

In short, language norms are rules of language usage that are abstracted from those utterances which conform to the underlying system.

Changing language norms: When we look at changing current language norms, we have to consider the relevant factors that are involved in these processes: norm guards ("Normenhüter"), norm propagators ("Normenverbreiter"), norm authorities ("Normeninstanzen"). I want to propose a model which is based on the model of Ulrich Ammon (2005: 33). Ammon defines the social force field of a standard variety ("soziales Kräftefeld einer Standardvarietät") in setting up four norm-constituting factors:

1. norm authorities: correctors
2. language codices: codifiers
3. model speakers/writers: model texts
4. language experts: professional judgements

I want to augment and vary this model in four steps (see Fig. 4).

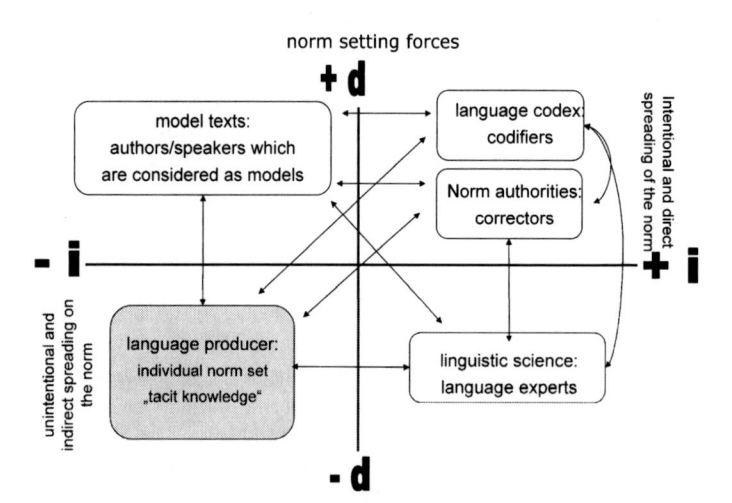

Figure 4: Adapted model of language norms (based on Ammon 2003: 33)

1.) In Ammon's model the language producer, the average user of a natural language is only considered as a grounding and surrounding factor to the four norm constituting factors (see above). The majority of a language community embeds the other four norm factors. In my opinion we have to take into account that the normal language user, the normal producer of utterances in a natural language is an important norm-constituting factor as well, especially when we look at the language producer as a whole, as a collective, not as several individuals with their idiosyncrasies in language use. Actually, I think we can propose the normal language user as the sovereign of the language norm. In the German language it is only at the level of orthography that we have an explicitly fixed norm, which is adopted by an official institution (Kultusministerkonferenz der Länder). Moreover, this norm holds only for the administrative bodies and for schools. Admittedly, not being in compliance with this orthographical norm is sanctioned, but the sanctions are of a different kind than the sanctions which are imposed by laws or prescriptions. There are no monetary fines or prison sentences in connection with breaking orthographic norms. What is to be done with a member of an administrative body who neglects orthographical norms?

All the other levels of the language systems (an exception is the level of orthoepy) are ruled by subsistent norms. These norms are set by the language sovereign, i.e. the language user producing utterances in everyday speech (or writing). It is clear that the norm-setting forces mentioned above (norm authorities, language codices, model speakers and language experts) are involved in constituting and holding up the language norms as well. But I think they are involved in this process to a lesser extent than is often assumed. They are not involved in the process of norm building first and foremost as norm authorities or language experts but as normal users of the natural language, i.e. as being part of the language sovereign. Primarily the normal language user doesn't want to norm the language. They want to communicate. Therefore language norms emerge as side effects of optimizing communication instead. What the other factors of the process of language norming contribute is in this respect secondary.

2.) Language codices, norm authorities (e.g. teachers, parents etc.) and model texts are spreading the language norms in a direct way. Language experts, linguists can only contribute to the forming and upholding of the language norm in an indirect way, by putting the findings of linguists in language codices or school books. *Language codices* are grammars, dictionaries and other commonly used and accepted references works of the German language (from handbooks of German grammar up to style guides). In my opinion these codices aren't constituting the language norm. Primarily they want to describe the language norm which is supposed to exist beforehand. Only the language user makes the codices a norm constituting factor. On the other hand it is true that the Duden publishing house doesn't resist being a norm authority. This is evident when we look at advertising slogans like *unentbehrlich für richtiges Deutsch* ('indispensible for correct German') (Duden grammar). But the Duden grammar isn't explicitly normative, it isn't a prescriptive grammar. The Duden grammar and the publisher are accepting their normative role willingly as they know that they aren't able to norm the levels of morphology, syntax and phonology in this explicit way. Therefore, language codices are part of the norming process in a direct way and in an intentional way (see for example the advertising by the publisher). But the authors of the Duden are well aware of the fact that this norming process is of a very different kind than the norming process associated with laws, prescriptions or decrees. The difference lies in the fact that the Duden authors do not have the power and authority to explicitly norm these levels of the German language. This specific relationship between describing a norm and being seen as a norm giver isn't relevant for the normal language users. They don't ask whether the Duden is a prescriptive or a descriptive grammar. They only seek advice in tricky language problems and they expect that kind of advice from the Duden. Therefore the language users take the Duden as a norm setting authority whether the authors of the grammar have intended that or not.

Norm authorities are for example teachers, parents, language advisers and critics like Bastian Sick or Wolf Schneider. These authorities play a different role in the norming process than the codices. Sometimes the so-called norm authorities have certain beliefs about language norms and these beliefs don't necessarily fit the norms we can find in the codices. Nils Langer and Winfred Davies have this in their study from 2006. It became obvious that teachers didn't accept some constructions which were in fact accepted by the Duden grammar, i.e. which were in fact part of the language norm. The majority of teachers didn't accept the connection of a relative clause with the temporal interrogative pronoun *wo* ('where'), even though the Duden does accept this construction with good reasons (*an dem Tag, wo wir uns getroffen haben*, 'on the day we met'). Therefore what norm authorities think about the language norm is sometimes more like an ideal norm. This ideal norm is at the best in accordance with the actual codified language norm. But there are sometimes considerable differences between the two. This leads us to the conclusion that this ideal norm sometimes lives a life of its own.

Model texts are those texts which the language community receives as models with respect to the language pattern chosen. Model texts give an orientation for the language norm. Therefore they can function like codices. The difference between model texts and codices lies in the fact that model texts are not designed and produced to promulgate, stabilize or spread the language norm. Sometimes the design and often the reception of codices do fulfil these functions. Model texts are produced to fulfil specific communicative tasks, whether this task is in the area of literary, institutional, scientific, religious or technical language. Therefore, model texts can function as language authorities which promulgate and spread language norms in an unintentional but direct way.

The language experts form a very small group of the language community. They reflect on the German language and on the process of norm setting in this language. When language experts – e.g. linguists – publish on topics of language norms they are joining in the discussion of setting norms in a intentional way. But it has to be considered that this small group of language producers isn't as important for the norming process as one would expect. Studies on the influence of grammarians since the early modern period have shown that language experts haven't had any considerable impact on the norming process. This holds true even if we concede that in some cases the grammarians were successful with their proposals in the long run (e.g. the suppression of the *tun*-periphrasis since Early High German times). To conclude we can say that the language experts are involved in the process of establishing new norms only in an indirect way (see Fig. 4). To be more precise language experts act as norm authorities to a lesser extent when they write as scientists in scientific journals. Only when their argumentations can reach the public (e.g. in codices like the Duden, in newspaper articles or in talk shows) their influence on the language norms is a direct one. Of course, this distinction is somewhat artificial as language experts (e.g. university professors) are norm authorities. In this role they do help promulgating and spreading language norms. But in my opinion we have to separate these two roles: the role of teaching, spreading the norm (teacher) and the role of analysing the norm (scientist).

3.) Codifiers, correctors (e.g. teachers, parents, language advisors, writers of language glosses), language experts are aware of their own norm-stabilising and norm-spreading role. With model speakers this is not the case. They don't produce their texts with the intention of promulgating and/or stabilising a language norm.

4.) The average language user, the Joe (or Jane?) Public of the German language normally acts unintentionally and indirectly with respect to language norms. He or she participates in the process of norm building by taking up new language patterns, by frequently using specific language patterns or by not using some language patterns which are either grammatical but not common or ungrammatical. Establishing new norms, stabilising and/or changing existing norms isn't the intention of the average language user. The norming processes caused by the average language users are therefore unintended consequences of the speaking/writing of the average language users (in the way of invisible-hand processes). It is not a question of a specific theory of language change. Whether you prefer optimality theory, the theory of naturalness or the like, in my opinion it is always the average language user who is responsible for establishing and upholding the emerging language norms.

2. Advantages of the violations of language norms

In which cases is the violation of language norms useful? Which conditions must prevail so that new language patterns get the chance of becoming grammatical, i.e. of entering the language system? To answer this question I want to take a look at two different cases. First I want to describe the path a new pattern takes in the language system (exemplified by syntactic constructions). Secondly I want to discuss one possible pathway of eliminating an established syntactic pattern from the language system.

Case 1: New language patterns enter the language system. Here a prototypical pathway is proposed:

1.) The new pattern must have some communicative advantage for the language users. For example a new syntactic construction must solve a specific communicative problem better than an existing syntactical pattern. This competition between different constructions can be seen on the basis of language economy. The construction fitting best the requirements of communication will win this competition in the long run. This doesn't mean that the old construction is abandoned immediately. Grammaticalisation theory has shown that this is not the case. The old construction is used beside the new one (with decreasing frequency), this is called layering and persistence in grammaticalisation theory. To give an example: In using reflexive passive constructions in German the speakers/writers have a communicative advantage. This advantage is given when the context of the construction is by default of a passive kind (e.g. in German scientific texts it is strongly recommended not to say 'I think' or the like but to demote the author and to make rather impersonal and general statements). When the writers of a scientific text have the standards of a scientific text type in mind, they will use passive constructions almost automatically. Therefore the reflexive passive gives them the opportunity to use specific verbs in a passive context which otherwise couldn't be used (e.g. inherent reflexive verbs like *sich beziehen auf*, *sich beschäftigen mit*, or reflexive used transitive verbs like *sich waschen*, *sich abkoppeln*, etc.). When the writers/speakers have to choose such a verb either they have to paraphrase the whole sentence not to use the uncommon reflexive passive or they can use the reflexive passive form. It is a communicative advantage that they don't have to abandon the passive pattern completely. In analogy to the procedural passive (Vorgangspassiv), a reflexive passive is used in the utterances. The communicative problem of staying in the passive context is solved.

Example: A student wants to write in a scientific essay about a special hypothesis proposed by a linguist, e.g. Noam Chomsky. He writes *Im Folgenden wird sich auf Chomsky bezogen* ('The following refers to Chomsky') instead of *Im Folgenden beziehe ich mich auf Chomsky* ('In the following, I will refer to

Chomsky') which would violate the Ich-proscription in scientific texts, or instead of *Im Folgenden wird eine Argumentation unter Rückgriff auf Chomsky verfolgt* ('The following pursues an argumentation based on Chomsky') which would be much longer.

2.) Regularity of the construction: The language users don't make use of every chance to optimize the communication by inventing a new construction. A new language pattern, a new syntactic construction must have some specific characteristics with respect to the underlying syntactical rules of well-formedness. Even if the language users aren't able to tell which regularity it is that the new construction conforms to, there has to be such a regularity or it wouldn't be possible for the construction to survive, to be established and to be – in the long run – a likely example of a new syntactic norm. Of course the average language users don't reflect on the underlying syntactical regularities of the constructions they use. Therefore, it is the task of the language experts to analyse these regularities, especially those ones which are responsible for establishing new constructions. In the case of syntactic regularities it is important to consider the fact that not just any regularity will meet the conditions of new norms. Only those syntactic regularities are possible ones which make statements about those constructions which are still ungrammatical even under the new conditions. Take for example the reflexive passive in German. The new syntactic regularity underlying this construction still excludes non-agentive or ergative verbs, e.g.

(1) a. *Die Kosten läppern sich.*
    'Costs mount up.'
    **Es wird sich geläppert.*
    '*It is mounted up.'
  b. *Es gehört sich, zuzuhören.*
    'Listening is good manners.'
    **Es wird sich gehört zuzuhören.*
    'Listening is good manners.'
  c. *Es versteht sich von selbst, dass die Theorie nicht alles lösen kann.*
    'Obviously this theory cannot solve everything.'
    **Es wird sich von selbst verstanden.*
    '*It is being understood...'

The passivization of those verbs is impossible as the new syntactical regularity for constructing reflexive passives in German sets a restriction for non-agentive or ergative verbs (s. below).

For constructions in the recipient passive the restriction lies in not permitting the *dativus ethicus* or the *dativus iudicantis*. For sentences with these dative noun-phrases the recipient passive isn't permissible.

(2) a. *Komm mir ja nicht nach 11 Uhr nach Hause.*
'Don't you dare come home after 11.'
**Ich kriege (ja nicht) nach 11 Uhr nach Hause gekommen.*
'Don't you dare come home after 11.'
b. *Du bist ihm zu nassforsch aufgetreten.*
'You acted too snappily for him.'
**Er bekommt zu nassforsch aufgetreten.*
'*He gets acted too snappily.'

3.) Acceptability of the construction and spreading of the construction through the language community: The acceptability of a language pattern is a much more complex phenomenon than is usually assumed. In a paper published earlier[10] I proposed that the most important criterion of acceptability is the unmarkedness of the construction with respect to its grammaticality status. This surely is a criterion. But it isn't – in my opinion – a sufficient criterion for defining the concept of grammatical acceptability. It is clear that the acceptability of a syntactic construction is a sign, a indication of a valid language norm. If we accept the operational definition of language norms as the intersection between the language system (*langue*) on the one hand and the actually produced utterances (*parole*) on the other, we can see that acceptable constructions are positioned in this intersection. But it is another question what it is that makes these constructions acceptable. Even asking test groups about the acceptability of the construction doesn't help to solve the problem. The test persons can only tell you what construction they accept, but not – that is in the normal case – *why* the construction is acceptable or unacceptable at all. In my opinion it is worth trying to answer this question by looking at the tacit knowledge of a speaker/writer. If someone is confronted with a new construction like *Das sieht man auch daran, wie sich hier geschminkt wird* (reflexive passive) ('This is also reflected by the way people use make-up.') this activates some routines[11] of checking the constructions. First of all we have to ask whether the language user is aware of the curiosity of the construction. If that is the case they have to decide whether this construction is marked/unusual in some way. If it's unmarked the construction will be acceptable for the average language user and no further checking of the construction is necessary. If the construction is marked in some way, the language user will have to decide what to do with this markedness. They have to judge whether this deviation is good, neutral or bad in terms of acceptability (e.g. posh language vs. sloppy language etc.). Of course it is possible that the language users say the new construction is indeed marked or unusual but practical, sensible; and therefore they dedide to accept it although it is marked. If they

---

[10] Hundt (2005: 19f.).
[11] The following argument is based on the model of Miyazaki (2001). I want to thank Vít Dovalil for his very insightful advice on this topic and for showing me the connections of this problem to the topic of language management, see especially Dovalil (2006).

dislike the construction – and this is in my opinion the interesting case – then they wouldn't refer to grammatical statements or to looking up the underlying rules in a grammar. The reasons for the markedness and therefore in consequence the reasons for the unacceptability are then formulated in statements like this: *Such sentences are only uttered by fools not knowing the basics of the German language; this is only said in southern Germany, bad language, not really German* etc. Sometimes – but I think very rarely – then grammars or the like are consulted to confirm these intuitive judgements. This means grammars are used and perceived as prescriptive norm-setting authorities whether they like it or not. For the checking process in the case of dubious constructions it is crucial that the tacit knowledge is rarely reflected. If in the checking process a syntactic construction is rejected as marked and as unacceptable, it can be expected that this construction will stay unacceptable for (maybe) a long time even if the codex has voted for its correctness in the meantime. It is evident that the average language user, the sovereign of the language norms, is guided rather by an ideal language norm than by the actual codex. This ideal norm and the codex don't have to be concordant with each other in every case. This discrepancy has recently been shown by the studies of Winifred Davies and Nils Langer (2006). They analysed 11 dubious constructions in a synchronic and in a diachronic perspective. It was obvious that the language codex wasn't the only guide for the language users, in this case for teachers as norm authorities. The connection of relative clauses with the temporal interrogative pronoun *wo* (*where*) wasn't accepted as well-formed by the majority of the teachers despite the fact that the Duden allows this construction. On the other hand the teachers believe that the codex allows the use of the preposition *wegen* with the dative case in general despite the fact that the codex votes in this case rather strictly in favour of the genitive case in the written standard language.[12] Only in spoken language and in some special cases in the written language it is in accordance with the norm to use the dative case.[13] These data show that not only the average language user but also some norm authorities follow their own ideal language norms rather than the explict codex. Therefore the acceptability of construction cannot be set by permissive or prohibitive acts in the codex alone.

---

[12] Davies/Langer (2006: 210f., 265f.).

[13] Examples: *Standarsprachlich mit Dativ in bestimmten Verbindungen u. wenn bei Pluralformen der Genitiv nicht erkennbar ist: – wegen etwas anderem, wegen manchem, wegen Vergangenem; wegen Geschäften. Standardsprachlich auch mit Dativ, wenn ein Genitivattribut zwischen 'wegen' und das davon abhängende Substantiv tritt: – wegen meines Bruders neuem Auto.* (Duden Rechtschreibung 2006: 1107; cf. also Duden Grammatik 2005: 619f.). 'Standard language: dative in certain combinations and if the genitive in plural forms cannot be distinguished: – due to something else, due to some, due to past things; due to business. Dative is further used in standard language if a genitive attribute is used between 'wegen' (due to) and the substantive depending on it: – due to my brother's new car'.

The main reasons for the fact that the language users are able to orient themselves to an ideal norm rather than to the actual codified norm are the following: a) the increase of the frequency of the construction. Those constructions heard or read more often are more familiar to the language users. The increase in frequency does not lead to increased acceptability in one case: If the violation of the language norm is evident even for the average language user as in cases like *Hier werden Sie geholfen* ('You will be assisted here.') – I think – a rising frequency of the construction doesn't have acceptability as its consequence. b) After a time of rising frequency of a construction there is a take-off phase in which the construction is used in a generalized way, i.e. the construction can now be used in contexts where it wasn't possible before (see for example the generalized applicability of the dative passive nowadays). In this case the average language user gets the impression that this construction has always been acceptable, i.e. that the construction has never been marked before. The take-off-phase is often associated with the appearance of the construction in model texts.

4.) Appearance of the construction in model texts: Describing the sequence of events as establishing a new norm is an idealization in itself. Looking at model texts we have a special problem. Speaking of model texts has meant so far 'model authors', 'accepted/canonical texts of the masse media' and the like. Maybe this holds true for some historical periods of the German language (although I would doubt that). Texts from M. Luther, J. W. v. Goethe or F. Schiller, T. Mann etc. could be seen as model texts of their time. For the present time speaking of model texts in this text-oriented manner isn't reasonable any more. Which texts can function as model texts nowadays? Literary texts aren't able to fulfil this task. In these texts the authors regularly play with and vary the syntactic patterns intentionally. Intentionally produced deviations from the language norms are typical of literary texts. If literary texts have to be omitted, are nationwide newspapers possible candidates for model texts (e.g. Süddeutsche Zeitung, Frankfurter Allgemeine Zeitung)? Or are the spoken texts of news anchormen model texts? Or the texts of the political or juridical discourse (Bundestag)? Or even schoolbooks? In my opinion neither at the level of orthography nor at other levels of the language system we can assume that the average language user takes those texts as model texts. The notion that the average language user seeks help in these texts, if he is in doubt about the correctness of a construction, has to be abandoned. Therefore the question which texts function as real model texts for the average language user is an open one. More important than model texts seem to be model speakers. To look at them – as U. Ammon does too – opens the way to take several varieties of a language, several user groups etc. into account. Surely Dieter Bohlen is accepted as a model speaker only for very few persons. But when we look at the standard variety of the German language as the variety with the highest prestige, as a minimally marked variety with respect to regional or social factors, we can identify certain groups of model speakers. Well-known politicians, anchormen in television, popular writers of editorial articles in nationwide newspapers are examples of such model speakers. They are often taken as model speakers whether they would agree or not. As a consequence, the texts of these model speakers can function as model texts in a secondary way. The prestige of the model speakers is transferred to their texts. So it is not – or at least only to a lesser extent – the language internal factors that are responsible for constituting the model texts but language-external ones like the popularity of the speaker/writer.

5.) Reactions of the norm authorities: The advantage in communication, the syntactic regularity, the acceptability, the appearance of the construction in model texts are always associated with some reactions of the norm authorities. Studies in the history of the German language have shown that both the reactions of the norm authorities (e.g. teachers) and the reactions of the language experts (e.g. grammarians) shouldn't be overrated. Norm authorities are always conservative in their attitude against new constructions. Therefore it is possible that some constructions are not accepted by the norm authorities despite the fact that they have been adopted in the codex in the meantime. The example of the relative particle *wo* was mentioned earlier in this paper (see above). I only want to give one more example of this construction. A sentence like *Wenn in unserem Leben etwas Tragisches passiert, kommt der Zeitpunkt, wo wir das Dunkel ins Auge fassen müssen.* ('If something tragic happens in our life, we reach the point where we have to face the dark.')[14]

The majority of teachers don't accept this construction. In this case they demand the 'correct' prepositional phrase construction: *der Zeitpunkt, an dem/zu dem/bei dem....* Of course it's no mystery why the connection of temporal relative clauses with the local interrogative pronoun is sensible and accepted by the codex. When we talk about time relations we have to fall back on locative notions, we have to talk metaphorically. For the judgement of the teachers this fact isn't relevant, they opt for one and only for one alternative (the majority, not all of them!). Examples like these show that there exist ideas about the valid norms of the standard language. On the other hand there is considerable fluctuation in the way these norms are realized. Even the mediators of the norm (e.g. teachers) are often guided by an ideal of that norm. This ideal is taken for granted and rarely – at least not always – checked against the codex.

> "Studies of the norm knowledge of teachers of German in Germany (e.g. Davies 2000a, 2005, and see below) show that Bellmann is right to assume that the standard as an idea is not in danger, although there is some disagreement, even amongst these language norm authorities as to which of the individual variants commonly used by native speakers are to count as standard."[15]

---

[14] Internet, see Duden Grammatik (2005: 1041).
[15] Langer/Davies (2006: 116).

If – at last – a construction is in the position that it is supported by the norm authorities it will spread more easily. But – to summarize – for the implementation of new norms the norm authorities are less important than could be expected.

6.) Getting into the codex: In the idealized sequence of the implementation of new norms a last step is the entry of the new construction into the codex. An example of this long entering process is the dative passive in German. In former editions of the grammars either we don't find a hint on the dative passive at all or it is described only in a marginal way. Nowadays the construction is fully accepted and therefore adopted by all grammars of the German language.

Case 2: Accepted and norm-conforming language patterns are eliminated from the language system.

The sequence of events proposed here is an idealized one, too. It differs in some ways from the sequence in case 1.

1. Criticism by the codifiers and by the norm authorities: Nils Langer (2000, 2001) analyses the example of the *tun*-periphrasis in the history of the German language. The judgement of grammarians and of authorities was responsible for the stigmatisation of the construction. Step by step this led to the elimination of the construction from language use.
2. Avoidance/non-appearance in model texts: As a consequence of stigmatisation, the *tun*-periphrasis wasn't used in model texts any more. Like this construction, other constructions are dependant on their prestige/stigma. The more one construction is stigmatized the less probable it is to find it in model texts.
3. An alternative construction exists: Eliminating one construction from the system is only possible if an alternative construction is at hand. This is an almost trivial statement, as for every construction in the German language a periphrasis and/or an alternative construction is possible. This holds true for the *tun*-periphrasis, which is well-established in oral communication up to today. This is also true for non-finite subordinate clauses which were abandoned at the end of the Early New High German period. Since then placing the finite predicate in the subordinate clause was obligatory.

Language experts, linguists and the like are only observers at both processes, the implementation of new constructions in the system as well as the elimination of construction out of the system. They can't determine which construction will survive in the system in the long run. Despite the success of grammarians at the elimination of the *tun*-periphrasis, it is the language sovereign who has to decide whether they want to follow the recommendations of the language experts and norm authorities or not. In many cases they don't, as we can see by the survival of the *tun*-periphrasis in oral communication.

3. From violating norms to the constitution of new norms

The reasons for the change of language norms are identical with the reason of language change in general. Peter von Polenz has stated and elaborated four factors of language change in detail (see v. Polenz 2000: 28-80).

1. linguistic economy
2. innovation
3. variation
4. evolution

If we accept that the driving forces for language change are also responsible for changing language norms, than we can conclude: language norms are *per se* instable, they are changing constantly, sometimes at a faster, sometimes at a slower rate. The changes in language norms are caused by the disposition of the language users to vary constantly in their language, to use innovative constructions on the one hand. On the other hand the principles of systemic and informational linguistic economy are at work. This kind of economy shouldn't be misunderstood. Economy in this case doesn't mean "get the most profit with the least effort". This is a shortcut and misleading statement. Economy here means the tension between shortness/minimal linguistic work on the one hand and expansion,[16] i.e. greater linguistic effort to achieve the communicative aims. When the principle of linguistic economy is at work, this means solving communicative problems in a most effective way and not in the shortest way possible. If users of the German language want to use verbs which take dative objects in a passival context, they have two options:

a) The old, so far the only construction is used further: The language users utter a construction in the procedural passive with the dative nominal phrase in the first position (*Ihm wird das Buch geschenkt*, 'He is given the book'.)
b) A new construction is invented. Of course this new construction doesn't replace the old one. It is a further option to solve the communicative problem. In grammaticalisation theory this is called layering. The old construction can survive in some cases for a very long time, it persists (persistence).

Case a) Maintenance of the old construction:

(3) Die Polizei entzog ihm den Führerschein, weil er betrunken Auto gefahren war (active voice)

---

[16] For the concept of linguistic economy and its application on morphological change see Nübling et al. (2006: 54ff.), Ronneberger-Sibold (1980), Werner (1987; 1989), Harnisch (1990).

'The police revoked his driver's licence because he had been driving under the influence of alcohol.'
Der Führerschein wurde ihm entzogen (passive voice)
'His driver's licence was revoked.'
Ihm wurde der Führerschein entzogen, weil er betrunken Auto gefahren war (passive voice)
'His driver's licence was revoked because he had been driving under the influence of alcohol.'

If the object (dative noun phrase) has to be put in the first position of the sentence, the construction (output) will be marked in some way: It differs from the standard pattern of German sentences:

Standard pattern:
    subject   + predicate   + (object)
    NP_{nom} + Verb +   + (NP_{acc})

The procedural passive of transitive verbs leads to this constructional pattern: *Der Rechenschaftsbericht wurde gelesen* ('The accountability report was read.').

Furthermore the SPO-pattern is in accordance with the regularly observed cline of agentivity and definiteness in German sentences (from left to right).[17]

(4)   *Polizist Maier*$_{(def.)}$ *bestraft einen Parksünder*$_{(indef.)}$ (active voice)
'Policeman Maier$_{(def.)}$ punishes a parking offender$_{(indef.)}$.'
Ein Parksünder$_{(indef.)}$ *wurde von Polizist Maier*$_{(def.)}$ *bestraft* (passive voice)
'A parking offender$_{(indef.)}$ is punished by policeman Maier$_{(def.)}$.'

The sentence above in the passive voice violates the cline of definiteness. Therefore this sentence is – with regard to the most frequent pattern in German – marked. Of course other factors are playing an important role in such marking processes. In some cases it's also a question of animate vs. inanimate participants. Often we have a decline from animate to inanimate participants in sentences (from the left to the right).

Sentences like the one above aren't ungrammatical, they aren't unacceptable either. But – I think – the neglecting of clines (see above) can lead to new solutions which preserve the clines. Therefore a new construction will emerge.

Case b) Invention and implementation of a new construction:

If a speaker/writer wants to combine a definite dative object on the one hand with an indefinite nominative subject in a sentence in the active voice we have the starting point for a new construction. To avoid the reversed cline of definite-

---

[17]   The decline of agentivity is usually observed in sentences with active voice. The decline of definiteness is usually to be expected in sentences with passive voice.

ness the speaker/writer tries to preserve the Nom-Acc-Case-Sequence as well as the cline of definiteness and 'invents' the new dative passive.

> Context: Although Paul Maier was drunk he drove his car. He was stopped by the police.
>
> (5) *Ein Polizist entzog ihm deshalb den Führerschein* (active voice). ('The police thus revoked his driver's licence.') The cline of definiteness in the sentence is reversed. Therefore the sentence is marked in some way.
> *Er bekam den Führerschein entzogen* (passive voice) ('He had his driver's licence revoked.')

This solution would guarantee the cline of definiteness in the sentence (as both the police officer and the driver are animate, the cline of animacy plays no role in this sentence). In addition to that the sequence of NP_{nom} + verb + (further NPs) is also guaranteed. Of course this is only one aspect of linguistic economy. New constructions sometimes have other communicative advantages: e.g. the more flexible sequencing of elements with regard to the information structure of the sentence. The new construction sometimes is an option to place known and new things in the sentence in a better sequence (theme-rheme, topic-comment etc.). This is the case in periphrastic constructions with the subjunctive II in counterfactual sentences. Here the periphrastic forms do have communicative advantages over their synthetic alternatives.

Periphrastic forms but also expanded forms like *dem Mann sein Hut* ('the man's hat'; possessive attribute in the dative case) are evidence that linguistic economy isn't always associated with the shorter construction, with less effort and so on. On the contrary, in these cases it is reasonable to use the longer construction, to take a higher effort into account. If we accept that in some cases it is a sign of linguistic economy to use longer and/or more complex constructions, then the often cited "genitive-apostrophe" in German is less mysterious. Forms like *Carla's Imbiss* are, from this point of view, economical, since they fulfil the speaker's/writer's need to have a clear distinction between the lexical and the grammatical morpheme in a construction. In this case the proper name is highlighted in contrast to the less important genitive case which is separated by the apostrophe.

Proposed steps of implementing a new construction:

It is clear that the steps of implementation so far described don't follow each other in this unproblematic manner in every case. Overlaps and an exchange of individual steps are possible. But as a general heuristic I think this algorithm could be useful.

48   Markus Hundt

Step 1: The communicative problem seeking a solution.
Step 2: Trial and error – several solutions of the communicative problem are proposed.
Step 3: One construction emerges as a solution which is widely accepted by the language sovereign and which is therefore spread by the language users.
Step 4: The appearance of the new construction in model texts.
Step 5: The new construction is mentioned in codices (grammars, dictionaries etc.).
Step 6: (possibly) The language experts react, e.g. by analysing the construction.
Step 7: (possibly) The norm authorities promulgate and spread the new, now norm-conforming construction.

In this algorithm – I think – the most important part is the uptake of the construction by the language sovereign. They are centre stage. The other steps (regularity analysis by language experts, reactions by the norm authorities and even the appearance in model texts) are secondary to this.

4. 'Anything goes' – No!

"The longer we look at a suspicious construction, the more examples of this construction we collect, the more acceptable, the more understandable, the more grammatically well-formed this construction seems to be." Especially those linguists who often struggle with constructions on the borderline of grammaticality will share this opinion – at least sometimes. But I think it isn't true. Take for example the following constructions. They don't get more grammatical even if we analyse them for several hours.

(6) a. *Hier werden Sie geholfen.* (V. Feldbusch/Pooth)
      'You will be assisted here.'
   b. * *Hier werden Sie erholt.* (Commercial)
      '*You will be relaxed here.'
   c. *Er kriegt zu spät nach Hause gekommen.*
      '*He obtains coming home late.'
      (active: *Du kommst ihm zu spät nach Hause.*)
      ('You are coming home too late for him.')
   d. *Es wird sich zusammengeläppert.*
      '*It is mounted up.'
      (active: *Die Kosten läppern sich zusammen.*)
      ('Costs mount up.')
   e. *Sie ist wegen der Mann$_{Nom.}$ nicht gekommen.*
      'She did not come due to the man.'

When we search for the regularities of new syntactical construction, when we ask whether they are covered by the norm or not, we always have to take into account that a syntactic regularity always tells us which constructions still aren't possible. In the case of the five examples above, there are certain restrictions which are responsible for the exclusion of these constructions from the norm.

(a) + (b) In the construction of the procedural passive, the former object in the accusative (active voice) is promoted to the position of subject in the nominative case in the passive sentence. Furthermore the subject of the sentence in the active voice demoted in the passive voice. To be accessible for the passive voice there has to be some kind of agentivity in the sentence in the active voice. This doesn't mean that the sentence in the passive voice is a projection of the active voice sentence (converses etc.). This only means that we have a criterion for the decision which verbs can access the passive voice and which cannot. The passive construction has to be seen as a construction on its own. Therefore we can say that only those verbs are accessible for the passive voice which are agentive at least to some extent. Ergative verbs aren't accessible for the passive voice in German. Agentivity, promotion of the accusative object, and demotion why the sentences (a) and (b) are ungrammatical. The promotion of a dative object (a) isn't possible in the procedural passive construction. If we want to do this, we have to choose another – already existing – construction: the dative passive. Verbs like *sich erholen* are inherently reflexive. The reflexive pronoun isn't an argument in the verb frame. Therefore we can't replace it by a real argument like *die Kunden/Sie*$_{nom}$. Therefore this argument can't appear as a nominative subject in the passive sentence. Either we have to change the verb or we have to use the impersonal passive.

(c) The dative passive is characterized by the promotion of the dative object (active voice) to the nominative subject (passive voice), by the demotion of the subject of the active sentence and by the use of the auxiliaries *bekommen, erhalten, kriegen*, which are – at least up to now – in a certain competition for the status of the one and only possible auxiliary in this construction. As for all passive constructions the verb involved must have some kind of agentivity coded. Therefore we can say: The sentence in the active voice must show a specific decline of agentivity (from left to right). If this isn't the case, the passive construction isn't accessible for the verb. This restriction excludes the free dative NPs from the promotion to subject position in the dative passive construction, e.g. *dativus ethicus* and *dativus iudicantis*.

(d) If we accept that the reflexive passive is a constructional pattern conforming to the norm (not every linguist would agree) then we can apply the restriction-rule to this construction as well. The reflexive passive is accessible for those verbs which are inherently reflexive (like *sich schämen, sich freuen, sich beziehen auf*) or at least that are read as inherently reflexive verbs in some contexts (like *sich abkoppeln, sich rüsten, sich waschen, sich vorbereiten* etc.). In the latter case as a first step the reflexive pronoun is interpreted as an inherent reflexive pronoun (part of the verb). In both cases this reflexive pronoun reminds the

user of the demoted subject (active voice), despite the fact that the reflexive pronoun in this passive construction isn't anchored in a proper way. The reflexive passive is accessible only for those verbs which support the cline of agentivity in the active voice sentence. This means verbs with a reverse agentivity aren't possible candidates for the reflexive passive: *sich gehören, sich läppern, sich zeigen, dass* etc.

(e) Prepositions are able to govern the accusative, the dative or the genitive case but not the nominative case (casus rectus). Therefore we can argue about the question whether the prepositions govern the genitive or the dative case. But we can't suggest that it governs the nominative case.

5. Summary

The main thesis of this paper was the following: In reconstructing and analysing language norms we have to take into account the language sovereign more than before. Speakers have a greater influence on the emergence, establishment and elimination of language norms than language codices, norm authorities, language experts and model speakers.

Language norms as we have defined them here are only very rarely prescriptive, fixed and institutionally-grounded norms. Only in orthography (and partly in orthoepy) there are fixed, explicit and prescriptive norms. In most cases language norms come into being as emergent, instable norms related to several levels of the language (regional, social, historical varieties etc.). In my opinion not only those norms should be called norms which are present in the codex at the end of the norming process; but all the other language norms (especially the emergent norms which aren't yet codified) which are sometimes called language rules.[18] There are differences between these two types, this much is true. But I think it is more the explicitness of the formulation of the norm and less the obligation which is associated with those norms and language rules that separates the two. They both function as guiding lines for the language production and reception of the speakers/writers. In separating the codified norms from the mere language rules we would focus only on the end point of the norming process. In addition to that – in my opinion – only a minority of the system levels and of the actually normed language patterns are fixed in codices. So we would neglect the majority of the normed language parts if we only take the codified ones into account.

As we have seen in this paper, the borderline of syntax can be helpful in analysing language norms. The area in which we have suspicious constructions, constructions which are on the path of grammaticalisation (and therefore on their way of getting into the norm) are good examples of the process of estab-

---

[18] For the very interesting discussions on this topic I want to thank my colleague Walter Haas (Fribourg, Suisse).

lishing and implementing language norms. To conclude this paper I want to give a short list of further constructions which can be analysed with regard to language norm questions:

1. reflexive passive constructions[19]
   Da wird sich dann auf das Bankgeheimnis berufen. (ZDF, 13.5.02)
   'Such cases refer to banking confidentiality.'
2. dative passive constructions[20]
   Wer seinen Führerschein entzogen bekommt, muss sich ... (Mannheimer Morgen 17.3.98)
   'If your driver's licence has been revoked, you will have to...'
3. the *tun*-periphrasis (partly correct in the standard variety[21])
   Singen tut sie überaus gern.
   'She does like to sing.'
4. possessive constructions with a dative NP
   (*dem Mann sein Hut*)[22] (not found in the IDS-Corpora)
   'the man's hat'
5. split constructions with a pronominal adverb
   (*Da kann ich jetzt auch nichts für*)[23]
   'It's not my fault.'

---

[19] See Hundt (2005: 29ff., 2002); Ágel (1997).
[20] See Diewald (1997), Askedal (1984, 2005), Wegener (1985), Eroms (1992), Hundt (2005: 31ff.), Lenz (2007), (2008).
[21] See DRGD (835f.): "**2. tun + Infinitiv**: Die Verbindung von *tun* mit einem reinen Infinitiv in Sätzen wie *Sie tut gerade schreiben* oder *Er tut das schon erledigen* ist eine umgangssprachliche überflüssige Erweiterung des Prädikats. Sie gilt in der Standardsprache nicht als korrekt. Nur bei vorangestelltem Infinitiv, also wenn das Verb besonders nachdrücklich hervorgehoben werden soll, ist die Erweiterung mit *tun* zulässig, weil dann das *tun* die syntaktische Funktion des Verbs übernehmen muss: *Singen tut sie gern. Gesehen habe ich sie schon, aber kennen tue ich sie nicht.* [...]." '**2. do + infinitive**: The combination of *do* and an infinitive in phrases such as *She is writing* or *He is taking care of it* is a colloquial redundant extension of the predicate. In standard German it is not considered to be correct. Only with a preceding infinitive, if the verb is particularly emphasized, is an extension with *do* possible. In this case *do* assumes the syntactic role of the verb: *She does like to sing. I did see her but I do not know her.* [...]' For the state of the art in research see: Langer/Davies (2006), Langer (2000, 2001), Elspaß (2005: 254-267); Fischer (2001). As an example I give one of the many sentences with this constructions (IDS-Corpora): *Den Haushalt besorgt sie selbständig und besorgt die Einkäufe.* [...] *Singen tut sie überaus gern. So gehörte sie 30 Jahre dem Madrigalchor an* [...]. (St. Galler Tagblatt, 16.6.2000) 'She takes care of the housework herself, and she does grocery shopping. [...] She does like to sing. In fact, she has attended the madrigal choir for 30 years.'
[22] Langer/Davies (2006: 158ff.); Elspaß (2005: 325-336); Ágel (1993).
[23] Hundt (2005), S. 37; Fleischer (2002); Klumpp (1997). Data from the IDS-Corpora: *Für den Ausschluß der Frankfurter Gesundheitspolitiker zeichne er als Gast nicht verant-*

6. progressive constructions (with *am, beim, im* etc.)[24]
Wir sind am Überlegen...; *wir sind am Verhandeln* (St. Galler Tagblatt, 21.12.98).
'We are contemplating..., we are negotiating'
7. double negation with the function of emphatic negation[25]

---

[24] *wortlich: 'Da kann ich jetzt auch nichts für.'.* (Frankfurter Rundschau, 10.12.1997) '*As a guest, he was not responsible for the exclusion of the Frankfurt health politicians: 'It is not my fault.*"

See Elspaß (2005: 268-275); van Pottelberge (2005, 2004); Krause (2002, 1997); Reimann (1999); Rödel (2003). Some examples from the IDS-Corpora: *Erste Gedanken gingen in Richtung «Waterdiver – Flawil taucht und schwimmt für Kinder», weiss der Organisator, noch definiert werden müsste die Gruppe der zu unterstützenden Kinder. Thomas Gebert: «Wir sind am Überlegen, ob wir allenfalls ein Tabu-Thema wie die (sexuelle) Misshandlung von Kindern aufgreifen und breit angelegt zur Sprache bringen wollen.».* (St. Galler Tagblatt, 2.7.1998) '*First thoughts included «Waterdiver – Flawil dives and swims for kids», knows the organizer, while the group of children to be supported is yet to be defined. Thomas Gebert: «We are contemplating to take up and raise a taboo subject such as (sexual) abuse of children in a far reaching campaign.».*'; *Wir schreiben in unserer Gemeinde alle zu besetzenden Ämter in Kommissionen oder Räten öffentlich aus. Jede Wahl auf allen drei politischen Ebenen steht allen Altersstufen offen. Wir sind am Zusammenstellen unserer Kantonsratsliste.* (St. Galler Tagblatt, 27.7.1998) '*In our community we call public elections for all open offices in commissions or councils. Each election on all three political levels is open to all age brackets. We are currently putting together the council list for our canton.*'; *Das Gemüse wird für Grossverteiler respektive Grossabnehmer zubereitet. Baumgartner: «Wir sind am Verhandeln für die Verarbeitung von weiterem Gemüse [...].* (St. Galler Tagblatt, 21.12.1998) '*The vegetables are prepared for major distributors or bulk buyers, respectively. Baumgartner: We are negotiating the processing of further vegetables [...].*'.

[25] See Langer/Davies (2006: 258ff.); Langer (2001); Elspaß (2005: 275-28); Lenz (1996); Donhauser (1996). The data from the IDS-Corpora usually reflect spoken language: *Er ist überzeugt, dass mit der Investition in Theaterbillette zu Gunsten der Sulger Jungbürger auch dem Stadttheater mehr geholfen ist als mit einer reinen Geldspende. Und: Manch einer der Jugendlichen zeige sich zwar von der Idee des Theaterbesuchs anfangs wenig begeistert, doch weiss Ziegler mit seiner über zehnjährigen Erfahrung als Gemeindeammann, dass das Programm bei den Jungbürgern «noch nie nicht angekommen» sei. Von allen 41 Jungbürgern der Politischen Gemeinde Sulgen nahmen 30 an der Jungbürgerfeier teil.* (St. Galler Tagblatt, 6.12.1999) '*He is convinced that the investment in theater tickets for the young adults of Sulgen also helps the local theater more than a donation would. Plus: Some teenagers might not be thrilled of the idea of going to the theater at the beginning. However, after more than ten years as a mayor, Ziegler knows that the program «has never not been well received». Out of 41 young adults of the political community of Sulgen, 30 participated in the election party.*'; *AUSSERWINKLER hat sich mittlerweile entschuldigt: "Der Arzt Ausserwinkler hat zu wenig bedacht, daß er als Politiker Ausserwinkler bewertet wird." Die Entschuldigung dürfte also sinngemäß so gelautet haben: "Liebe Burgenländer, ich hab' nie nicht gesagt, daß Ihr immer angesoffen seid, ich hab nur gemeint, daß sich Eure Leber höchstens noch zum Backen eignet."* (Salzburger Nachrichten, 10.3.1993) '*Meanwhile,*

... *ich hab' nie nicht gesagt, daß Ihr immer angesoffen seid* ... (Salzburger Nachrichten 10.3.93)
'I never said you people are always drunk...'

8. *weil*-V2-subordinate clauses[26]

Der war zurechnungsfähig, weil er hat vor der Gendarmerie noch seinen Namen gewusst (Oberösterreichische Nachrichten, 14.6.1997)
'He was sane and fit to plead, since he remembered his name at the police station.'

9. using the relative particle *wo* in relative clauses[27]

Ich bin dankbar für jeden Tag, wo ich mich noch nützlich machen kann (St. Galler Tagblatt, 2.9.98)
'I am grateful for every day on which I am able to contribute.'

6. Literature

Ágel, Vilmos. 1993. "Dem Jubilar seine Festschrift: Ein typologisches Kuckucksei in der deutschen Substantivgruppe". *Im Zeichen der ungeteilten*

---

[26] *Ausserwinkler apologized: "The doctor Ausserwinkler neglected that he is judged as the politician Ausserwinkler." Thus, the apology will have been more or less like this: "Dear Burgenländer, I never said that you people are always drunk, I just meant your livers can only be used for cooking".'.*

See Hundt (2005: 38f.); Elspaß (2005: 296-316); Wegener (1999, 2000); Uhmann (1998); Pasch (1997); Selting (1999). Restricted to spoken language, very rare in written language: *Vor dem Welser Gericht erklärte er sich gestern als "zur Tatzeit im Vollrausch unzurechnungsfähig". Dies widerlegte sein Opfer, das starke Prellungen erlitten hatte, indem es sagte: "Der war zurechnungsfähig, weil er hat vor der Gendarmerie noch seinen Namen gewußt."* (Oberösterreichische Nachrichten, 14.6.1997) *'Yesterday, before the court of Wels, he declared himself as "not fit to plead at the time of the offense due to intoxication". The victim who had suffered bad bruises proved him wrong by stating: "He was sane and fit to plead, since he remembered his name at the police station."'.*

[27] See Langer/Davies (2006: 130ff.); Davies (2000); DRGD (944). Examples from the IDS-corpora: *Kaum waren die Faltprospekte verschickt, kamen die ersten Bestellungen. Noch jetzt vergeht kaum ein Tag, wo weitere Personen Solarstrom ordern.* (St. Galler Tagblatt, 22.7.1997) *'As soon as the leaflets were sent out, the first orders came in. Even today people order solar electricity almost every day.'*; *Ich rate jedem, bis zum 65. Altersjahr zu arbeiten. Ich bin dankbar für jeden Tag, wo ich mich noch nützlich machen kann.* (St. Galler Tagblatt, 2.9.1998) *'I recommend working until you are 65 years of age. I am grateful for every day on which I can contribute.'*; *Wir hoffen und wir freuen uns auf den Tag, wo wir die vielen Flüchtlingshelfer als erste Besucher in unsere Heimat einladen und unsere Dankbarkeit äussern können.* (St. Galler Tagblatt, 3.11.1998) *'We hope and we are looking forward to the day on which we will be able to invite the large number of refugee help organizations as first visitors to our homeland and express our gratitude.'.*

Philologie. Festschrift für Professor Dr. sc. Karl Mollayzum 80. Geburtstag ed. P. Bassola et al., 1-18. Budapest: ELTE.

Ágel, Vilmos. 1997. "Reflexiv-Passiv das (im Deutschen) keines ist. Überlegungen zu Reflexivität, Medialität, Passiv und Subjekt". *Sprache im Fokus. Festschrift für Heinz Vater zum 65. Geburtstag* ed. C. Dürscheid, 147-187. Tübingen: Niemeyer.

Ágel, Vilmos. 2000. "Syntax des Neuhochdeutschen bis zur Mitte des 20. Jahrhundert". *Sprachgeschichte. Ein Handbuch zur Geschichte der deutschen Sprache und ihrer Erforschung. 2. Teilband* ed. W. Besch, A. Betten, O. Reichmann & S. Sonderegger, 1855-1903. Berlin & New York: de Gruyter.

Ammon, Ulrich. 2005. "Standard und Variation: Norm, Autorität, Legitimation". *Standardvariation. Wie viel Variation verträgt die deutsche Sprache* ed. L. M. Eichinger & W. Kallmeyer, 28-40. Berlin & New York: de Gruyter.

Askedal, John Ole. 1984. "Grammatikalisierung und Auxiliarisierung im sogenannten 'bekommen/kriegen/erhalten-Passiv' des Deutschen". *Kopenhagener Beiträge zur Germanistischen Linguistik* 22. 5-47.

Askedal, John Ole. 2005. "Grammatikalisierung und Persistenz im deutschen "Rezipienten-Passiv" mit bekommen/kriegen/erhalten". *Grammatikalisierung im Deutschen* ed. T. Leuschner, T. Mortelmans & S. D. Groodt, 211-228. Berlin & New York: de Gruyter.

Coseriu, Eugenio. 1970. *Sprache. Strukturen und Funktionen*. Tübingen: Niemeyer.

Davies, Winifred V. 2000. "Linguistic Norms at School. A survey of secondary-school teachers in a central German dialect area". *Zeitschrift für Dialektologie und Linguistik* 67. 129-147.

Davies, Winifred V. & Nils Langer. 2006. "'Gutes' Deutsch – 'Schlechtes' Deutsch von 1600 bis 2005". *Sprachreport* 3. 2-9.

Diewald, Gabriele. 1997. *Grammatikalisierung. Eine Einführung in Sein und Werden grammatischer Formen*. Tübingen: Niemeyer.

Donhauser, Karin. 1996. "Negationssyntax in der deutschen Sprachgeschichte: Grammatikalisierung oder Degrammatikalisierung?". *Deutsch – typologisch* ed. E. Lang & G. Zifonun, 201-217. Berlin & New York: de Gruyter.

Duden. 2005. *Richtiges und gutes Deutsch* (Duden Band 9). Mannheim.

Duden. 2005. *Die Grammatik* (Duden Band 4). Mannheim.

Duden. 2006. *Die deutsche Rechtschreibung* (Duden Band 1). Mannheim.

Duden. 2005. *Das Aussprachewörterbuch* (Duden Band 6). Mannheim.

Dovalil, Vít. 2006. *Sprachnormenwandel im geschriebenen Deutsch an der Schwelle zum 21. Jahrhundert. Die Entwicklung in ausgesuchten Bereichen der Grammatik*. Frankfurt: Lang.

Elspaß, Stephan. 2005. *Sprachgeschichte von unten. Untersuchungen zum geschriebenen Alltagsdeutsch im 19. Jahrhundert.* Tübingen: Niemeyer.

Eroms, Hans-Werner. 1992. "Das deutsche Passiv in historischer Sicht". *Deutsche Syntax. Ansichten und Aussichten* ed. L. Hoffmann, 225-249. Berlin & New York: de Gruyter.

Eroms, Hans-Werner. 2000. *Syntax der deutschen Sprache.* Berlin & New York: de Gruyter.

Fischer, Annette. 2001. "Diachronie und Synchronie von auxiliarem *tun* im Deutschen". *Zur Verbmorphologie germanischer Sprachen* ed. S. Watts, J. West & H.-J. Solms, 137-154. Tübingen: Niemeyer.

Fleischer, Jürg. 2002. *Die Syntax von Pronominaladverbien in den Dialekten des Deutschen. Eine Untersuchung zu Preposition Stranding und verwandten Phänomenen.* Stuttgart: Steiner.

Gloy, Klaus. 1975. *Sprachnormen I. Linguistische und soziologische Analysen.* Stuttgart: Frommann-Holzboog.

Gloy, Klaus. 1998. "Sprachnormierung und Sprachkritik in ihrer gesellschaftlichen Verflechtung". *Sprachgeschichte. Ein Handbuch zur Geschichte der deutschen Sprache und ihrer Erforschung. 1. Teilband* ed. W. Besch, A. Betten, O. Reichmann & S. Sonderegger, 396-406. Berlin & New York: de Gruyter.

Harnisch, Rüdiger. 1990. "Morphologische Irregularität – Gebrauchshäufigkeit – psychische Nähe. Ein Zusammenhang im empirischen Befund und in seiner theoretischen Tragweite". *Naturalists at Krems. Papers from the Workshop on Natural Phonology and Natural Morphology* ed. J. Mendez Dosuna & C. Pensado, 53-64. Salamanca: Universitätsverlag.

Hundt, Markus. 2002. "Formen und Funktionen des Reflexivpassivs im Deutschen". *Deutsche Sprache* 30. 124-166.

Hundt, Markus. 2005. "Grammatikalität – Akzeptabilität – Sprachnorm. Zum Verhältnis von Korpuslinguistik und Grammatikalitätsurteilen". *Corpuslinguistik in Lexik und Grammatik* ed. F. Lenz & S. Schierholz, 15-40. Tübingen: Niemeyer.

Klumpp, Franziska. 1997. "Zu den Ursachen der Ungrammatikalität von Präpositionsstranden im Deutschen". *Neuphilologische Mitteilungen* 98(2). 147-159.

Krause, Olaf. 1997. "Progressiv-Konstruktionen im Deutschen im Vergleich mit dem Niederländischen, Englischen und Italienischen". *Sprachtypologie und Universalienforschung* 50. 48-82.

Krause, Olaf. 2002. *Progressiv im Deutschen. Eine empirische Untersuchung im Kontrast mit Niederländisch und Englisch.* Tübingen: Niemeyer.

Langer, Nils. 2000. "Zur Verbreitung der *tun*-Periphrase im Frühneuhochdeutschen". *Zeitschrift für Dialektologie und Linguistik* 47. 287-316.

Langer, Nils. 2001. *Linguistic Purism in Action. How auxiliary tun was stigmatized in Early New High German*. Berlin & New York: de Gruyter.

Langer, Nils & Winifred V. Davies. 2006. *The Making of Bad Language*. Frankfurt: Lang.

Lenz, Alexandra (2007): "Zur variationslinguistischen Analyse regionalsprachlicher Korpora." *Sprachkorpora – Datenmengen und Erkenntnisfortschritt* ed. W. Kallmeyer & G. Zifonun, 169-202. Berlin & New York: de Gruyter.

Lenz, Alexandra (2008): "*Wenn einer etwas gegeben bekommt* – Ergebnisse eines Süprachproduktionsexperiments zum Rezipientenpassiv". *Dialektale Morphologie, dialektale Syntax* ed. F. Patocka & G. Seiler, 155-178. Wien: Edition Präsens.

Lenz, Barbara. 1996. "Negationsverstärkung und Jespersens Zyklus im Deutschen und in anderen europäischen Sprachen". *Deutsch – typologisch* ed. E. Lang & G. Zifonun, 183-200. Berlin & New York: de Gruyter.

Mattheier, Klaus J., ed. 1997. *Norm und Variation*. Frankfurt: Lang.

Milroy, James. 1999. "The consequences of standardisation in descriptive linguistics". *Standard English. The widening debate* ed. T. Bex & R. J. Watts, 16-39. London & New York: Routledge.

Milroy, James & Lesley. 1991. *Authority in Language. Investigating language prescription and standardisation*. London & New York: Routledge.

Miyazaki, Satoshi. 2001. "Theoretical Framework for Communicative Adjustment in Language Acquisition". *Journal of the Asian Pacific Communication* 11:1. 39-60.

Nübling, Damaris et al. 2006. *Historische Sprachwissenschaft des Deutschen. Eine Einführung in die Prinzipien des Sprachwandels*. Tübingen: Niemeyer.

Pasch, Renate. 1997. "WEIL mit Hauptsatz – Kuckucksei im DENN-Nest". *Deutsche Sprache* 25/3. 252-271.

Reimann, Ariane. 1999. *Die Verlaufsform im Deutschen. Entwickelt das Deutsche eine Aspektkorrelation?* Bamberg: Universitätsverlag.

Rödel, Michael. 2003. "Die Entwicklung der Verlaufsform im Deutschen". *Muttersprache* 113. 97-107.

Ronneberger-Sibold, Elke. 1980. *Sprachverwendung – Sprachsystem: Ökonomie und Wandel*. Tübingen: Niemeyer.

Selting, Margret. 1999. "Ahd. *wanta* + Verbletzt-/Verbzweitstellung gwd. *weil* + Verbletzt-/Verbzweitstellung – historische Kontinuität oder neuerer Sprachwandel". *Zeitschrift für germanistische Linguistik* 27. 167-204.

Uhmann, Susanne. 1998. "Verbstellungsvariation in *weil*-Sätzen. Lexikalische Differenzierung mit grammatischen Folgen". *Zeitschrift für Sprachwissenschaft* 17. 92-139.

van Pottelberge, Jeroen. 2005. "Ist jedes grammatische Verfahren Ergebnis eines Grammatikalisierungsprozesses? Fragen zur Entwicklung des *am*-Pro-

gressivs". *Grammatikalisierung im Deutschen* ed. T. Leuschner, T. Mortelmans & S. D. Groodt, 169-191. Berlin & New York: de Gruyter.
van Pottelberge, Jeroen. 2004. *Der am-Progressiv. Struktur und parallele Entwicklung in den kontinentalwestgermanischen Sprachen.* Tübingen: Niemeyer.
von Polenz, Peter. 1999. *Deutsche Sprachgeschichte vom Spätmittelalter bis zur Gegenwart. Bd. III: 19. und 20. Jahrhundert.* Berlin & New York: de Gruyter.
von Polenz, Peter. 2000. *Deutsche Sprachgeschichte vom Spätmittelalter bis zur Gegenwart. Band 1: Einführung. Grundbegriffe. 14. bis 16. Jahrhundert.* Berlin & New York: de Gruyter.
von Wright, Georg Henrik. 1963. *Norm and Action. A Logical Enquiry.* London: Routledge.
Wagner, Melanie. 2005. *An investigation into lay knowledge of an perception of linguistic norms in modern German on the basis of an empirical sociolinguistic study in the Moselle Franconian dialect area.* Wales.
Wegener, Heide. 1985. "Er bekommt widersprochen. Argumente für die Existenz eines Dativpassivs im Deutschen". *Linguistische Berichte* 96. 127-139.
Wegener, Heide. 1999. "Syntaxwandel und Degrammatikalisierung im heutigen Deutsch? Noch einmal zu weil-Verbzweit". *Deutsche Sprache* 27. 3-26.
Wegener, Heide. 2000. "*Da, denn* und *weil* der Kampf der Konjunktionen. Zur Grammatikalisierung im kausalen Bereich". *Deutsche Grammatik in Theorie und Praxis* ed. R. Thieroff, M. Tamrat, N. Fuhrhop & O. Teuber, 69-81. Tübingen: Niemeyer.
Werner, Otmar. 1987. "Natürlichkeit und Nutzen morphologischer Irregularität". *Beiträge zum 3. Essener Kolloquium über Sprachwandel und seine bestimmenden Faktoren* ed. N. Boretzky, W. Enninger & T. Stolz, 289-316. Bochum: Brockmeyer.
Werner, Otmar. 1989. "Sprachökonomie und Natürlichkeit im Bereich der Morphologie". *Zeitschrift für Phonetik, Sprachwissenschaft und Kommunikationsforschung* 42. 34-47.

Beate Henn-Memmesheimer (Mannheim)

Ephemera and Tradition-Founding Grammatical Constructions
Staging and Acceptance

1. Introduction

New grammatical constructions are developed in various domains of cultural space (e.g., in sciences, in administrations, in new media) and established with specific meanings. Some of them are carried over with altered meanings into different cultural domains, while others disappear as ephemeral trends. Examples of patterns in communication studies and political science established in the last few years include: *kommunizieren* as a transitive and passive verb, as in *etwas wird gut/missverständlich kommuniziert*; *abheben* with the preposition *auf*; in the field of administration, the preposition *in* followed by a year; in comics and cartoons, verbs without endings such as *flatter, seufz*; in the sciences – in scientific and scholarly texts – the formation *nichtsdestotrotz*, originally a facetious form[1], which has appeared in the meantime in my colleagues' publications and in students' papers as a hallmark of weighty scientific argumentation[2]. In the following study, the scope of quantitative and qualitative methods of describing new linguistic conventions will be exemplified. On a systemic level, the innovations can be related to existing standardized patterns and explained. On the basis of larger corpora, temporal developments such as establishments and trends can be ascertained quantitatively and represented by growth-curves (gradients). These developments can be qualitatively analyzed through interpretative methods. It will be shown that new grammatical patterns become linguistic currency for the sake of specific meanings, and that these meanings change with their dissemination into new domains. On the level of personal action, conjectures can be used as motives for the implementation or the abandonment of syntactic patterns. This will be typified both in theory and methodologically using the example of a new media-specific syntagm: in chat rooms between 2000 and 2009, a specific type of verb phrase was staged, disseminated and generally accepted before partially being abandoned again.

---

[1] From *nichtsdestoweniger* and *trotzdem*, cf. Gauger 2004.
[2] According to surveys from seminars, in which students are no longer familiar with *nichtsdestoweniger*.

2. A history of dissemination: the spread of new verb phrases in different domains

In the first half of the twentieth century, verb forms without endings were already in sporadic use,[3] and with the Mickey Mouse translations of Erika Fuchs starting in 1951, they became popular, productive word formation patterns:

(1) *grübel, flatter, seufz, ächz*
(2) iterative: *grübel, grübel; flatter, flatter*

These are usually interpreted as calques.[4] Diffused through comics, they belong to the significant characteristics of this type of literature. These formations appeared at the very latest in the 1970s in the oral utterances of young comic fans in Zurich as well as Berlin.[5] Meanwhile, verb phrases without an inflected verb are used in diverse forms in the written texts of online chat rooms.[6] The documents in question derive from corpora collected from 2002, 2004 and 2007 with regionally differentiated names: Berlin-Brandenburg (hereafter *BB*), Hessennetz (*H*), Pälzer unner sich (*P*), Bayern (*B*).[7]

(3) ***grins*, *freu*, *sing*, *anstups*, *knuddel*, *snief*, *anschiel*, *wink*, *wunda*** [from *sich wundern*],[8] ***schäm*** (B, 11.01.07, 13:24:57)[9]
(4) with graphemic iterations: ***knuddddddddddlllllllllllllll*** (B, 11.01.07, 14:11:17), with lexeme iteration: ***freufreu*** (H, 14.04.02, 20:33:49)
(5) in acronymic variations: ***g*** (abbreviates *grins*)[10]
(6) with syntactic extensions: ***freudig-kuck*** (BB, 09.05.04, 12:37:48), ***liebguck*** (B-B, 14.04.02, 15:25:52), ***frechgrins*** (B, 14.04.02, 16:54:20), acronymic: ***fg*** (B, 14.04.04, 15:44:20), ***nichtfreu*** (H, 22.09.02, 00:58:11), ***ganzdollfreu*** (B, 14.04.02, 18:26:13), ***handstandmach*** (BB, 14.04.02, 15:49:21), ***kopfschüttel*** (H, 22.09.02, 1:15:40), ***andreas hand geb***(B, 14.04.02, 21:03:11), ***Coolfun auch ma vom eis leckenlass*** (BB, 14.04.02, 19:58:21), ***sich ganz nah an nervi setz und ihn**

---

[3] Götz 2006.
[4] Cf. Schlobinski (2001: 3/4, note 3), where verbs without endings are regarded, and justifiably so, as a new phenomenon, in spite of *knall!*, cited in Adelung 1782, which will not be interpreted analogously to the constructions thematized here.
[5] Private communication: Daniel Süss, Barbara Schmugge, Institut für Angewandte Psychologie der Hochschule für Angewandte Wissenschaften Zürich.
[6] Cf. Schlobinski 2001, Henn-Memmesheimer 2004.
[7] See the Spin-Chat-Korpus described in Henn-Memmesheimer 2004, supplemented with material from 2004, 2007 and 2009. See below for more specific characteristics.
[8] Documents from Spin-Chat, cited in Henn-Memmesheimer 2004, Zetzsche 2008.
[9] Linguistic units that are objects of this study are in italics, with the exception of those cited from chat and only documented in writing; these units are bolded.
[10] Documents from Spin-Chat, cited in Henn-Memmesheimer 2004, Zetzsche 2008.

ganz ganz süß anguck* (BB, 14.04.02, 00:41:37), **heulend chanel verlass** (BB, 14.04.02, 02:53:16)[11]

Formal changes with the transition to the new medium consist of inserting a structure sign: «*», development of the construction through expansion via verb supplements and information, as well as coalescence and reduction to the point of univerbation and acronym. Around 2004, one finds complex phrases in oral utterances with verbs in the last position:

(7)   *Was macht ihr mit der Weihnachtsfeier? Nur mal so in die Runde frag.* (undocumented evidence, 2004).

Here a medial change and an expansion of the domain for this type of syntagms take place. At the same time, it can be shown in the chat corpus of 2004 that they begin to disappear from usage.

The adoption of these syntagms in literary texts constitutes the next medial change. Being a symptom of his entanglement in internet communication, they are used to cite reflexively and also to symptomize the addiction and confusion of a novel figure. For the first-person narrator, it is a way of distancing himself from the mainstream's demands, of emotional postures iconified by hasty, short statements that breach the education-oriented standard language: syntagms containing verbs without endings, *Herzklopf* and *Geldverdienmist* (Kehlmann 2009, PP. 138, 134), appear among other constructions considered to be chat- and forum-specific.

3. Syntactic development

Chat participants indicate the special status of utterances such as those mentioned in (6) in several ways:

– through structure signs,
– through verbs without endings,
– through verbs placed in the last position.

With surprising new forms, chatters follow a "maxim of explicitness for written texts"[12] which comprises part of their standard language, as Zifonun's grammar and others have confirmed. This is necessary because "content for communicative purposes" must be "made available solely with written means".[13] The designation of certain text functions with punctuation is not easily imparted, whether it be in school or at the university. One need only think, for example, of the difficulty of implementing the designation of words used metalinguistically

---

[11]   For a detailed description of the syntax of these syntagms within the framework of dependency grammar, see Henn-Memmesheimer 2004.
[12]   Zifonun et al. (1997: 253).
[13]   Ibid.

with italics, or the designation of cited statements with quotation marks. By contrast, the usage of asterisks is conventionalized in the chat texts from 2002 for the designation of a kind of stage direction. With asterisks, chatters offset actions accompanying utterances from other utterances, since, due to the medium of communication, these actions can only be presented verbally. There is no corresponding phenomenon to be found in standard texts, barring the italicization of stage directions in dramatic texts.

Syntagms with 'uninflected' verbs are indeed described as standard language; however, verbs with an infinitive ending are usually meant in this context:

(8) Syntagms without personal, modal or temporal markers, ending with a verb: *Anfangen, jetzt aber anfangen! sofort kommen, alle mal herhören, vor Gebrauch schütteln, den Tisch abgeräumt*, etc.[14]

Also, by the same token, syntagms ending with a verb:

(9) Syntagms ending with a verb: *wie gut er doch tanzt! mit welch einer Ausdauer sich alle amüsiert haben! was du dir jetzt schon wieder denkst!*[15]

Standard grammars confirm the specific status, as well as the modes, respectively, of such constructions. Weinreich treats examples ending with a verb, as in (9), as exclamations[16], while Zifonun attributes the same examples to the "exclamatory mode", examples with infinite verb forms as in (8) to the "demanding", "exclamatory", "interrogative" and "optative" modes. In captions, Zifonun also ascribes the latter examples to the "declarative mode".[17] The syntagms with uninflected verbs documented in chats, which lack both inflected form and infinite endings, belong exclusively to the declarative mode. They operate on utterances and thematize an action, relevant to text or to conversation, which can only be conveyed verbally under the conditions of comics or chat. In the following example, this function is especially clear:

(10) 11.01.07, 23:42:03 [BB]   ~krYa~: *wer saugtn hier *asteri anguck**,[18]

where the interrogative mode of the statement, aside from being signaled by the interrogative pronoun, is designated by the asterisked syntagm, but not by the structural sign (question mark).

---

[14] Examples from Zifonun et al. (1997: 141f., 613, 654).
[15] Examples from Weinrich (2003: 893).
[16] Weinrich (2003: 8.3.4, 892f.), see also Zifonun et al. (1997: D2, 648: "Verbletzt-Formtypen im Fragebereich" 669, 674).
[17] Zifonun et al. (1997: D2, 613, 654, 669, 674).
[18] In this context, *saugen* means 'to download music'.

The utterances placed within asterisks are strongly formalized to the point of abbreviation: *grins*, *g*, *frech grins*, *frechgrins* *fg*. The complex, expanded syntagms are very strictly organized in their syntactic form as well: they are marked by asterisks, and their constituent elements always have an identical sequence. Described in terms of syntactic relations from left to right, the elements are: 1. modals[19], 2. dative object, 3. accusative object, 4. prepositional object, 5. prepositional adverbial, 6. adverbial with an adverbial head, 7. adverbial with an adjectival head, 8. uninflected verb as predicate. The individual positions can be empty. Many writers apparently see the parts as being so fixed and integrated that they write them into one word. The emergence of such complexly integrated phrases can be described in terms of process as grammaticalization. We have

1. graphic reduction to the point of acronyms,
2. morphological reduction: Ø as verb morpheme,
3. coalescence: writing as one word to the point of univerbation,
4. topologization: firm position of the constituent elements of the syntagm according to syntactic relations,
5. semantic reduction and synsemantisation: reduction to the designation of an action accompanying the utterance of the particular chatter.

More or less grammaticalized forms are found side by side: *grinst frech* next to *frech grins*, *frechgrins* and *fg*.

Furthermore, the stereotypical configuration of constituent elements described in terms of syntactic relations found here corresponds to the configuration postulated in the universal grammar and appearing in a certain phase of language acquisition. It is also the 'salient arrangement' described in functional semantics or categorial grammar, for example, that of Zifonun.[20] According to optimality theories, it may also be the optimal, unmarked sequence in the verbal phrase[21] (however, these theories are only typified by partial aspects of the structures described above).

4. Formation and breakdown tendency of a chat convention – observations

In the examples before 2000 from the literature (e.g. Beißwenger 2000), there are many deviations from verbs without endings, verbs in the last position, and utterances in asterisks. In 2002 the convention appears very stable, the afore-

---

[19] Used here to mean, on the level of lexical categories: *modal particle*, on the level of syntactic relations: *modals*.
[20] Cf. Zifonun et al. (1997: 1300, 1324: on the realization of primary components, 102 on the relationship between sequences and salient arrangement.
[21] E.g., Müller (2000: 242).

mentioned characteristics form a consolidated collocation: asterisks as structural signs are consistently placed in nearly all phrases that have the syntactic characteristics of verbs without an ending and verbs in the last position. The adverbial, adjectival and substantivial expansions of the verb phrase have the same configuration almost everywhere. In the corpora of 2004 and 2007, however, signs of a convention breakdown crop up that will be examined until 2009. Upon inspection of corpus excerpts, one notices that uninflected verbs are used less frequently and that verb phrases with uninflected verbs are not structured as regularly as before. A great number of variants appear side by side:

(11) 11.01.07, 22:54:59 [BB]   assos: *schulterzuck*
      11.01.07, 23:41:15 [BB]   assos: *neue geb*
      11.01.07, 23:41:44 [BB]   *~asteri~*: seh schon g*

In other cases, asterisks are not used:[22]

(12) 11.01.07, 23:37:53 [BB]   *~asteri~*: schultern zuck+
      11.01.07, 00:23:18 [B]   Mochlos: weglach
      11.01.07, 00:23:21 [B]   authateia: grinst frech

There are also usages of double asterisks in meanings conventional to chat, with infinite and finite verb phrases, as well as with substantivial phrases (in this case, an acronymic substantivial phrase):

(13) 11.01.07, 04:03:57 [BB]   Phili: *reküss*
      11.01.07, 00:44:50 [B]   zestos*agori*20*: jettchen was ist mit genau? bin nicht mitgekommen *schäm*
      11.01.07, 16:56:57 [H]   *~InDiana~*: *UrlaubNeigtSichDemEndeZu* :(
      11.01.07, 13:24:57 [P]   !BrachoS83!: *fährt sich mit der Hand über sein Kinn*
      11.01.07, 13:59:28 [B]   nai1976: <<<<<<schweigt ...... ~XuXu~ *gfG*[23]

In the preceding examples, asterisks have the function (among others) of ornamenting proper names. This usage will be taken up again in 6.4. In the quantitative analysis in chapter 5, however, only messages will be analysed.

How can the tendencies of changes be quantitatively and qualitatively conceived?

---

[22] The plus symbol, «+», could be interpreted as an intended asterisk, «*», perhaps because the writer accidentally let go of the control key too soon, but this investigation will follow the formal differentiations.

[23] XuXu is a username, gfG is an acronym for ganz freches Grinsen.

5. Quantitative analysis of the development of intra-chat conventions

5.1 Hypothesis and corpus

The expectation of convention formation and convention breakdown can be conceived in the following hypotheses:

1. Until 2002 and 2004, there is a tendency to greater distance from standard language and a tendency to consolidate intra-chat conventions.
2. From 2004 to 2007, there is a tendency to greater proximity to standard language and a tendency to dissolve intra-chat conventions.
3. This tendency continues beyond 2007.

Therefore, statements will be made on developments between 2002 and 2009. The population comprises of messages composed in chat rooms during this time in the online community of the firm SPIN-AG. The firm can be reached at the web addresses http://www.spin.de and www.spin-ag.de, respectively. Access is free, and registration must merely be verified by a valid e-mail address.[24] Spin has approximately 1.2 million members and approximately 120 million hits per month. 24-hour records were selected as a sample from the years 2002, 2004, 2007 and 2009 from the Spin rooms Berlin-Brandenburg, Hessennetz, Pälzer unner sich, and Bayern.[25] Although users still look at the chat room of Palatinate, it was discontinued after 2009 due to lack of participation. There are 103,600 lines of chat altogether. A line counts as that which is between two enter-signs (¶). A line is composed of the date, time, name of the chat room, name of the chatter, and the message. These types of lines are reproduced in shortened form in examples (10) to (12). In the Excel spreadsheets in which the corpus was transcribed and which forms the basis of the computations, there is a column for the date and time, the name of the chat room, the chatter's name, and the message. The prerequisite for the processing of such a large corpus is the isolation of elements that can be read and quantified by the computer program Excel and its operating macros.[26]

---

[24] Cf.: http://de.wikipedia.org/wiki/Spin.de, as well as http://www.spin-ag.de (visited on 01.03.2008).
[25] Regional differentiation will not be pursued in the following investigation.
[26] The Excel macros were generated by Ernst Eggers of the Studienseminar Mainz. The calculations were carried out by Sarah Zetzsche (Zetzsche 2008), and reviewed and adjusted by Ernst Eggers. I thank Tilmann Deutler, Universität Mannheim, and Raoul-Martin Memmesheimer, Harvard University, Cambridge, Mass., for their critical review and consultation.

5.2 Quantifiable indicators for intra-chat conventions and their development

In our research, the usage of asterisks in messages allows us to use them as indicators for the stability of conventions. Indeed, they fulfill the following requirements: the asterisks are frequent; they have specific meaning in this type of text that they do not have in standard language and that cannot be fulfilled by other means; they are easily and automatically detectable, in contrast to other intra-chat characteristics including verbs in the last position and uninflected verbs. The chart in Table 1 arises from asterisk usage in messages.

Table 1: Decrease in asterisk expressions

	2002	2004	2007	2009
Corpus size: Total lines	32885	32232	28262	16118
Lines with self-written messages	22928	23084	20065	10208
Self-written messages with asterisks Absolute frequency Relative frequency	2578 11,24 %	2544 11,02 %	1862 9,28 %	726 7,11 %
Relative change of the percentage of asterisk-expressions compared to the prior value (rate of change)		−2 %	−15,8 %	−23,4 %

Over the years in question, a decrease in messages marked with asterisks can be observed. The points in the figure below indicate the percentage of lines with asterisks found in the sample, and the confidence intervals show the probability with which lines containing asterisks appear during the years from which the samples were taken. The confidence intervals (based on 2σ) are calculated at the confidence level $1-\alpha = 95{,}5\,\%$. For 2002, the confidence interval is then [10,8 %; 11,7 %], for 2004, it is [10,6 %; 11,4 %], for 2007, it is [8,9 %; 9,7 %]. Between 2002 and 2004, the decrease is not significant, because it still falls inside the confidence interval. However, the decrease between 2004 and 2007, and between 2007 and 2009 is significant (see Figure 1). The displayed confidence intervals in Figure 1 (0,45 % for 2002; 0,4 % for 2004; 0,4 % for 2007; 5% for 2009) are for the confidence level $1-\alpha = 95{,}5\,\%$. For the rate of change ↓(-15,8 %), cf. commentary in the text.

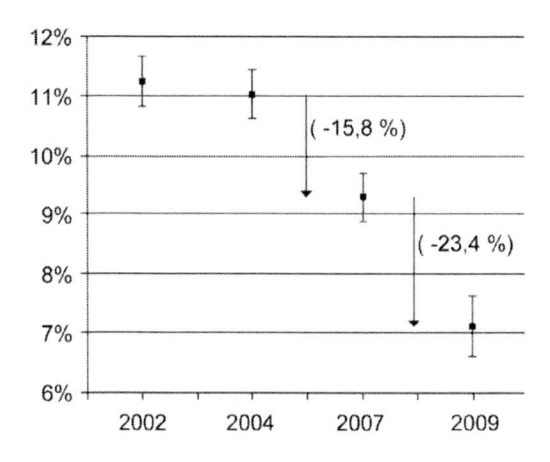

Figure 1: Decrease in the percentage of messages with asterisks (cf. Table 1)[27]

This development can be clarified through an illustration of the rate of change (also called 'gradient analysis'), which takes the percentage of the year 2004 as base value and sets it to 100 %: the percentage of messages with asterisks decreases by 15,8 % from 2004 to 2007 and even more by 23,4% from 2007 to 2009 (see also Table 1).

The indicator *asterisk placement* can be further differentiated, since chatters use the structural sign of double asterisks (*...*) very consistently in 2002 to designate actions accompanying utterances. The occurance of simple asterisks in a message is an indicator that these signs' usage is only perfunctory, i.e., only at the beginning or at the end of a syntagm, as in the example (10).We have no quantifiable data from the time before 2002 in the following image results (cf. Figure 2). From 2004 to 2009, the percentage of messages with asterisks generally declines. The percentage of messages with only one asterisk increases from 2002 to 2007 then decreases slightly from 2007 to 2009 but still remains above the level of 2004. The percentage of messages with two asterisks decreases. The use of three, four, or more than four asterisks in a message plays practically no role in our statistics.

---

[27] The displayed confidence intervals (0,45 % for 2002; 0,4 % for 2004; 0,4 % for 2007) are for the confidence level 1-α = 95,5 %. For the rate of change ↓(−15,8 %), cf. commentary in the text.

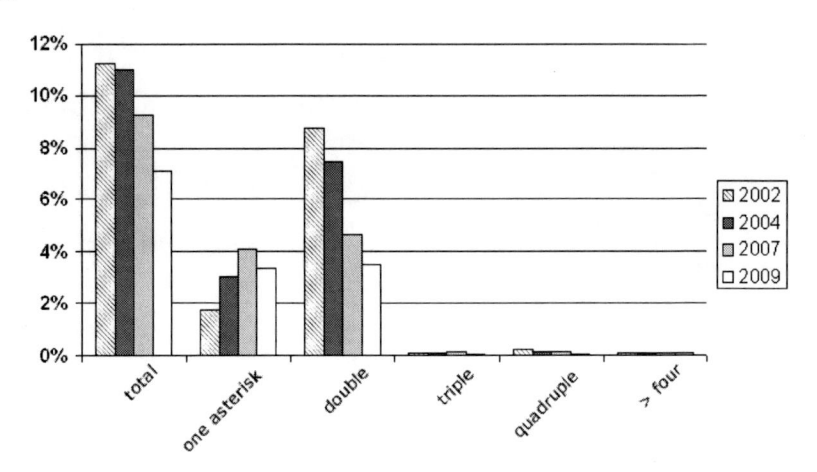

Figure 2: Percentage of self-written messages with asterisks

The development can also be clarified here based on rates of change (cf. Figure 3).

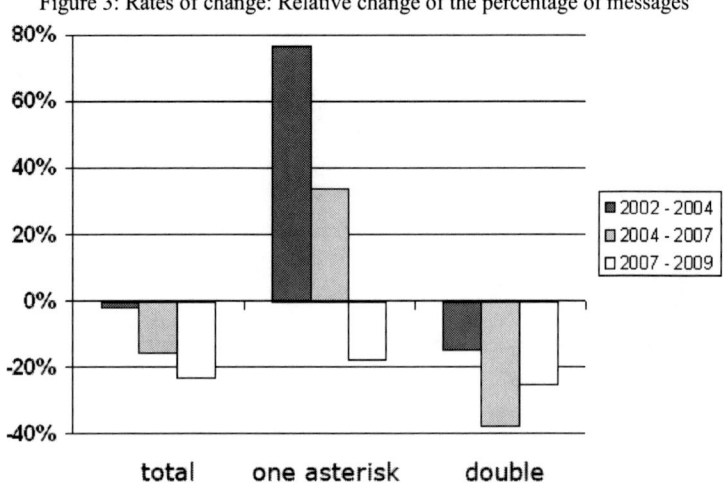

Figure 3: Rates of change: Relative change of the percentage of messages with asterisks, each measured relative to the prior inquiry

To this end, first the percentages from 2002 are set to 100 %. From 2002 to 2004, the percentage of double asterisks decreases by 14,8 %.[28] Setting the percentages from 2004 to 100 % reveals a decrease in percentage of double asterisks of 37,4 %. Setting the percentages from 2007 to 100% reveals a decrease in percentage of double asterisks of 25,3% from 2007 to 2009. Taken together, we see a 'negative growth' of the intra-chat convention of double asterisk usage and of asterisk usage altogether. A positive growth in the usage of simple asterisks, which does not correspond to intra-chat conventions, is seen from 2002 to 2004 with +90 %, from 2004 to 2007 with a lesser growth of 33,7 %, and from 2007 to 2009 a negative growth applies, i.e. the usage of asterisks decreases in general (Figure 3 and Table 2).

Table 2: Rates of change

Percentages	*Percent of lines with asterisks, of lines with messages*	*Percent of lines with simple asterisks, of lines with messages*	*Percent of lines with double asterisks, of lines with messages*
2002	11,24%	1,74%	8,77%
2004	11,02%	3,08%	7,46%
2007	9,28%	4,12%	4,67%
2009	7,11 %	3,38 %	3,49 %
Development of percentages	*Of lines with asterisks*	*Of lines with simple asterisks*	*Of lines with double asterisks*
2002-2004	-2,00%	76,50%	-14,90%
2004-2007	-15,60%	33,80%	-37,40%
2007-2009	- 23,4 %	- 18,0 %	- 25,3 %

The following significance can be read out from Figure 4, which summarizes the information in Figures 2 and 3 and shows confidence intervals and rates of change.

---

[28] Values that Excel outputs, rounded to a decimal place after the fact.

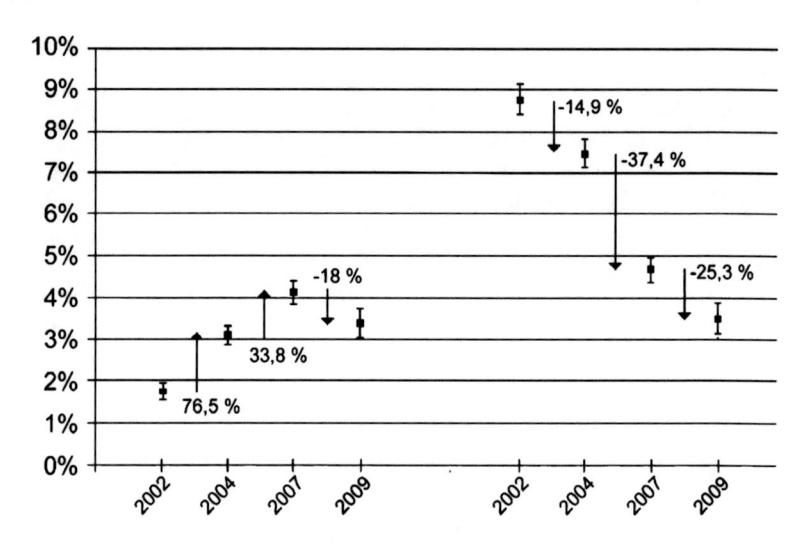

Figure 4: Development of the usage of one and two asterisks with entry of rates of change ↑(X%)

Taking the confidence interval into consideration yields the following results: based on 2002, the percentage of lines with an asterisk increases to 76,5 % (arrow) on average, the gain accounts for at least 53 % and 100 % at most. Based on 2004, the percentage of lines with an asterisk increases to 33,8 % (arrow) on average, the gain accounts for at least 17,2 % and 50,3 % at most. Based on 2007, the percentage of lines with an asterisk decreases to 18% (arrow) on average, the loss accounts for at least 46,9% and 69,5% at most. Based on 2002, the percentage of lines with two asterisks decreases to 14,9 % (arrow) on average, the loss accounts for at least 6,6 % and 23 % at most. Based on 2004, the percentage of lines with two asterisks decreases to 37,4 % (arrow) on average, the loss accounts for at least 28,8 % and 46,1 % at most. Based on 2007, the percentage of lines with two asterisks decreases to 25,3% (arrow) on average, the loss accounts for at least 51,5% and 72% at most.

For one as well as for two asterisks, the values differ significantly. We note the following as a final result and as a correction and specification of the statement formulated in the hypothesis (in 5.1): the increase of messages with one asterisk decelerates and reaches its peak in 2007, while the breakdown of the double-asterisk convention accelerates until 2007, and continues slightly slower until 2009.

5.3 Quantitative analysis of *grins* and its variations in 2002: The development of a convention through quantitative analysis

The aforementioned examples (1) to (13) are relevant for a structural description, but on the majority are not possible for quantitative analysis. *Grins* and its variations are adequately frequent and, therefore, promising for a qualitative analysis. In 2002, *grins,* or a variation thereof, appears in 1371 lines with messages (6 %); in 2004, they appear in 1697 lines (7,35 %); in 2007, in 1280 lines (6,4 %) and in 2009 in 258 lines (2,5%). The following variations are documented (see Table 3):

Table 3: *grins*-variations

grins	heftig grins	*sfg...
grins intelligently	saufrechgrins	
grins silently		*grins*
grins*	grins*	*grinst frech*
grinsel	angrins*	*grinst*
grinselt	g*	*dich angrins*
grinst	gg*	*dichangrins*
grinst diabolisch	ggg*	*fiesgrins*
grinst dreggisch	ggg...*	*frechgrins*
grinst einzigartig frech	sfg...*	*frechzuniederbayerrübergrins*
grinst extrem frech	... ggg*[29]	*ma fies grins*
grinst frech	fg...*	*schadenfroh grins*
grinst frecher		*fg* / *FG*
grinst ganz frech	*grins	*fg... *, *FG... *
grinst hessisch frech	*grinsel	*g*
grinst ma	*fiesgrins	*gg*
grinst mal	*fg	*ggg*
grinst mal eben mit	*fg...	*gggg...*
grinst mal frech	*g / *G	*grinsäää*
grinst noch frecher	*gg	*gb* / *bg*
grinst rotzfrech	*ggg	*gfg*
grinst sich eins	*ggg...	*sfg*, *s..sfg*
fgrins		
fresch grins		"grins"

For the following analysis, only the variations that appeared in more than 1 % of the messages containing *grins* (in at least one of the four years) are drawn upon.

---

[29] ...: Iteration of the last graphem.

Table 4: Table for the statistically relevant / applicable *grins*-variations[30]

Year:	2002		2004		2007		2009	
Lines with *grins*-variations:	1371		1697		1280		258	
	Z	h	Z	h	Z	h	Z	h
fg | *FG*	166	12,1 %	263	15,2 %	72	5,8 %	10	3,9 %
*fg...	35	2,6 %	75	4,3 %	43	3,4 %	16	11,2 %
*g | *g | *G	73	5,3 %	266	15,4 %	253	20,3 %	87	33,4 %
g	345	25,2 %	352	20,4 %	206	16,5 %	55	21,3 %
*gg	22	1,6 %	69	4,0 %	18	1,4 %	11	4,3 %
gg	131	9,6 %	126	7,3 %	63	5,1 %	4	1,6 %
ggg	60	4,4 %	18	1,0 %	10	0,8 %	1	0,4 %
gggg...	55	4,0 %	3	0,2 %	7	0,6 %	2	0,8 %
grins	14	1,0 %	18	1,0 %	26	2,1 %	0	0 %
sfg, *s..sfg*	37	2,7 %	44	2,6 %	31	2,5 %	1	0,4 %
g*	4	0,3 %	3	0,2 %	39	3,1 %	1	0,4 %
Grins	63	4,6 %	14	0,8 %	30	2,4 %	20	7,8 %
grins silently	0	0,0 %	0	0,0 %	24	1,9 %	0	0 %
grinst frech	317	23,1 %	353	20,5 %	351	28,1 %	0	0 %
grinst rotzfrech	0	0,0 %	61	3,5 %	0	0,0 %	0	0 %
Σ	1371	100 %	1657	100 %	1280	100 %	258	100 %

Table 4 shows that in 2002, the variations *g*, *gg*, *ggg*, *gggg...*, *fg*/*FG*, *sfg*/*s..sfg* account for 58 % of all incidences of *grins*-variations. Acronyms without asterisks do not appear, *grins* without asterisks accounts for 4,6 % of the total incidences of *grins*-variations, the inflected form *grinst* appears exactly five times (0,4 %), the simply inflected form *grinst frech* without asterisks accounted for 23 % of the total incidences of *grins*-variations. The last part, "Breaks with convention", shows that acronyms beginning with one asterisk account for 9,5 %, do not appear or remain at 0,3 % of all *grins*-variations (see Table 3). For this reason, the usage of acronyms with double asterisks can be identified as an intra-chat convention in 2002.

---

[30] The absolute frequencies are listed in the Z columns, and the relative frequencies are listed in the h columns.

5.4 Quantitative development of the usage of *grins* and its variants until 2009: Liberalization of a convention

In Table 3, the values from 2004 to 2009 are already entered. The following image emerges for *g*, the most often employed variation (Figure 5).

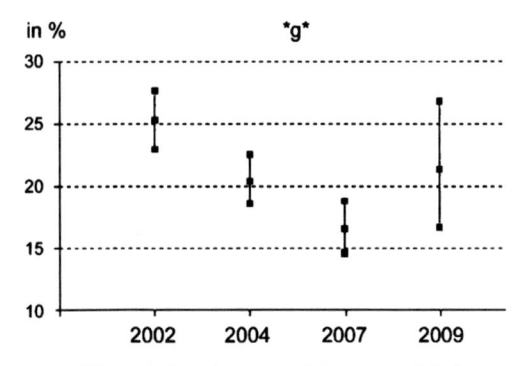

Figure 5: Development of the usage of *g*

In 2002 *g* appears 345 times in our corpus, it makes up 25,2 % of all 1371 *grins*-variations. The confidence interval entered in the figure amounts to 22,9-27,6 %. In 2004 *g* appears 352 times and only makes up 20,4 % of all 1697 incidences of *grins*-variations, and the confidence interval amounts to 18,5-22,4 %. With a total of 1280 incidences of *grins*-variations, the 206 incidences of *g* in 2007 correspond to 16,5 % and a confidence interval of 14,5-18,5 %. With a total of 1280 incidences of *grins*-variations, the 55 incidences of *g* in 2009 correspond to 21,3 % and a confidence interval of 16,6-26,8 %. The apparent increase in 2009 is, when compared to 2007, not significant. We conclude that with its confidence interval entries, the figure clearly illustrates that the decrease until 2007 is significant; as the values of the following or prior year, respectively, lie outside the confidence interval. The decrease of a central element of intra-chat conventions of 2002 is therefore quantitatively documented.

In terms of the other acronymic syntagms that had turned out to be conventionalized elements in chat for 2002, Figure 6 appears for *fg*/*FG* (in the order of their frequency in 2002).

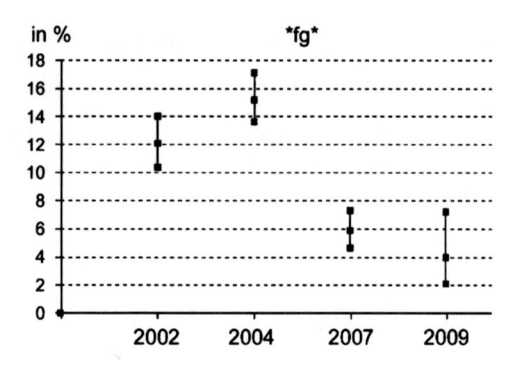

Figure 6: Development of the usage of *fg*/*FG*

The data (cf. commentary on Figure 5): Absolute incidences in 2002: 166, relative 12,1 %, confidence interval: 10,4-14 %; absolute incidences in 2004: 263, relative 15,2 %, confidence interval: 13,6-17,1 %; Absolute incidences in 2007: 72, relative 5,8 %, confidence intervals: 4,6-7,3 %,; Absolute incidences in 2009: 10, relative 3,9%, confidence intervals: 2,1-7,1%. The data are significant here, as well: an increase until 2004, a decrease until 2007 and 2009. – For the development of *gg* see Figure 7.

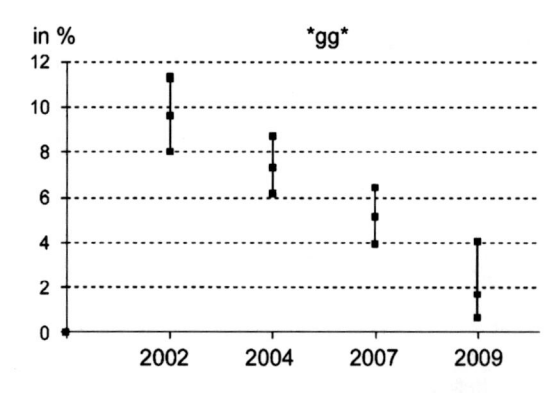

Figure 7: Development of the usage of *gg*

The data (cf. commentary on Figure 5): Absolute incidences in 2002: 131, relative 9,6 %, confidence interval: 8,0-11,3 %; Absolute incidences in 2004: 126, relative 7,3 %, confidence interval: 6,1-8,7 %; Absolute incidences in 2007: 63, relative 5,1 %, confidence interval: 3,9-6,4 %; Absolute incidences in 2009: 4, relative 1,6%, confidence interval: 0,6-4%. The development is significant: compared to 2002 a decrease until 2004 that continues until 2009. – For *ggg...*, i.e. for 3 or more g in double asterisks see Figure 8.

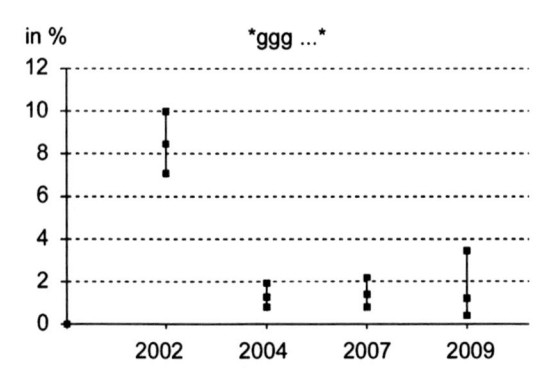

Figure 8: Development of the usage of *ggg...*

The data (cf. commentary on Figure 5): Absolute incidences in 2002: 115, relative 8,4 %, confidence interval: 7,0-10 %; Absolute incidences in 2004: 21, relative 1,2 %, confidence interval: 0,8-1,9 %; Absolute incidences in 2007: 17, relative 1,36 %, confidence interval: 0,8-2,2 %; Absolute incidences in 2009: 3, relative 1,2%, confidence interval: 0,4-3,4%. The decrease from 2002 to 2004 is significant, and from 2004 to 2009 there are no further changes. – For *sfg*/*s...fg*, i.e. with an s or iterated s, acronymic for *sehr frech grins*, see Figure 9.

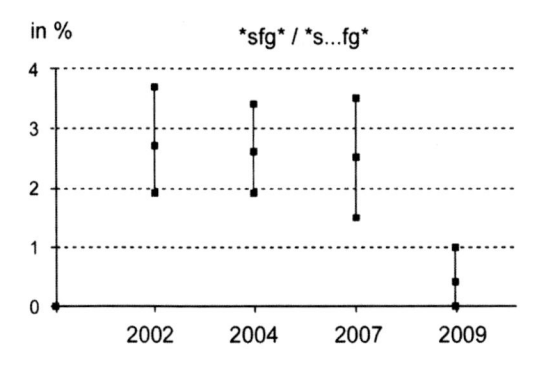

Figure 9: Development of the usage of *sfg* / *s...sfg*

The data (cf. commentary on Figure 5): Absolute incidences in 2002: 37, relative 2,4 %, confidence interval: 1,9-3,7 %; Absolute incidences in 2004: 44, relative 2,6 %, confidence interval: 1,9-3,4 %; Absolute incidences in 2007: 31, relative 2,5 %, confidence interval: 1,7-3,5 %; Absolute incidences in 2009: 1, relative 0,4%, confidence interval: 0-1%. From 2002 to 2007, there is no significant development to be accounted for here; the decrease in 2009 is significant, however cannot be interpreted at the moment due to a lack of data from following years.

A development in the opposite direction can be observed with *g/*G (see Figure 10).

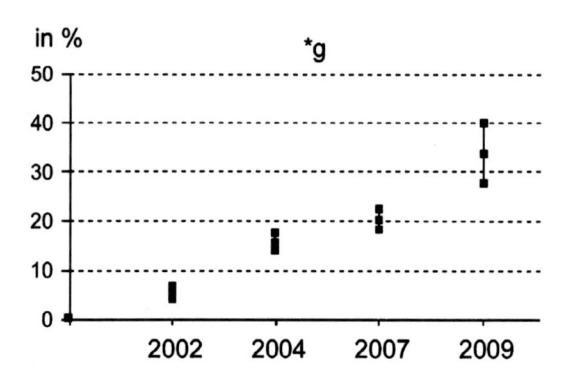

Figure 10: Development of the usage of *g / *G

The data (cf. commentary on Figure 5): Absolute incidences in 2002: 73, relative 5,3 %, confidence interval: 4,2-6,7 %; Absolute incidences in 2004: 266, relative 15,4 %, confidence interval: 13,7-17,3 %; Absolute incidences in 2007: 253, relative 20,3 %, confidence interval: 18,1-22,7 %; Absolute incidences in 2009: 87, relative 33,7%, confidence interval: 28-40%.

Similarly, we have a clear increase with $g*$ in 2007, which apparently did not correspond to the conventions in 2002, 2004 and 2009 (see Figure 11). When searching for reasons, it becomes clear that the increase stems from two particular chatters in Berlin-Brandenburg, who chat with each other and used $g*$ 32 and 5 times, respectively. Compared to a total of only 39 incidences in 2007, the use of $g*$ can still be considered scarce.

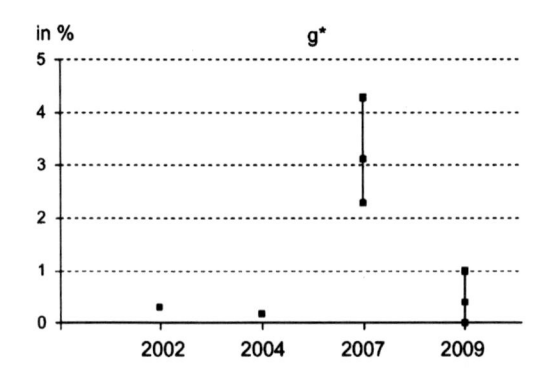

Figure 11: Development of the usage of *g**

The data (cf. commentary on Figure 5): Absolute incidences in 2002: 4, relative 0,3 %, confidence interval: 0-0,6 %; Absolute incidences in 2004: 3, relative 0,2 %, 0-0,4 %; Absolute incidences in 2007: 39, relative 3,1 %, confidence interval: 2,2-4,3 %; Absolute incidences in 2009: 1, relative 0,4%, confidence interval: 0-1%. – For the development of the formally standard-oriented phrasing *grinst frech* see Figure 12.

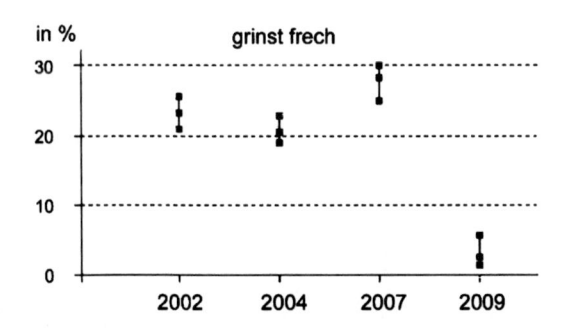

Figure 12: Development of the usage of *grinst frech*

With 317 incidences in 2002, *grinst frech* makes up 23,1 % of all *grins*-variations; with 353 incidences in 2004, 20,5 % of all *grins*-variations; with 351 incidences in 2007, 28,1 % of all *grins*-variations, with 7 incidences in 2009, 2,7% of all *grins*-variations.[31] In all three years, *grinst frech* takes the leading

---

[31] Confidence intervals: 2002 [20,9 %; 25,5 %], 2004 [18,9 %; 22,8 %], 2007 [25 %; 30 %], 2009 [1,3%; 5,6%].

position. That the percentage of a phrasing close to standard language is the highest in 2007 confirms the general tendency to greater proximity to standard language since 2004. The decrease in 2009 cannot be explained on a grammatical basis.

The syntagm *grins* (no Figure) is uninflected and formally noticeable without asterisks. With the following statistics it can be counted as a convention (owing to its frequency) in 2002, but not in 2004. Absolute incidences in 2002: 63, relative 4,6 %, absolute incidences in 2004: 14, relative 0,8 %, absolute incidences in 2007: 30, relative 2,4 %, absolute incidences in 2009: 20, relative 7,8%[32]. The increase in 2009 can be seen as an example for the general abandonment of the asterisk's usage.

Taken together, we note the following as a final result and as a correction and specification of the statement formulated in the hypothesis (in 5.1): most of the examples mentioned already document the tendency in 2004 to liberalization of intra-chat conventions and a tendency to greater proximity to standard language.

5.5 Another parameter: length of statements

Another parameter that can be measured well is the length of statements. Their development is drawn upon here in order to support the overall tendency.[33] Calculated in terms of all self-written messages in 2002, we have: 13,7 symbols per statement; in 2004 and 2007: 18,2 and 18,5 symbols per statement, respectively. The result speaks for the change of a characteristic determined to be typical for chat between 2002 and 2004 in the literature.

5.6 An ephemerally appearing occurence in quantification

grinst rotzfrech, a standard language-oriented phrasing, appears 61 times in 2004 and makes up 3,5 % of all *grins*-variations. In 2002, 2007 and 2009 this phrasing does not appear at all. A single chatter on 09.05.2004 in Hessennetz entered it 24 times between 11:59:08 and 12:46:03, then another 33 times between 17:32:09 and 19:40:42. At 22:08:30 and 22:49:34, two other chatters use it again. Since we are only investigating one day from each year, this clearly indicates a limit for statements about ephemeral patterns and short-term (daily) modes.

---

[32] Confidence intervals: 2002 [3,6 %; 5,9 %], 2004 [0,5 %; 1,4 %], 2007 [1,6 %; 3,4 %], 2009 [5%; 11,8%].

[33] The calculations of statement length were carried out by cand. phil. Marlen Jens in 2009 in the context of a research term paper.

6. Qualitative analysis of the development of chat-specific verb phrases

6.1 System and system development: syntax and semantics

The quantitative analysis was explicated based on minimal chat-specific syntagms. The smallest syntagm was *g*, the most frequent was **g** after *grinst frech*. For 2002, the quantitative analysis reveals a very consequent usage of chat-specific syntagms (as described in chapter 3) that are marked by a specific usage of structural signs and specific grammaticalizations including: graphic, morphologic and semantic reductions as well as coalescence and topologization. Due to their consequent and narrow usage in form and function in (almost exclusively) chat-rooms, these syntagms can be understood as chat-specific conventions. Hence, a decrease in usage indicates an easing of conventional use.

For a formal, well-distinguishable Excel-based analysis, high-frequent syntagms were selected. A qualitative analysis that follows up on the present quantitative analysis can incorporate further syntagms that, for different reasons, are not quantifiable: e.g., because they are too seldom, like those in (6) and (15) to (20),[34] or because they cannot be found automatically, rather only upon complex processing of the text, which could not be made consistently.

(15) <- *schnitzel ess* (P, 09.05.04, 19:54:44)
(16) *assos*[35] *egal an Kopp knall* ^^ (BB, 11.01.07, 11-23:30:10)
(17) <<<<<<<<<nickt zustimmend Xetsipotos[36] (B, 11.01.07, 19:34:30)
(18) *hmmm ich liebe diese freundlichkeit under den chattern. *tränenweg wichvorbegeisterung** (H, 09.05.04, 14:17:30)
(19) <-- *sich auf ihre tortellini freut* (B, 09.05.04, 17:19:10)
(20) <-- *sich grad Wasser für tortelline hingestellt hat* (B, 09.05.04, 17:10:51)

These syntagms can be read as further proof for the tendency to dissolve intra-chat conventions insofar as they maintain certain features without consistently using all of them. We are dealing with the following: non-chat-specific word order conventions that retain asterisks (18), chat-specific word order (non-inflected verbs in the last position) without asterisks (15, 16), chat-specific word order (verbs in the last position) without asterisks but with standard inflected endings (19, 20) and various usages of symbols (15-17, 19-20). The verb phrase

---

[34] Zetsche (2008) compiles all variants of verb phrases containing *feix, freu, gähn, grins, grummel, guck, handgeb/-reich, knubu, knuddel, kopfschüttel, lach, lol, muah, re-, rofl, schau, schrei, sing, wein/heul/schnief*. The documented evidence is too scarce for confident calculations.
[35] Username made anonymous.
[36] Username made anonymous.

patterns described in detail in part 3 can be assumed to follow intra-chat convention prototypically, despite an increase in variations.[37]

The semantics of these chat-specific verb phrases likewise demonstrate a prototypical core area and a more complex image than the quantitatively investigated patterns above provide. In the core area, the described syntagms are used in order to described actions or moods, which are to be staged alongside statements, but can only be represented verbally and in writing due to the medium of communication. They are adequately demarcated, clearly and formally, from other statements (see above, parts 2 and 3). The verb phrases marked with asterisks are largely semantically unambiguous, even if only one asterisk is employed. In the examples (15), (16), (17), (19) and (20), however, other symbols are used instead of asterisks. Apparently, what matters is only the differential aspect: the situation's staging is defined by the usage of any symbol in order to introduce the staging graphically and semantically highlighted into the text, as the following examples illustrate (21-24):

(21) <-------fand alba besser als F1 (BB, 14.04.02, 18:04:20)
(22) <<<<<<<<< nimmer weiter weiss (B, 11.01.07, 14:01:08)
(23) <<< wach is, nur gerad am futtern is "g" (B, 11.01.07, 13:49:20)
(24) *ganz traurig um sich her schaut* (BB, 11.01.07, 11-12:06:18)

When analyzing the semantics of chat symbols, the notion of unambiguous codifications and stable conventions must be abandoned and replaced by a differentiated analysis of fluctuating symbols.

6.2 Symbol, function, and loss of salience

When linguistic studies negotiate verbs without endings, acronyms, and special symbols on the level of symbol selection that chatters agree upon, one explanation often comes to the fore: the speed and brevity that the medium supposedly compels. Here, we allow the argument for the fast sequence of contributions. The practical-functional explanation may explain part of the history: acronyms are de facto shorter than the written-out variants. The placing of asterisks, however, may offer the reader the advantage of quick ascertainability of the structure of the message. But for the writer, owing to the complex string of keystrokes (shift key – asterisk – acronym – shift key – asterisk), the time saved compared to typing a short string of letters is almost completely cancelled out. The practical functional explanation has to be replaced, or at least complemented, by a communicative explanation. The usage of asterisks or other symbols offers the recipient the advantage of a faster comprehension of the messages' structure.

---

[37] Approaches to a quantification can be found in Zetsche 2008, who compiled lists of verb phrases formally marked with asterisks or other graphic symbols.

Throughout all kinds of text, the asterisk is a marginal symbol. By contrast, the asterisk is so popular in chats that in 2007 it still appeared, simply, doubled or multiple times, in 9 % of all messages (5.2). The accumulation of this formal element alone is particularly noticeable for that reason. It was able to become salient[38] and characteristic for chat in the perception of users. As a result, its sheer frequency, as well as the specific rules of its usage, became salient. Double asterisks were thus used with great consistency and uniformity. The correct handling of double asterisks identified the text as appropriate and the chatter as a member of the chat community. In 2002, the asterisk is a part of verb phrases with uninflected verbs, i.e. of a syntagm that is likewise marginal throughout all types of German texts, and for that reason its appearance is striking. The verb phrase is not only salient, but also has a special meaning developed from a tradition that reaches back to the 1920s. In its cultural meaning, it is linked to the literary genre of comics, to an attitude that is anti-traditional and critical of school-learning.

The asterisked syntagm with an uninflected verb in chats becomes syntactically expandable and associated with the properties of chat texts, which distinguish these syntagms from the norms of standard language stipulated by schools. Symbols that are used and iterated in such a specific way become stylistic features. Chat was considered a medium of youth culture in 2002, and the phrasings employed there were a symbol of quick, unconventional, spontaneous writing. Because of their specific syntax, syntagms with asterisks had become an especially salient, stylistic feature that established the user as a competent chatter with regard to group distinction.

In the data from 2004, however, a tendency to dissolve asterisk usage already emerges. This can be explained by a loss of salience within chats, which results from the broad usage of these syntagms. The construction in the form conventional for chat has lost its conspicuousness and distinctiveness; it is no longer understood to be funny, spontaneous, or eccentric. It no longer lends itself (to the extent that it previously did) to staging interesting actions of a person, to being an indicator of style. Fittingly, a diffusion of longer syntagms without verb inflection is taking place in spoken language concurrently with the

---

[38] On the term *salience*: salience is described substantially in Gestalt psychology. There is a tradition reaching back to the first decades of the twentieth century of investigating pre-rational 'impulse factors' that make objects noticeable. It is shown that social norms also influence what may draw attention and what must be overlooked. Cf. Hofstätter 1972, s.v. *Aufmerksamkeit*. In biopsychology, salience is explained in terms of incentive salience, cf. Birbaumer/Schmidt (1996: 640). In pragmatic theories that thematize language as an institution and language usages as a coordinational problem, salience is the prerequisite for coordination (cf. Schelling 1960, Lewis (1969: 13-14, 35-36), Clark (1985: 179-231), Clark 1996). In semantics, v. Heusinger 1997 uses the term *salience* in conjunction with the definition of that which is meant by noun phrases, which is elaborated there. On salience and group perception, cf. Blanz 1998.

verifiable liberalization of intra-chat convention we have discussed: *Was macht ihr denn mit der Weihnachtsfeier? Nur mal so in die Runde frag* (undocumented evidence, 2004). Dissemination is necessarily accompanied by loss of salience and distinctiveness.

6.3 Tendency to standard forms

A loss of salience in non-standard forms need not result in a turn toward standard language. One can also imagine rapidly changing modes of non-standard forms. In the quantitative analysis, the trend toward the standard clearly begins to show. This trend exists generally in online communities: Facebook as well as StudiVZ presents people with their profiles, out of which stable social contacts, professional and private, may develop. The presented characteristics are attributed to the users over the long-term. Owing to its codification and enforcement by schools, the standard language of German is recognized by all users even if they are not adequately familiar with it and provides for orientation.[39] The situational, lackadaisical play with language is being pursued less demonstratively and less intensively within these online communities. This tendency towards standard language is also noticeable in chat rooms since many of the writers use the aforementioned communities in addition to chat (informal survey among students).[40]

6.4 The asterisk

There is indeed a liberalization of the convention of double asterisks. In messages, the formal element «*...*» is no longer employed with the consistency and unified function typical for 2002. What clearly remains constant is the general popularity of asterisks and their playful usage in one other syntagm. Asterisks as part of personal designations do not experience a change in usage: The percentage of nicknames with asterisks relative to the total amount of names neither decreases from 2002 to 2004, nor decreases significantly from 2004 to 2007. Furthermore, the pattern of asterisk usage in names remains stable: in 50 % of the names, two asterisks are used, while merely one asterisk is used in slightly more than 20 % of the names. In the examples (made anonymous) numbered (10) to (12), one finds the following ornamentations of self-designations:

---

[39] On the orientational function of school-enforced language standards, cf. Bourdieu 1984.
[40] Another explanation for the approximation to standard language could be the age of the chatters: some users have aged five years while using chat. That chatrooms are also used by thirty-year-olds can be read in the usernames with numbers. The analysis of the 30-40-50 CHAT-SET chat room, however, shows a decrease of conventions since 2002, as well.

(25) zestos*agori*20*
(26) *@*|Aristos|*@*
(27) *~asteri~*

With these ornaments, the asterisk attains a meaning that will stay in the game as long as it makes proper names more noticeable and as long as participants are interested in this particular functional differentiation. This applies for every linguistic form.

7. Ephemera and 'exapted' syntagms

The thematic concept *ephemer* was taken literally because of the corpus structure: 'for the day', one documented day from 2002, 2004, 2007, 2009, respectively. Normally the term is interpreted metonymically to mean, 'for a short time'. Other corpora that could show this quality might be packs of data collected in short time intervals, e.g., press releases from databases, which one can analyze with other means, with trend curves, etc. For that reason, we only pointed out one syntagm (*grinst rotzfrech*), which, although part of standard language, could be shown in our corpus as an example of an ephemeral incidence, an event only taken up in the short-term by others (5.8).

The focal points of our analysis of tradition-founding grammatical constructions were a type of syntagm developed about 90 years ago in a literary genre and its differentiation in several media. The syntagm's development was described in part 3 as grammaticalization. In part 2, absorption into various discursive traditions and the functional shift attending them were shown. With a gesture to evolutionary theory, the adoption of linguistic forms and their transferral to new contexts and media can be referred to as 'exaptation'.[41] Adoption with a functional shift is the essential characteristic of developmental processes that can be documented with the term 'exaptation'.

For syntax theory, this means the following: there are 1) standard syntagms, 2) syntagms in comics, 3) chat-specific syntagms (that can be explained as both extensions of comic-specific syntagms and as grammaticalizations of standard forms at the same time) and 4) syntagms, which lack certain features of chat-specific grammaticalization and which are also closer to standard syntagms.[42] Newer and older syntagms are used side by side and employed with different meanings. Structurally speaking, this is a matter of functional differentiation. At the beginning of the last decade comic-specific syntagms were used and extended specifically in chat rooms. During the decade, these chat-specific syn-

---

[41] Cf. Traugott 2004, where the usage of this term is not only understood as a gesture or a metaphor.

[42] There is no need to interpret the syntagms categorized under 4) as degrammaticalizations of the syntagms under 3), but rather as renewal of characteristics of standard syntagms.

tagms were modified so that the current usage of syntagms (which were originally used in chat rooms at the beginning of the last decade) indicate a selection from a new repertoire (in a structural, paradigmatic sense – the competition between older and newer symbols), that has to be approached and interpreted from a new perspective.

8. Literature

Behaghel, Otto. 1923-1932. *Deutsche Syntax. Eine geschichtliche Darstellung.* Heidelberg: Winter.
Beißwenger, Michael. 2000. *Kommunikation in virtuellen Welten. Sprache, Text und Wirklichkeit.* Stuttgart: ibidem.
Birbaumer, Niels & Robert F. Schmidt. 1996. *Biologische Psychologie.* Berlin, Heidelberg & New York: Springer.
Blanz, Matthias. 1998. *Wahrnehmungen von Personen als Gruppenmitglieder. Untersuchungen zur Salienz sozialer Kategorien.* Münster, New York & München: Waxmann.
Bourdieu, Pierre. 1984. *Ce que parler veut dire.* Paris: Fayard.
Crystal, David. 2004. *Language and the Internet.* Cambridge: Cambridge University Press.
Clark, Herbert H. 1996. *Using Language.* Cambridge: Cambridge University Press.
Clark, Herbert H. 1985. "Language Use and Language Users". *Handbook of Social Psychology. Vol. II. Special Fields and Applications* ed. G. Lindzey, 179-231. New York: Random House.
Duden. 2005. *Die Grammatik.* Mannheim: Duden.
Gauer, Hans Martin. 2004. "Nichtsdestotrotz". *Was wir sagen, wenn wir reden* ed. H. M. Gauger, 143-145. München & Wien: Hanser.
Götz, Eva Maria. 2006. "Die Sprache Entenhausens. Mickey-Mouse-Übersetzerin schuf eine Sprachkultur voller Witze". Deutschlandfunk. Kalenderblatt, December 7, 2006. http://www.dradio.de/dlf/sendungen/kalenderblatt/571143/
Henn-Memmesheimer, Beate. 2004. "Syntaktische Minimalformen: Grammatikalisierungen in einer medialen Nische". *Morphologie und Syntax deutscher Dialekte und Historische Dialektologie des Deutschen* ed. F. Patocka & P. Wiesinger, 84-118. Wien: Praesens.
Henn-Memmesheimer, Beate. 2006. "Grammatikalisierungen in verschiedenen Diskurstraditionen". *Grammatische Untersuchungen. Analysen und Reflexionen. Gisela Zifonun zum 60. Geburtstag* (Studien zur deutschen Sprache 36) ed. E. Breindl, L. Gunkel & B. Strecker, 533-551. Tübingen: Narr.
Heusinger, Klaus v. 1997. *Salienz und Referenz. Der Epsilonoperator in der Semantik der Nominalphrase und anaphorischer Pronomen* (Studia Grammatica 43). Berlin: Akademie.

Hofstätter, Peter, ed. 1972. *Psychologie*. Frankfurt: Fischer.
Jäger, Ludwig. 2000. "Die Sprachvergessenheit der Medientheorie. Ein Plädoyer für das Medium Sprache". *Sprache und neue Medien* ed. W. Kallmeyer, 9-30. Berlin & New York: de Gruyter.
Jakobs, Eva Maria. 1998. "Mediale Wechsel und Sprache. Entwicklungsstadien elektronischer Schreibwerkzeuge und ihr Einfluss auf Kommunikationsformen". *Medien im Wandel. Neues in alten, Altes in neuen Medien* ed. W. Holly & B. U. Biere, 187-209. Opladen & Wiesbaden: Westdeutscher Verlag.
Kehlmann, Daniel. 2009. *Ein Roman in neun Geschichten*. Reinbek: Rowohlt.
Lehmann, Christian. 2005. "New Reflections on grammaticalization and lexicalisation". <http://www.uni-erfurt.de/sprachwissenschaft/personal/lehmann/CL Publ/New reflections.pdf>
Lehmann, Christian. 1989. "Grammatikalisierung und Lexikalisierung". *Zeitschrift für Phonetik, Sprachwissenschaft und Kommunikationsforschung* 42. 11-19.
Lewis, David Kellog. 1969. *Convention. A Philosophical Study*. Harvard: University Press.
Müller, Gereon. 2000. *Elemente der optimalitätstheoretischen Syntax*. Tübingen: Stauffenburg.
Neuland, Eva. 2003. "Doing Youth: Zur medialen Konstruktion von Jugend und Jugendsprache". *Jugendsprache – Jugendliteratur – Jugendkultur. Interdisziplinäre Beiträge zu sprachkulturellen Ausdrucksformen Jugendlicher* ed. E. Neuland, 261-273. Frankfurt: Lang.
Neuland, Eva. 2006. "Variation im heutigen Deutsch: Perspektiven für den Unterricht". *Variation im heutigen Deutsch: Perspektiven für den Sprachunterricht* ed. E. Neuland, 9-27. Frankfurt: Lang.
Nübling, Damaris. 2006. *Historische Sprachwissenschaft. Eine Einführung in die Prinzipien des Sprachwandels*. Tübingen: Narr.
Schelling, Tomas C. 1960. *The Strategie of Conflict*. Cambridge: University Press.
Schlobinski, Peter. 2001. "*knuddel – zurueckknuddel – dichganzdollknuddel*. Inflektive und Inflektivkonstruktionen im Deutschen". *Zeitschrift für Germanistische Linguistik* 29,2. 192-218.
Traugott, Elisabeth Clos. 2004. "Exaptation and Grammaticalisation". *Linguistic Studies based on Corpora* ed. M. Akimoto, 133-156. Tokio: Hituzi Syobo Publishing Co.
Wahrig. 2006. *Deutsches Wörterbuch*. Gütersloh & München.
Weinrich, Harald. 2003. *Textgrammatik der Deutschen Sprache*. Hildesheim, Zürich & New York: Olms.

Zetzsche, Sarah. 2008. *Von FEIX bis WEIN. Konventionen und Moden in Chats zwischen 2002 und 2007.* Wissenschaftliche Arbeit im Rahmen der Ersten Staatsprüfung für das Lehramt an Gymnasien. Mannheim.

Zifonun, Gisela, Ludger Hoffmann, Bruno Strecker et al. 1997. *Grammatik der deutschen Sprache* (Schriften des Instituts für deutsche Sprache 7). Berlin: de Gruyter.

<http://www.duckipedia.de/index.php/Erika_Fuchs [2007]>

Ulrich Busse (Halle-Wittenberg) & Anne Schröder (Bielefeld)
Problem areas of English grammar between usage, norm, and variation

1. Introduction

The amazing commercial success of books such as Bastian Sick's *Der Dativ ist dem Genitiv sein Tod* and its sequels (2004-2009) in Germany indicates that the general public and thus the 'normal' language users are worried about or at least interested in what is to be considered 'correct' usage. Similar phenomena can also be observed for the English-speaking world. The 'bestseller' *Eats, Shoots and Leaves. The Zero Tolerance Approach to Punctuation* by Lynne Truss (2003) may serve as a recent example. However, these books were written by journalists, and linguists are usually very critical about such works. But even prior to the works above, David Crystal had the idea of soliciting the public opinion on problems of grammatical usage. In his book *The English Language* (2003: 27-29), he reports on the top ten complaints about grammar, which listeners sent in to the BBC radio series *English Now* in 1986. Among these complaints were such pronounced statements as the following:

– *Hopefully* should not be used at the beginning of a sentence.
– *Different*[*ly*] should be followed by *from* and not by *to* or *than*.

These two issues are interesting insofar as the first one concerns a rather recent development in the English language whereas the second has been described as a classic example of divided or even disputed usage in modern standard English.

Undisputedly, what lay people think about grammar in terms of norm and variation, and what linguists make of this topic can, at times, be very different things. However, if both educated native and non-native speakers alike are insecure about a question of divided usage, depending on the kind of problem they often consult dictionaries and grammar books or usage guides. The latter, in particular, can be regarded as authoritative all-in-one-reference works (see Busse and Schröder 2006: 460-462).

In this study, we will therefore take a detailed look at the two above-mentioned 'problem areas' of English grammar in use from three different perspectives, namely by investigating their representation in selected usage guides, reference grammars, and small and large electronic corpora, in order to find out whether these different types of reference works go about describing usage differently and in how far this ties in with usage frequencies as observable in modern electronic corpora.

To this end, we looked at a broad sample of usage guides,[1] including both older and also fairly recent publications, such as *The King's English* (1906), Fowler's *Modern English Usage* (1926), *The Cambridge Guide to English Usage* (2004), and peripheral, semi-humorous ones, such as *Between You and I. A Little Book of Bad English* (2003), in order to cover both the historical dimension and present usage and also to have different methodological approaches, ranging from the more prescriptive to the more descriptive end of a continuum (see also Busse and Schröder 2006).

The grammars under investigation include the three comprehensive grammars of present-day standard English: Quirk et al. (1985) = CGEL, Biber et al. (1999) = LGSWE, Huddleston & Pullum (2002) = CaGra.

They can all be described as modern reference grammars,[2] subscribing to a descriptive treatment of standard English. However, in terms of theoretical underpinning and adherence to corpus data they show the differences displayed in Table 1 (adapted from Mukherjee 2006: 339[3]).

Table 1: Some major differences between the reference grammars consulted

	CaGra	LGSWE	CGEL
object of inquiry	'international standard English'	'four core registers'	'common core'
preference for multiple analysis and gradience	no	no	yes
database	intuitive, collected, corpus	LSWE corpus	intuitive, collected, corpus

The corpora to be analysed are the *British National Corpus* (BNC) for present-day spoken and written British English and the Brown and LOB corpora from 1961 and their updates known as Frown and F-LOB for British [BrE] and American English [AmE]. These four corpora allow for two different kinds of comparison, namely on a synchronic level for regional variation between the two national varieties of AmE and BrE, but also on an admittedly short-term

---

[1] For a list of the usage guides investigated, see reference list 5.1.

[2] In his *Encyclopedia of Language*, Crystal defines the term *reference grammar* as follows: "A grammatical description that tries to be as comprehensive as possible, so that it can act as a reference book for those interested in establishing grammatical facts (in much the same way as a dictionary is used as a 'reference lexicon' [...])" (1987: 88). Among the "best known" examples given, Quirk et al. (1985) features alongside Otto Jespersen's seven-volume *Modern English Grammar* (1909-49).

[3] For further details see Mukherjee (2006).

diachronic level for language change between the two synchronic stages of 1961 in comparison to the state of affairs 30 years on in 1991/92 (see Figure 1, adapted from Mukherjee 2002: 31).[4]

	AmE	BrE
1961	Brown	LOB
1991/92	Frown	F-LOB

Regional variation (horizontal) / Diachronic variation (vertical) / Synchronic variation

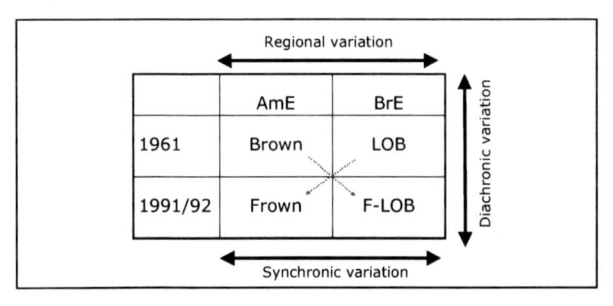

Figure 1: The four matching corpora of written edited American and British English

Finally, the World Wide Web will be incorporated as a data base.

The paper at hand thus addresses the following three research hypotheses:

1. It can be assumed that both over time and synchronically within the different types of reference works a different methodological approach towards the treatment of norm and variation has taken place; i.e. prescriptivism vs. descriptivism.
2. Presumably, some parts of grammar are presented as being more subject to the acceptability of variation than others; i.e. long-standing vs. recent controversies on usage.
3. According to their practical and theoretical footing, the usage guides and the grammars will reflect the usage frequencies to be found in present-day small and large computer-readable text collections of spoken and written English to different extents; i.e. do reference works accurately reflect usage frequencies?

---

[4] In a recent article, Christian Mair characterized the four matching corpora as "small and tidy" (2006a: 355f.) and argued for the complementary role of small and "big and messy" corpora such as the COBUILD monitor corpus – the *Bank of English* – which has "now exceeded the 400-million-word limit" (355). Mair regrets that not much dialogue is going on between the scholars working within these different traditions. However, the *British National Corpus* BNC consisting of approximately 100 million words (10 million spoken and 90 million written BrE from the 1990s) can be regarded as having integrated these two different traditions in corpus design.

2. How should usage be recorded?

In his outline of the meaning and history of the term *usage* in linguistics, Allen points out that the term itself can be used both neutrally and also with strong attitudinal overtones. "It occurs neutrally in such terms as *formal usage, disputed usage,* and *local usage,* and it has strong judgemental and prescriptive connotations in such terms as *bad usage, correct usage, usage and abuse,* and *usage controversies*" (Allen 1992: 1071).

Herbst et al. define the term *usage* as "the custom of speech as established by the speakers of a speech community in relation to frequency or usualness in the occurrence of certain forms" (Herbst et al. 1991: 29; our translation).[5] The important notion is that the speech community establishes the custom or practice. Herbst et al. go on by saying that usage is an important category because there are forms which are both grammatical or well-formed and acceptable, but which are nonetheless not very commonly used in a speech community. Thus, important distinctions are established between the concepts of grammaticality or well-formedness, acceptability, and frequency.

In addition to these factors, they introduce the concept of *divided usage*. Quirk et al. in the CGEL (1985) discuss this phenomenon in greater detail, and describe it as two synonymous constructions, which are equally frequent, as for example the following:

(1) *He stayed a week* vs. *He stayed for a week.* (See Quirk et al. 1985: 31; our emphasis)
(2) *I consider her my friend* vs. *I consider her as my friend.* (ibid.)
(3) *I don't know whether I can be there.* vs. *I don't know if I can be there.* (ibid.)

Quirk et al. argue that the choice of one or the other in each of these pairs cannot be linked to any specific variety of English, such as varieties according to field of discourse, varieties according to medium, varieties according to attitude, etc. Nonetheless,

> "attempts have been made to find a basis for at least some of this seemingly random variation (often called 'free variation'). For example, it has been claimed that certain language varieties (termed 'randomly distributed dialects') define groups of speakers who are not associated regionally or sociologically, the groups being characterized by linguistic features that are related systematically" (CGEL 1985: 31).

Whereas cases like (1) to (3) are fairly uncontroversial, and may thus occur in speech and writing as true alternatives in free variation, often below the level of the speaker's or writer's consciousness, cases like *split infinitives* or *preposition*

---

[5] The German original reads as follows: "Durch die Sprecher einer Sprachgemeinschaft etablierter Sprachgebrauch in Hinblick auf die Häufigkeit bzw. Üblichkeit des Auftretens bestimmter Formen" (Herbst et al. 1991: 29).

stranding should be regarded as instances of *disputed usage*, because here the variants are either clearly marked or unmarked in their usage value, making their distribution in the most extreme case complementary. As a result of this, individual speakers, the speech community, public opinion or usage manuals often have a specific attitude towards or opinion about a variant (construction) and pass unfavourable judgements on the less usual, acceptable, favourable, etc. form, turning it into a shibboleth, which can lead to stigmatisation of this form and its users and thus to a kind of linguicism.

With regard to modern reference grammars compiled on corpus evidence, cases like those above are handled by describing usage differences. This goes in particular for the *Longman Grammar of Spoken and Written English*, which focuses "on describing the actual patterns of use and the possible reasons for those patterns" (LGSWE 1999: 19) and indicates the preferences of speakers or writers for alternatives, but does not argue about their correctness.

The compilers of the LGSWE admit that throughout their grammar "several traditional usage controversies" are discussed in passing: "However, our primary goal is to describe the patterns of use across the breadth of English grammar, rather than focusing on a handful of usage issues" (ibid.). In the abbreviated student version they give the following reason for doing so: from the viewpoint of communication, i.e. of making oneself understood, usage controversies are not important, but they can be crucial for the social perception of the communicative skills of speakers or writers, because value judgements are made on the basis of 'good' or 'bad' grammar. "These judgments, in turn, may have an influence on actual patterns of use" (LSGSWE 2002: 7). To this they add the interesting note that "most cases of variation within standard English [...] do not attract attention from ordinary language users. However, speakers do tend to be aware of some aspects of disputed usage and sometimes have strong opinions about what forms are 'correct'" (ibid.).

Crystal (1997) goes about defining the term *usage* in this way:

> "The collective term for the speech and writing habits of a community, especially as they are presented descriptively with information about preferences for alternative linguistic forms. Linguists emphasize the importance of describing the facts of usage as a control on the claims made by grammars, and contrast this emphasis with the prescriptive attitudes of traditional grammar, whose rules often bore no relationship to what people actually did with their language" (Crystal 1997: 405).[6]

This definition highlights the question of whether this issue should be treated in a prescriptive or in a descriptive way and what is to be taken as a reference point. Even though it is usually not mentioned explicitly,

> "guidance tends to centre on standard English, a form assumed to be shared, used, and accepted by educated speakers throughout the English-speaking world, despite

---

[6] For the sake of uniformity, the capitals of the keywords have been rendered as lowercase letters.

great variety in accent, grammar, and vocabulary; it is based partly on intellectual argument and partly on received opinion" (Allen 1992: 1072).

If standard and usage are equated, this allows for two different procedures in codifying the language:

1. A change in usage, i.e. the collective linguistic habits of a speech community, is codified in linguistic reference works, and thus entails (in the long run) a change of descriptive linguistic norms and standards.
2. An observed usage or change in usage is not sanctioned by authorities and hence this custom or practice is regarded as odd, wrong or as bad usage and labelled accordingly.

In the past, the latter procedure was common practice in traditional grammars and many usage guides. Nowadays, as shown for reference grammars, scholarly linguistic description is based on the evidence of large electronic corpora and on usage panels, but even with large corpora it can be difficult to assess usage objectively. This has to do with data selection, because the type of data will affect and hence skew the results.

> "Establishing current majority usage is not as straightforward as it sounds, even in the age of mass media, because it rests on the need to be sure of what constitutes currency and majority. Until the development of databases, scholarly evidence consisted of collections of citations, generally from printed sources. Depending on the range of sources studied, the evidence has tended to have a literary or formal bias; usage criticism based on it does not therefore take adequate account of ordinary English spoken and written communication. Even computer corpora are collected mainly from the language in print, although conversational texts do exist [...]" (Allen 1992: 1073).

An important strand of current dictionaries and grammars is corpus-based and professes to describe usage accurately. However, if questions of data selection and interpretation make it almost impossible to describe – let alone assess – usage objectively, this problem becomes even more difficult for usage guides, because on which evidence or on whose authority should they base their decisions and recommendations or even 'verdicts' (see e.g. MEU-3)?

If we take the most recent example, the CEU (2004), the preface has the following to say about the different kinds of evidence and authority on which guidance in questions of style and usage rests:

1. Large databases, i.e. the 100 million word *British National Corpus* (BNC), and the *Cambridge International Corpus of American English* with 140 million words. These corpora include enough samples of spoken discourse to show patterns of divergence. "Negative attitudes to particular idioms or usage often turn on the fact that they are more familiar to the ear than the eye, and the constructions of formal writing are privileged thereby" (CEU 2004: vii).

This answers the problem addressed above in that corpus design has an important impact on frequency patterns and further descriptions based on them.
2. Population surveys by using questionnaires on doubtful or disputed usage. The results, which are quoted in some entries, show "insights into people's willingness to embrace particular spellings or usages" (viii).
3. "Attitudes to usage often reflect what's said in the relevant authorities" (ibid.). In terms of lexis, the large national dictionaries, i.e. the *Oxford English Dictionary* (1989), for British English, and *Webster's Third New International Dictionary* (1961) together with smaller dictionaries and usage guides such as Fowler and others count as authorities. For grammatical problems of usage, modern reference grammars such as the *Comprehensive Grammar of the English Language* (1985), the *Introduction to Functional Grammar* by Halliday (1985, 1994) and the *Longman Grammar of Spoken and Written English* serve the function of "authorities" (ibid.).
4. Issues of editorial style are treated with regard to national style guides, such as the *Chicago Manual of Style* (2003) and the *Oxford Guide to Style* (2002).
5. A large range of (undisclosed) linguistic primary and secondary sources serves as additional evidence.

This listing shows that guidance in the CEU rests upon a number of scholarly sources and not on the personal preference of its editor. Apart from corpus evidence, dictionaries, usage guides, grammars, and scholars are regarded as authorities. However, the inclusion of dictionaries, grammars and previous usage guides as 'received wisdom' bears the dangers of circularity and of introducing a diachronic perspective into the description of present-day English.

The further we go back in history, the fewer of these sources were available and perhaps not even desirable to earlier editors of reference works. In former days, grammars and dictionaries were compiled on the basis of citation slips that reflected the readings of their editors, or as regards the OED on the results of a large-scale reading programme.

3. 'Problem areas' of English grammar

After having outlined the difficulties and possible pitfalls of recording usage in reference works, the next part of the article will be devoted to a close analysis of two notorious cases of divided or even disputed usage, namely the treatment of *hopefully* as a sentence adverbial and the preposition following *different*.

3.1 Hopefully

As pointed out in the introduction, the use of *hopefully* as a sentence adverbial is a very recent development, although Burchfield notes that "since at least the 17c., certain adverbs in *-ly* have acquired the ability to qualify a predication or assertion as a whole" (MEU-3: 703). We thus find *hopefully* in the original (and literal) sense of 'full of hope' or 'in a hopeful manner' (e.g. *They travelled hopefully* and *They set to work hopefully*) as well as in the sense of 'it is hoped' or 'I am hopeful that' (e.g. *Hopefully business will pick up*), where it functions as a sentence adverbial.

Other adverbs are used in a similar fashion. Thus in *Frankly, we don't want them; frankly* is used as a sentence adverb and may be paraphrased as 'if I may speak frankly'. Or in *Unhappily, there are times when violence is the only way in which justice can be secured; unhappily* means 'it is an unhappy fact that' and not 'in an unhappy manner'. And finally in *Quite seriously, all the vital functions ... rise and set with the sun; seriously* expresses 'to speak seriously'. But while no stylistic objections have been raised to the use of other adverbs as sentence adverbials, such as the ones mentioned or *(un)fortunately, actually* etc., basically all usage guides and reference grammars under investigation note that "since the 1960s *hopefully* has been the favourite bugbear of language purists" (BYI: 60).

Some reference works attempt to give an explanation for the strong opposition against specifically just this one of the sentence adverbials. Among the explanations given we find:

a. Possible ambiguity as in *They will leave hopefully in the morning*, where *hopefully* could either mean 'with optimism' or 'I hope that' (e.g. GEU: 641).
b. Its sudden rise in the early 1960s (e.g. CEU: 254), making it "a relatively recent newcomer to the ranks of the sentence adverbs" (BYI: 61); (see also CaGra: 768: fn.33).
c. The fact that it is said to have come to British English from the United States (e.g. BYI: 61; CPW-2: 162; CPW-3: 232 and GEU: 343).

Especially the last two points of explanation can be verified by looking at corpus data. If the occurrences of *hopefully* in the Brown, Frown, LOB and F-LOB as well as in the BNC are compared, we get the distribution displayed in Table 2.

Table 2: Use of *hopefully* in British and American standard English

	literal meaning		sentence adverbial		ambiguous	total
Brown	6	75.00 %	1	12.50 %	1	8
LOB	11	100.00 %	-	0 %	0	11
Frown	3	33.33 %	5	55.56 %	1	9
F-LOB	1	8.33 %	11	91.67 %	0	12
BNC	242	12.98 %	1602	85.89 %	21	1865

As Table 2 illustrates, the use of *hopefully* as a sentence adverbial is unattested in the LOB Corpus, i.e. in the British English of 1961, while we find one instance of this use in contemporary American English in the Brown Corpus. In both varieties, however, the majority of the uses of *hopefully* in this period is in its literal meaning.

The situation seems to be reversed with regard to the uses of *hopefully* in the 1990s. In the majority of the cases, *hopefully* is now used as a sentence adverbial. This is true for both varieties of English, but while in American English only 55 % of the tokens are used as sentence adverbials, in British English more than 90 % of the tokens are used in this function. That this is not due to the fact that the overall number of tokens is comparatively low can be shown by the results from the BNC: in more than 85 % of the 1865 instances of *hopefully* in this corpus it is also used as a sentence adverbial.

As we can see from the analysis of this 'problem area' in the reference works and the corpora, the reference works under investigation are surprisingly up-to-date. Publications prior to 1970 (i.e. QE, KE, MEU-1 and MEU-2) cannot mention the new use of *hopefully*, as indeed it seems to have only been introduced in the 1960s, as most reference works correctly note. The corpus data also suggest that the development may have originated in the US, although the size of the corpora is probably too small to state this with certainty. Its rapid spread in British English, however, may explain why the new use has faced such strong opposition. From 1973 onwards, the new use of the adverb is discussed and it is noticed that "the new use of *hopefully* will establish itself as a new idiom" (CPW-2: 162).

In fact, the corpus data confirm that in present-day English both varieties use *hopefully* primarily as a sentence adverb, and most reference works see the usefulness of the new meaning, which is adequately summarised in the CGEL in a long note:

> "Since, however, the 'general view' in *hopefully* is usefully distinguished thereby from the purely individual viewpoint in *I hope,* the disjunct has considerable convenience, as can be seen in the following textual example from an administrator's note put before a committee: 'My assistant has arranged for the matter to be considered by an ad hoc working party, and *hopefully* a proposal will be ready in time for our next meeting. *I hope* this approach will be acceptable to members.' The two italicized parts are not identical in force and could not in fact be interchanged; the former ventures to express a general hope, attributed by the writer to the committee as a whole, or even a general assessment of probability ('It is likely that a proposal...'); the latter expresses the writer's personal hope that his action will be approved" (CGEL: 627).

The reference works, however, may be wrong in believing that "the fuss over this word has died down" (GEG: 204), as in fact usage guides up to today find it necessary to comment on this construction. This may possibly be attributed to two facts. Either modern editors still find it important enough to warrant an entry or a comment, or, which is perhaps more likely, they think that potential users might expect an entry on this example of divided usage in a usage manual professing guidance in cases of doubt.

3.2 Different from/than/to

This is also true with regard to the second 'problem area' we investigated. In English, there is the question of which preposition is to follow *different,* as there are three possible variants. The blank space in *Bob's approach was different ... Jo's* could be filled in by either *from, than* or *to.*[7] All of these solutions are grammatically correct. However, their degree of acceptance seems to vary. In this case it is stated that preference is not a matter of individual speakers but rather of national varieties.

This issue triggers yet another question, which is put forward in the GEG at the beginning of the entry: "Can anyone say anything new about this old grammatical shibboleth?" (GEG: 124). And, indeed, the choice of preposition with *different* has not only been commented on in the reference works under investigation but has also been discussed and investigated in numerous linguistic publications (e.g. Mair 2006a: 368/369; Mair 2006b: 18-20 and 25-28; Mair 2007: 236-239; Busse/Schröder 2006: 468/469; Schmied 2006: 314/315; Hundt 1998:106; and Kennedy 1998: 194, to name but a few). As Christian Mair observes:

> "Sometimes anecdotal observations [...] are repeated again and again, gaining a life of their own and solidifying into a body of folk-linguistic knowledge whose truth is taken for granted and no longer challenged even in scholarly publications" (Mair 2006b: 18).

If this type of evidence is included and repeated in reference works, this can lead to circularity as pointed out in Section 2.

The original complete objection against any other preposition than *from* (because of the analogy with the verb *to differ from* and for etymological reasons)[8] can be found in QE:[9]

> "A correspondent stigmatises the expression '*different to,*' which he shows (I own I was not aware of it) has become very common of late. Of course such a combination is entirely against all reason and analogy. 'Compare', says the writer, 'any other English words compounded of this same Latin preposition, for example, *distant, distinct,* and it will be seen that *from* is the only appropriate term to be employed in connection with them.' The same will be seen, I venture to add, by substituting the verb *to differ* in places where *different,* which in fact is only its participle, is thus joined" (QE: 232).

---

[7] Example taken from Peters (1995: 203).
[8] Because etymologically *different* embodies the Latin prefix *dis-* ('away from').
[9] In this reference work the construction with *than* is not commented on.

But objections of this kind are not expressed in any of the later publications, and it is believed that in the 20th century a preference for *different from* developed in British English while "in the same period *different than* has flourished in AmE" (MEU-3: 212).[10]

However, corpus evidence shows that *different from* is the dominant form both in British *and* in American English (see Table 3).

Table 3: Choice of preposition with *different* in British and American standard English[11]

	from		*than*		*to*	
Brown	40	76.9 %	12	23.1 %	0	---
LOB	38	86.4 %	2	4.5 %	4	9.1 %
Frown	41	93.2 %	3	6.8 %	---	---
F-LOB	51	86.4 %	---	---	8	13.6 %

Thus "one thing is clear: [...] contrary to claims, American and British English are rather similar, and little seems to be happening diachronically" (Mair 2006b: 25). The two varieties only seem to differ in their secondary preference, which is *different to* in British English and *different than* in American English. However, the figures obtained for the interesting variants, i.e. *different to* and *different than*, in the four corpora investigated are too low to allow for a definite judgement concerning their distribution.

Fortunately, we can have recourse to findings by Mair (2006b) from the World Wide Web which corroborate the ones obtained via traditional corpus linguistic methods. As Table 4 illustrates, *different from* is the most frequent variant in American English and British English and the two varieties differ in their secondary preference. A similar study undertaken by Schmied (2006: 315) confirms these results.[12]

---

[10] The entire quote reads: "The commonly expressed view that *different* should only be followed by *from* and never by *to* or *than* is not supportable in the face of past and present evidence or of logic, though the distribution of the construction is not straightforward. (a) History. The OED lists examples of each of the three constructions from the dates indicated: *different from* 1590, *different to* 1526, *different than* 1644. In the 20c. a marked preference for *different from* has been shown in BrE; in the same period *different than* has flourished in AmE, but so too has *different from*. In both countries, in all kinds of circumstances, *different to* has been widely perceived as a credible alternative [...]." (MEU-3: 212)

[11] Figures for Brown and LOB based on Kennedy 1998; see also Mukherjee 2002: 24.

[12] See Mair also (2006a: 368/369) and (2007: 238/239) for similar results.

Table 4: Choice of preposition with *different* in major regional varieties of standard English[13]

	from abs.	in %	than abs.	in %	to abs.	in %	Total abs.	in %
.us	194,000		85,200		6,060		285,260	
.edu	1,450,000		343,000		33,100		1,826,100	
.gov	787,000		152,000		6,050		945,050	
.nasa.gov	11,000		3,180		235		14,415	
Total US	2,442,000	79.52	583,380	19.0	45,445	1.48	3,070,825	100
.ca	253,000	76.0	68,700	20.64	11,200	3.36	332,900	100
.uk	469,000	71.17	33,000	5.0	157,000	23.83	659,000	100
.au	171,000	60.25	14,800	5.22	98,000	34.53	283,800	100
.nz	45,400	67.36	4,290	6.37	17,700	26.27	67,390	100
.za	28,700	66.42	2,910	6.74	11,600	26.84	43,210	100

The analysis of the World Wide Web data also reveals that *different from* is the dominant form not just in British and American English but in all major varieties of English. In addition, we can see that the secondary preference observed for British and American English spreads to the varieties influenced by them respectively. Thus, we find a preference for *different than* in Canada, whereas in Australia,[14] New Zealand, and South Africa *different to* is the preferred secondary variant.[15]

We can thus state that some of the reference works under investigation are mistaken, for instance, when in 1906 it is claimed that *different to* "is undoubtedly gaining ground, and will probably displace *different from* in no long time"

---

[13] Table adapted from Mair 2006b: 27.

[14] However, Peters believes *different than* to be frequent in Australian English, at least in some syntactical constructions (CEU: 153; Peters 1995: 203).

[15] In terms of settlement history, these 'Southern Hemisphere varieties of English' have been influenced most strongly by British English. For instance, in pronunciation they also have a number of features in common, which makes them the 'English' rather than the 'American' type of mother tongue varieties of English (see Trudgill and Hannah 2002: 5f.).

(KE: 162) or when *different than* is claimed to be *the* American variant (e.g. quote above, see footnote 10). Thus, they do not describe the distribution and variation accurately. The majority of the works, however, take a rather tolerant position and judge the use of all three prepositions as more or less permissible.[16] Only very few reference works attempt to describe the regional distribution of the three variants, most notably CEU. In some reference works, e.g. MEU-3, CGEL and CEU, a qualified contextual look is taken, showing that *different than* may be more elegant than the use of *different from* in comparative constructions such as: *Bob's approach was different ... than we expected* as opposed to the clumsy *... from the one that we expected.*

4. Conclusion

Our analysis of the reference works with regard to the two 'problem areas' investigated in this study cannot substantiate Crystal's critique that the rules presented in grammars often bear no relationship to actual language behaviour ([4]1997: 405; see also above). We would therefore answer in the affirmative the question put forward at the beginning of the present paper (see p. 83), i.e. do reference works accurately reflect usage frequencies? We found the reference works to reflect usage frequencies to an unexpectedly high degree. Especially with regard to the use of *hopefully,* we noted that the usage guides and the reference grammars are surprisingly up-to-date. Concerning *different from/to/than*, we found that the reference works are a little less accurate, but that especially the later publications attempt to describe the distribution of the variants.

This is directly connected to our first research hypothesis – the problem of descriptivism vs. prescriptivism. In accordance to our previous diachronic study (see Busse and Schröder 2006) we found that the more recent a usage guide is, the more descriptive its treatment of variation in use will be.[17] However, hardly any guide is prescriptive or descriptive *per se*, but the treatment of individual items differs to some degree. As concerns the differences between usage guides and reference grammars, we noted that in usage guides the normal language user can easily find information on constructions of divided usage, as this is where their major interest lies. In the reference grammars the various constructions of divided usage are 'hidden' under abstract entries such as *adjective complementation* and *comparative constructions* (e.g. for *different* in CaGra), and usually explained in various chapters. Their major interest lies on general syntactic phenomena rather than in describing differences in divided usage between individual lexical items. If a language user is concerned or insecure about the value or usage of a construction and seeks advice, he or she will be quite at a loss with

---

[16] See Busse/Schröder (2006: 468/469) for a more detailed discussion.
[17] There are, however, some exceptions to this rule, as for instance the recently published, semi-humorous guide *The Grouchy Grammarian* by Thomas Parrish (2002) and BYI.

the reference grammars as clear viewpoints of the 'correctness' of a construction are seldom given. However, we claim that the border between the two types of reference books investigated is getting blurred. It seems as if grammars increasingly feel the need to treat constructions of divided usage and to comment on them, even if they do so mostly in footnotes and in form of reported opinions (see Busse/Schröder 2009 for details).

And finally, our second initial research hypothesis (see p. 83) and the question whether long-standing cases of disputed usage are treated differently from more recent ones cannot be answered with any claim to generalization, because two cases make up just a small sample. But even within this limit differences can be made out: *hopefully* is dealt with more descriptively than the question of *different*. This may be due to the fact that it represents a fairly recent phenomenon, which therefore does not feature in the older guides and thus in the more prescriptive reference works. Another side effect of 'missing evidence' from older usage guides is that the assessment of present-day usage is not hampered by the introduction of a historical dimension and by circularity from quoting predecessors as authorities.

5. References

5.1 Usage guides

BYI = Cochrane, James. 2003. *Between You and I. A Little Book of Bad English*. Cambridge: Icon Books.

CEU = Peters, Pam. 2004. *The Cambridge Guide to English Usage*. Cambridge: Cambridge University Press.

CPW-1 = Ernest Gowers. 1946. *The Complete Plain Words*. London: His Majesty's Stationary Office.

CPW-2 = *The Complete Plain Words* revised by Bruce Fraser. 1973. London: Her Majesty's Stationery Office.

CPW-3 = *The Complete Plain Words* revised by Sidney Greenbaum and Janet Whitcut. 1986. London: Her Majesty's Stationery Office.

GEG = Howard, Godfrey. 1993. *The Good English Guide: English Usage in the 1990s*. London: Macmillan.

GEU = Greenbaum, Sidney & Janet Whitcut. 1988. *The Longman Guide to English Usage*. Harlow: Longman.

KE = Fowler, Henry W. & Francis G. Fowler. 1906. *The King's English*. Oxford: Clarendon Press.

MEU-1 = Fowler, Henry W. 1926. *A Dictionary of Modern English Usage*. Oxford: Oxford University Press.

MEU-2 = *A Dictionary of Modern English Usage* revised by Ernest Gowers. 1965. Oxford: Oxford University Press.

MEU-3 = *The New Fowler's Modern English Usage* revised by Robert W. Burchfield. 1996. Oxford: Oxford University Press.
QE = Alford, Henry. 1880. *The Queen's English. Notes on Speaking and Spelling*. Fifth edition. London: Strahan.

5.2 Reference grammars

CaGra = Huddleston, Rodney & Geoffrey K. Pullum. 2002. *The Cambridge Grammar of the English Language*. Cambridge: Cambridge University Press.
CGEL = Quirk, R., S. Greenbaum, G. Leech & J. Svartvik. 1985. *A Comprehensive Grammar of the English Language*. London: Longman.
LGSWE = Biber, D., S. Johansson, G. Leech, S. Conrad & E. Finegan. 1999. *Longman Grammar of Spoken and Written English*. Harlow: Pearson Education.
LSGSWE = Biber, D., S. Conrad & G. Leech. 2002. *Longman Student Grammar of Spoken and Written English*. Harlow: Pearson Education.

5.3 Corpora

BNC = *British National Corpus* (c. 10 million words of spoken and c. 90 million words of written British English).
Brown = *Brown Corpus* (1 million words of edited written American English published in 1961).
F-LOB = *Freiburg-Lancaster-Oslo/Bergen Corpus* (1 million words of edited written British English published in 1991; intended to replicate the LOB Corpus).
Frown = *Freiburg-Brown Corpus* (1 million words of edited written American English published in 1992; intended to replicate the Brown Corpus).
LOB = *Lancaster-Oslo/Bergen Corpus* (1 million words of edited written British English published in 1961; modelled after the Brown Corpus).

5.4 Secondary sources

Allen, R. E. 1992. "Usage". *The Oxford Companion to the English Language* ed. T. McArthur, 1071-1078. Oxford: Oxford University Press.
Busse, Ulrich & Anne Schröder. 2006. "From Prescriptivism to Descriptivism? 140 Years of English Usage Guides: Some Old and New Controversies". *Anglistentag 2005 Bamberg: Proceedings* ed. C. Houswitschka et al., 457-473. Trier: WVT.
Busse, Ulrich & Anne Schröder. 2009. "Fowler's *Modern English Usage* at the Interface of Lexis and Grammar". *Exploring the Lexis-Grammar Interface* (Studies in Corpus Linguistics 35) ed. U. Römer & R. Schulze, 69-87. Amsterdam: Benjamins.

Crystal, David. 1987. *The Cambridge Encyclopedia of Language.* Cambridge: Cambridge University Press.
Crystal, David. 1997. *A Dictionary of Linguistics and Phonetics.* Fourth edition. Oxford: Blackwell.
Crystal, David. 2003. *The English Language.* Second edition. London: Penguin.
Herbst, T., R. Stoll & R. Westermayr. 1991. *Terminologie der Sprachbeschreibung.* Ismaning: Hueber.
Hundt, Marianne. 1998. *New Zealand English Grammar – Fact or Fiction? A Corpus-based Study in Morphosyntactic Variation.* Amsterdam: Benjamins.
Kennedy, Graeme. 1998. *An Introduction to Corpus Linguistics.* London: Longman.
Mair, Christian. 2006a. "Tracking Ongoing Grammatical Change and Recent Diversification in Present-day Standard English: The Complementary Role of Small and Large Corpora". *The Changing Face of Corpus Linguistics* ed. A. Renouf & A. Kehoe, 355-376. Amsterdam: Rodopi.
Mair, Christian. 2006b. *Standard English in the Twentieth Century: History and Variation.* Cambridge: Cambridge University Press.
Mair, Christian. 2007. "Change and Variation in Present-day English: Integrating the Analysis of Closed Corpora and Web-based Monitoring". *Corpus Linguistics and the Web* ed. M. Hundt, N. Nesselhauf & C. Biewer, 233-247. Amsterdam: Rodopi.
Mukherjee, Joybrato. 2002. *Korpuslinguistik und Englischunterricht. Eine Einführung.* Frankfurt: Lang.
Mukherjee, Joybrato. 2006. "Corpus Linguistics and English Reference Grammars". *The Changing Face of Corpus Linguistics* ed. A. Renouf & A. Kehoe, 337-354. Amsterdam: Rodopi.
Parrish, Thomas. 2002. *The Grouchy Grammarian. A How-Not-To Guide to the 47 Most Common Mistakes in English Made by Journalists, Broadcasters, and Others Who Should Know Better.* Hoboken & New Jersey: Wiley & Sons.
Peters, Pam. 1995. *Cambridge Australian Style Guide.* Cambridge: Cambridge University Press.
Schmied, Josef. 2006. "New Ways of Analysing ESL on the WWW with WebCorp and WebPhraseCount". *The Changing Face of Corpus Linguistics* ed. A. Renouf & A. Kehoe, 309-324. Amsterdam: Rodopi.
Sick, Bastian. 2004-2009. *Der Dativ ist dem Genitiv sein Tod.* Vols. 1-4. Cologne: Kiepenheuer und Witsch.
Trudgill, Peter & Jean Hannah. 2002. *International English: A Guide to the Varieties of Standard English.* London: Arnold.
Truss, Lynne. 2003. *Eats, Shoots and Leaves: The Zero Tolerance Approach to Punctuation.* London: Profile Books.

Renata Szczepaniak (Hamburg)

Während des Flug(e)s/des Ausflug(e)s? German Short and Long Genitive Endings between Norm and Variation

1. Introduction

This article addresses the formal variation between the short genitive *-s* and the long genitive *-es* in contemporary German, e.g. in *während des Flug(e)s/Ausflug(e)s* 'during the flight/the excursion', which can be traced back to a diachronic norm change. For the most part, the Old High German (OHG) norm *-es*, i.e. the obligatory way of expressing strong genitive singular, has gradually given way to the New High German (NHG) norm *-s*. The resulting present-day variation between *-es* and *-s* is one of the most problematic cases within the normative German grammar. This has made it difficult to satisfactorily describe the distribution of these two formal variants (s. Duden-Grammatik 2005). This article will document this norm change and, based on the analysis of written corpora of contemporary German, it also will offer a phonological explanation of the diachronic development as well as of the present-day variation, taking into account the parameters of the phonological word, its size and its shape.

2. The strong genitive suffix in Old High German

The *es*-ending developed into a norm, i.e. the obligatory way of expressing strong genitive singular, during the OHG period. As a legacy of the Germanic language, the OHG nominal system comprised a series of declension classes with different types of so-called stem suffixes and different inflectional endings, also for genitive singular. However, the original (Indo-)Germanic dependency of the suffix on the inflectional stem gradually disappeared, and so *-es* became an obligatory genitive singular marker as it spred to new stem classes: First, only the OHG masculine and neuter nouns of the *a*-declension (the so-called *a*-stems), the masculine nouns of the *i*-declension (the *i*-stems), and the neuter nouns of the *iz/az*-declension (the *iz/az*-stems) marked genitive singular with *-es*, see Table 1.

In the course of OHG's development, the few *u*-stems that survived attracted the *es*-genitive, since they changed into the *i*-stems, or less frequently, into the *a*-stems, e.g. *u*-class > *i*-class: *sunu, sunes, suni* 'son'. The same happened to the *nt*-stems, OHG *friunt* 'friend' and *fiant* 'enemy' and the *r*-stems and the monosyllabic consonantal (athematic) stems. Here, the initial variation between two genitive singular forms (the original one without any ending, and the new one, -*es*) eventually disappeared in favour of the *es*-suffix, e.g. masculine *r*-stem: *fater/fater-es* 'father; gen.' or masculine athematic stem *man/mann-es* 'man/human being; gen.' (Braune/Reiffenstein 2004: 183-217). Before the end of the OHG period, the members of the unproductive declension classes (the *u*-, *er*-, *nt*- and the monosyllabic consonant stems) completely changed into the productive classes (mainly the *a*- and *i*-stems). Due to this general reorganisation of the OHG nominal system, the genitive -*es* rose to the level of an obligatory and formally stable inflectional ending in the so-called strong declension[1], i.e. -*es* became a norm (Figure 1).

Table 1: OHG declension

declension class	masculine nouns	neuter nouns
a-class:	*fisk-es* 'fish'	*swert-es* 'sword'
i-class:	*liut-es* 'people, folk'	——
iz/az-class:	——	*lamb-(ir)-es* 'lamb'

es-genitive (Germanic legacy)

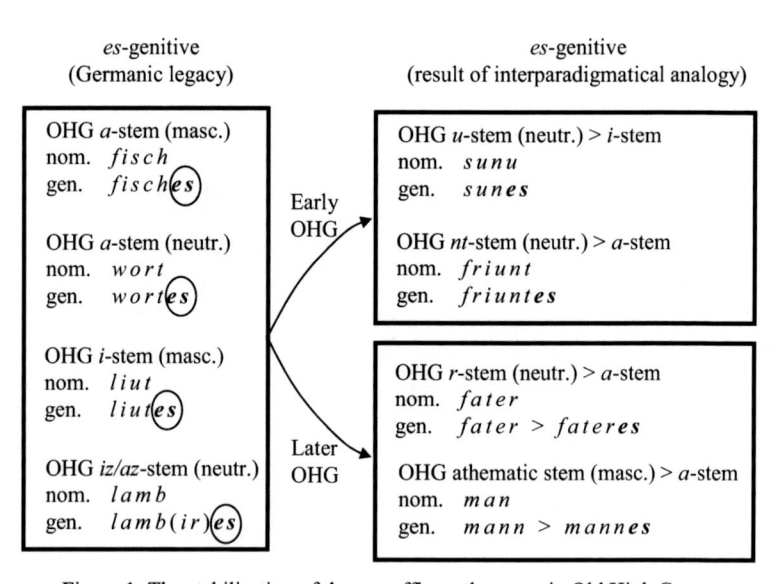

OHG *a*-stem (masc.)
nom. *fisch*
gen. *fisch(es)*

OHG *a*-stem (neutr.)
nom. *wort*
gen. *wort(es)*

OHG *i*-stem (masc.)
nom. *liut*
gen. *liut(es)*

OHG *iz/az*-stem (neutr.)
nom. *lamb*
gen. *lamb(ir)(es)*

Early OHG

Later OHG

es-genitive (result of interparadigmatical analogy)

OHG *u*-stem (neutr.) > *i*-stem
nom. *sunu*
gen. *sunes*

OHG *nt*-stem (neutr.) > *a*-stem
nom. *friunt*
gen. *friuntes*

OHG *r*-stem (neutr.) > *a*-stem
nom. *fater*
gen. *fater* > *fateres*

OHG athematic stem (masc.) > *a*-stem
nom. *man*
gen. *mann* > *mannes*

Figure 1: The stabilisation of the *es*-suffix as the norm in Old High German

---

[1] The weak declension, as it was called by Jacob Grimm, consists of the Germanic *n*-stems and exhibits *n*-containing suffixes in oblique cases, including the genitive singular.

Because all OHG vowels display full quality regardless of their position within a word, the phonetic/phonological shape of the OHG strong genitive differs from its later form in Middle High German (MHG). It contains a full vowel in OHG, but the later reduction of unstressed vowels, beginning in MHG, led to the present-day form with a schwa [əs].[2]

3. The genitive suffix in Middle High German: The role of the phonological word

While the strong genitive (henceforth "genitive") was formally stable in OHG and contained a vowel (most frequently *e*) followed by an *s*, it underwent certain phonological processes in MHG that led to the rise of a new, vowel-less variant, *-s*. Before explaining this phenomenon in detail (section 3.2), I will give a short description of the increasing significance of the phonological word in the diachronic phonology of German, which has directly affected the strong genitive.

3.1 The phonological word in the history of the German language

As a constituent in the prosodic hierarchy, the phonological word (ω) is located between the phonological foot (F) and the phonological phrase. This hierarchy is governed by a series of principles leading to the strictly unchangeable order of its individual layers (see Selkirk 1984, Nespor/Vogel 1986, Hall 1999 among others). For the purposes of this article, only a part of this hierarchy needs to be discussed, from the phonological syllable (σ) upwards to the phonological word. The example in Figure 2 illustrates the phonological hierarchy of the words *Wolke* 'cloud' and *Phantasie* 'imagination'.

The phonological word is the smallest prosodic constituent constructed on the basis of phonological as well as morphological information, i.e. by mapping the morphological structure onto the phonological one. A phonological word contains at least one morpheme. Conversely, the whole morpheme is contained in one phonological word (Hall 1999).

---

[2] In the OHG period, the most frequently occurring graphic form is <es> (Braune/Reiffenstein 2004: 84, 201). At the end of the ninth century, the form <as> appears in Old Bavarian due to the general vowel change from *e* to *a* in final syllables in this dialect (Braune/Reiffenstein 2004: 62; Schatz 1907: 104). This graphic deviation can also be observed in other OHG dialects (Franck 1971: 172, Schatz 1927: 203f.). Only very sporadically does the graphic variant <is> appear in the Late OHG period (Schatz 1927: 203).

```
monopedal, bisyllabic    ω           bipedal, trisyllabic        ω
phonological word:       |           phonological word:         / \
                         F                                    Fₛ   F_w
                        / \                                   / \   |
                       σ   σ                                 σ   σ   σ

                      vɔl  kə                              fan  ta  ziː

                   Wolke 'cloud'                       Phantasie 'imagination'
```

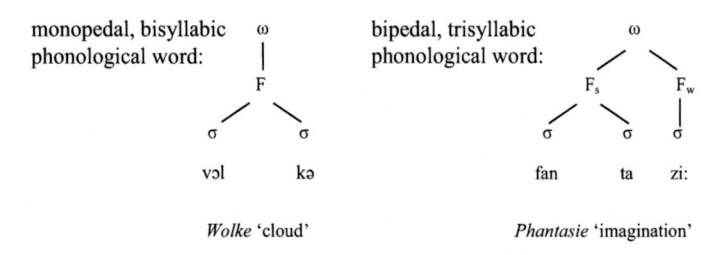

Figure 2: The phonological hierarchy (syllable, foot, and word)

Throughout the history of the German language, the phonological word has continuously increased in importance. Over the course of German's typological change from syllable language to word language, the phonological word has replaced the phonological syllable as the central phonological constituent (for details, see Szczepaniak 2007). In the OHG period, the phonological syllable played the most important role in phonological processes, as is typical of syllable languages. As such, these processes, e.g. the *i-umlaut* and other vocalic changes, led to optimisation of the syllable or were related to it. As early as the Later OHG period, the phonological syllable had gradually lost its role and had been replaced by the phonological word. The subsequent stage in the history of German (from MHG to NHG) has been characterised by an increasing optimisation of the phonological word and an enhancement of both its size and its form, which has had a direct impact on the genitive ending.

The size of the phonological word has been regulated in that the number of feet and syllables has been reduced. This has been achieved through the phonological reduction and subsequent deletion of unstressed vowels. Since MHG, the unmarked phonological word is monopedal and disyllabic, i.e. it contains only one phonological foot with at most two syllables (see Figure 2). This prosodic ideal has many morphological consequences, e.g. for the plural. In NHG nouns, the syllables are organised in such a way that a monopedal phonological word does not contain more than two of them. Thus, if a lexical morpheme contains only one syllable as in *Tür* 'door', an additional grammatical morpheme has to be syllabic, e.g. *-en* in *Tür+en* [tyː.ʀən] 'doors' (it does not apply for the *s*-plurals). After a disyllabic lexical morpheme as in *Straße* 'street', only a non-syllabic inflectional ending *-n* is possible, e.g. *Straße+n* [ʃtʀaː.sən] 'streets' (Eisenberg 1991). The situation is almost the same with the masculine/neuter genitive singular ending. While it can vary between syllabic and non-syllabic after a monosyllabic lexical morpheme as in *Wort+(e)s* 'word, gen.sg.', it is always non-syllabic after a disyllabic lexical morpheme as in *Himmel+s* 'heaven, gen.sg.' (see below).

The form of the phonological word has also been subject to optimisation. There are many strategies to optimise the internal form, to strengthen the edges of the phonological word and to increase its coherence. All of these processes help make the phonological word recognisable as such, often at the expense of the syllable. Such strategies that increase the recognisability of the phonological word help the hearer to decode the information contained in the word (for more details see Szczepaniak 2007, in press; Nübling/Szczepaniak 2008).

The fact that the genitive ending was also directly affected by the processes of word optimization (it underwent vowel reduction) contributes to the syntagmatic disequilibrium between stressed and unstressed syllables.

Additionally, there have been many strategies to strengthen the edges of the phonological word. One of the processes emphasising the right edge was the ENHG consonant epenthesis, e.g. MHG *mâne* > ENHG *mond* 'moon' (sic!). Word-final extrasyllabic consonants, i.e. consonants in the syllable coda with a lower degree of consonantal strength (CS) than their left-hand neighbours, exhibit a similar marking function. As the following example shows, the short genitive ending -*s* after plosives functions as an extrasyllabic consonant: (*des*) *Abends* 'evening, gen.sg.'.

The phonological parameter of CS refers to the degree to which pulmonic air flow is impeded on its way through the mouth or the nose: the larger the physical barrier, the higher the CS, see Figure 3. Thus, plosives exhibit the highest CS, followed by fricatives, nasals, and liquids (see Vennemann 1988). Inversely proportional to CS is the phonological parameter of sonority, which can be defined as a parameter of loudness, referring to the acoustic intensity of a sound.

◄──────── increasing sonority ──────── increasing consonantal strength ────────►

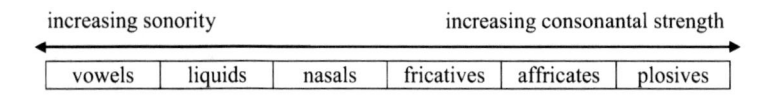

| vowels | liquids | nasals | fricatives | affricates | plosives |

Figure 3: Consonantal strength and sonority

3.2 The rise of the short genitive

The short genitive arose in MHG as a consequence of two types of word-optimising vowel deletion. The first type led to word optimisation through regulation of word size (see Table 2). Generally, phonological words containing more than two syllables were shortened by vowel deletion. In this way, the size of the phonological word was reduced, with few exceptions, to a maximum of one disyllabic foot. The phenomenon has led to a regular appearance of the non-syllabic genitive after disyllabic stems in NHG, e.g. *des Vaters* 'father, gen.sg.', *des Abends* 'evening, gen.sg.' or *des Bodens* 'ground, gen.sg.'. In these words, only the short genitive can appear so that the whole word is not larger than an unmarked monopedal, disyllabic word, e.g. [bo:.dəns]_ω.

Table 2: Reduction of the size of the phonological word in MHG

	[σσσ]_ω	>	[σσ]_ω
MHG	fa.te.res	>	fa.ters
MHG	en.ge.les	>	en.gels
MHG	â.ben.des	>	â.bends

The second type of vowel deletion emphasized the structure of the phonological word by making the stressed syllable heavy, i.e. by adding at least one consonant to an empty coda, e.g. *spi.les* > *spils* 'game, gen.sg.' (Wilmanns 1911: 356). This deletion was blocked after stems with long vowels, e.g. MHG *mâles* > *mâls 'mark, gen.sg.'. Whereas this prosodic regularity was given up as early as in ENHG, another fact must be taken into account: In MHG, vowel deletion, and therefore the short genitive, was possible only after liquids. In ENHG, the short genitive also began to occur after stronger consonants (fricatives and plosives), where it functions as an extrasyllabic consonant, e.g. *kruges* > *krugs* 'jug, pitcher' (see also Figure 4 on p. 114).

4. The genitive suffix in New High German

As already mentioned, the norm change from the long *-es* to the short *-s* began as early as MHG. During this time, the short, vowel-less variant developed. Since that period, the shift from long ending to short ending has continued. In this study, a corpus-based analysis of present-day variation is conducted with the purpose of determining the internal factors.

The Duden-Grammatik (2005: 199-203) states that the short genitive should be considered the norm (in Duden-Grammatik: *Normalfall*) in contemporary German. The long ending is either phonologically conditioned (morpheme-final sibilant, e.g. *Fisch* 'fish', *Fisch+es* 'fish, gen.') or lexically motivated. In lexical borrowings, the short ending is preferred, e.g. *des Konflikts* 'conflict, gen.'. The behaviour of lexical borrowings provides an additional argument for considering the short genitive to be the norm. According to the Duden-Grammatik, there is no clear preference for one ending over another after nouns whose stem ends with a stressed vowel followed by one or more consonants, e.g. *Gift* 'poison' or *Verzicht* 'resignation'. Nouns with a full vowel in the last syllable that does not carry the main stress are said to have a tendency toward the short ending, e.g.

Vortrag 'presentation', *Hauptbahnhof* 'main train station'. Only the short ending appears with derivational suffixes such as *-tum, -ling, -lein, -chen*, and *-ig*.

The statements from the Duden-Grammatik suggest that there is a deep phonological dependency of the genitive form on the phonological word structure. Here, this assumption will be proved in a corpus-linguistic approach. Conversely, the present-day distribution can also help explain the way the dominance of the short genitive has increased throughout the history of German.

For the purposes of this article, a corpus analysis was conducted using the database of the Cosmas II, Corpus Search System of the *Institut für Deutsche Sprache* in Mannheim.[3] On the basis of the annotated corpus TAGGED, native or (borrowed but) phonologically fully assimilated masculines and neuters were arranged in lists according to morphological complexity: simplexes, derivatives with unstressed and stressed prefixes, derivatives with suffixes, and compounds. This systematisation also takes phonological nature into account. German nominal simplexes (except unassimilated borrowings) create simple (mostly monopedal and monosyllabic) phonological words, e.g. *Buch* 'book' [[buːx]$_F$]$_\omega$ or *Straße* 'street' [[ʃtʀaː..sə]$_F$]$_\omega$ (see Figure 2). The complexity of the phonological structure increases with the morphological one. Only derivatives with unstressed suffixes (like *-er* in *Lehr+er* 'teacher' [[leː.ʀə]$_F$]$_\omega$) still constitute simple phonological words, as do derivatives with unstressed prefixes. However, an unstressed prefix increases the complexity because it is an unparsed syllable that is not able to create a phonological foot of its own, e.g. *Ver+stand* 'intellect, reason' [<fɐ>[ʃtant]$_F$]$_\omega$. Derivatives with stressed prefixes (*An+ruf* 'telephone call' [[an]$_F$]$_\omega$[[ʀuːf]$_F$]$_\omega$) and derivatives with stressed suffixes (*Reich+tum* 'wealth' [[ʀaɪç]$_F$]$_\omega$[[tuːm]$_F$]$_\omega$) exhibit the same phonological complexity as compounds (*Kunst+werk* 'piece of art' [[kʊnst]$_F$]$_\omega$[[vɛɐk]$_F$]$_\omega$). A stressed prefix or stressed suffix constitutes its own phonological word as does each member of a compound. Thus, both derivatives with stressed affixes and compounds each comprise at least two phonological words (see Raffelsiefen 2000). Table 3 summarises the phonological and morphological structure of German nouns.

---

[3] First, research was conducted using the annotated corpus TAGGED. Unfortunately, this corpus is too small (approx. 26 million words) to lead to any conclusions about the distribution of the short and long genitive endings. For that reason, a second research series was conducted using the biggest corpus of Cosmas II, the so-called "all public corpora of written language" (henceforth "public corpus"). One part of it, the "archive of written corpora", contained 5,776,397 texts at the time of research (February 2007).

Table 3: The morphological and phonological structure of NHG nouns

Morphological structure	Example	Phonological structure
Simplex:	*Buch* 'book'	$[[\sigma]_F]_\omega$
Derivative with unstressed suffix:	*Lehrer* 'teacher'	$[[\sigma\sigma]_F]_\omega$
Derivative with unstressed prefix:	*Verstand* 'intellect'	$[<\sigma>[\sigma]_F]_\omega$
Derivative with stressed prefix:	*Anruf* 'telephone call'	$[[\sigma]_F]_\omega[[\sigma]_F]_\omega$
Derivative with stressed suffix:	*Reichtum* 'wealth'	$[[\sigma]_F]_\omega[[\sigma]_F]_\omega$
Compound:	*Kunstwerk* 'piece of art'	$[[\sigma]_F]_\omega[[\sigma]_F]_\omega$

(increasing phonological complexity ↓)

Because the derivatives with unstressed and stressed suffix (*Léhr+er*, *Réich+tùm*) regularly take the short genitive ending, they were excluded from the corpus research. However, they are considered in the final discussion of the norm change in section 4.5. Table 4 presents the total number of the investigated nouns. Additionally, it provides information about their phonological complexity.

Table 4: The total number of nouns investigated

Morphological structure	Total number	Phonological complexity
Simplexes:	162	simple monopedal phonological word (the unmarked case)
Derivatives with unstressed prefixes:	61	complex monopedal phonological word (the marked case)
Derivatives with stressed prefixes:	99	two phonological words
Compounds:	~ 660	at least two phonological words

The following analysis consists of two steps. First, the parameters responsible for the formal variation between *-s* and *-es* in simplexes will be elaborated (section 4.1). The focus of sections 4.2 – 4.5 lies on the general tendency toward the short genitive as depending on the size of the phonological word.

4.1 Simplexes

In order to analyse the formal behaviour of simplexes, individual searches in the public corpus of Cosmas II (see footnote 3) were undertaken for both genitive variants (the short and long ending) of each noun. Here, a total of 91 masculine and 71 neuter simplexes with more than 100 appearances in Cosmas II were considered. The analysis took into account the number and the quality of final consonants, and the vowel quantity. Tables 5 and 6 show all analysed simplexes with the relative frequency of the short ending -s (the absolute number of short ending occurrences divided by the absolute number of all occurrences of the genitive form). The closer the value of the relative frequency to 1, the stronger the tendency toward the short genitive. For simplexes, the slightly lower relative frequency value reflects a tendency toward the long genitive. Here, the ending -s cannot be seen as a norm. In the rest of this section, a closer look is taken at the parameters of variation between -s and -es. It will be shown that the frequency of the short ending varies very widely depending on syllable structure.

Table 5: All masculine simplexes and the relative frequency (rf) of the short ending

	noun	rf		noun	rf		noun	rf		noun	rf
1	Bach	0,85	24	Krieg	0,16	47	Schirm	0,62	70	Tag	0,11
2	Berg	0,44	25	Krug	0,83	48	Schlag	0,35	71	Teich	0,36
3	Brand	0,19	26	Lärm	0,98	49	Schlauch	0,5	72	Teil	0,88
4	Bund	0,01	27	Leib	0,03	50	Sieg	0,06	73	Text	0,04
5	Darm	0,6	28	Lohn	0,37	51	Sinn	0,35	74	Tisch	0,09
6	Dienst	0,01	29	Mond	0,04	52	Sohn	0,06	75	Tod	0,01
7	Feind	0,02	30	Mord	0,01	53	Spott	0,68	76	Traum	0,61
8	Fisch	0,11	31	Müll	0,99	54	Spruch	0,58	77	Trost	0,09
9	Flug	0,35	32	Mut	0,06	55	Staat	0,33	78	Turm	0,62
10	Freund	0,02	33	Ort	0,26	56	Stab	0,32	79	Wald	0,02
11	Frost	0,4	34	Pfahl	0,98	57	Stahl	0,98	80	Weg	0,13
12	Gang	0,46	35	Plan	0,59	58	Stamm	0,21	81	Wein	0,48
13	Geist	0,01	36	Rang	0,06	59	Stand	0,06	82	Wert	0,2
14	Grund	0,06	37	Rat	0,26	60	Staub	0,6	83	Wind	0,2
15	Hang	0,41	38	Raub	0,09	61	Stein	0,85	84	Wirt	0,39
16	Hof	0,32	39	Raum	0,3	62	Stern	0,89	85	Wunsch	0,02
17	Hund	0,02	40	Ring	0,7	63	Stier	0,71	86	Zahn	0,47
18	Kampf	0,06	41	Ruf	0,46	64	Stock	0,61	87	Zaun	0,48
19	Kauf	0,71	42	Rumpf	0,27	65	Stoff	0,22	88	Zoll	0,82
20	Kern	0,98	43	Saal	0,38	66	Streit	0,82	89	Zorn	0,9
21	Klang	0,51	44	Sand	0,62	67	Strom	0,71	90	Zug	0,2
22	Koch	0,97	45	Sarg	0,1	68	Stuhl	0,79	91	Zweck	0,92
23	Kopf	0	46	Schein	0,87	69	Sturm	0,95			

Table 6: All neuter simplexes with the relative frequency (rf) of the short ending

#	noun	rf	#	noun	rf	#	noun	rf	#	noun	rf
1	Amt	0,18	19	Fleisch	0,07	37	Korn	0,81	55	Schaf	0,29
2	Bad	0,05	20	Geld	0,01	38	Land	0	56	Schiff	0,24
3	Bein	0,32	21	Gold	0,03	39	Laub	0,29	57	Schnitt	0,64
4	Bett	0,1	22	Grab	0	40	Leid	0,65	58	Schwein	0,58
5	Bier	0,37	23	Haar	0,15	41	Licht	0,68	59	Seil	0,59
6	Bild	0,03	24	Haupt	0,01	42	Lied	0,08	60	Spiel	0,86
7	Blatt	0,07	25	Heer	0,04	43	Lob	0,06	61	Stück	0,54
8	Blech	0,9	26	Heft	0,22	44	Loch	0,58	62	Tal	0,26
9	Blut	0,07	27	Heil	0,91	45	Mahl	0,63	63	Tier	0,11
10	Boot	0,39	28	Heim	0,49	46	Meer	0,06	64	Tuch	0,31
11	Brett	0,2	29	Hirn	0,96	47	Moor	0,22	65	Volk	0,06
12	Brot	0,09	30	Hoch	1	48	Obst	0,05	66	Weib	0,06
13	Ding	0,45	31	Horn	0,94	49	Ohr	0,38	67	Werk	0,38
14	Dorf	0,06	32	Huhn	0,73	50	Paar	0,1	68	Wohl	0,68
15	Fach	0,52	33	Jahr	0	51	Pferd	0,02	69	Wort	0,03
16	Feld	0,02	34	Kalb	0,27	52	Rad	0,08	70	Zelt	0,15
17	Fell	0,73	35	Kind	0,01	53	Rind	0,13	71	Ziel	0,62
18	Fett	0,27	36	Kleid	0,1	54	Rohr	0,18			

1) The parameter of vowel quantity

In Table 7 the relative frequency of the short genitive is given, taking into account vowel length. The short genitive is equally less frequent than the long one after short as well as after long stressed vowels. Hence, there is no correlation in contemporary German between genitive form and vowel length.

Table 7: Mean relative frequency of the short genitive ending after short and long stressed vowels

Short genitive after ...	Mean relative frequency
... a short stressed vowel:	0.38
... a long stressed vowel:	0.35

The difference between these two genitive forms is still marginal even if the quality of the final consonant is taken into account (see Table 8). For example, the difference for vowels followed by a nasal is very small (0.08), with a higher value for short stressed vowels. This means that the short genitive ending appears slightly more frequently after a short stressed vowel, e.g. *des Klang(e)s* 'sound. gen.sg.' (short vowel) vs. *des Wein(e)s* 'wine, gen.sg.' (long vowel).

German Short and Long Genitive Endings between Norm and Variation 113

Table 8: Mean relative frequency of the short genitive ending
(parameters: vowel quantity and consonant quality)

Final consonant:	Mean relative frequency of the short ending after ... a short stressed vowel (example):		Mean relative frequency of the short ending after ... a long stressed vowel (example):	
[ɐ/R]	—		0.16	(des Haars/es)
[l]	0.85	(des Zolls)	0.71	(des Pfahls)
nasals	0.63	(des Lärms)	0.55	(des Weins)
fricatives	0.43	(des Kochs)	0.45	(des Kaufs)
affricates	0.11	(des Kampfs/es)	—	
plosives	0.23	(des Betts/es)	0.19	(des Leids/es)
[st]	(0.4)	(des Frosts/es) (only one lexeme)	0.04	(des Diensts/es)

2) The parameter of the quality of the final consonant

However, what is striking in Table 8 is the difference in the relative frequency of the short genitive depending on the final consonant. This is summarised in Table 9a, where the consonants are arranged according to their CS, from the weakest consonant [R], which is normally vocalised at the end of the word, to the strongest consonant class, the plosives. In Table 9b, the results are listed in order of the increasing value of the relative frequency:

Table 9a: The mean relative frequency of the short genitive ending (in order of increasing CS)

Final consonant:	Mean relative frequency of the short ending (example)	
[ɐ/R]	0.21	(des Haar(e)s)
[l]	0.74	(des Pfahls)
nasals	0.60	(des Lärms)
fricatives	0.44	(des Kochs)
affricates	0.11	(des Frost(e)s)
plosives	0.21	(des Bett(e)s)
[st]	0.11	(des Dienst(e)s)

Table 9b: The mean relative frequency of the short genitive ending (in order of increasing value)

Mean relative frequency of the short ending:	Final consonant:
0.74	[l]
0.60	nasals
0.44	fricatives
0.21	plosives
0.21	[ɐ/R]
0.11	affricates
0.11	[st]

↓ increasing CS

Table 9b shows that the tendency toward the short genitive decreases with increasing CS of the final consonant. It is very high after [l] and becomes weaker after nasals, fricatives, and plosives. The short genitive ending seems to be very rare after [ɐ/ʀ], the affricate [pf][4] as in *Kampf* 'struggle', and the ending *-st* as in *Frost* 'frost'.

Obviously, the CS has a big impact on the choice of the genitive variant. The short genitive prevails in lexemes with a final *l* and with nasals, and it becomes less frequent with an increasing CS, i.e. with fricatives, affricates, and plosives. This suggests that the syllable structure plays the decisive role in determining the form of the genitive singular. This appears to have been the case since MHG (see above, section 3.2).

Because simplexes are at most monosyllabic, the non-syllabic genitive ending is incorporated into the coda. In combination with weak consonants (*l* or nasals), the non-syllabic *-s* does not disturb the steady decrease in sonority in the syllable coda. The fact that the short genitive also occurs (even if less frequently) after strong consonants (fricatives, affricates and plosives) can be explained by the diachronic tendency of German to optimise the phonological word. After a lexeme-final plosive, the non-syllabic genitive ending becomes an extrasyllabic element, which noticeably distorts the sonority curve in the coda. It leads to a secondary sonority increase in the syllable coda, as shown in Figure 4. The ensuing deterioration of the syllable structure simultaneously optimises the form of the phonological word by marking its right edge.

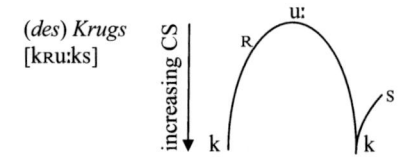

Figure 4: Syllable structure with an extrasyllabic element
(example (*des*) *Krugs* 'jug, pitcher; gen.sg.')

The current correlation between the occurrence of the short genitive ending and the CS clearly corresponds with the diachronic path of the norm change, where *-s* occurred first after weak final consonants and later after stronger final consonants. This can be explained through the increasing tendency toward the optimisation of the phonological word at the expence of the syllable.

---

[4] For reasons of morphological transparency, the short genitive ending does not appear after the affricate [ts] or after other sibilants, as observed in the Duden-Grammatik (see above), e.g. *Schatz+es* 'treasure; gen.sg.' [ʃatsəs] > **Schatzs* [ʃats:]. In such cases, there is no possibility of showing the morpheme boundary by means of a long consonant *[ʃats:]. This is also confirmed by the public corpus of Cosmas II: *Schatzes* (470 appearances) vs. *Schatzs* (0 appearances) (26.10.2007).

In light of the above, the fact that the long genitive is still preferred with nouns ending in the affricate [pf] (*des Kampfes* 'struggle, gen.sg.') and the consonant cluster [st] (*des Geistes* 'ghost, gen.sg.') is not very surprising. The affricate [pf] makes the syllable structure already very complex and marked, because the second part of the affricate, *f*, exhibits lower CS than the first part, *p*. Hence, *f* functions as an extrasyllabic element. Here, the non-syllabic genitive-*s* makes the syllable almost too complex and, hence, it tends to be avoided.

Interestingly, the short genitive ending is also very infrequent with a final [ɐ], a vocalised *r* (see Table 9b). The long genitive form enables the *r* to be realised as a consonant due to resyllabification, e.g. *Tier* [tiːɐ] 'animal' – *Tieres* [tiː.Rəs] 'animal, gen.sg.'. Here, the opposition between the realisation of a word-final and a word-medial consonant helps to highlight the word boundary, where the vocalised *r* clearly marks the word end, cf. *auslautverhärtung* in *Kind* [kɪnt] 'child' – *Kind+er* [kɪn.dɐ] 'children'.

3) The number of final consonants

The third possible phonological parameter that can explain the variation between genitive endings is the number of final consonants. In the database, the number of final consonants varies between one and three, e.g. *Huhn* 'chicken' (1), *Pferd* 'horse' (2), and *Obst* 'fruit' (3). The results shown in Table 10 suggest that the number of final consonants strongly influences the genitive form.

Table 10: Mean relative frequency of the short ending depending on the number of final consonants

Number of lexeme-final consonants	Mean relative frequency	
one consonant	0.42	(*des Huhns*)
two consonants	0.29	(*des Pferd(e)s*)
three consonants	0.09	(*des Obst(e)s*)

The smaller the word-final consonantal group, the more frequent the short genitive ending. However, it should be kept in mind that the larger the group, the more restricted the consonantal quality. There are hardly any lexemes with two final consonants ending with a liquid (such as *Kerl* 'fellow').[5] In contrast to Ta-

---

[5] There are some polysyllabic words (in the southern variant of standard German) ending with *-rl* where *-l* is a diminutive suffix, e.g. *Tüpferl* 'dot'. Because of their polysyllabicity, they exhibit only the short genitive ending. Besides *Kerl* 'fellow', there are a handful of infrequently used monosyllabic words ending with *-rl*, e.g. *Quirl* 'whisk, kitchen device' and *Schwirl* (a kind of songbird). A search in the public corpus of Cosmas II returns 471 results for *Kerl* with the short genitive ending and none with the long genitive

ble 7, a strong tendency toward the short ending can be observed in nouns with a short vowel and only one final consonant, see Table 11.

Table 11: Mean relative frequency of the short ending depending on vowel quantity (with one final consonant)

Vowel quantity	Mean relative frequency
short vowel:	0.49
long vowel:	0.34

Interestingly, the gender of the simplex also appears to have some significance. Table 12 shows that masculines demonstrate a greater tendency toward the short genitive than the neuters.

Table 12: Mean relative frequency of the short ending depending on gender

Gender	Mean relative frequency
masculine:	0.41
neuter:	0.31

This correlation appears to be even more relevant when vowel quantity is considered, as in Table 13. Both masculines with short and those with long vowels display a significantly stronger tendency toward the short genitive ending than neuter lexemes.

Table 13: Mean relative frequency of the short ending depending on gender and vowel quantity

Gender:	*Mean relative frequency of the short ending after* ... a short stressed vowel:	... a long stressed vowel:
masculine:	0.42	0.40
neuter:	0.32	0.31

Gender also appears to be a significant parameter of genitive variation when combined with phonological parameters such as vowel quantity and number of

---

ending. Due to the low frequency of the other two words, no genitive forms could be found in Cosmas II (26.10.2007).

final consonants. Table 14 shows that the short ending occurs more frequently after masculines with a short vowel.

Table 14: Mean relative frequency of the short ending (parameters: vowel quantity, number of final consonants, and gender)

Vowel quantity:		Mean relative frequency of the short ending			
		Masculines (example):		Neuters (example):	
a short stressed vowel	C CC CCC	0.52 0.37 0.12	(des Bachs) (des Kerns) (des Kampf(e)s)	0.44 0.25 —	(des Blechs) (des Amt(e)s)
a long stressed vowel	C CC CCC	0.45 0.17 (0.01)	(des Kaufs) (des Mond(e)s) (des Dienst(e)s) (only one lexeme)	0.32 (0.01) (0.05)	(des Beins) (des Haupt(e)s) (des Obst(e)s) (only one lexeme)

The higher relative frequency of masculines with the short ending can also be observed when consonant quality is taken into account. As shown in Table 15 (on p. 118), masculines ending in [l], but not those ending in a nasal, exhibit a higher mean relative frequency of the short ending than their neuter counterparts.

To sum up, the frequency of short genitive ending after simplexes is not very high (the mean relative frequency for all simplexes is 0.37). Whether -s will be chosen or not, depends on phonological and morphological factors. Among phonological factors, the size of the phonological word is the most important. Polysyllabic (mostly bisyllabic) monopedal phonological words take only the non-syllabic ending -s. For monosyllabic words, the quality of the final consonant and, by extension, the syllable structure are very important. This variation can be explained by the strong diachronic tendency of German to emphasise and regulate the phonological word. Vowel quantity appears to be important, when combined with the number of final consonants. Stems with a short vowel and one final consonant tend to attract the short ending more than those with a long vowel.

Interestingly, gender proves to influence the genitive ending variant, too. Masculines occur more often with the short genitive than the neuters.

Table 15: Mean relative frequency of the short ending
(parameters: final consonant quality and gender)

Final consonant:	Mean relative frequency of the short ending after	
	Masculines:	Neuters:
[ɐ/ʀ]	(0.71)[6]	0.16
[l]	0.83	0.66
nasals	0.58	0.66
fricatives	0.43	0.44
affricates	0.11	—
plosives	0.25	0.17
[st]	0.13	(0.05)

4.2 Derivatives with unstressed prefixes

In general, tendency toward the short genitive is stronger in derivatives with unstressed prefixes, e.g. *Verstand* (mean relative frequency 0.67) than in simplexes (mean relative frequency 0.37). In NHG, there are several unstressed prefixes: *Be-*, *Ge-*, *Er-*, *Ver-*, *Zer-*, and *Ent-/Emp-*. Figure 5 (on p. 119) shows that only derivatives with final plosives (and *-st*) oscillate between the short and long genitive endings. Derivatives with final liquids, nasals and fricatives obviously tend toward the short ending.

The fact that relative frequency decreases with increasing CS supports the diachronic scenario already described in section 3. The range of consonants after which the short genitive ending can occur is in a state of constant growth, gradually encompassing consonants of increasing CS and leading to deterioration of the syllable and optimisation of the phonological word. Only derivatives ending with *-st* mostly exhibit the long *-es*, due to their very complex coda. Regarding this type of derivatives, the short genitive can be seen as more advanced in acquiring the status of the norm (as it is in the case of simplexes). It is almost obligatory, i.e. for most derivatives, *-s* is the only acceptable and expectable genitive form (for a wider discussion of the notion of linguistic norm see Hundt 2009).

---

[6] Because of the high relative frequency of the short ending with the only masculine lexeme in the database ending with *r* (*Stier* 'bull'), additional searches were performed for two other lexemes meeting the same morphological and phonological criteria: *Speer* 'spear' and *Flur* 'hall, corridor'. It should be noted that these are the only frequent lexemes of this type in German, and that the relative frequency of the short genitive ending is very high for these lexemes (0.92 for *Speer* and 0.70 for *Flur*).

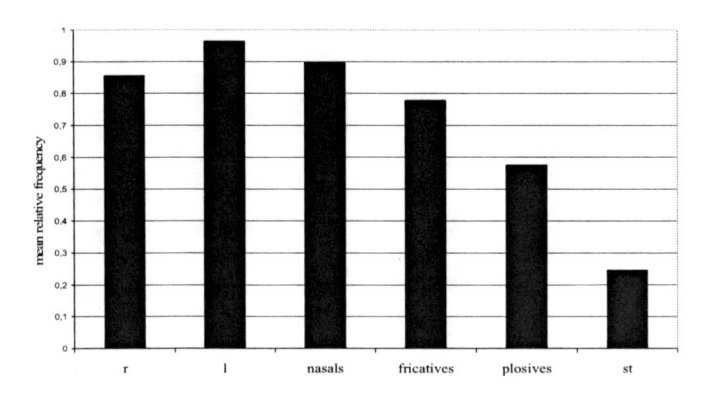

Figure 5: Mean relative frequency of the short genitive depending on CS
(for derivatives with unstressed prefix)

4.3 Derivatives with stressed prefixes

In German, derivatives with stressed prefixes have the same phonological structure as compounds. Since stressed prefixes (*Ab-, An-, Auf-, Aus-, Durch-, Ein-, Gegen-, Rück-, Über-, Um-, Un-, Unter-, Ur-, Voll-, Vor-, Weg-, Wider-, Zu-,* and *Zusammen-*) each constitute their own phonological word, the whole derivative contains two phonological words. The prefixes bear the main stress, i.e. they constitute the strong phonological word (ω_1), e.g. *Ursprung* 'origin' [uːɐ̯]$_{\omega 1}$-[ʃpʀʊŋ]$_{\omega 2}$ (see above, section 4).

The obvious tendency of these derivatives toward the short genitive ending is presented in Figure 6 (on p. 120). The mean relative frequency for all those derivatives is as high as 0.78.

Only a small number of derivatives with final plosives get mostly *-es*: *Abstand, Aufstand, Aufwand, Ausstand, Gegenstand, Umstand, Untergrund, Vorort, Vorstand, Widerstand, Zustand*. With the exception of *Vorort* 'suburb', all of these lexemes exhibit the final consonant cluster [nt]. The homorganic status of this consonant cluster could be responsible for their deviation from the norm, *-s*. Its status as a semi-geminate may discourage the tendency toward vowel deletion as in *Gegenstandes* > *Gegenstands* 'object/item' (see GILLES 2006 on semi-geminates).

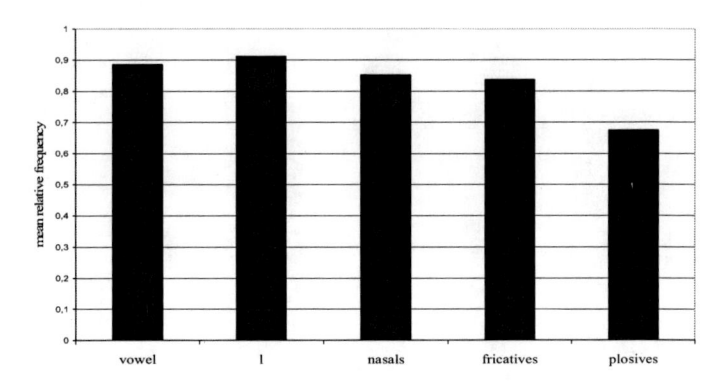

Figure 6: Mean relative frequency of the short genitive ending
for derivatives with stressed prefixes (parameter: CS)

4.4 Suffixation

Depending on their phonological shape, German suffixes can be divided into two phonological types. Suffixes beginning with a vowel, e.g. *-er* and (the no longer productive) *-icht*, are not able to constitute their own phonological word. They are incorporated into the phonological word of the preceding lexical morpheme, e.g. *Lehr+er* 'teacher' [le:.ʀɐ]$_\omega$ and *Kehr+icht* 'sweepings' [ke:.ʀɪçt]$_\omega$. This leads to a polysyllabic monopedal phonological word, which, for phonological reasons, can take only the short ending, e.g. *Lehrers* and *Kehrichts*.

The second group contains consonantal suffixes, e.g. *-tum* (*Reichtum* 'wealth'), *-ling* (*Lehrling* 'apprentice'), *-sal* (*Scheusal* 'monster'). Those suffixes continue to maintain phonological-word status, e.g. [ʀaɪ̯ç]$_\omega$[tu:m]$_\omega$. In the course of grammaticalization, they lost their original lexical meaning and acquired a more abstract one as is characteristic for derivational suffixes. Their formal development, however, has not been completed (for details on their phonological development, see Szczepaniak 2007). Although they maintain phonological-word status, these derivational suffixes show a very strong tendency toward the short ending. The Duden-Grammatik even declares it obligatory (see section 4). The relative frequency of the short genitive ending for *Reichtum* as well as for *Lehrling* is 0.997. As will be shown in the next section, compounds exhibiting the same phonological structure (one compound contains at least two phonological words) do not tend as strongly toward *-s*. There must be an additional factor leading to the regular occurrence of the short ending in words containing them. We will return to this question in the next section.

4.5 Compound nouns

For two practical reasons, the following analysis of compounds is limited to a few selected examples. First of all, the total number of appearances in Cosmas II is not as high as that of simplexes or derivatives. In many cases, it does not reach 100 hits. In order to produce statistically significant results, the analysis includes only compounds with at least 100 appearances. Secondly, it would require a great deal of time to analyse many compounds of each noun considered in this study. For the purposes of this article, two representative cases will be discussed (the nouns *Kampf* 'struggle' and *Werk* 'opus'). Both nouns, *Kampf* and *Werk*, tend toward the long genitive when used separately. This is why their relative frequency is so low (see Figures 7 and 8).

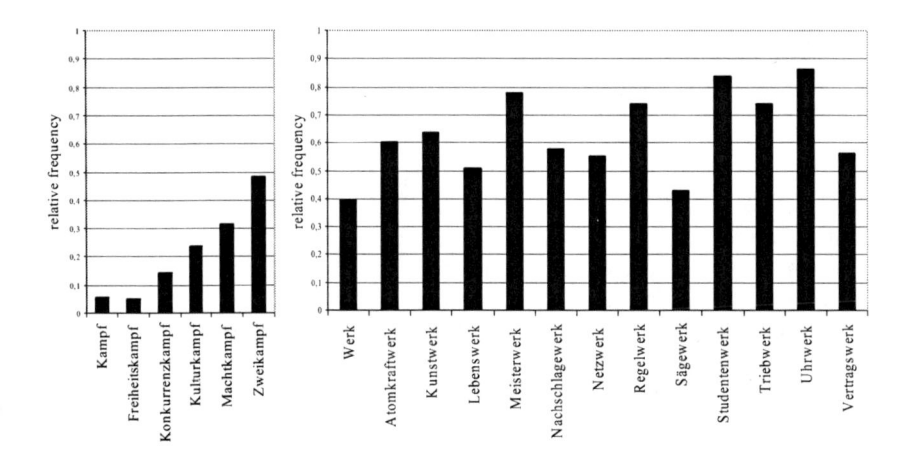

Figure 7: Relative frequency of short genitive ending by *Kampf* and compounds with *Kampf*

Figure 8: Relative frequency of the short genitive ending by *Werk* and compounds with *Werk*

Although the nouns tend to the long genitive when occurring separately, the respective compounds exhibit a very strong tendency toward the short form. This clearly suggests that longer words favour the short ending. Remember that compounds contain at least two phonological words, whereas a simplex comprises only one simple phonological word, e.g. $[Kampf]_\omega$ 'struggle' vs. $[Macht]_\omega[kampf]_\omega$ 'power struggle'.

Figure 9 shows a comparison between the frequency of the short genitive in the simplex *Stand*, *-stand* derivatives with unstressed and stressed prefixes, and compounds with *-stand*.

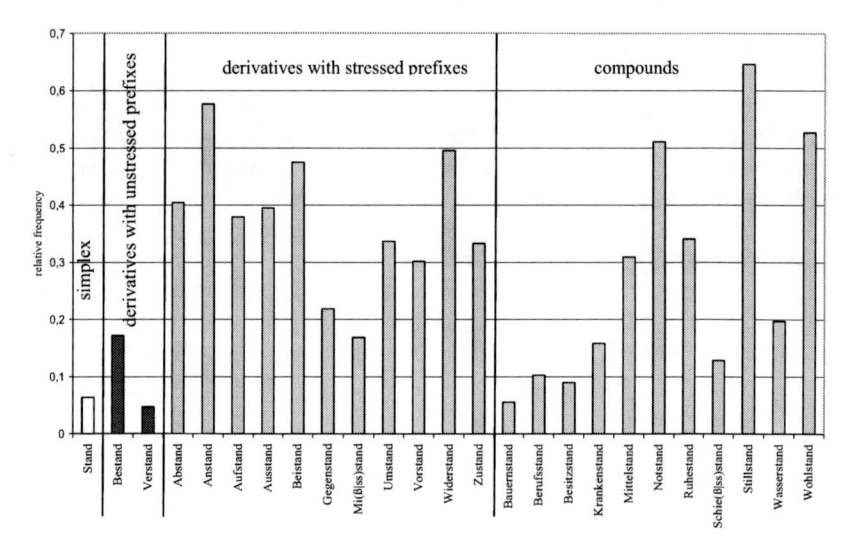

Figure 9: Relative frequency of the simplex *Stand*, derivatives
with *-stand*, and compounds with *-stand*

The tendency toward the short genitive increases from simplex to derivatives with unstressed prefix. It is also stronger in compounds than in derivatives with unstressed prefixes but weaker than in those with stressed prefixes. The mean relative frequency of the short ending in these words confirms this observation, as shown in Table 16.

Table 16: Mean relative frequency of the short ending with *Stand* and related words

	Mean relative frequency
Simplex (*Stand*):	0.06
Derivatives with unstressed prefix:	0.11
Derivatives with stressed prefix:	0.37
Compounds:	0.28

These results suggest that the probability of the short genitive increases with the size of the phonological word. Thus, the long ending most frequently occurs with a monopedal phonological word (simplexes). Its frequency gradually decreases with the more complex type of derivatives with unstressed prefixes which are the unparsed unstressed syllables, e.g.. *ver-*, preceding the phonological foot: [<ver>[stand]_F]_ω. The short genitive is fairly frequent with compounds and derivatives with stressed prefixes. Both types consist of two phonological words. However, the tendency toward the short genitive is even stronger with derivatives with stressed prefixes (and also with derivatives with stressed suffixes such as *-tum*). This might suggest that a higher degree of morphological fusion (here: derivation) favours the short genitive. This, in turn, has an impact on the phonological representation: Stressed affixes, although separate phonological words, are always combined with other lexical morphemes (also separate phonological words). Thus, they constitute a special kind of phonological word which never occurs on its own. As a result, they are gradually losing their status as phonological words. By choosing the short genitive, the derivates with stressed prefixes tend to behave as if they simply were very long single phonological words. The same applies to the stressed suffixes. Here, the short genitive is already the only choice. Additionally, some compounds exhibit a very strong tendency toward the short genitive, possibly due to their high token frequency and their degree of lexicalization (see *Stillstand* 'stagnancy' in Figure 9).

5. Summary

In contemporary German, the degree of obligatoricity of the short genitive depends on phonological factors. First of all, the frequency of the short genitive ending correlates positively with the phonological word size. Thus, the short ending appears more often in compounds and derivatives than in morphological simplexes. This is due to phonological complexity: Compounds and derivatives with stressed prefixes contain more than one phonological word each, whereas the derivatives with unstressed prefixes comprise only one but nevertheless complex phonological word. The simplest phonological words allow both variants, unless they contain two syllables. In the latter case only the short genitive is possible, otherwise very marked trisyllabic words would arise (**des Abendes* instead of the correct form *des Abends*) (see Table 17 on p. 124).

Additionally, the frequency of *-s* after monosyllables depends on the quality of the final consonant. The lower its consonantal strength, the higher the possibility of the short ending, e.g. *des Pfeils* 'arrow', *des Steins* 'stone' vs. *des Teiches* 'pond', *des Weges* 'way'. The number of final consonants and vowel quantity influence the ending, but only to a minor degree. The data suggest that gender is also important. Masculine simplexes exhibit a slightly stronger tendency toward *-s* than neuters.

Table 17: The morphological and phonological structure of NHG nouns

Morphological structure	Example	Phonological structure	
Simplex:	*Stand* 'class, condition'	$[[\sigma]_F]_\omega$	-es
Derivative with unstressed suffix:	*Lehrer* 'teacher'	$[[\sigma\sigma]_F]_\omega$	
Derivative with unstressed prefix:	*Bestand* 'inventory'	$[<\sigma>[\sigma]_F]_\omega$	
Compound:	*Kontostand* 'account balance'	$[[\sigma]_\omega[\sigma]_\omega]_\omega$	
Derivative with stressed suffix:	*Reichtum* 'wealth'	$[[\sigma]_\omega[\sigma]_\omega]_\omega$	
Derivative with stressed prefix:	*Aufstand* 'insurgence'	$[[\sigma]_\omega[\sigma]_\omega]_\omega$	-s

The high complexity of factors influencing the choice of the genitive form is responsible for the speaker's uncertainity of the right genitive form and, thus, for the high number of doubtful cases (see Klein 2006, 2009). The genitive variation ranges from zero variation (-s after disyllabic words) through gradual variation (e.g. strong tendency toward -s derivatives with unstressed prefix and towards -es after simplexes ending in plosives) to free variation between both endings (e.g. after simplexes ending in nasals).

Finally, the norm change from OHG to NHG has proven to be sensitive to both the size and the shape of the phonological word. The new, nonsyllabic ending is a result of the phonological tendency of German to optimise the phonological word, which has been very strong since MHG. The first step was in the MHG period, when the vowel was dropped after disyllabic stems as in *fateres > faters*. The following development was driven by the same forces. Today, the complex phonological words of compounds and derivatives show a strong tendency toward the short ending. In this way, the whole word remains as small as possible. Because of their optimal size, monosyllabic simplexes do not take the short genitive as frequently. Originally, it occurred under convenient syllabic conditions, i.e. when a well-formed sonority curve was guaranteed. In the course of the typological change of German toward a word language, the short genitive has occurred more and more frequently after strong consonants, optimising the phonological word and simultaneously leading to syllable deterioration.

The new (emerging) norm, the short ending -s, can be considered the result of the phonological-typological change of German from a syllable language to a word language.

6. References

6.1 Primary sources

Cosmas II. http://www.ids-mannheim.de/cosmas2

6.2 Secondary references

Braune, Wilhelm & Ingo Reiffenstein. 2004. *Althochdeutsche Grammatik I. Laut- und Formenlehre.* Tübingen: Niemeyer.
Duden-Grammatik. 2005. *Duden. Die Grammatik. Unentbehrlich für richtiges Deutsch.* Mannheim: Dudenverlag.
Eisenberg, Peter. 1991. "Syllabische Struktur und Wortakzent. Prinzipien der Prosodik deutscher Wörter". *Zeitschrift für Sprachwissenschaft* 10,1. 37-84.
Franck, Johannes. 1971. *Altfränkische Grammatik. Laut- und Flexionslehre.* Göttingen: Vandenhoeck & Ruprecht.
Hall, T. Alan. 1999. "The phonological word: a review". *Studies on the phonological word* ed. T. A. Hall & U. Kleinhenz, 1-22. Amsterdam & Philadelphia: Benjamins.
Gilles, Peter. 2006. "Phonologie der *n*-Tilgung im Moselfränkischen ('Eifler Regel'). Ein Beitrag zur dialektologischen Prosodieforschung". *Perspektiven einer linguistischen Luxemburgistik. Studien zur Diachronie und Synchronie* ed. C. Moulin & D. Nübling, 29-68. Heidelberg: Winter.
Hundt, Markus. 2009. "Normverletzungen und neue Normen". *Deutsche Grammatik – Regeln, Normen, Sprachgebrauch* ed. M. Konopka and B. Strecker, 117-140. Berlin, New York: de Gruyter.
Klein, Wolf Peter. 2006. "Sprachliche Zweifelsfälle als linguistischer Gegenstand. Zur Einführung in ein vergessenes Thema der Sprachwissenschaft". *Linguistik online* 16. http://www.linguistik-online.com/16_03/klein.html
Klein, Wolf Peter. 2009. *"Auf der Kippe?* Zweifelsfälle als Herausforderung(en) für Sprachwissenschaft". *Deutsche Grammatik – Regeln, Normen, Sprachgebrauch* ed. M. Konopka & B. Strecker, 141-165. Berlin, New York: de Gruyter.
Nespor, Maria & Irene Vogel. 1986. *Prosodic Phonology.* Dordrecht: Foris.
Nübling, Damaris & Renata Szczepaniak. 2008. "On the way from morphology to phonology. German linking elements as indicators of the phonological word". *Morphology* 18. 1-25.
Raffelsiefen, Renate. 2000. "Evidence for word-internal phonological words in German". *Deutsche Grammatik in Theorie und Praxis* ed. R. Thieroff et al., 43-56. Tübingen: Niemeyer.
Schatz, Josef. 1907. *Altbairische Grammatik. Laut- und Flexionslehre.* Göttingen: Vandenhoeck & Ruprecht.

Schatz, Josef. 1927. *Althochdeutsche Grammatik*. Göttingen: Vandenhoeck & Ruprecht.
Selkirk, Elisabeth. 1984. *Phonology and syntax. The relation between sound and structure*. Cambridge, Mass.: MIT Press.
Szczepaniak, Renata. 2007. *Der phonologisch-typologische Wandel des Deutschen von einer Silben- zu einer Wortsprache*. Berlin & New York: de Gruyter.
Szczepaniak, Renata (in press) "Phonologisch-typologische Entwicklung des Deutschen und des Luxemburgischen im Kontrast". *Kontrastive germanistische Linguistik* ed. A. Dammel, S. Kürschner & D. Nübling. Hildesheim: Olms.
Vennemann, Theo. 1988. *Preference laws for syllable structure and the explanation of sound change*. Berlin & New York: de Gruyter.
Wilmanns, Wilhelm. 1911. *Deutsche Grammatik. Gotisch, Alt-, Mittel- und Neuhochdeutsch. Erste Abteilung. Lautlehre*. Straßburg: Trübner.

Stephan Elspaß (Augsburg)
Regional Standard Variation in and out of Grammarians' Focus

1. Standard Variation in German

As more and more dialects and regiolects in the German-speaking countries have fallen into disuse (except in Switzerland and Liechtenstein), more and more people are unable to speak any other variety of their national language than its standard variety. Another consequence of this change is that the standard variety increasingly has to provide for formal as well as informal communicative contexts, whereas only half a century ago, the standard was more or less restricted to writing or to formal discourse. Inevitably, Standard German has developed more register variation in recent decades (Schwitalla 2008).

Informal registers of 'everyday' spoken German, in particular, display regional variation to a considerable extent – the more informal, the more regional they are (Kappel 2007). But even standard languages are not free from variation. They can have more than one standard variety, and yet formal registers of standard varieties are full of variants, as the plethora of 'Englishes' and their standard variation shows. Contrary to a widespread folk linguistic belief, there is no such thing as a completely homogeneous speech-community, as "the only fully standardised language is a dead language" (Milroy & Milroy 1985: 22).

In German linguistics, the notion of "standard varieties" has met with some approval. In the last two decades, it has become widely accepted that mainly Switzerland, Austria and Germany have developed "national varieties of German" in a pluricentric setting after World War II (von Polenz 1999: 412–453), although this politically very correct view may not quite have reached speakers' minds and influenced their own beliefs about their standard (Scharloth 2005). Still under debate, therefore, is whether this concept does full justice to the actual language situation *within* the German-speaking countries. Some linguists argue that variants of 'national varieties' do not stop at national borders, that there is, for instance, not much more linguistic difference between Standard German in the northern and the southern parts of Germany than between German in Southern Germany and German in Switzerland or Austria. They favour models of 'pluri-areal German' ("pluriareales Deutsch", Wolf 1994: 74, Scheuringer 1997: 343–344) or 'regional pluricentricity' ("regionale Plurizentrität", Reiffenstein 2001: 88; cf. also Koller 1999: 154).

Research into the variation of Standard German has largely been restricted to pronunciation and lexis, and it has resulted in authoritative handbooks, such as Ammon et al. (2004) and König (1989), to name the two most prominent works.[1] Variation in grammar, however, has gone almost unnoticed. There is no work on grammar comparable to these two handbooks. The lack of a codex or handbook does not mean that speaker-writers do not use different variants in standard grammar, even if folk linguistic belief – itself being deeply rooted in a standard language ideology (Milroy & Milroy 1985: 22–23) – will have it that a fully standardised German language does exist. As for grammar, one sometimes gets the impression that even grammarians wish that their field of research was free from variation.

The present paper will explore the extent of regional grammatical variation in Standard German and investigate how regional variants in grammar get into grammarians' focus (if they do at all). I will present two brief case studies and discuss the possible consequences for the study of present-day grammar.

2. Regional Variation in Standard German Grammar

Ursula Götz' (1995) article on regional variants of Standard German in Germany was probably the first exclusive study on this topic. Having leafed through three contemporary grammars of German, she identified 46 grammatical phenomena which were marked as being regional. Five of them she then checked against ten other grammars. The result of her study was that, in general, grammars did not or not sufficiently consider regional variation. Three of Götz' examples, which can also be found in later editions of the Duden grammar and other grammars, are the use of double perfect and double past perfect (1), plural forms (2), or strong instead of weak verb forms (3).

(1)   *Wir **haben** uns alle schon so daran **gewöhnt gehabt***
      we have us all already so PRO-to used (to it) had
      'All of us had already got used to it so much.'
      standard variants: *hatten ... gewöhnt* or *haben ... gewöhnt*
      ("im Oberdeutschen" 'in upper German', Duden 1984: 152, 1998: 153)

(2)   *Wägen*
      carriage-PL
      'carriages'
      standard variant: *Wagen*
      ("südd." 'southern German', Duden 1984: 243, 1998: 234)

---

[1]   A second edition of Ammon et al. (2004) is in preparation. A new survey on standard regional pronunciation in all German-speaking countries is presently being undertaken in the "Deutsch heute" project at the *Institut für Deutsche Sprache* in Mannheim, cf. <http://www.ids-mannheim.de/prag/AusVar/Deutsch_heute/> (24 April 2010).

(3) Dann *frug* er ...
Then ask-PST-SG he ...
'Then he asked ...'
standard variants: *fragte*
("landsch." 'regional', Duden 1984: 135, 1998: 136)

There are four general problems with entries in grammars of the kind shown here. Firstly, they are usually not based on corpora or other empirical studies. One simple reason for this is that to date nobody has undertaken to build a corpus of regional Standard German, nor has anybody so far carried out a systematic survey of non-dialectal regional variation in German grammar. Secondly, handbook entries such as "im Oberdeutschen" 'in upper German' or "südd[eutsch]" 'southern German' do not disclose whether the regional variant in question is considered *Standard* German or not. "Oberdeutsch", for instance, usually refers to dialect. Example (1), however, certainly is a sentence written in (literary) Standard German. Thirdly, from unspecific entries such as "landsch[aftlich]" 'regional' it is not even clear in which specific region the variant is supposed to be employed. And fourthly, the entry notes are often simply incorrect. *Wägen* is not only a variant of 'southern German', but also of German in Austria and probably also in Switzerland (cf. AdA 2003ff.: "Plural").

In recent years, Austrian and Swiss scholars have presented further evidence of grammatical variation of Standard German in Austria and Switzerland. Works on Standard German grammar in Austria remain scattered, however, and concentrate on rather specific phenomena (e.g. Sellner 2006). Dürscheid & Hefti (2006) devote an entire paper to syntactical features of Standard German in Switzerland such as filling the vorfeld with the adverb *bereits* 'already' (4), the use of subordinate clauses with verb-first position and without *dass* 'that' (5), or ellipsis of correlating *es* 'it' in the vorfeld (6):

(4) *Bereits liegt in den Alpen Schnee*
Already lies in the Alps snow
'There is snow already in the Alps.'
standard variant: *In den Alpen liegt bereits Schnee*

(5) *Gut, gibt's Karton*
good (that) exists it cardboard
'It's a good thing that there is/we have cardboard.'
standard variant: *Gut, dass es Karton gibt*

(6) *Kommt dazu, dass ...*
(it) comes in addition that ...
'There is also the fact that .../Moreover, ...'
standard variant: *Es kommt dazu, dass ...*

To sum up, regional grammatical variation in Standard German has been rather neglected in grammaticography, particularly in Germany, and its study has only recently emerged as a field of research in its own right.

3. Pinpointing 'Standard Language'

To give the reader an idea of the range of grammatical variation in Standard German, I will first present an exemplary list of phenomena. The variants listed here are established as being standard by employing a restrictive definition of standard language: A standard form is a linguistic form which is commonly used in printed or online newspaper texts. The list comprises examples of the different use of linking elements in compounds (7), verb complements (8), prepositions in verb complements (9), reflexive pronouns (10), gender (11), deverbal noun formation (12), and auxiliaries with analytical tense forms of the stative verbs *sitzen* '(to) sit', *stehen* '(to) stand', *liegen* '(to) lie' (13).

(7) *Zugmitte/Zugsmitte*
 train + middle/train + s-LINK + middle
 'centre/middle of the train'
(8) *etw. bei jdm beantragen/etw. jdm beantragen*
 sth. PREP OBJ (bei) apply/sth. DAT OBJ apply
 'to apply for sth. to sb.'
(9) *für das Examen lernen/auf das Examen lernen*
 PREP OBJ (für) the exams work/PREP OBJ (auf) the exams work
 'to study for the exams'
(10) *das Wetter ändert/das Wetter ändert sich*
 the weather changes/the weather changes REFL PRON
 'the weather changes'
(11) *das E-Mail/die E-Mail*
 the-NEUTR e-mail/the-FEM e-mail
 'the e-mail'
(12) *der Entscheid/die Entscheidung*
 the-MASK decide-ROOT/the-FEM decide-ROOT + DER-SUFF -ung
 'the decision'
(13) *ich bin gesessen/ich habe gesessen*
 I sein-FIN sit-PAST PART/I have-FIN sit-PAST PART
 'I have sat'

A narrower view of standard language would only consider the language use in non-regional newspapers (Eisenberg 2007: 217). This view is not adopted here, as there are no clear criteria to establish whether a given newspaper can be regarded as regional or not, and as it is not clear whether the local news section of a given newspaper would then have to be rated 'non-standard' in contrast to the money section or the national sports section of the same newspaper. A wider notion of standard language includes other printed or online texts, or even spoken language. If we embraced this notion, it would extend our list considerably, e.g. to phenomena like the *tun*-construction (*ich tu ... sammeln* 'I will collect/will be collecting/am collecting ...'), which can be heard in all regions, or e.g. the use of the auxiliary verb with analytical forms of the verb *anfangen* '(to) begin, start'. (The use of *sein* '(to) be' with *anfangen*, e.g. *ich bin angefangen zu...* 'I have started to ...' is typical of spoken German in the north-west of Germany.)

4. Case Studies

In the following sections, I will concentrate on two syntactic phenomena, the *am*-progressive and discontinuous constructions of pronominal adverbs in German. I will not strive at a detailed grammatical analysis of these two phenomena. Although both have come into grammarians' focus only quite recently, a range of studies has been published since (particularly on the *am*-progressive). The aim of the following two case studies is rather to look at the way in which grammars and linguistic studies deal with the two constructions with respect to their normative status and the depiction of their areal distribution.

4.1 The *am*-progressive

From a typological point of view, German usually counts as a language without grammatical means to express aspect. This notion changed when grammarians discovered the *am*-construction and its spreading in contemporary German. Thus, in his 1991 article on grammaticalization phenomena in contemporary German, Lehmann noted that "in a couple of West German dialects [...], a progressive aspect has come into use" (Lehmann 1991: 513). The *am*-construction consists of a merged form of the preposition *an* 'at' and the definite article (*am*), a nominalized infinitive form of mostly durative verbs (e.g. *schlafen* 'to sleep') and a finite form of *sein* 'to be'. It is frequently used to express the progress of an action (e.g. *Sie ist am Schlafen.* 'She is sleeping.'), but can also convey a habitual meaning (e.g. *Sie ist in dieser Fabrik am Arbeiten.* 'She works in this factory.', cf. Reimann 1999: 97, Elspaß 2005a: 271–273).

Only few grammars ignore the *am*-progressive altogether (Engel 1996, Wahrig 2002, Weinrich 2003). Most grammars acknowledge its existence and, like Lehmann, some recognize that it provides a means to express progressive aspect (e.g. Zifonun et al. 1997: 1878, Hentschel & Weydt 2003: 44, Wellmann 2008: 245). What the grammars disagree about is whether it is Standard German or not. Zifonun et al. (1997: 1880), Duden (2001: 63), Helbig & Buscha (2001: 80), Hentschel & Weydt (2003: 44) and Eisenberg (2004, vol. I: 200) attribute it to spoken language and/or colloquial use. Duden (1998: 91) and Duden (2005: 434; 2009: 427) declare it fit for use in Standard German, whereas Duden (2007: 62) is not sure. Several studies have been published in the last ten years which present copious examples from newspapers as well as fictional texts, of the *am*-construction used as a progressive form (Reimann 1999, Krause 2002, Van Pottelberge 2004), thus leaving no doubt that the *am*-progressive actually has achieved the status of 'norm of use' ("Gebrauchsnorm", cf. Eisenberg 2007) in Standard (Written) German. As for its regional distribution and its varietal status, the three studies agree that the *am*-progressive is certainly not restricted to substandard varieties in the west of Germany, as Lehmann stated and as Duden (2001: 63, "landschaftliche Umgangssprache (vor allem im Rheinland und Westfalen)" 'regional colloquial language/regiolect, particularly in the Rhineland and in Westphalia') and Eisenberg (2004, vol. I: 200, "bestimmte Varietäten des Gesprochenen (‚Ruhrgebietsdeutsch')" 'certain spoken varieties ("Ruhr area German")') have it. Helbig & Buscha (2001: 80), Duden (1998: 91) and Duden (2005: 434; 2009: 427) are right in declaring that the *am*-progressive has become a widespread grammatical form in spoken German, but it may be too generalized to state that the *am*-progressive is accepted as a standard form in *all* German-speaking regions. To shed more light on this aspect, both a look at the history of this construction and the present-day regional distribution of different forms of the *am*-progressive can be helpful. As for its historical development, the *am*-construction in fact spread out from (North) Western parts of Germany (Elspaß 2005a: 269–270), where it can certainly be considered a contact phenomenon (cf. Dutch *aan't* + INF + *zijn*, Low German *an't* + INF + *sien/wesen*), and from German in Switzerland (Van Pottelberge 2004: 220–221). It can be argued that its rise is connected to the fall of the *tun*('to do')-construction, which over centuries was used to convey aspectual meaning in German (Elspaß 2005a: 273–275). With respect to its present-day distribution, different forms of the *am*-progressive have to be taken into account. Due to a lack of a corpus or a survey on standard grammatical variation in German (cf. Dürscheid, Elspaß & Ziegler in print), I will present two maps from the *Atlas zur deutschen Alltagssprache* (AdA 2003ff.) 'Atlas of colloquial everyday language' (cf. Elspaß 2007), which is the most up-to-date atlas on non-dialectal language variation in the German-speaking countries and regions. Colloquial everyday language is, of course, not the same as Standard German. The maps can nevertheless give an accurate picture of the areal distribution of certain variants. For the purpose of this paper, it suffices to show the different grades of acceptance of two forms of the *am*-progressive which differ in complexity.

Map 1 shows the overall distribution of the 'simple' *am*-progressive (*am* + INF + *sein*: *Sie ist am Schlafen.* 'She is sleeping.'), map 2 the distribution of a more complex "transitive" form (*am* + DIR OBJ to INF + INF + *sein*: *Ich bin die Uhr am Reparieren.* 'I am repairing the watch.', cf. Ebert 1996: 49–50).

Whereas map 1 displays a widespread use of the simple form in Germany, East Belgium and Switzerland (but not in Austria, South Tyrolia, and a hesitant acceptance in eastern parts of Germany), the more complex transitive form in map 2 is clearly restricted to the regions in which the *am*-construction originated. The results of this small investigation on the actual use of the *am*-construction combined with the evidence from the studies mentioned above can be summed up as follows:

1. The *am*-progressive in its simple form is a variant of Standard German.
2. The result of the comparison between the distribution of the simple and the more complex transitive form indicates an ongoing standardization process. (Whether these can be seen as different stages of a grammaticalization process, is a disputed matter, cf. Lehmann 1991 and Van Pottelberge 2005.)
3. German has a grammatical form 'aspect' (cf. Glück 2001: 13).

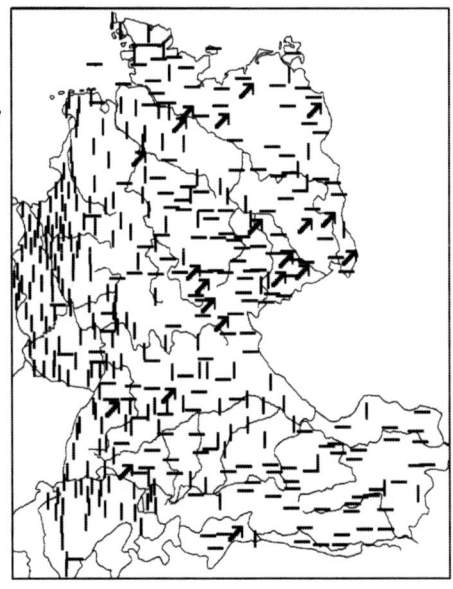

Map 1: Progressive construction with *am* + verbal noun + *sein* in colloquial German: *sie ist schon am Schlafen* 'she is already sleeping' (source: AdA 2003ff.)

die Uhr am reparieren

| has always been customary
↗ has become customary recently
— not customary

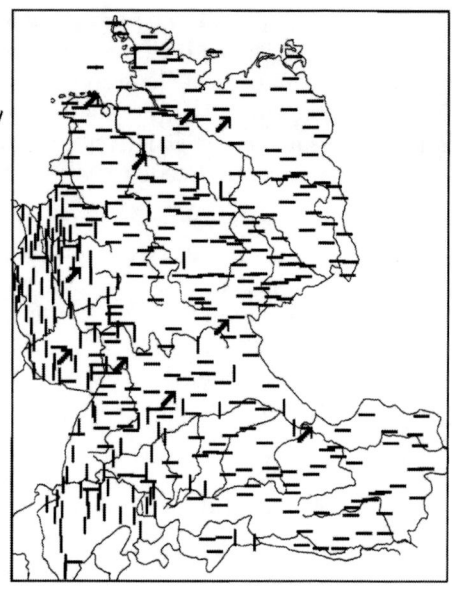

Map 2: Progressive construction with direct object + *am* + verbal noun + *sein* in colloquial German: *ich bin die Uhr am Reparieren* 'I am repairing the watch' (source: AdA 2003ff.)

4.2 Discontinuous Pronominal Adverbs

Pronominal adverbs (PAs), also called 'prepositional adverbs' in grammars and the research literature, consist of a PRO-adverb (*da-* 'there' *wo-* 'where' and, rarely, *hier-* 'here') and a preposition. If the preposition begins with a consonant, PAs with *da-* and *wo-* drop historic *-r* (OHG/MHG *dar*, *war*), thus *davon* 'thereof', *damit* 'therewith', *wofür* 'wherefore' etc. PAs containing a preposition beginning with a vowel have retained *-r* as a linking element, e.g. *darauf* 'thereupon'. Most grammarians consider such univerbal PAs as the only standard forms of PAs in German. Historically, it is uncertain whether they derived from discontinuous forms such as *dar ... von*. At any rate, discontinuous forms are well documented in earlier periods of High and Low German (Fleischer 2008, Negele 2010a: 123–144). German dialects in the north(west) and central western areas have preserved the discontinuous forms, mostly in the form *da/wo/hier ...* PREP; they are usually called 'split PAs' (cf. Fleischer 2002a: 137–211 for details). This variant has attracted considerable attention from syntacticians, who considered it a form of preposition stranding in German. Whether split PAs in German and similar constructions in Dutch (Haeseryn 1989) are structurally similar to preposition stranding in English, is rather disputed (cf. Fleischer 2002b: 117–120, Negele 2010a: 158–163) and, in any case, not relevant in the context of this paper. More recent structural variants in German dialects include 'doubling constructions' with *da-*, which take a 'long' form (e.g. *da ... davon, da ... daran*) and a 'short' form (e.g. *da davon/dadavon, da daran/dadaran*; cf. Fleischer 2002a: 212–329, 2002b: 125–127). Doubling constructions containing *-r-* can be shortened (e.g. *da ... dran, da dran/dadran*).

With the decline of the dialects, however, such alleged 'non-standard' forms, i.e. split PAs and doubling constructions, have emerged in standard contexts. Again, standard grammars either totally ignore these variants (e.g. Engel 1996; Duden 1998; Helbig & Buscha 2001; Hentschel & Weydt 2003; Wellmann 2008), or they mark them as colloquial (Duden 2005: 587; Duden 2009: 581) or right away as non-standard (Zifonun et al. 1997: 2085; Duden 2001: 695; Wahrig 2002: 301; Duden 2005: 886, 897; Duden 2007: 739; Duden 2009: 872, 883).

But are they really *non*-standard (cf. Negele 2010b)? In general, if several grammars bother to mention such variants, this may be a good indicator that the standard question has not yet come to a final conclusion and that it is worth investigating the status of the variants in question. Unlike the *am*-construction, the research literature is not full of examples from printed texts of the mass media. But as (14) to (18) show, examples can be found, although mostly in reported speech.

(14) Sechzig Jahre. **Da** kann der Schröder sich eine Scheibe **von** abschneiden.
*... **this** can (the) Schröder himself a slice **from** of-cut*
'Sixty years. Schröder can take a leaf from this book.'
(Kölner Stadt-Anzeiger, 28.06.2002, p. 36, on the diamond wedding anniversary of former chancellor Helmut Schmidt and his wife Loki Schmidt)

(15) **Da** *darf man gar nicht* **drüber** *nachdenken*
this must one not **this-over** about-think
'You don't want to think about it.'
(headline from Osnabrücker Zeitung, 03.06.2003, on the consequences of fowl pest for farmers)

(16) *"Sein Weg" heißt das 176-Seiten-Opus der Stern-Redakteure Rüdiger Barth und Bernd Volland. Ein Porträt, keine Autobiografie: "**Da** bin ich einen Tick zu jung **für**", meint der 29-Jährige.*
*... a portrait, no autobiography: "**this** am I a bit too young **for**"*
'... A portrait, no autobiography: "I am a bit too young for this."'
(Süddeutsche Zeitung, 15./16./17.4.2006, p. 56, on a book presentation by soccer star Michael Ballack)

(17) *Die Firma produziert regelmäßig bis zur Ärgerlichkeit platte Unterhaltungsfilme für die ältere Zielgruppe. Keiner der Anwesenden in dieser Runde kann **da** was **dafür**. Aber den Kopf hinhalten müssen jetzt alle. Am meisten natürlich Gudrun Landgrebe.*
... nobody of those present in this group can **this** anything **this-for** ...
'... Nobody of those present here can be blamed for this. ...'
(Süddeutsche Zeitung, 17.06.2005, p. 17, interview by Eva Marz with actress Gudrun Landgrebe about her new film)

(18) *Ein Wahlrecht mit 16? **Da** halte ich nichts **davon**!*
this think I nothing **this-of**
'A right to vote at the age of 16? I don't think much of this!'
(Internet edition of Die Oberpfalz, March 2008, transcript of interviews in an opinion poll, http://www.dieoberpfalz.de/schwandorf/wahlumfrage-2008-kk.html [24 April 2010])

It appears that these PA variants are becoming 'norms of use' in standard contexts via written representations of reported speech, and via phrases containing these forms, in particular. This would by no means be a premature assumption. Language change via reported speech and other forms of orality in newspaper texts, i.e. standard in the narrowest sense (see section 3.1 above), is not unusual (cf. Schwitalla 2008). In a comparative study of newspaper language from 1965, 1982 and 2001/02, Betz (2006) found that various syntactic phenomena which are considered 'typical' of spoken German, such as V2 subordinate clauses with *weil* ('because'), aposiopesis, left and right dislocation etc., appear only or significantly more often in the most recent text group (2001/02). Standard language texts in the new media are even more open to variation. A simple search via one of the internet search engines renders 11,500 hits for *da halte ich nichts davon* (doubling construction) and even 254,000 hits for *da halte ich nichts von* (split construction) alone, all of which seem to have been written by competent speaker-writers in Standard German contexts (24 April 2010).

Why do linguistic forms such as the split PA, which have been stigmatized for at least 250 years (cf. Elspaß 2005b: 39–40), gradually re-emerge in standard contexts? Or why have substandard varieties been so reluctant to adopt the standard form? As with many other substandard variants (e.g. *wie* 'than' after comparative, cf. Elspaß 2005b: 35–36), a functional explanation is plausible. From a processual point of view, splitting and the 'long' doubling constructions have a clear advantage in that the anaphoric and topical PRO element usually occurs at the beginning of an utterance (and *wo-* has to be in the initial position), thus adjacent to the point of reference, whereas the preposition or the 'doubled' constituent containing the preposition tends to appear close to the content word to which the PA is a complement; this is particularly noticeable in examples (14) to (16). Thus, to use splitting or 'long' doubling constructions makes it easier to plan and process a sentence, and an optimal balance between its two functions and syntactic requirements is achieved (cf. Ronneberger-Sibold 1993: 216–218).

One aspect remains to be addressed in the context of this paper: What do grammarians tell us about the regional distribution of the PA variants, and how do they know about it? Grammars which mention the construction variants of the PA in German concentrate on the split form and the 'long' doubling construction with a dropped *a* (*da* ... *drin*). As for the regional distribution of the split form alone, we find in grammars as well as in the research literature "strikingly different statements on its occurrence" (Fleischer 2002b: 121). The grammars either contain no information about its distribution (e.g. Wahrig 2002: 301; Eisenberg 2004, vol. II: 198) or rather vague information: the split construction is supposed to be "regional verbreitet, besonders im Nordwesten" 'regionally distributed, particularly in the northwest' (Eroms 2000:136), "umgangssprachlich, besonders norddeutsch" 'colloquial, particularly northern German' (Duden 2001: 695; Duden 2007: 739), or "regionalsprachlich im Norden" 'regiolectal in the north' (Zifonun et al. 1997: 2085).

Again, as we do not have regionally balanced corpora of Standard German (yet), we have to rely on data from colloquial German. Two maps from the *Atlas zur deutschen Alltagssprache* (AdA 2003ff.) can provisionally cast some light on the actual regional distribution of discontinuous pronominal adverb constructions in Standard German. Map 3 shows the distribution of the variants for *davon/....* (*Davon halte ich nichts.* 'I don't think much of this.'), map 4 the distribution of the variants for *daran/...* (*Daran habe ich nicht gedacht.* 'I haven't thought of that.')

Map 3 and map 4 display a clear pattern, which resembles the equivalent dialect maps, but differs in one significant respect: Map 3 and the dialect maps (cf. Fleischer 2002a: Appendix, maps 1 and 4) show a preference for the split construction in the north and for the doubling constructions in the centre and in the south, but the split construction has gained ground. In present-day colloquial 'everyday' language, split PAs cover the entire northern part of Germany north of the Main river. On the other hand, map 4 shows that doubling constructions have moved further to the north, they virtually cover the entire German-speaking countries (cf. Fleischer 2002a: Appendix, maps 4 and 7).

138   Stephan Elspaß

davon (halte ich nichts)

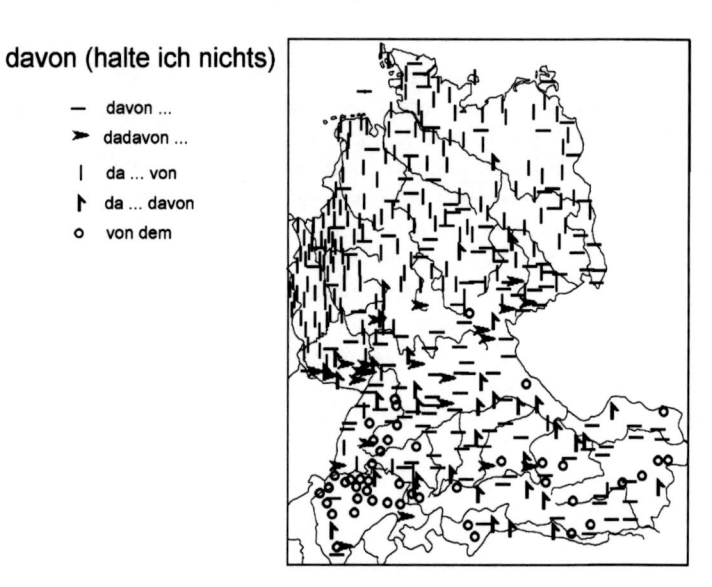

— davon ...
➤ dadavon ...
| da ... von
▶ da ... davon
o von dem

Map 3: Variants of the pronominal adverb *davon* in colloquial German:
davon halte ich nichts 'I don't think much of this' (source: AdA 2003ff.)

daran (habe ich nicht gedacht)

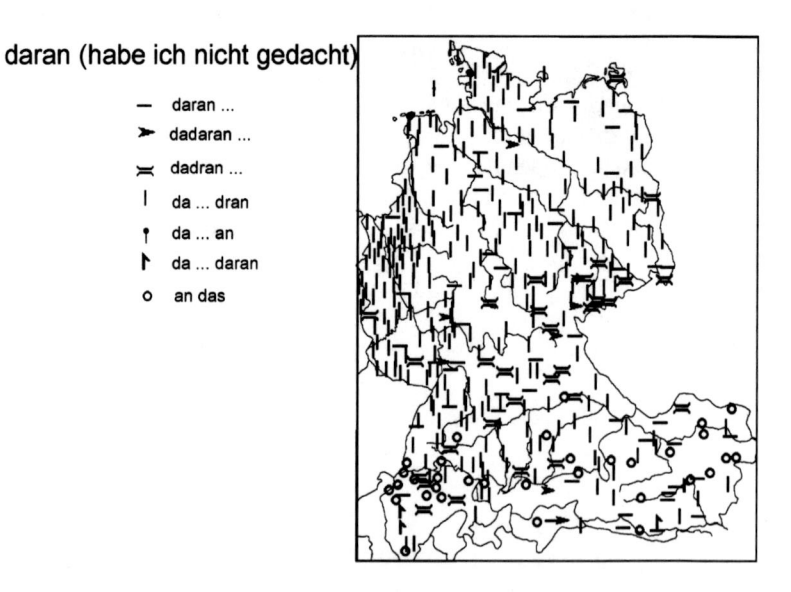

— daran ...
➤ dadaran ...
⇒ dadran ...
| da ... dran
↑ da ... an
▶ da ... daran
o an das

Map 4: Variants of the pronominal adverb *daran* in colloquial German: *daran habe ich nicht gedacht* 'I haven't thought of that' (source: AdA 2003ff.)

Together with Fleischer's findings (cf. Fleischer 2002b: 132), these results render strong empirical evidence against Eisenberg's (2004, vol. II: 198) assumption of a complementary distribution. (Interestingly, Eisenberg talks about 'dialects', but gives examples in Standard German in a Standard German grammar.) He supposes that PAs are split when the preposition begins with a consonant (*da ... von*), whereas prepositions with initial vowel lead to the long doubling construction with dropped *a* (*da ... dran*). At first glance, map 4 may support Eisenberg's assumption for prepositions with initial vowel, as the doubling construction occurs in all German-speaking countries and regions. For central and southern German regions, however, the use of the 'short' doubling construction (*dadran ...*) is also reported, and speakers in Switzerland, Austria and South Tyrolia apparently prefer a totally different construction with a preposition and a following demonstrative pronoun (*an das*). As for prepositions with initial consonant, map 3 clearly shows that Eisenberg's assumption cannot be confirmed. In Saxony and south of the river Main line, the split construction is only rarely used. Speakers clearly seem to prefer the univerbal PA, doubling constructions or (again in Switzerland, Austria and South Tyrolia) the construction with a preposition and a following demonstrative pronoun (*dem*).

Considering the little attention these constructions have drawn in grammars, a particular entry in the Wahrig grammar (2002: 301) is noteworthy. The author mentions two 'incorrect' PA variants, the split construction (*da ... für*) and the 'short' doubling construction (*da dafür ...*). As maps 3 and 4 show, the latter variant is indeed a rare one with a rather small regional distribution. Why did the author select this one and why did he not mention the more frequent 'long' doubling construction (*da ... dafür*)? Possibly this is simply due to biographic reasons. The author has, as his CV discloses, actually lived and worked for most of his life in central German regions where he probably has come across the two variants which he mentions, but probably not with the 'long' doubling construction.

5. Conclusion

The decline of regional varieties such as dialects and regiolects in the German-speaking countries (except Switzerland and Liechtenstein) has consequently led to more 'standard variation' and has virtually washed up grammatical forms into standard language use in German, which previously – sometimes merely a few decades ago – were considered non-standard. Grammarians and corpus linguists, however, do not yet seem to have responded adequately to these far-reaching developments. To date, neither a reference work nor even a corpus of regional German grammar exists, and there is still a lack of broad empirical studies on regional variation of Standard German. The lack of empirically based data is particularly noticeable in grammars of Standard German. Grammar book writers often ignore regional variation in grammar altogether. When regional variants are actually featured in grammar books, their selection seems to be based on a) the adoption of entries from other (or just earlier editions of the same) grammar books or b) the more or less haphazard acquaintance of the grammar book writers with certain variants that happened to be in their linguistic focus at some stage(s) in their lives. It appears that a lot of entry notes on variants' regional distribution are similarly insufficient. Due to a lack of adequate corpora or surveys, such notes are usually not based on empirical, but on rather anecdotal evidence. Finally and more importantly, I would argue that most grammarians have not resolved the standard question in their treatment of regional variants. Grammarians' judgements on the 'standardness' of a given variant often appear to be established on subjective and/or stylistic grounds. The result of such practices is a sometimes confusing array of statements on the normative and stylistic status as well as the distribution of regional variants, as I tried to demonstrate in the two case studies.

The aim of this paper was to address some key grammaticographical problems with regard to regional variation. In conclusion, it is necessary to bring regional standard variation more into grammarians' focus. From a practical point of view, it appears inevitable that a whole new – nationally and regionally balanced – corpus of Standard German will have to be constructed, which can serve as a basis for studies on the grammatical variation in German as well as a variational reference grammar of Standard German (cf. Dürscheid, Elspaß & Ziegler in print [2010]).

6. References

AdA (2003ff.). *Atlas zur deutschen Alltagssprache* ed. S. Elspaß & R. Möller. <http://www.uni-augsburg.de/alltagssprache> (24 April 2010).

Ammon, Ulrich, Hans Bickel, Jakob Ebner, Ruth Esterhammer, Markus Gasser, Lorenz Hofer, Birte Kellermeier-Rehbein, Heinrich Löffler, Doris Mangott, Hans Moser, Robert Schläpfer, Michael Schloßmacher, Regula Schmidlin & Günter Vallaster. 2004. *Variantenwörterbuch des Deutschen. Die Standardsprache in Österreich, der Schweiz und Deutschland sowie Liechtenstein, Luxemburg, Ostbelgien und Südtirol.* Berlin & New York: de Gruyter.

Betz, Ruth. 2006. Gesprochensprachliche Elemente in deutschsprachigen Zeitungen. Radolfzell am Bodensee: Verlag für Gesprächsforschung. <http://www.verlag-gespraechsforschung.de/2006/betz.htm> (24 April 2010).

Duden 1984/1998/2005/2009. *Duden 4. Grammatik der deutschen Gegenwartssprache.* Mannheim: Dudenverlag.

Duden. 2001/2007. *Duden. Richtiges und gutes Deutsch. Wörterbuch der sprachlichen Zweifelsfälle.* Mannheim, Leipzig, Wien & Zürich: Dudenverlag.

Dürscheid, Christa & Inga Hefti. 2006. "Syntaktische Merkmale des Schweizer Standarddeutsch. Theoretische und empirische Aspekte". *Schweizer Standarddeutsch. Beiträge zur Varietätenlinguistik* ed. C. Dürscheid & M. Businger, 131-161. Tübingen: Narr.

Dürscheid, Christa, Stephan Elspaß & Arne Ziegler. In print [2010]. "Grammatische Variabilität im Gebrauchsstandard: das Projekt 'Variantengrammatik des Standarddeutschen'". *Grammar & Corpora/Grammatik und Korpora 2009. Third International Conference/Dritte Internationale Konferenz, Mannheim, 22.-24.9.2009* ed. M. Konopka, F. Štícha, J. Kubczak, C. Mair & U. H. Waßner: Tübingen: Narr.

Ebert, Karin H. 1996. "Progressive Aspect in German and Dutch". *Interdisciplinary Journal for Germanic Linguistics and Semiotic Analysis* 1. 41-62.

Eichhoff, Jürgen. 1977-2000. *Wortatlas der deutschen Umgangssprachen.* Bern: Francke/München: Saur.

Eisenberg, Peter. 2004. *Grundriß der deutschen Grammatik.* Vol. 1: *Das Wort.* Vol. 2: *Der Satz.* Stuttgart: Metzler.

Eisenberg, Peter. 2007. "Sprachliches Wissen im *Wörterbuch der Zweifelsfälle.* Über die Rekonstruktion einer Gebrauchsnorm". *Aptum. Zeitschrift für Sprachkritik und Sprachkultur* 3/07. 209-228.

Elspaß, Stephan. 2005a. *Sprachgeschichte von unten. Untersuchungen zum geschriebenen Alltagsdeutsch im 19. Jahrhundert* (Reihe Germanistische Linguistik 263). Tübingen: Niemeyer.

Elspaß, Stephan. 2005b. "Language norm and language reality. Effectiveness and limits of prescriptivism in New High German". *Linguistic Purism in the Germanic Languages* (Studia Linguistica Germanica 75) ed. N. Langer & W. V. Davies, 20-45. Berlin & New York: de Gruyter.

Elspaß, Stephan. 2007. "Variation and Change in Colloquial (Standard) German – The *Atlas zur deutschen Alltagssprache (AdA)* Project". *Standard, Variation und Sprachwandel in germanischen Sprachen/Standard, Variation and Language Change in Germanic Languages* (Studien zur deutschen Sprache 41) ed. C. Fandrych & R. Salverda, 201-216. Tübingen: Narr.

Engel, Ulrich. 1996. *Deutsche Grammatik.* Heidelberg: Groos.

Eroms, Hans-Werner. 2000. *Syntax der deutschen Sprache.* Berlin & New York: de Gruyter.

Fleischer, Jürg. 2002a. *Die Syntax von Pronominaladverbien in den Dialekten des Deutschen. Eine Untersuchung zu Preposition Stranding und verwandten Phänomenen.* Stuttgart: Steiner.

Fleischer, Jürg. 2002b. "Preposition Stranding in German Dialects". *Syntactic Microvariation* (Meertens Institute Electronic Publications in Linguistics 2) ed. S. Barbiers, L. Cornips & S. van der Kleij, 116-151. Amsterdam:

Meertens Institute. <www.meertens.knaw.nl/books/synmic/pdf/fleischer.pdf> (24 April 2010).

Fleischer, Jürg. 2008. "Die Syntax von Pronominaladverbien in der Sprachgeschichte des Deutschen: eine vorläufige Bestandsaufnahme". *Die Formen der Wiederaufnahme im älteren Deutsch: Akten zum Internationalen Kongress an der Université Paris Sorbonne (Paris IV), 8. bis 10. Juni 2006* (Berliner Sprachwissenschaftliche Studien 10) ed. Y. Desportes, F. Simmler & C. Wich-Reif, 199-235. Berlin: Weidler.

Glück, Helmut. 2001. "Die Verlaufsform in den germanischen Sprachen, besonders im Deutschen". *Valenztheorie. Einsichten und Ausblicke* ed. W. Thielemann, 81-96. Münster: Nodus.

Götz, Ursula. 1995. "Regionale grammatische Varianten des Standarddeutschen". *Sprachwissenschaft* 20. 222-238.

Helbig, Gerhard & Joachim Buscha. 2001. *Deutsche Grammatik. Ein Handbuch für den Ausländerunterricht*. München: Langenscheidt.

Haeseryn, Walter. 1989. "Gesplitste en ongesplitste voornaamwoordelijke bijwoorden". *Neerlandica Extra Muros* 52. 12-18.

Hentschel, Elke & Harald Weydt. 2003. *Handbuch der deutschen Grammatik*. Berlin & New York: de Gruyter.

Kappel, Péter. 2007. "Überlegungen zur diatopischen Variation in der gesprochenen Sprache". *Zugänge zur Grammatik der gesprochenen Sprache* (Reihe Germanistische Linguistik 269) ed. V. Ágel & M. Hennig, 215-244.. Tübingen: Niemeyer.

König, Werner. 1989. *Atlas zur Aussprache des Schriftdeutschen in der Bundesrepublik Deutschland*. Vol. 1: *Text*. Vol. 2: *Tabellen und Karten*. Ismaning: Hueber.

Koller, Werner. 1999. "Nationale Sprach(en)kultur der Schweiz und die Frage der 'nationalen Varietäten des Deutschen'". *Sprachgeschichte als Kulturgeschichte* (Studia Linguistica Germanica 54) ed. A. Gardt, U. Haß-Zumkehr & T. Roelcke, 133-170. Berlin & New York: de Gruyter.

Krause, Olaf. 2002. *Progressiv im Deutschen. Eine empirische Untersuchung im Kontrast mit Niederländisch und Englisch* (Linguistische Arbeiten 462). Tübingen: Niemeyer.

Lehmann, Christian. 1991. "Grammaticalization and related changes in contemporay German". *Approaches to Grammaticalization. Vol. II: Focus on types of grammatical markers* ed. E. Traugott & B. Heine, 493-535. Amsterdam & Philadelphia: John Benjamins.

Milroy, James & Lesley Milroy. 1985. *Authority in Language. Investigating Language Prescription and Standardisation*. London & New York: Routledge & Kegan Paul.

Negele, Michaela. 2010a. *Varianten der Pronominaladverbien im Neuhochdeutschen – Grammatische und soziolinguistische Untersuchungen*. Ph.D. Augsburg.
Negele, Michaela. 2010b. "Diskontinuierliche Pronominaladverbien in der Alltagssprache des jüngeren Neuhochdeutschen – Standard oder Substandard?". *Historische Textgrammatik und Historische Syntax des Deutschen. Traditionen, Innovationen, Perspektiven* ed. A. Ziegler & C. Braun, 1063-1081. Berlin & New York: de Gruyter.
Polenz, Peter von. 1999. *Deutsche Sprachgeschichte vom Spätmittelalter bis zur Gegenwart. Band III: 19. und 20. Jahrhundert*. Berlin & New York: de Gruyter.
Reiffenstein, Ingo. 2001. "Das Problem der nationalen Varietäten. Rezensionsaufsatz zu Ulrich Ammon: Die deutsche Sprache in Deutschland, Österreich und der Schweiz. Das Problem der nationalen Varietäten, Berlin/ New York 1995". *Zeitschrift für deutsche Philologie* 120. 78-89.
Reimann, Ariane. 1999. *Die Verlaufsform im Deutschen. Entwickelt das Deutsche eine Aspektkorrelation?* Ph. D. Bamberg [Mikrofiche].
Scharloth, Joachim. 2005. "Asymmetrische Plurizentrizität und Sprachbewusstsein. Einstellungen der Deutschschweizer zum Standarddeutschen". *Zeitschrift für Germanistische Linguistik* 33:2. 236-267.
Scheuringer, Hermann. 1997. "Sprachvarietäten in Österreich". *Varietäten des Deutschen* (Jahrbuch des Instituts für Deutsche Sprache 1996) ed. G. Stickel, 332-345. Berlin & New York: de Gruyter.
Schwitalla, Johannes. 2008. "Sprachwandel durch gesprochene Sprache in öffentlichen Texten nach 1945". *Questions on Language Change* ed. M. C. Almeida, B. Sieberg & A. M. Bernardo, 27-48. Lissabon: Colibri.
Sellner, Manfred B. 2006. "'Trotz', 'wegen' und 'während' im Österreichischen Deutsch. Eine Pilotstudie". *Zehn Jahre Forschung zum Österreichischen Deutsch: 1995–2005. Eine Bilanz* ed. R. Muhr & M. Sellner, 49-64. Frankfurt: Lang.
Van Pottelberge, Jeroen. 2004. *Der am-Progressiv. Struktur und parallele Entwicklungen in den kontinentalgermanischen Sprachen* (Tübinger Beiträge zur Linguistik 478). Tübingen: Narr.
Van Pottelberge, Jeroen. 2005. "Ist jedes grammatische Verfahren Ergebnis eines Grammatikalisierungsprozesses? Fragen zur Entwicklung des *am*-Progressivs". *Grammatikalisierung im Deutschen* (Linguistik – Impulse und Tendenzen 9) ed. T. Leuschner, T. Mortelmans & S. de Groodt, 169-191. Berlin & New York: de Gruyter.
Ronneberger-Sibold, Elke. 1993. "Funktionale Betrachtungen zur Diskontinuität und Klammerbildung im Deutschen". *Sprachwandel und seine Prinzipien. Beiträge zum 8. Essener Kolloquium über „Sprachwandel und seine Prinzipien" vom 19.10.-21.10.1990 an der Ruhruniversität Bochum* (Bochum-

Essener Beiträger zur Sprachwandelforschung 14) ed. N. Boretzky & A. Barassek, 206-236.. Bochum: Brockmeyer.

Wahrig. 2002. *Grammatik der deutschen Sprache. Sprachsystem und Sprachgebrauch* by L. Götze & E. W. B. Hess-Lüttich. Gütersloh & München: Wissen Media.

Wolf, Norbert Richard. 1994. "Österreichisches zum österreichischen Deutsch. Aus Anlaß des Erscheinens von Wolfgang Pollack: Was halten die Österreicher von ihrem Deutsch? […]". *Zeitschrift für Dialektologie und Linguistik* 61. 66-76.

Weinrich, Harald. 2003. *Textgrammatik der deutschen Sprache.* Hildesheim, Zürich & New York: Olms.

Wellmann, Hans. 2008. *Deutsche Grammatik. Laut. Wort. Satz. Text.* Heidelberg: Winter.

Zifonun, Gisela, Ludger Hoffmann, Bruno Strecker et al. 1997. *Grammatik der deutschen Sprache* (Schriften des Instituts für deutsche Sprache 7). Berlin: de Gruyter.

Jürg Fleischer (Marburg)

Norm and variation in the relative order of accusative and dative personal pronouns in German
Evidence from corpora (18th-21st century)

1. Introduction

While German word order is generally said to be 'free', according to many reference grammars and individual linguists, the relative order of accusative and dative personal pronouns is fixed. The pronominal cluster usually occurs at the left edge of the so-called *Mittelfeld*, i.e., after the inflected verb in main clauses and after the subordinator or relative pronoun in dependent clauses, respectively; in addition, the pronominal cluster can be placed after a subject positioned in the *Mittelfeld*. Within the pronominal cluster, the order of accusative and dative personal pronouns is said to be rigid: the accusative usually precedes the dative[1] (see, for instance, Lenerz 1977: 68, Grundzüge 1981: 734, Wegener 1985: 252, Grammatik der deutschen Sprache 1997: 1519-1520, Duden Grammatik 2009: 871):

(1) *Anna will ihn*$_{ACC}$ *ihr*$_{DAT}$ *morgen übergeben* (Duden Grammatik 2009: 871)
     'Anna wants to give her it tomorrow'

In contrast to personal pronouns, for full noun phrases the 'unmarked' order is dative before accusative, according to Lenerz (1977). Certainly, inverse order is possible for full noun phrases, but certain conditions (not treated in any detail here) have to be met; for example, depending on, among other criteria, the topicality, definiteness and length of the noun phrases (see Lenerz 1977: 63), or depending on the animacy of the noun phrases or the verbal classes (see Grammatik der deutschen Sprache 1997: 1520-1521), the dative noun phrase can occur after the accusative noun phrase. Thus, while there is some variation with two full noun phrases, no variation seems to exist with two personal pronouns:[2]

---

[1] It should be emphasized that this holds only for personal pronouns, with which this paper is exclusively concerned; demonstrative pronouns, for instance, are usually placed after personal pronouns, regardless of case. In addition, some special regularities seem to hold for the third person reflexive pronoun *sich*, which cannot be treated here (note, however, that reflexive usage of first and second person pronouns is not distinguished from other functions and is thus included here).
[2] If one of the noun phrases is nominal and the other pronominal, the relative order is pronominal before nominal, regardless of case (see, for instance, Lenerz 1977: 68-69, Grammatik der deutschen Sprache 1997: 1518).

(2) a. *Ich habe [dem Kassierer]*$_{DAT}$ *[das Geld]*$_{ACC}$ *gegeben* (Lenerz 1977: 43)
  b. *Ich habe [das Geld]*$_{ACC}$ *[dem Kassierer]*$_{DAT}$ *gegeben* (Lenerz 1977: 43)
  'I have given the money to the cashier'
(3) a. *Ich habe es*$_{ACC}$ *ihm*$_{DAT}$ *gegeben* (Lenerz 1977: 68)
  b. **Ich habe ihm*$_{DAT}$ *es*$_{ACC}$ *gegeben* (Lenerz 1977: 68)
  'I have given it to him'

However, the data situation with respect to the order of accusative and dative personal pronouns has not remained uncontested. Firstly, it is quite often stated that clitic pronominal forms can provide exceptions to the "accusative before dative" rule (see, for instance, Lenerz 1977: 68, Grundzüge 1981: 734, Wegener 1985: 253, Grammatik der deutschen Sprache 1997: 1520):

(4) *Gib mir's* (Lenerz 1977: 68)
  'Give it to me'

Then, Lenerz (1993: 141-142) discusses several counterexamples and states that the "accusative before dative" rule possibly only holds for certain pronouns, probably those of the third person (further counterexamples are also discussed in Grammatik der deutschen Sprache 1997: 1520):

(5) *wenn Paul mir ihn so beschreibt* (Lenerz 1993: 142)
  'if Paul describes him to me that way'

Finally, according to the Duden Grammatik (2009: 871), the dative-before-accusative order occurs in some regional varieties (see section 4).

In the remainder of this paper I examine the relative order of accusative and dative pronouns in Modern German. Based on corpus searches I examine whether there is variation between two word orders and, if so, how that variation can best be described. In section 2, the methodology and the corpora analyzed are discussed. In section 3, I present the findings of different corpora searches and I try to deduce some descriptive generalizations from the distributional patterns found. In section 4, the corpus findings are compared with modern dialect data, where considerable variation can be observed. In section 5, the emergence of the modern norm is discussed. Finally, in section 6, I provide a short outlook with respect to the factors responsible for the word-order patterns.

2. Methodology and corpora

To begin with, it is necessary to briefly consider the number of theoretically possible combinations of accusative and dative personal pronouns. In Table 1, Standard German accusative and dative personal pronoun forms are given. As becomes clear from this table, there is a gender distinction in the third person singular, which is absent in other persons. This leaves us with eight different personal pronouns. However, there are some homonymous forms: the pronoun *sie* stands for the third person feminine singular accusative as well as for the third person plural accusative, and *ihm* stands for the third person singular dative of both the masculine and neuter gender. As for case syncretism, Table 1 shows that the first and second person plural forms are homonymous: *uns* and *euch*, respectively, are accusative as well as dative. In addition, *sie* and *es/(')s* are accusative as well as nominative (the latter case is not included in the table).

Table 1: Standard German accusative and dative personal pronouns

		Accusative	Dative
Singular	1st	*mich*	*mir*
	2nd	*dich*	*dir*
	3rd masc.	*ihn*	*ihm*
	3rd fem.	*sie*	*ihr*
	3rd neut.	*es, (')s*	*ihm*
Plural	1st	*uns*	*uns*
	2nd	*euch*	*euch*
	3rd	*sie*	*ihnen*

In (written) present-day Standard German, variation between different forms can occur at only one place in the paradigm, namely in the third person singular neuter: the phonetically fuller form *es* can be replaced by the clitic form *'s* (usually spelled with an apostrophe). To be sure, many other clitic forms exist in colloquial registers (even in ones close to the standard) and in dialects (see, for instance, Wiese 1996/2000: 248-249, Nübling 1992: 251-300); but *'s* is the only clitic form to find an orthographic expression in written Standard German.

The accusative and dative forms provided in Table 1 can theoretically all be combined with each other in clauses displaying an accusative and dative personal pronoun. This is illustrated in Table 2, where each empty cell represents a possible combination of an accusative and dative personal pronoun.

In sum, there are 64 theoretically possible combinations (true, this figure diminishes somewhat if homonymous forms are counted only once; on the other hand, it could be augmented to 72 by counting *es* and *(')s* separately). Since for each of these combinations two word orders, namely, accusative before dative and dative before accusative, are logically possibly, we are potentially dealing with 128 different possibilities. Some of the theoretically possible combinations seem to be quite unlikely, for instance, combinations of the accusative and dative of the same (and hence coreferential) first or second person pronoun. However, even such unlikely combinations can be shown to exist, as the following example illustrates. It displays the combination of the first person singular accusative and dative in both theoretically possible word orders:

(6) *Früher steckte ich mir immer, bevor ich mit dem Training begann, die Zunge heraus, um mir mich erst einmal ganz nahe zu bringen, bevor ich mich mir wieder entfremden konnte* (Heinrich Böll, *Ansichten eines Clowns*)
'Earlier I stuck my tongue out at myself before I began my training in order to bring me really close to myself for a start before I could alienate me from myself again'

This amazing example shows that it is necessary to check all theoretically possible word orders, including the *a priori* unlikely ones.

Table 2: possible combinations of accusative and dative pronouns

Acc. \ Dat.		Sing. *mir*	Plur. ... *ihnen*
Sing.	*mich*		
	dich		
	ihn		
	sie		
	es, (')s		
Plur.	*uns*		
	euch		
	sie		

In order to contrast the normative rules found in prescriptive grammars of Standard German discussed in section 1 with actual written Standard German language use, I will present findings from corpus searches in different corpora provided by the Institut für Deutsche Sprache in Mannheim.[3] I analyzed corpora representing 20th/21st-century Standard German from Germany (including both the former German Democratic Republic and the Federal Republic of Germany), Austria and Switzerland. Most corpora consist of newspaper texts. In addition, I included one corpus consisting of a selection of prose works by Johann Wolfgang von Goethe (1749-1832), arguably the most important German writer ever. Table 3 provides information about the corpora analysed.

---

[3] All corpora can be accessed via the following homepage: <https://cosmas2.ids-mannheim.de/cosmas2-web>.

Table 3: Corpora analyzed[4]

Short	Corpus name	Genre	Running words	Date
mk	Mannheimer Korpora 1+2	fiction, non-fiction, daily and weekly newspapers	2,530,403	1946–1974
bzk	Bonner Zeitungskorpus	daily newspaper	3,053,390	1949–1974
sgt	St. Galler Tagblatt	daily newspaper	103,448,343	1997–2001
sbn	Salzburger Nachrichten	daily newspaper	112,355,956	1991–2000
goe	Goethes Werke	novel, autobiographical, critical and scientific writing	1,411,645	1772–1842

Example (6) above and all other corpus examples in the remainder of this paper are quotations from the Institut für Deutsche Sprache corpora (unless otherwise indicated). All corpus examples are quoted along with some information appearing in the KWIC view provided in the COSMAS searches.

The 20th/21st-century corpora analyzed are heavily newspaper-biased. Only the Mannheimer Korpora 1 and 2 are to any extent balanced: besides newspaper texts they contain a range of fiction and non-fiction texts. Even here, however, many genres are lacking. All other 20th/21st-century corpora consist solely of newspaper texts (which, it is true, could – and should – be classified in more detail: for example, it is clear that the language of the sports section can differ notably from the language of the business section). In this respect, it must be noted that these corpora are not representative of 'Standard German', but stand to a large extent for Standard German as it can be found in newspapers, mostly from the 1990s.

As already indicated, the 20th/21st-century corpora cover different national varieties: the Bonner Zeitungskorpus was designed to represent the language of two major newspapers, from the Federal Republic of Germany (*Die Welt*) and the German Democratic Republic (*Neues Deutschland*); the Salzburger Nachrichten corpus samples the language of an Austrian newspaper, thus illustrating the Austrian national variety, and the same is true of the St. Galler Tagblatt corpus for the Swiss national variety. As can be seen by comparing the figures in the running words column, the Austrian and Swiss national varieties are considerably overrepresented. This is intentional, because findings from Austrian and

---

[4] The information in Table 3 is drawn from <https://cosmas2.ids-mannheim.de/cosmas2-web/action.openArchive.do?index=0> and the subsequent links as of August 13th, 2008.

Swiss dialects suggest that a word order different from Standard German is widespread at the dialectal level (see section 4).

The data from the different corpora could not be retrieved using the corpora's tagging systems, which proved to be impractical for my purposes: although in the STTS tag set – which is available for some IDS corpora – there is one tag identifying personal pronouns ('PPER'), no information with respect to case is provided. Thus, when searching for combinations of two personal pronouns using twice the tag identifying personal pronouns, most of the hits include one nominative form, which is undesired. For that reason it proved to be easier to search specifically for individual combinations of accusative and dative forms. The data was thus obtained by searching for all possible combinations individually, that is *mich mir* & *mir mich*, *dich mir* & *dir mich* etc., were all searched for separately by using their standard orthographic forms.[5] The results were then checked manually and irrelevant examples had to be sorted out. Since the accusative forms *sie* and *es*/*(')s* are homonymous with nominatives, there was an especially large number of irrelevant examples in combinations with one of these forms. Special care was necessary when dealing with the third person singular neuter accusative form: here the existence of the shortened *(')s* form and its different orthographical representations had to be taken into account by looking at combinations like *es mir* & *mir es*, *'s mir* & *mir's*, *s mir* & *mir s*, *mirs* etc. With *(')s*, unfortunately, it proved to be impossible to systematically find all relevant examples using the search instruments provided by the Institut für Deutsche Sprache corpora.[6]

---

[5] Using the methodology as outlined above is not unproblematic: most importantly, deviant orthographies are not covered. For 20th/21st-century Standard German this seems not to be much of a problem, since standard orthographic norms can be taken for granted in newspapers and other published texts from the second half of the 20th century onwards. However, the further into the past one searches, the more problematic the issue becomes. For Goethe, although there are considerable deviances from present day Standard German orthography in general, I found no evidence that personal pronouns differ from present-day usage with respect to their spelling. Still, the danger of having overlooked some orthographically deviant forms cannot be entirely excluded.

[6] Specifically, it was impossible to retrieve examples displaying clitic *s* attached to the word preceding the dative pronoun, either with or without apostrophe (an example would be *gabs ihm*): it would have been necessary to search for all words ending in *s* which preceded the dative pronominal forms, which would have generated far too many irrelevant hits. Therefore, I can unfortunately not exclude the possibility that some relevant examples have been overlooked. A few relevant examples could be found using another electronic edition of the works of Goethe (see note 10), which, ironically, provides a much less sophisticated search syntax.

3. Results

The results of the 20th/21st-century corpora searches are quite uniform: in each corpus the accusative-before-dative order is found in almost 99 % of the relevant examples. The other order – dative before accusative – is rare: in the Mannheimer Korpus 1 + 2 I found only two examples (as opposed to more than three hundred examples for the reverse order); in the Bonner Zeitungskorpus I found three (as opposed to over a hundred examples for the accusative-before-dative order); the Salzburger Nachrichten corpus contains 16 examples of dative-before-accusative order (here the number of examples for the accusative-before-dative order exceeds 1,600); and in the St. Galler Tagblatt corpus I found 25 examples for dative before accusative[7] (here the accusative-before-dative order is found in more than 1,900 examples). The following examples illustrate the very rare dative-before-accusative order:

(7) *bei der nächsten Übung rollt ein Junge ihr ihn blitzschnell zu* (ND 17.07.1969)
'in the next exercise a boy rolls it towards her lightning fast'

(8) *Wir können uns es aber nicht leisten* (Salzburger Nachrichten, 29.01.1998)
'We cannot afford it, however'

(9) *In Österreich war das Niveau nicht so hoch, wie ich mir es vorgestellt hatte, deshalb wollte ich weg* (St. Galler Tagblatt, 14.10.1997)
'In Austria the standards were not as high as I had expected, that's why I wanted to leave'

In sum, exceptions such as (7)-(9) notwithstanding, the generalization given by prescriptive grammars as quoted in section 1 is borne out quite impressively by the 20th/21st-century corpus findings: in Standard German as represented by the corpora analyzed, there is only marginal variation between the two logically possible word orders. In accordance with prescriptive grammars, the order of dative before accusative is extremely rare.

Quite a different picture emerges from the Goethe corpus: In the prose writings included in the corpus, the order of dative before accusative occurs in 119 examples, which makes up about 30 % of all relevant examples (of which there are somewhat more than 400). The dative-before-accusative order is by no means infrequent (see below for examples). There is thus a remarkable differ-

---

[7] In this figure, the following example is not included: *Ich hoffe, sehr verehrte Herren, ich habe Ihnen uns Frauen etwas näher bringen können.* (St. Galler Tagblatt, 07.11.2000) 'I hope, gentlemen, that I was able to give you an understanding of us women.' Here the accusative pronoun *uns* is an apposition to the full noun phrase *Frauen* and therefore is not counted as a pronominal noun phrase.

ence between the 18th/19th-century language of Goethe's prose writings and the 20th/21st-century Standard German corpora.

In the remainder of this section I will discuss how occurrences of the dative-before-accusative order are best described from a descriptive point of view. Since, in the corpora analyzed, variation between the two word orders is found to a significant extent only in the Goethe corpus, I will restrict my discussion to this data base.

As already indicated in section 1, one factor often said to favor dative-before-accusative order is cliticization, which applies to the third person singular neuter accusative *es* in Standard German, as discussed in section 2 (see, for instance, Lenerz 1977: 68, Grundzüge 1981: 734, Wegener 1985: 253, Grammatik der deutschen Sprache 1997: 1520). At first sight this factor seems to play an important role in the Goethe corpus. Cliticization is reflected orthographically in the third person singular accusative neuter form *(')s*; of the 119 examples for the dative-before-accusative order in the Goethe corpus more than 50 display clitic *(')s*. This is illustrated by the following examples, which also show that the pronoun in question can be spelled with or without an apostrophe:

(10) *ich will dir's nur sagen, ich habe aus der Flasche getrunken* (Goethe, H[amburger] A[Ausgabe, Vol.] 7 (2006): 604)
'I just want to tell you, I drank from the bottle'

(11) *ich habe dirs schon so oft gesagt und geschworen; wir wollen es nicht mehr sagen und schwören, nun soll es werden* (Goethe, HA 6 (2006): 338)
'I have said and sworn it to you so often already; let us not say and swear it any longer, now it must come true'

However, cliticization is not observed in all instances of the dative-before-accusative order; beside clitic *(')s* other accusative forms can also occur after the relevant datives.[8] As a matter of fact, the distribution observed in the Goethe corpus can best be described by referring to the pronouns involved: almost all examples for the dative-before-accusative order include one of the datives *mir*, *dir* or *ihr*. In the Goethe corpus, only one example of this order features another dative pronoun, namely *ihnen*:

(12) *hätte ich jungen Männern zu raten, die sich höherer Staatskunst und also dem diplomatischen Fache widmen, so würde ich ihnen es als Handbuch anrühmen, um sich daraus zu vergegenwärtigen, wie man*

---

[8] One could of course hypothesize that all accusative forms following the datives in (12)-(17) are clitic; however, here the limitations of a written language corpus show up: the orthography provides no unequivocal indication that accusative forms such as *es*, *ihn* or *sie* are clitic, although we cannot exclude it, either (see also Behaghel 1932: 74, who points out that the third person singular masculine form *ihn* is often cliticized in "living pronunciation").

unzählige Fakta sammelt und zuletzt sich selbst eine Überzeugung bildet (Goethe, HA 12 (2006): 339)
'if I had to advise young men who devote themselves to higher statesmanship and thus to diplomacy, I would recommend it to them as a handbook from which to envision how to collect countless facts and eventually construct a conviction of one's own'

The following examples illustrate the dative pronouns *mir*, *dir* and *ihr* in the dative-before-accusative order. Note that for the third person singular accusative neuter pronoun it is not only clitic *(')s*, but also full *es* that can occur after one of the relevant datives, as illustrated by (15) and (16):

(13) *so wollte er doch von mir ein für allemal auch einen Heiland g[e]zeichnet[9] haben, wie ich mir ihn vorstellte* (Goethe, HA 10 (2006): 15)
'he nevertheless wanted to have a Savior painted by me, as I imagined Him to myselfh'

(14) *Sperata ist mein; nur der Tod soll mir sie nehmen* (Goethe, HA 7 (2006): 584)
'Sperata is mine; only death shall take her from me'

(15) *treten Sie mir es ab* (Goethe, HA 7 (2006): 546).
'cede it to me'

(16) *ich vermache dir es zurück, Lotte, und bitte dich, es zu ehren* (Goethe, HA 6 (2006): 122)
'I bequeath it back to you, Lotte, und I beg you to honor it'

(17) *ich hatte den "Wakefield" auf der Zunge, allein ich wagte nicht, ihr ihn anzubieten* (Goethe, HA 10 (2006): 457)
'I had "Wakefield" on the tip of my tongue, but I did not dare to offer it to her'

If we take a closer look at the dative pronouns attested with both word orders, it turns out that for some of them the dative-before-accusative order is more frequent than for others. Table 4 gives the relevant figures for the dative pronouns in the Goethe corpus for which both word orders are attested. As becomes clear from this table, in the Goethe corpus it is only with the forms *mir* and *dir* that the dative-before-accusative order dominates; for *ihr* this order occurs in less than a fifth of all examples, whereas for *ihnen* it is marginal. Thus, for the third person plural and feminine singular the accusative-before-dative order is much more frequent than the reverse order.

---

[9] The Institut für Deutsche Sprache Goethe Korpus provides the form *gzeichnet*, which is a typographic error: a comparison with the quoted print edition shows that *gezeichnet* is correct.

Table 4: Occurrences and frequency of the order of dative pronouns in the Goethe corpus

	ACC > DAT	DAT > ACC	% DAT > ACC
mir	63	98	61 %
dir	6	15	71 %
ihr	31	5	14 %
ihnen	37	1	3 %

As for accusative pronouns, only some of them are attested in the dative-before-accusative order, namely *mich, ihn, sie* and *es/(')s*. The occurrences of these pronouns in the two orders and the frequency of the dative-before-accusative order are illustrated in Table 5.[10]

Table 5: Occurrences and frequency of the order of accusative pronouns in the Goethe corpus

	ACC > DAT	DAT > ACC	% DAT > ACC
mich	41	1	2 %
ihn	7	21	75 %
sie (sg.)	31	17	35 %
sie (pl.)	35	4	10 %
es	159	21	12 %
(')s	?	53	?

As one can see, with a single exception, all of the accusative pronouns attested after a dative pronoun are third person forms. The exception is an example in which the first person singular accusative form *mich* is preceded by the third

---

[10] For *(')s* two serious problems must be discussed. First, it was impossible to automatically retrieve examples displaying clitic *(')s* written together with the preceding word (see note 6); such examples would be relevant here. Then, I encountered the following problem when working with the Goethe corpus as provided by the Institut für Deutsche Sprache: when searching for clitic *(')s* preceding dative pronouns, the search orders *s mir* or *'s mir* etc. led to no hits. For instance, the following example could not be found by searching for *'s ihm* in the Institut für Deutsche Sprache's Goethe corpus, although it is found when searching for *gab's ihm*: *Ich zuckte die Achseln und gab's ihm zu* (Goethe, HA 6 (2006): 46) 'I shrugged my shoulders and admitted it to him'. Because of this problem, I cannot provide the raw figure for the ACC > DAT order for *(')s* (and hence also not the frequency) in Table 5; the respective cells are filled with a question mark. In an electronic CD-ROM edition of Goethe's writings published by the Digitale Bibliothek, which also contains the texts provided in the Institut für Deutsche Sprache Goethe corpus (among others), the search order *s ihm* (but not *'s ihm*) finds the example just quoted; this is why I used this electronic edition to circumvent some problems (see note 12).

person singular feminine dative form *ihr*.[11] Of the third person accusative forms, it is clitic *(')s* for which most examples display the dative-before-accusative order. This is followed by *ihn* with 75 %, while all other accusative forms occur more frequently in the accusative-before-dative order.

To sum up so far, we can state that it seems to be the datives *mir* and *dir*, on the one hand, and the accusatives of the third person, on the other, which are most often found in the dative-before-accusative order. The most typical example of the dative-before-accusative order thus consists of *mir* or *dir* plus an accusative form of the third person.

It is interesting now to look at different combinations of individual forms. Table 6 provides the figures for the two orders and the frequency of dative before accusative in combinations of *mir* and third person accusative pronouns.[12]

Table 6: Occurrences and frequency of the word order with *mir* in the Goethe corpus

	ACC > DAT	DAT > ACC	% DAT > ACC
ihn	1	21	95 %
sie (sg.)	12	15	56 %
sie (pl.)	10	4	29 %
es	34	17	67 %
(')s	–	41	(100 %)

Here, the accusative pronouns *(')s* and *ihn* and are most likely to follow the dative pronoun; compared to these *es* and *sie* occur less often in this order (it remains to be investigated whether the differences between singular and plural *sie* are systematic). As one can see, the relative frequencies of the dative-before-accusative order varies depending on the accusative pronoun. For instance, whi-

---

[11] This example is: *auch Angelika war angekommen; an einer großen gedeckten Tafel hatte man ihr mich rechter Hand gesetzt* (Goethe, HA 11 (2006): 425) 'Angelika had arrived too; at a large set table they had sat me to the right of her'.

[12] Since it was impossible to find examples displaying clitic *(')s* preceding the dative pronouns in the Institut für Deustche Sprache's Goethe corpus (see notes 6 and 10), the relevant data in Tables 6-8 is supplemented by the results of searches in the Digitale Bibliothek text edition. These searches were limited to the texts also available in the Institut für Deutsche Sprache Goethe corpus and to *(')s* in connection with the datives *mir*, *dir* and *ihr;* two examples for the serialization *(')s dir* but no additional examples for the serializations *(')s mir* and *(')s ihr* were found and added to the data base. The figures for the ACC > DAT order for *(')s* in Tables 6-8 were attained in this way. Even based on this supplementary data, however, the possibility that some examples of clitic *s* attached to the preceding word without apostrophe have not been found cannot be excluded; the frequencies for *(')s* in Tables 6-8 are therefore given in brackets.

le there are 21 examples for the order *mir ihn*, which is illustrated by (18), there is only one example for the reverse order *ihn mir*, which is (19):

(18) *er soll mein Gatte werden, was man auch für Pläne macht, mir ihn zu rauben* (Goethe, HA 7 (2006): 535)
'he is supposed to become my husband, no matter what plans are made to rob me of him'

(19) *an einen Ruhepunkt, an einen stillen Ort, wie ich ihn mir nur hätte wünschen können* (Goethe, HA 11 (2006): 15)
'to a place of rest, to a quiet place, as I could only have wished it'

For the second person singular dative form, *dir,* the number of examples attested in the corpus is much smaller. Table 7 presents the figures for the two word orders for *dir* and the third person accusative pronouns as well as the frequency of the dative-before-accusative order.

Although the number of examples is small, the pattern can be seen to correspond to some extent with what we know from the first person: clitic *(')s* is most likely to occur in the dative-before-accusative order, *es* less so (for the other pronouns the number of examples is too small to support generalizations).

Table 7: Occurrences and frequency of the word order with *dir* in the Goethe corpus

	ACC > DAT	DAT > ACC	% DAT > ACC
ihn	1	–	0 %
sie (sg.)	1	1	50 %
sie (pl.)	–	–	–
es	3	4	57 %
(')s	2	10	(83 %)

Finally, the occurrences of *ihr* and the third person accusative pronouns in the two word orders and the frequency of the dative-before-accusative order are given in Table 8. Here again, the absolute number of examples is quite small; still, the fact that clitic *(')s* seems more likely to follow the dative pronoun than the full form *es* does is compatible with the findings from *mir* and *dir.*

Table 8: Occurrences and frequency of the word order with *ihr* in the Goethe corpus[13]

	ACC > DAT	DAT > ACC	% DAT > ACC
ihn	–	1	100 %
sie (sg.)	–	–	–
sie (pl.)	4	–	0 %
es	15	1	6 %
(')s	–	2	(100 %)

To sum up, for the Goethe corpus we can state that it is the datives *mir* and *dir*, followed by *ihr*, which most often precede the accusative pronouns. Among the accusative forms, it is clitic *(')s* which most often occurs after the dative pronoun, followed by *ihn*, *sie* and *es*. These generalizations can be formalized in the following hierarchies: (1.) *mir*, *dir* > *ihr* > other datives and (2.) *(')s* > *ihn* > *sie*, *es* > other accusatives.

It remains to be investigated whether these hierarchies can be confirmed or reformulated in more detail when other data are taken into account.

4. Modern dialectal variation

The results attained so far can be compared with modern German dialect data. Interestingly, patterns quite different to Standard German are attested in some dialects. In many Upper German dialects, among them those spoken in Switzerland and Austria, dative before accusative is the usual order, at least with respect to the frequent clitic forms (see, for instance, Nübling 1992: 275, Werner 1999: 104 on the Alemannic dialects of Switzerland or Pohl 1989: 61 on a Bavarian dialect of Austria; Weiß 2005: 180-181 provides a brief survey of Bavarian dialects spoken in Germany, Austria and Italy). The following examples illustrate the dative-before-accusative word order for Zurich German, an Alemannic dialect spoken in Switzerland, and for Carinthian German, a Bavarian dialect spoken in Austria:

(20) *Ich wär froo, wänn du mer en morn chöntisch ggee* (Werner 1999: 106)
 'I would be glad if you could give it to me tomorrow'
(21) *i gi:b eam's* (Pohl 1989: 61)
 'I give it to him'

In modern Central German dialects, both orders are possible, depending on the combination of pronouns. For an East Hessian dialect spoken in Thuringia,

---

[13] The combination of *ihr* with the first person singular accusative form *mich* is disregarded here; this combination is attested once in dative-before-accusative order (see note 11), whilst the reverse order, *mich ihr*, is attested eleven times.

Weldner (1991: 198-199) states that the dative-before-accusative order occurs with dative pronouns of the first and second person singular in combination with third person accusative pronouns, while other third person accusatives follow the dative pronouns. There seems thus to be a split between the first and second person of the dative, on the one hand, and all other datives, on the other. According to Reis (1894: 503), in the Rhine-Franconian dialect of Mainz we find dative before accusative in *mir es, dir es* and *ihr es*, but accusative before dative in *es ihm, es uns, es euch*. In this dialect we find thus a split between the datives of the first, second and third person feminine singular pronoun on the one hand, and all other dative pronouns on the other. The following examples illustrate this situation:

(22) *er hot mer's gesagt* (Reis 1894: 503)
 'he told me'
(23) *ich hab 's 'em gewwe* (Reis 1894: 503)
 'I gave it to him'

In Low German dialects, finally, the order direct before indirect object[14] seems to be preferred for personal pronouns (at least, this is what can be deduced from Born's [1978: 58] description of a Westphalian dialect). This can be illustrated with the following example:

(24) *Nu häff'k et di säggt* (Born 1978: 58)
 'Now I've told you'

To sum up, for the German dialects we find the following basic distributional pattern: dative before accusative predominates in the south; both word orders occur in the Central German area, displaying a split either between the first and second person singular of the dative as opposed to the other forms or between the first, second and third person feminine singular dative as opposed to the other forms; in the north, accusative before dative predominates. Interestingly, similar differences between Old Saxon and the Old High German dialects can be observed as early as the 8th/9th century (see Fleischer 2005: 32-33).

Comparing the dialectal data just presented to my corpus findings can prove illuminating. As we have seen in section 3, in the modern Standard German corpora there seems to be almost no variation with respect to pronoun order. This also holds for the Austrian and the Swiss corpora although it does not correspond to the patterns found in Swiss and Austrian dialects. It thus seems that the modern Swiss and Austrian standard data are in conflict with that of their dialects.

---

[14] As is well known, most Low German dialects lack an accusative-dative distinction altogether (see Shrier 1965: 431). For this reason, I refer here not to case forms, but to semantic roles.

The picture is different for the 18th/19th-century Goethe data. The distribution observed in the two West Central German dialects discussed above is quite similar to Goethe's usage: as reported in section 3, for Goethe, dative-before-accusative order occurs most often with the first and second person of the dative singular, which matches the indications provided by Weldner (1991). In addition, in the language of Goethe, the third person singular feminine dative form also sometimes occurs in the dative-before-accusative order, albeit only in a minority of examples. This comes quite close to the system of the dialect of Mainz described by Reis (1894); note that Mainz is quite close to Goethe's native Frankfurt.

To conclude, the distribution to be observed in the Goethe corpus seems to be quite close to that reported for around Goethe's dialectal origin. The 20th/21st-century corpora, however, irrespective of their geographical source, all exhibit only the accusative-before-dative order, which corresponds to the northern dialectal pattern.

5. Discussion: emergence of the present-day norm

The accusative-before-dative order is clearly dominant in modern Standard German from the second half of the 20th (and the first years of the 21st) century as – and insofar as – it is represented by the different corpora analyzed. On the other hand, in 18th/19th-century German represented by the language of a selection of Goethe's prose works, about 30% of all examples display the inverse word order. This finding suggests that the distribution observed in 20th-century Standard German is a relatively recent development. This is confirmed by the information given by Behaghel (1932) and Ebert (1999). Behaghel (1932: 73-75), covering the whole historical period of German, provides many (though isolated) examples, which confirm that dative-before-accusative word order used to be widespread in earlier epochs of German in at least some combinations. The same can be deduced from Ebert (1999: 119-120), who covers the period between 1300 and 1750. According to Ebert (1999: 120), the dative-before-accusative order was still frequent in the work of the preclassical and classical period writers Gellert, Lessing and the young Goethe. I conclude therefore that the important period for the emergence of the modern accusative-before-dative norm is the 19th (and possibly the 20th) century.

Interestingly, there are some remarks in prescriptive grammars that pertain to our problem. Johann Christoph Adelung (1732-1806), arguably the most influential 18th-century German grammarian (and the first to have written an Education Ministry-commissioned grammar for use in secondary schools; see Naumann 1986: 98) makes the following statement:

"Sind beyde Casus Pronomina, so wird der Accusativ gemeiniglich dem Dative vorgesetzet: *sage es mir*; *schicke ihn uns*. [...] Indessen ist es oft gleichgültig, welches

Pronomen voran gesetzet wird: [...] *ich will ihn dir*, oder *dir ihn anvertrauen*; *er gab es mir*, oder *er gab mir es, mirs.*" (Adelung 1782, 2: 519; italics mine) 'If both case forms are pronouns, the accusative is usually put before the dative: *sage es mir*; *schicke ihn uns.* [...] However, it is often immaterial which pronoun is put before the other one: [...] *ich will ihn dir*, or *dir ihn anvertrauen*; *er gab es mir*, or *er gab mir es, mirs.*'

Adelung prefers the order of accusative before dative, but also accepts the reverse order. Note that his examples for the dative-before-accusative order all involve the first and second person singular of the dative, the accusative pronouns occurring in this serialization being *ihn, (')s* and *es*. This matches Goethe's usage quite closely (see section 3).

In the 19th century, the picture changes. Two widespread 19th-century prescriptive grammars are less permissive than Adelung (and, unfortunately, also more parsimonious with examples). In the grammars of Johann Christoph August Heyse (first edition 1814) and of Karl Ferdinand Becker (first edition 1837), we read:

"Z.B. Ich habe es ihm gesagt; er gab es mir (nicht: ihm es, mir es) [...]" (Heyse 1849: 515) 'For example, *Ich habe es ihm gesagt*; *er gab es mir* (not: *ihm es, mir es*) [...]'

"Bei den Personalpronomen geht der Sachkasus dem Personenkasus immer voran z.B. *Ich habe Dich ihm empfohlen.*" (Becker 1870: 466) 'With personal pronouns the accusative always precedes the dative, e.g., *Ich habe Dich ihm empfohlen.*'

Both 19th-century prescriptive grammarians demand the serialization that has since become standard, while Adelung, who also prefers it, leaves some room for the reverse order. One might therefore gain the impression that the prescriptive rules found in the grammars by Heyse and Becker have made their way into the present-day Standard German norm.

At this point, the question arises as to whether we have here an example of successful norm imposition by prescriptive grammarians, which has recently been the object of an inspiring study by Davies/Langer (2006). As they emphasize, "[s]cholarly views on the effectiveness of grammarians in the selection and non- or de-selection of linguistic features range from a "yes" via "a little" to "no" [...]" (Davies/Langer 2006: 72). The crucial question is whether the purported imposition of a norm can be successfully demonstrated. Ultimately, the question asked by Takada (1998: 15, 296) has to be answered: Do prescriptive grammar rules parallel actual language usage or do they lag behind them or precede them? Only in the latter case can one speak of a norm imposition proper. To effectively prove such a case, it would be necessary to compare prescriptive statements with contemporaneous usage.

In the case at hand, we have seen that there are prescriptive rules in two 19th-century grammars, whereas a late 18th-century grammar is still somewhat more permissive. However, in contrast to constructions such as periphrastic *tun* or the double negation, against which very strong words were raised in prescriptive grammars (see Langer/Davies 2006: 211-224, 241-260 on these two constructions), one does not get the impression that the grammarians or the public paid much attention to our problem. It is safe to say that no major prescriptive crusades were fought against the dative-before-accusative word order; for prescriptivists the ordering of accusative and dative pronouns was not a major battlefield. For instance, in the (in)famous *Allerhand Sprachdummheiten* (first edition 1891) by Gustav Wustmann (1844-1910), one of the most widespread of the books denouncing language usage breaking prescriptive norms, which was reprinted many times far into the 20th century, this phenomenon is not mentioned. With the exception of the three grammarians' statements quoted above, I have to date found no other prescriptive remarks in 18th and 19th-century grammars. Thus, to put it bluntly, prescriptive grammarians seem to have cared much about the *tun* periphrasis and double negation, but they seem to have cared little about the order of accusative and dative pronouns.

For this reason, I think that the emergence of the present-day norm ought not be attributed solely to prescriptive activities, but needs instead to be seen in another context. From general history we know that the north of the German language area became increasingly important and dominant during the 19th century, especially in its second half. The German north is the area where Low German dialects were originally at home (eventually being replaced by Standard German in a long – and not entirely concluded – process). As we have seen, in Low German, the direct-before-indirect-object order seems to be preferred for personal pronouns. It could thus turn out that the present-day norm has adopted a feature originally characteristic of Low German due to northern dominance in the 19th century. This finding would not be isolated: most importantly, it is well known that present-day norms for the oral realization of Standard German are heavily north-biased, as was already remarked upon by 19th-century observers (see Polenz 1999: 259).

It thus seems that the order of object pronouns confirms the importance of the north in the formation of present-day Standard German. On the other hand, even a figure as important as Goethe, whose works dominated German intellectual life in the 19th century, was unable to impose his usage onto the emerging norm. To some extent this runs counter to an older view (still found in many textbooks on the history of German), which stresses the importance of so-called Weimar classicism (see Elspaß 2005: 4), but it is in line with more recent findings according to which the influence of the Weimar classics on 19th-century Standard German is not as large as was earlier thought (see Ernst 2004: 3087).

6. Outlook: syntactic, semantic or phonological criteria?

In this outlook I briefly discuss factors that could determine the order of accusative and dative personal pronouns in German. As Primus (1998: 422) emphasizes, word order of recipient and patient noun phrases is "a multi-factor phenomenon". In the literature (both on word order in general and on the order of German pronominal objects in particular), it has been proposed that syntactic, semantic and phonological factors may play a role.[15] Some of them are briefly discussed in what follows.

According to a typological study by Primus (1998) two basic hierarchies are responsible for the order of direct and indirect objects, namely, the Thematic Hierarchy and the Case Hierarchy (for both hierarchies only the portion relevant to our phenomenon is reproduced):

Thematic Hierarchy (according to Primus 1998: 432):
Proto-Recipient > Proto-Patient

Case Hierarchy (according to Primus 1998: 436):
accusative argument > dative argument

In Standard German the unmarked word order of full noun phrase objects is determined by the Thematic Hierarchy, whereas for the serialization of pronouns the Case Hierarchy is decisive: "Light pronominal arguments are ordered along the Case Hierarchy [...] to the exclusion of the Thematic Hierarchy [...]" (Primus 1998: 445). For present day Standard German this predicts that accusative pronouns always precede dative pronouns, which corresponds quite well to the results from the 20th/21st-century Standard German corpora presented in section 3. By referring to one of the two hierarchies, the Upper German data can also be easily modeled: here, as with full noun phrases, the Thematic Hierarchy is decisive. Note, however, that this analysis cannot be extended to the language of Goethe and the Central German dialect data, in which a sizeable number of examples display the dative-before-accusative order.

To model the Goethe and the Central German dialect data another semantic hierarchy that suggests itself might be taken into consideration. This is the Animacy or Personal Hierarchy, which is given here in its form as proposed by Siewierska (only the portion relevant for our purposes is reproduced here):

---

[15] In addition, according to e.g. Lenerz (1977), pragmatic factors also play a role with full noun phrases in German (see section 1). As for pronouns, however, I think pragmatic factors are less important; for instance, since personal pronouns are usually used anaphorically, they almost always refer to entities already established in the discourse, which is quite different from full noun phrases.

Personal Hierarchy (according to Siewierska 1988: 30):
1st p. > 2nd p. > 3rd p.

By referring to this hierarchy we can neatly explain the split between the datives of the first and second person of the singular and all other datives if we additionally allow singulars to be ranked as more animate than plurals.

Besides the syntactic rule discussed above, the Standard German pattern is often explained by referring to phonological criteria. According to Wegener (1985: 253-254) and the Grammatik der deutschen Sprache (1997: 1519-1520), the fact that accusative pronouns precede dative pronouns in Standard German is not due to their case, but rather to their phonological form. In this view, the fact that we predominantly find accusative-before-dative ordering in Standard German is just an epiphenomenon of phonological factors. According to the Grammatik der deutschen Sprache (1997: 1519), phonetically weaker, unmarked forms precede phonetically fuller, marked forms. Specifically, the following rules can be stated (see Grammatik der deutschen Sprache 1997: 1519-1520): monosyllabic words precede disyllabic words (thus, the disyllabic dative *ihnen* never occurs before the monosyllabic accusatives); words with final vowels precede words with final consonants (thus, the accusative *sie* precedes the datives, which all have a coda); words with short vowels precede words with long vowels (thus, *mich, dich, es, uns, euch* precede *mir, dir, ihm, ihr, ihnen*). Only clitic *(')s* can follow the dative pronoun, forming one phonological word with it.[16]

According to these rules, combinations containing the accusative *ihn* and one of the datives *mir, dir, ihr* or *ihm* are expected to allow both word orders, since these pronouns all display a long vowel and a coda. As a matter of fact, this can explain why an example such as (7) displays the dative-before-accusative order (see Grammatik der deutschen Sprache 1997: 1520). On the other hand, the phonological criteria can explain only a handful of the instances of dative-before-accusative order encountered in the 20th/21st-century Standard German corpora analyzed: in the Mannheimer Korpora 1+2 and in the St. Galler Tagblatt, not a single example (out of three and 25, respectively) displays one of the datives *mir, dir, ihm* and *ihr* preceding *ihn*; in the Bonner Zeitungskorpus one example (out of three; shown as [7] above) displays such a combination, and in the Salzburger Nachrichten three (out of 16) examples are explicable so. One might expect variation in combinations where both orders are equally good from the point of view of the phonological criteria. However, in the 20th/21st-century corpora, the orderings *mir ihn, dir ihn, ihm ihn* and *ihr ihn* are extremely rare to non-existent, although nothing would speak against them from the point of view of the phonological factors.

---

[16] Note that this is somewhat unexpected since clitic *s* is arguably the "weakest" of all pronominal forms, consisting of only one segment. As a matter of fact, *s* could cliticize to the word preceding the pronominal cluster as easily as to the dative pronoun.

Nor can the phonological factors model the results of the 18th/19th-century Goethe corpus. Again, we would expect, for example, that the serializations *mir ihn* and *ihn mir* would be roughly equally frequent; however, as we have seen in Section 3 *mir ihn* is by far the more frequent (the examples for combinations of *ihn* with *dir*, *ihm* and *ihr* are too few to allow any conclusions to be drawn). On the other hand, *sie* and *es* ought to precede *mir*, *dir*, *ihm* and *ihr* regularly, but this is the case only for *ihm* and not for *mir*, *dir* or *ihr*.

On the other hand, there is one clear result: the clitic *(')s* regularly follows *mir*, *dir* and *ihr*. As for *mir* and *dir*, this could be attributed to the Personal Hierarchy; but if the Personal Hierarchy were the only decisive criterion one would expect the third person singular masculine pronoun *ihm* to occur at least as often in the dative-before-accusative order as the third person singular feminine pronoun *ihr*, which is not the case. However, as can be immediately seen, the three dative pronouns preceding clitic *(')s* regularly share a phonological property: all have the same rhyme and coda, namely /iːr/. It might therefore turn out that this phonological environment is an important favorable factor for cliticization.

To sum up, it seems that phonological as well as syntactic and semantic factors play a role in the ordering of personal pronoun objects in German: an interplay between these factors, rather than any single one of them, seems to determine the word order. Most importantly, the differences between 18th/19th-century German represented by the Goethe corpus findings and 20th/21st-century Standard German represented by the other corpora, and differences between the dialects could all be modelled as a re-ranking of the different criteria (which can, of course, be formulated as OT constraints). To assess the relative importance of the different factors in different varieties, however, more and more decisive data is needed. It seems quiet certain, that in addition to the phonological, syntactic and semantic criteria discussed in the literature so far, the Personal Hierarchy must be considered. Given that this hierarchy is known to determine the serialization of German full noun phrases (see, e.g., Grammatik der deutschen Sprache 1997: 1514) and given that it is well-established from many cross-linguistic studies (although its importance for the serialization of recipient and patient is controversial; see Primus 1998: 458-460), this does not come as a surprise.

7. References

7.1 Electronic text edition

Goethe, Johann Wolfgang von. 2006. *Leben und Werk.* Sonderband Digitale Bibliothek. Berlin: Directmedia [CD-ROM].

7.2 Secondary sources

Adelung, Johann Christoph. 1782. *Umständliches Lehrgebäude der Deutschen Sprache, zur Erläuterung der Deutschen Sprachlehre für Schulen. Zweyter Band.* Leipzig: Breitkopf. [reprint Hildesheim & New York 1971: Olms.]

Becker, Karl Ferdinand. 1870. *Ausführliche deutsche Grammatik als Kommentar der Schulgrammatik. Zweiter Band.* Prag: Tempsky. [reprint: Hildesheim & New York 1969: Olms.]

Behaghel, Otto. 1932. *Deutsche Syntax: eine geschichtliche Darstellung. Band IV: Wortstellung. Periodenbau.* Heidelberg: Winter.

Born, Walter. 1978. *Kleine Sprachlehre des Münsterländer Platt.* Münster: Regensberg.

Davies, Winifred V. & Nils Langer. 2006. *The making of bad language: lay linguistic stigmatisations in German: past and present.* Frankfurt: Lang.

Duden Grammatik. 2009. *Die Grammatik.* 8th edition, revised. Mannheim, Leipzig, Wien & Zürich: Dudenverlag.

Ebert, Robert Peter. 1999. *Historische Syntax des Deutschen 2: 1300-1750.* Berlin: Weidler.

Elspaß, Stephan. 2005. *Sprachgeschichte von unten: Untersuchungen zum geschriebenen Alltagsdeutsch im 19. Jahrhundert.* Tübingen: Niemeyer.

Ernst, Peter. 2004. "Die sprachliche Leistung und Wirkung der deutschen Klassik". *Sprachgeschichte. Ein Handbuch zur Geschichte der deutschen Sprache und ihrer Erforschung. 4. Teilband* ed. W. Besch et al., 3070-3092. Berlin & New York: de Gruyter.

Fleischer, Jürg. 2005. "Zur Abfolge akkusativischer und dativischer Personalpronomen im Althochdeutschen und Altniederdeutschen (8./9. Jahrhundert)". *Syntax Althochdeutsch – Mittelhochdeutsch: eine Gegenüberstellung von Metrik und Prosa* ed. F. Simmler, 9-48. Berlin: Weidler.

Heidolph, Karl-Erich, Walter Flämig & Wolfgang Motsch (Leitung eines Autorenkollektivs). 1981. *Grundzüge einer deutschen Grammatik.* Berlin: Akademie.

Heyse, Johann Christoph August. 1849. *Theoretisch-praktische deutsche Grammatik oder Lehrbuch der deutschen Sprache. Zweiter Band.* Neu bearbeitet von Karl Wilhelm Ludwig Heyse. Hannover: Hahn. [reprint Hildesheim & New York 1972: Olms.]

Lenerz, Jürgen. 1977. *Zur Abfolge nominaler Satzglieder im Deutschen.* Tübingen: Narr.

Lenerz, Jürgen. 1993. "Zu Syntax und Semantik deutscher Personalpronomina". *Wortstellung und Informationsstruktur* ed. M. Reis, 117-153. Tübingen: Niemeyer.

Naumann, Bernd. 1986. *Grammatik der deutschen Sprache zwischen 1781 und 1856.* Berlin: Erich Schmidt.

Nübling, Damaris. 1992. *Klitika im Deutschen: Schriftsprache, Umgangssprache, alemannische Dialekte*. Tübingen: Narr.

Pohl, Heinz-Dieter. 1989. *Kleine Kärntner Mundartkunde mit Wörterbuch*. Klagenfurt: Heyn.

von Polenz, Peter. 1999. *Deutsche Sprachgeschichte vom Spätmittelalter bis zur Gegenwart. Band III: 19. und 20. Jahrhundert*. Berlin & New York: de Gruyter.

Primus, Beatrice. 1998. "The relative order of recipient and patient in the languages of Europe". *Constituent order in the languages of Europe* ed. A. Siewierska, 421-473. Berlin & New York: de Gruyter.

Reis, Hans. 1894. "Syntaktische studien im anschluss an die mundart von Mainz". *Beiträge zur Geschichte der deutschen Sprache und Literatur* 18. 475-510.

Shrier, Martha. 1965. "Case systems in German dialects". *Language* 41. 420-438.

Siewierska, Anna. 1988. *Word order rules*. London, New York & Sidney: Croom Helm.

Takada, Hiroyuki. 1998. *Grammatik und Sprachwirklichkeit von 1640-1700: zur Rolle deutscher Grammatiker im schriftsprachlichen Ausgleichsprozeß*. Tübingen: Niemeyer.

Wegener, Heide. 1985. *Der Dativ im heutigen Deutsch*. Tübingen: Narr.

Weiß, Helmut. 2005. "Syntax der Personalpronomen im Bairischen". *Bayerische Dialektologie. Akten der Internationalen Dialektologischen Konferenz 26.-28. Februar 2002* ed. S. Krämer-Neubert & N. R. Wolf, 179-188. Heidelberg: Winter.

Weldner, Heinrich. 1991. *Die Mundart von Barchfeld an der Werra*. Stuttgart: Steiner.

Werner, Ingegerd. 1999. *Die Personalpronomen im Zürichdeutschen*. Stockholm: Almqvist & Wiksell.

Wiese, Richard. 1996/2000. *The phonology of German*. Oxford: Clarendon.

Zifonun, Gisela, Ludger Hoffmann, Bruno Strecker et al. 1997. *Grammatik der deutschen Sprache*. Berlin: de Gruyter.

Christa Dürscheid & Nadio Giger (Zürich)

Variation in the case system of German – linguistic analysis and optimality theory

alle grammatischen ausnahmen scheinen mir nachzügler alter regeln, die noch hier und da zucken, oder vorboten neuer regeln, die über kurz oder lang einbrechen werden.[1]

1. Preliminary remarks

This paper focuses on different kinds of case variation and uses optimality theory (abbreviated as OT) to analyze the phenomena in question. Thus, the realms of both sociolinguistics and grammar are entered and combined. A model of the different varieties of German as well as a brief overview of the German case system are presented in section 2. In section 3, we introduce a classification of different types of variation by focussing on case phenomena. Then, in section 4, a concept of OT is suggested that theoretically describes the relationship between the grammatical features and the distribution of variants within the varieties of a language. This OT concept is also used in section 5 for the analysis of case variation in dative plural NPs in different varieties of German. Finally, we plead for the combination of OT and a system linguistic presentation to be a fruitful approach that has to be pursued further.

As to the different varieties of standard German, it is assumed that the *Standardsprache* ('standard language') is the codified standard language as it is written down in grammars and dictionaries. Within this paper, it will be referred to as *codified standard German*. The codices we take as a basis are the *Duden* grammar of 2009 and the *Zweifelsfälle-Duden* ('Duden for cases of doubt') of 2007. In addition to this, the standard language is also constituted by the *Gebrauchsstandard* ('standard language in use') (cf. Ammon 1995: 88), which includes non-codified variants that are used in newspaper articles, for instance. Furthermore, we consider the spoken and written *Umgangssprache* ('colloquial German') as the non-dialectal non-standard language. It consists of regional varieties as well as of varieties that differ from the standard language socio-stylistically. Following Barbour/Stevenson (1990: 144), we suggest a rough division between *standardnaher Umgangssprache* ('colloquial standard German'), i.e.

---

[1] Jacob Grimm (1847): Ueber das pedantische in der deutschen sprache. In: Kleinere Schriften, Volume 1, Berlin 1879, S. 330. The quotation can be translated as follows: all grammatical exceptions seem to be remnants of old rules still flickering here and there or harbingers of new rules befalling us sooner or later.

colloquial German that is – structurally – relatively close to the standard language, and *dialektnaher Umgangssprache*, i.e. colloquial German that is relatively close to dialects.[2] It has to be underlined that the varieties that are focussed on in the following analysis can overlap. Particularly as for case variation, it is obvious that all variants of the standard language also appear in non-dialectal colloquial German, but not vice versa.[3]

Regarding the notion of case, it is assumed that all phrases carrying case are assigned abstract case as a grammatical feature and have a head that can be case-marked. This case marking of the head (= *morphologischer Kasus* 'morphological case', cf. Gallmann 1996: 298) refers to the presence of a morphosyntactic feature that can, but does not have to be realized morphologically by means of a case suffix. If a noun carries the grammatical feature of case, but has no case suffix, the case marking is not visible and thus non-overt (cf. (*das*) *Buch_* '(the) book' NOM). If there is a case suffix, however, the case marking is visible and thus overt (cf. (*des*) *Buch-es* 'of (the) book' GEN). Following Gallmann (1996), we regard case-marked heads as case specified. They are different from case indifferent heads, which are not case-marked even if the phrase in which they appear is assigned abstract case. This will be shown in section 5, where NPs are discussed which lack case specification.

2. Some notes on the German case system

The German case system still has case specified as well as overtly case-marked word forms. This can be shown with the paradigm of *der Junge* 'the boy': *der Junge* NOM, *des Jungen* GEN, *dem Jungen* DAT, *den Jungen* ACC. Although it is only the difference between the nominative and the oblique cases that the noun marks morphologically by means of the suffix *-n*, there are still different forms of all four definite articles (cf. *der* NOM, *des* GEN, *dem* DAT, *den* ACC 'the'). In addition to that, there are NPs in German with a noun that is case-marked, but without a suffix, and with a definite article without unambiguous case marking. This is the case for all feminine singular nouns in definite NPs (cf. the paradigm of *die Lehrerin* 'the teacher': *die Lehrerin* NOM, *der Lehrerin* GEN, *der Lehrerin* DAT, *die Lehrerin* ACC). In such a paradigm, the classification as nominative or accusative can only be deduced from the syntac-

---

[2] Instances of colloquial German are, for example, forms of expression as they may appear in chat communication. Such non-dialectal colloquial German exists in the German-speaking part of Switzerland as well. Therefore, we assume a bipolar model consisting of dialects as one pole as well as of Swiss High German as another pole. The latter is heterogeneous in itself as it includes codified standard German, the *Gebrauchsstandard* as well as non-dialectal colloquial German. Thus, colloquial German in Switzerland is not only constituted by dialects, but also by colloquial Swiss High German.

[3] Note that for our analysis, we do not take German dialects into consideration. Case variants in learner varieties and are not included in the analysis either.

tic context (cf. *Das Mädchen besucht die Lehrerin* 'The girl goes to see the teacher' or 'It is the girl that the teacher wants to go and see').

This large variability concerning case marking is connected with the fact that the inflectional paradigms of the nouns are, to a certain extent, in competition with each other. German grammars vary as to the exact amount of inflectional paradigms, using different criteria to classify them. Some assume three main classes (i.e. strong, weak and mixed inflection), some differentiate between up to 30 subclasses (cf. Hentschel/Weydt 2003: 150–155). With reference to the *Duden* grammar (2009: 194), we classify four main types of nominal inflectional paradigms in singular and one type in plural. In the inflectional paradigm of weak singular nouns, there is a formal distinction between the nominative and the oblique cases by means of the suffix *-en* (cf. *der Prinz_* 'the prince' NOM vs. *den Prinz-en* 'the prince' ACC). In the strong paradigm in singular, there is a genitive suffix *-(e)s* (cf. *des Kreis-es* 'of the circle' GEN), but no suffix for all other forms (cf. *der Kreis_* 'the circle' NOM) since the dative suffix *-e* (cf. *dem Kreis(-e)* 'the circle' DAT) has become obsolete. It is only used in lexicalised forms (cf. *zu Hause* 'at home') and in idiomatic expressions (cf. *im Grunde genommen* 'basically'). In these collocations, the dative suffix *-e* is still the norm that has been laid down in the codices, but else, it is no longer customary in the present-day language.

In the course of the following discussion, we will only focus on the nouns of the strong and of the weak inflection in singular for it is above all in these two inflectional paradigms where variation of case marking appears. An example of this is presented in (1a'), where the accusative noun *Student* 'student' has no case suffix *-en*, a pattern that is ungrammatical in codified standard German, but that can be found in the *Gebrauchsstandard* and in colloquial German. Moreover, the sentences in (1) make clear that the syntactic function can – albeit not generally – be deduced from the case form: the form of the article (cf. *den* 'the' ACC) indicates that the NP at the beginning of the sentence is the direct object and not the subject. The same applies if the nominal case suffix is omitted (cf. 1a') or if the noun is never overtly case-marked (cf. 1b).

(1) Case inflection:
  a. *Den Studenten* (weak inflection) *sieht der Lehrer.*
     'The student [object] sees the teacher [subject].'
  a'. *Den Student_ sieht der Lehrer.*
     'The student [object] sees the teacher [subject].'
  b. *Den Mann* (strong inflection) *sehe ich.*
     'The man [object] see I [subject].'

Not only the accusative object, but also genitive and dative objects can be placed in front of the finite verb. Under certain conditions, these cases can also be classified as direct objects (cf. Wegener 1986). However, we will not use the term 'direct object' because objects in German can be differentiated sufficiently by means of their case. In English, where nominal objects are not case-marked, it is reasonable to make a difference between a direct object and an indirect object, i.e. an object that is linked with the verb by a preposition (cf. *I give the book to Mary*).

Let us now turn to case assignment. In German, verbs, adjectives, nouns and prepositions assign case to an NP. All four types of case assigners are illustrated in (2) in bold print:

(2) The four categories of case assigners in German:

a. *einer Sache* GEN ***überdrüssig*** [adjective] *sein*

'to be tired of something GEN'

b. *das **Buch*** [noun] *des Kindes* GEN

'the child's GEN book'

c. ***mit*** [preposition] *dem Kind* DAT

'with the child DAT'

d. *jemanden* ACC ***treffen*** [verb]

'to meet someone ACC'

Note that case assignment by the noun is different from case assignment by the other parts of speech. The noun in standard German assigns only genitive case, a different case category is not possible. In colloquial German, however, a noun can be preceded by a dative NP and a possessive pronoun that links them both (cf. *dem Kind* DAT *sein Buch* 'the child DAT its book', i.e. 'the child's book'). The conditions under which such an adnominal dative can appear have already been described in detail (cf. Zifonun 2003, Dürscheid 2007) and are not part of the discussion here. According to the *Duden* grammar (2009: 1212), the dative possessive construction is characteristic of spoken language, but it cannot be used in written language. In the scope of case assignment by verbs, adjectives and prepositions, genitive, dative as well as accusative case are possible (cf. *jemandem* DAT *helfen* 'to help somebody DAT', *jemanden* ACC *treffen* 'to meet somebody ACC', *sich einer Sache* GEN *erinnern* 'to remember something GEN'), but not nominative. This case is exclusively linked with certain structural positions, that is to say the subject position as well as the position of a predicative nominative (cf. *Er* NOM *ist Lehrer* NOM 'He NOM is a teacher NOM').

Furthermore, case assignment can also be motivated semantically (cf. *an die Wand* ACC *hängen* 'to hook on the wall ACC' vs. *an der Wand* DAT *hängen* 'to be attached to the wall DAT'). The choice of the case category that is assigned depends on the meaning that is conveyed, which can be described with the thematic roles of GOAL with accusative and of LOCATION with dative case. It is possible that there is no change of meaning even if the case assigner varies as to the case category that it governs. This is the case when dative is used instead of genitive case (cf. *wegen des schlechten Wetters* GEN/*wegen dem schlechten Wetter* DAT 'because of the bad weather GEN/DAT'). Dative case in such phrases is outside the norm defined by the *Duden* grammar, except for constructions with such prepositions as *entlang* (see section 3).

3. A typology of case variation

In order to classify the different types of case variation, we make use of a theory by Jacobs (2007). This might be surprising at first glance since Jacobs focuses on the classification of orthographic variation exclusively. However, as will be shown, Jacobs' approach can be transferred to case variation. Case variation can be understood as variation of case assignment and as variation of case marking. The former refers to the case assigner and the phrase that is assigned case. It means the choice of a case category that is assigned, for instance accusative (cf. *Ich rufe dich* ACC 'I call you ACC') or dative case (cf. *Ich rufe dir* DAT 'I call you DAT'). The latter refers to the head of a phrase: on the one hand, there can be variation of case forms since the noun can be used with a case suffix (cf. *den Studenten* 'the student' ACC) or without a case suffix (cf. *den Student_* 'the student' ACC). On the other hand, the syntactic word in the head position can be with or without the grammatical feature of case, that is to say it can be case specified (cf. *Orchester ohne einen Dirigenten* 'orchestra without a conductor') or case indifferent (cf. *Orchester ohne Dirigent_* 'orchestra without conductor'), which can also lead to the variation of case forms. Jacobs (2007) suggests the following four different types of variants:

1) disambiguating variants
2) construction-based variants
3) free variants
4) system-based variants

1. disambiguating variants

According to Jacobs (2007: 47), word pairs such as *Moor* 'marsh' and *Mohr* 'Moor' are disambiguating variants because the difference in meaning is indicated via the spelling. In the case system, there is also such a semantically motivated variation, namely in the context of the prepositions *an* 'to', *auf* 'on', *hinter* 'behind', *neben* 'next to', *über* 'over', *unter* 'under', *vor* 'in front of' and *zwischen* 'between' if these prepositions are used with a locative meaning. This aspect has already been illustrated in section 2. The case assigned by the preposition in these PPs indicates if there is a change of location or not.

There can also be a semantically motivated alternation of the case category governed by the verb if the verb describes a physical influence, as the two sentences *Ich schneide mich* ACC *in den Finger* 'I cut me ACC in my finger', i.e. 'I cut my finger' and *Ich schneide mir* DAT *in den Finger* 'I cut me DAT in my finger', i.e. 'I cut my finger' illustrate. In both examples, the accusative NP, on the one hand, is in competition with the dative NP. The dative NP, on the other hand, can be paraphrased, together with the PP *in den Finger* 'in the finger', as *in meinen Finger* 'in my finger'. Thus, the accusative NP refers to a person affected by the verbal action (i.e. the NP is the argument with the thematic role of PATIENT). The dative NP, however, expresses a partial patientivity that only refers to a part of the body (cf. Duden 2007: 762). This also explains why the verb cannot be followed only by the dative NP (cf. **Ich schneide mir* DAT 'I cut me DAT'). Therefore, it is obligatory to mention the affected part of the body.

Furthermore, there are verbs varying as to the assignment of dative and accusative case without the necessity of another NP or PP in addition to the dative NP. According to the *Zweifelsfälle-Duden* (2007: 780), the verb *rufen* 'to call', for instance, assigns accusative, but also dative case in regional varieties if the meaning is 'to ask for somebody by calling him or her', but not 'to call somebody over'. It has already been postulated that there are semantic differences between the accusative and the dative object, but we will not resume this discussion in this paper. However, it can be stated that alternating between case categories can serve to indicate differences in meaning. As the choice of the case category is normally motivated by government and not by semantics, there are few contexts where this option is made use of.

A further phenomenon that can be connected with disambiguation is the morphological realisation of case. According to Wegener (2007), the omission of the suffix *-en* in weak masculine nouns with accusative or dative case serves to avoid homonymy. In Wegener's view, the noun *Dirigent* 'conductor' in the phrase *Orchester ohne Dirigent_* 'orchestra without conductor' has no suffix to rule out the possibility of confusing it with the plural form *ohne Dirigenten* 'without conductors'. In addition to the fact that the possibility of misunderstanding this example is far-fetched anyway – an orchestra has normally only one conductor – , there are similar examples where singular and plural forms do not coincide, but where there is a reduced nominal form nevertheless (cf. *Ich kenne einen Student_* 'I know a student'). In our view, the noun *Dirigent* 'conductor' in the example *Orchester ohne Dirigent_* is a syntactically motivated and thus a construction-based variant anyway, where the noun is not case-marked at all and thus case indifferent (see below).

Wegener (2007: 42 f.) suggests furthermore that also the diachronic change of the noun from the weak into the strong inflectional paradigm is motivated semantically. She points out that weak masculine nouns almost always carry the semantic feature [+ animate]. Nouns with the feature [– animate] tend to break out of this paradigm. This aspect indeed explains the transition of nouns such as *Funke* 'spark', *Gedanke* 'thought', *Wille* 'will' and *Friede* 'peace' into the strong inflectional paradigm. However, it should not be forgotten that the feature [+/– animate] is only one factor determining the change into another inflectional paradigm. According to Köpcke (2005), further factors referring to the final sound of the word (i.e. +/– schwa), its pronunciation and its syllabic structure have to be taken into consideration. Without doubt, these features are stronger than the semantic feature [+/– animate]. This can be illustrated with such examples as *Patient* 'patient', *Student* 'student', *Dozent* 'lecturer' and *Dirigent* 'conductor', which are all in the paradigm of words of non-German origin (cf. Duden 2009: 213). Although they carry the feature [+ animate], they all tend to give up the weak inflectional paradigm and to change to the strong inflectional paradigm when it comes to the case forms for accusative and dative case in singular.

It also has to be noted that such a tendency is mentioned in the *Duden* grammar (cf. 2009: 214), but it also has to be pointed out that these masculine nouns have to show weak inflection in the codified standard language (see further below). The same is the case for other nouns in this paradigm, such as *Automat* 'machine' or *Planet* 'planet', which have the semantic feature [– animate], but also have to show weak inflection (cf. Duden 2009: 213). The only noun with the feature [– animate] in this paradigm for which strong inflection is grammatical according to the *Duden* grammar (2009: 214) is *Magnet* 'magnet' (cf. *den Magneten*/*den Magnet_*), which supports Wegener's aforementioned view.

2) construction-based variants

Jacobs (2007: 48) regards spellings such as <milch> and <Milch> 'milk' as construction-based variants since it is just the one or the other spelling that is possible in a specific grammatical construction (cf. *Kuhmilch* 'milk of a cow' vs. *Milch holen* 'to get milk'). Construction-based variants in the case system are, for instance, case specified and case indifferent nouns. The aforementioned phrase *Orchester ohne Dirigent_* 'orchestra without conductor' is an example of a case indifferent variant. Neither an article nor an adjective precede the noun *Dirigent* 'conductor'. Further examples are *wegen Umzug_ geschlossen* 'closed for removal', *gemäss Artikel_ 20* 'according to article 20' and *das Verhältnis zwischen Arzt und Patient_* 'the relationship between doctor and patient'. Case indifference is the common denominator in all of these constructions, where the noun does not only lack a case suffix, but it is not case-marked at all. As there is no adjectivally inflected word form, the noun does not carry the grammatical feature of morphological case.

Like Gallmann (1996), we assume that the case specification of the noun is regulated by adjectivally inflected word forms. More exactly, this means that in an NP[4], an inflected determiner[5] and/or an inflected adjective carry the grammatical feature of morphological case. By means of congruence, this feature is transferred to the noun, making it case specified as well (cf. *Orchester ohne ein-en gut-en Dirigent-en* 'orchestra without a good conductor'). Of course, the noun can be case specified, but still without a case suffix (cf. *ohne ein-en gut-en Artikel_* 'without a good article'). If the adjectival inflection is missing, however, since there is neither a determiner nor an adjective (or only an adjective that is not inflected, such as *prima* 'great'), the noun is case indifferent (cf. *ohne prima Dirigent_* 'without great conductor').

This regularity is also recorded in the *Duden* grammar, where case indifference in singular is declared as acceptable (cf. Duden 2009: 964). In plural, however, case indifference is not considered acceptable, the dative suffix *-n* of the noun has to be realized even if the noun is not preceded by a determiner or an adjective (cf. Duden 2009: 967). This means that the plural noun has to be case specified in codified standard German without there being an adjectivally inflected word form (cf. *Eis mit Früchte-n/*mit Früchte_* 'ice-cream with fruits'). According to Gallmann (1996: 305), this phenomenon can be explained by a second principle of case specification, which we name *genuine case specification*: a nominal head can carry the feature of morphological case even if no adjectivally inflected word precedes the noun. Thereby, the case feature percolates directly from the phrase to the head, so it is not transferred via congruence with the article or with the adjective. Because of this genuine case specification of the nominal head, the syntactic word in the head position is also genuinely case specified (cf. *ein Abend mit Konzerte-n* 'an evening with concerts'). Since such a phenomenon of case specification is only possible in certain constructions, it is an instance of construction-based variation. This option of case specification seems to apply to NPs in plural, but also to proper names without an article (cf. *Peters Buch* 'Peter's book') for the proper name is also assigned morphological case without there being an adjectivally inflected word form (e. g. an article).

In a word, the following can be stated: because of the presence or absence of adjectivally inflected word forms and/or because of genuine case specification (or genuine case indifference), case specified and case indifferent nouns can be

---

[4] Gallmann analyzes the distribution of the case feature within a DP carrying case. Slightly simplifying matters, we will continue using the concept of NP.

[5] The original term *Artikelwort* 'article word' according to the *Duden* grammar (2009: 249 ff.) corresponds with the term *determiner* in most English grammars. Hence, it will be used throughout the paper. The term *Artikelwort* is synonymous with the traditional term *Begleiter* 'word accompanying the noun' and refers to demonstrative and indefinite determiners as well as to the article, but it excludes pronouns, such as the personal pronoun, which is traditionally termed as *Stellvertreter* 'word replacing the noun'.

considered construction-based variants. Contrary to that, the next type of variation enables the speaker to choose freely from various forms of realisation within a certain frame.

3) free variants

As Jacobs (2007: 50) points out, one can choose between spelling variants such as <Friseur> and <Frisör> 'hairdresser', as they do not differ semantically and as both are correct within the norm. In analogy to that, the long (cf. *-es*) and the short suffix (cf. *-s*) for the genitive case are free variants. That is because both suffixes are acceptable in German if the noun ends in a stressed vowel plus one or more consonants (cf. *Giftes/Gifts* 'poison' and *Erfolges/Erfolgs* 'success'). Another case of free variation can be made out when it comes to nouns which still appear with weak inflection, but the change of which into the strong inflectional paradigm has also been accepted by the norm. These are nouns such as *Oberst* 'colonel', where the genitive forms *des Obersten* [weak] as well as *des Obersts* [strong] are equally acceptable according to the *Duden* grammar (2009: 224 and 237). Contrary to an example such as *Bär*, the variation of these forms of the lexeme *Oberst* is not connected with a difference in meaning.[6] Thus, to speak with Jacob Grimm (see the introductory quotation), there are new rules that have already befallen us. The same applies to the pronouns *jemand* 'somebody' and *niemand* 'nobody', which can appear with or without a suffix in an accusative or dative position (cf. Duden 2007: 491).

After this discussion of free variation of case marking, free variation of case assignment will now be focussed on. There are prepositions governing dative as well as genitive case without a difference in meaning (cf. *entlang dem Fluss* DAT 'along the river DAT'/*entlang des Flusses* GEN 'along the river GEN'). In the context of the preposition *plus* 'plus', even three cases – dative, accusative and genitive case – are acceptable (cf. Duden 2009: 613). Further prepositions with such a variation of dative and genitive case are, for instance, *dank* 'thanks to', *entgegen* 'contrary to', *gemäss* 'according to' and *nahe* 'near' (cf. Di Meola 1998). However, variation of case assignment with these prepositions is not accepted in the codified standard language yet (see section 2). Because of that, they do not belong to the scope of free variation. Instead, they are classified as system-based or variety-based variants, respectively. This type of variation, overlying all others, will now be explained.

4) system-based variants

In his explanations about system-based variation, Jacobs (2007) lays the emphasis on the fact that formal differences with reference to spelling can be attributed

---

[6] The variant with weak inflection (cf. *des Bären* GEN) means 'bear', whereas the variant with strong inflection (cf. *des Bärs* GEN) is only possible with the technical meaning of the noun as *Maschinenhammer* 'ram' (cf. Duden 2009: 224).

to the use of the forms in different varieties. As an example, he mentions the difference in the spelling of <ß> between the standard German of Germany (cf. *heißen* 'to be called') and the standard German of Switzerland (*heissen* 'to be called'). We call such and other instances variety-based variants as differences can be found between the national varieties of German (e.g. between the codified standard in Germany and Switzerland) as well as within different varieties of a national variety (e.g. between the standard and colloquial German of Germany or of Switzerland). In the German case system, this type of variation appears on the level of case assignment (cf. *jemanden* ACC *anrufen* 'to call somebody ACC' in standard German vs. *jemandem* DAT *anrufen* 'to call somebody DAT' in the colloquial German of West and South Germany and of Switzerland). However, variety-based variants can also be found on the level of case forms, for instance when it comes to the realisation of the genitive case suffix *-es* or *-s* (cf. *des Ausgang-es* vs. *des Ausgang-s* 'of the exit'). Provided that there is free variation, the long form is preferred in the standard German of Switzerland (cf. Dürscheid/Hefti 2006: 135), whereas the short form is preferred in the standard German of Germany.

Further cases of variety-based variation can be found between technical language and everyday language (cf. *des Herzes* 'of the heart' GEN in technical language vs. *des Herzens* 'of the heart' GEN in colloquial language) or between specific dialects (cf. the variation of case forms in *bei die Mutter* DAT 'with the mother DAT' vs. *bei der Mutter* DAT 'with the mother DAT'). The variation of such nouns as *Student* 'student' between weak and strong inflection, as it was mentioned above, is another instance of variety-based case variation. According to the *Duden* grammar (cf. 2009: 214), only the variants with weak inflection are part of the codified standard language. Furthermore, it can be shown that a variant can belong to more than one type of variation. The change of case assignment of the verb *rufen* 'to call' (see above), for instance, is caused by semantics and is thus an instance of disambiguating variation. Simultaneously, its variation of case assignment is variety-based as the use of *rufen* assigning dative case is only acceptable in specific regional varieties. The adnominal dative (see above) is also variety-based as it is preferred in spoken language. At the same time, it is construction-based since as an alternative for the genitive attribute, it can only be in prenominal position.

There might be further classes that would have to be amended, but most case variants can be subsumed under these four types. The following two sections will show how some phenomena in the large area of case variation can be described by means of OT. First of all, there will be some remarks about OT.

4. Norm, variation and optimality theory

In OT, it is assumed that languages follow general (system linguistic) regularities, also known as constraints. It is also assumed that constraint conflicts can occur, meaning that the relevant constraints are violable. Consequently, linguistic regularities are by no means absolute rules, but strong tendencies at best (cf. Businger 2010: 155). In an OT competition, a set of candidates with the same meaning, the same surface structure (i.e. S-structure) or the same numeration (i.e. the same lexical material) is confronted with a ranking of constraints (cf. Müller 2000: 12). These constraints are universal, but what is parameterized is their ranking for each language or variety. The constraint profile of each candidate is shown in a table, indicating which constraints it fulfils, which ones it violates and how many times it violates a constraint. The higher a constraint is ranked, the more heavily its violation weighs. The candidate with the best constraint profile is the winner of the competition and thus the optimal candidate, which can violate one or more constraints once or several times and is still grammatical.

The question of what the characteristics of the optimal candidate are will now be focussed on. The answer depends on how the term *optimality* is defined and thus on the kind of competition. If optimality is – in the sense of the classical OT modelling – equated with the term of *grammaticality*, only the optimal candidate is determined as the grammatical structure and all further structures in the same set of candidates are ungrammatical. According to Müller (2000: 241), the idea of optimality can also be connected with the concept of *unmarkedness*.[7] The optimal candidate is then grammatical as well as completely unmarked. All further structures in the same set of candidates are graded in accordance with their constraint profile and their ranking indicates their degree of markedness. The worse their constraint profile is, the lower they are placed in the ranking list of all candidates and the more marked they are. In our view, both concepts of optimality (i.e. grammaticality/ungrammaticality as well as unmarkedness/markedness) can be combined in one single OT competition. In Müller's approach (2000: 241 ff.), this is made possible by a splitting up of the constraint hierarchy into a matrix hierarchy and a subhierarchy. Within the matrix hierarchy, grammatical and ungrammatical candidates can be differentiated. If there is more than one grammatical structure in a set of candidates, the grammatical candi-

---

[7] The concept of *unmarkedness* is to be understood as *grammatical unmarkedness* in OT and to be differentiated from *morphological unmarkedness*. *Grammatical unmarkedness* means the degree of acceptability in the scope of grammaticality: the less marked a candidate is, the more acceptable it is (cf. Müller 2000: 242 f.). *Morphological markedness*, however, means the presence of case suffixes as a morphological marking of the case feature. Therefore, nouns with non-overt case marking are not morphologically marked with respect to case.

dates are graded in accordance with their constraint profile by means of the subhierarchy, which is a hierarchy of constraints within a complex constraint of the matrix hierarchy. The violation of a constraint in the subhierarchy is indicated with a question mark. The candidate with the best constraint profile is grammatical as well as completely unmarked and the ranking of all other grammatical candidates reflects their degree of markedness.

In contrast to Müller, it is assumed here that the concepts of grammaticality/ungrammaticality and unmarkedness/markedness can be captured in only one competition with only one constraint hierarchy. Each candidate has its constraint profile because of its features in reference to this constraint hierarchy. A comparison of all constraint profiles leads to a ranking list of all candidates. The optimal candidate is, like in Müller's account, grammatical as well as completely unmarked. A boundary of grammaticality indicates which candidates – on the basis of their constraint profiles – are still or no longer grammatical. The advantage of this concept of OT competitions is the following: if language phenomena of different varieties are compared, an OT competition can demonstrate that the different varieties have the same constraint ranking and thus the same tables, but that the boundary of grammaticality in the tables is at a different position for each variety. It is in exactly this way that case variation can be analyzed (see section 5).

The potential of OT has been used more and more for analyzing and describing not only languages, but also variation within varieties of a language. Herrgen (2005), for instance, makes use of OT to explain the variation of verbal morphology in various regional varieties of German and pleads for OT to be used as a paradigm to describe areal linguistic dynamics (cf. Herrgen 2005: 278). In a more recent analysis on areal linguistic variation and OT, Herrgen (2009: 109) remarks that only few studies on this matter have been published. It is the aim of this paper to help fill this gap. We regard OT as suitable to analyze the relationship between the grammatical features and the distribution of variants within the varieties of a language, or even to account for the variational distribution in a language by means of the grammatical features of different variants. However, we assume that differences between varieties are not only based on constraint ranking differences (Herrgen 2009: 111 f.), but also on different positions of the boundary of grammaticality within a table with the same constraint ranking for all varieties, as it was mentioned before. An example of such an analysis is demonstrated in the next section.

5. Variation in dative plural noun phrases

In section 5.1, specific types of dative plural NPs with nominal heads ending in -e, -el or -er (cf. *Leute*, 'people' *Artikel* 'article' and *Wälder* 'forests') are described that are taken into consideration. In section 5.2, the relevant constraints and their ranking are suggested. In the same section, the competitions and tables of the different phrase types are presented. In line with the OT concept, it is assumed that the same constraint ranking applies to all relevant varieties. Also, we use the concept of the varying positions of the boundaries of grammaticality for the different varieties. This means that varieties close to the codified standard language, such as the *Gebrauchsstandard*, have fewer grammatical candidates whereas varieties far from the standard language, such as colloquial German, have more of them.

5.1 Phenomena

As to the relevant NPs, a difference will be made between three types. These are illustrated in scheme 1 and commented afterwards. In order to illustrate that all examples are assigned dative case, the NPs are embedded into PPs. It is thus not the whole PP, but only the NP embedded in the PP that has to be taken into consideration.

Scheme 1: case variation in dative plural NPs

Types of phrases	Possibility of case specification by means of an adjectivally inflected word form	Structural features of the NP

type I phrases	no	– without determiner/adjective
		  Ex.: *mit Konzerten* 'with concerts'
		– as an expression of measurement or quantity and without a partitive attribute (cf. Duden 2009: 175, 983)
		  Ex.: *nach 80 Metern* 'after 80 metres'
		– with an attributive adjective that is not inflectable
		  Ex.: *mit prima Artikeln* 'with great articles', *mit Schweizer Alpenkräutern* 'with Swiss alpine herbs', *mit 126 Spielen* 'with 126 games'

type II phrases	yes	– with a determiner with strong inflection
		  Ex.: *mit allen Artikeln* 'with all articles'
		– with an adjective with strong inflection
		  Ex.: *mit netten Leuten* 'with nice people'

type III phrases	yes	– with an determiner and an adjective, both with strong inflection
		  Ex.: *mit einigen guten Artikeln* 'with some good articles'
		– with two determiners, both with strong inflection
		  Ex.: *mit allen seinen Kindern* 'with all his children'

Type I phrases consist of NPs in which case specification of the noun by an adjectivally inflected word form is not possible because such a word form is missing or the adjective is not inflectable. The latter applies to adjectives such as *prima* 'great', to cardinal figure adjectives such as *zehn* 'ten' as well as to derivatives of geographic proper names ending in *-er* such as *Schweizer* 'Swiss'. As it has been discussed already, nouns in such syntagms must be case specified in codified standard German. However, there are four exceptions. According to the *Zweifelsfälle-Duden* (2007: 989, 994) and the *Duden* grammar (2009: 967), a plural noun can also be case indifferent (i) in a phrase with an expression of measurement or quantity and with a partitive attribute (cf. *in dreißig Meter_ Höhe* 'in a height of thirty metres'), (ii) in the collocation *aus aller Herren Länder_* with a prenominal genitive attribute (literally 'from the countries of all lords', i.e. 'from all the world'), (iii) in a phrase with an attribute with the preposition *von* 'of' describing a quality (cf. *eine Art von Hosenträger_* 'a kind of braces/suspenders') and (iv) in a phrase with the preposition *ab* with the meaning of 'as from' (cf. *ab drei Monate_* 'as from three months'). This possibility of free variation shows that also the codified standard language has the tendency to have genuine case indifference in plural NPs under certain conditions.

Otherwise, only nouns with genuine case specification are correct in such phrases, and the noun has to appear with the dative case suffix *-n* according to the *Duden* grammar (cf. Duden 2009: 967), even if there is no adjectivally inflected word form preceding it. Such syntagms are, for instance, expressions of measurement or quantity, but without a partitive attribute (cf. *nach 80 Metern/*Meter_* 'after 80 metres'),[8] NPs without a determiner or without an adjective (cf. *mit Konzerten/*Konzerte_* 'with concerts'), NPs with an attributive adjective that is not inflectable (cf. *mit Schweizer Alpenkräutern/*Alpenkräuter_* 'with Swiss alpine herbs') as well as NPs with a cardinal figure adjective, but without a noun of real measurement (cf. *mit 126 Spielen/*Spiele_* 'with 126 games').

In our OT analysis, we focus on NPs without an adjectivally inflected word form that can only have a genuinely case specified noun in the codified standard language (cf. *nach 80 Metern/*nach 80 Meter_* 'after 80 metres'), but that can also appear with a genuinely case indifferent noun in the *Gebrauchsstandard* and in colloquial German (cf. *nach 80 Meter_*).[9] In addition to that, it is assumed

---

[8] There is one exception in codified standard German: phrases with the preposition *ab* 'as from' can also have case indifferent nouns (cf. *ab drei Monate_/Monaten* 'as from three months', cf. Duden 2009: 967).

[9] We include expressions of measurement without a partitive attribute as the exceptional variation *ab drei Monate_/ab drei Monaten* 'as from three months' is only one particular case in the codified standard. Consequently, NPs with prenominal genitive attributes

that genuinely case specified nouns in an NP without an adjectivally inflected word form also have a suffix (cf. *mit Artikeln* 'with articles'). This means that nouns without a case suffix in an NP without an adjectivally inflected word form are always genuinely case indifferent only (cf. *mit Artikel_* 'with articles').

The **type II and type III phrases** have in common that the nouns are preceded by determiners and/or inflectable adjectives. Thus, there is the possibility of case specification by adjectivally inflected word forms. In type II phrases, there is one determiner or adjective with strong inflection in the NP whereas in type III phrases, there are two of them. In the *Gebrauchsstandard* and in colloquial German, it can be observed that determiners and adjectives with strong inflection can appear in two inflectional paradigms, one paradigm providing the suffix *-en* (cf. *mit netten Leuten* 'with nice people'), the other paradigm providing the suffix *-e* (cf. *mit nette Leuten* 'with nice people'). The suffix *-en* identifies the dative case unambiguously as there is no other inflectional suffix that is formally identical in the plural paradigm of strong adjectival inflection. The inflectional suffix *-e*, however, does not identify the dative case unambiguously since the suffix *-e* also appears in a nominative (cf. *Es sind nett-e Leute* 'They are nice people') and in an accusative form (cf. *Er traf nett-e Leute* 'He met nice people'). Plural nouns ending in *-e*, *-el* or *-er* show a similar variation since they can be with the dative case suffix *-n* as well as without a case suffix. This distribution leads to the following functional differentiation: the nominal case suffix *-n* identifies the dative case unambiguously in a plural paradigm whereas the nominal dative plural case form without a case suffix does not identify the dative case unambiguously.

If the sets of candidates of type II and type III phrases are formed with such lexemes as *all* 'alle', *some* 'einige' or *gut* 'good', there is also the possibility of candidates appearing with determiners and/or adjectives that are not inflected (see c_5 in table 4 as well as c_9 in table 5). In these NPs, there is no case specification by an adjectivally inflected word form.

5.2 Constraints and competitions

As it has become apparent, the three types of phrases have different structural features, so their sets of candidates cannot be in the same OT competitions. However, the constraints and their ranking are the same for all three types of phrases. Therefore, the OT competitions of a set of candidates for all relevant varieties can be summarized in one single table. This serves as an overview of the possibilities of case variation in standard and colloquial German. In general, it can be stated that the varieties differ in the following way: the closer to the codified standard language a variety is, the higher its boundary of grammatical-

---

would also have to be included. However, for the sake of brevity, this type of syntagm is excluded from our OT analysis.

ity is in the table. For the illustration of the case marking in dative plural NPs, we will use the following four constraints:

(3) Constraints for the OT competitions:
CASESPEC:
The nominal head of the NP is case specified.
IDENTPLUR:
The NP is identifiable unambiguously as a plural NP.
DATMARK:
A case specified word form in the NP marks the dative case in plural morphologically and also identifies the dative case unambiguously.
MARLIN:
The morphological marking of the case feature identifying the dative case in plural unambiguously appears linearly.

The constraint CASESPEC demands that the head of an NP carries the grammatical feature of case and that it is thus case specified either because of genuine case specification or by congruence with an adjectivally inflected word form. In accordance with the constraint IDENTPLUR, the NP has to be identifiable as a plural NP by means of its lexical (e.g. because of a quantifier) or its morphological structure (e.g. because of the suffixes in the NP). DATMARK refers to each case specified word form in the NP, thus including determiners, adjectives with strong inflection and nouns (cf. *mit einig-en gut-en Artikel-n* 'with some good articles'). According to this constraint, each of these case forms has to mark the dative case morphologically in such a way that it can be identified unambiguously. Thus, every missing unambiguous marking of the dative case of a case specified word form violates DATMARK.

As demanded by the constraint MARLIN, the morphological marking identifying the dative case unambiguously (i.e. the inflectional suffix *-en* for determiners and adjectives with strong inflection and the nominal inflectional suffix *-n*) has to manifest itself linearly, that is to say at the determiner first, then at the adjective and finally at the noun. MARLIN also demands that a case specified word form can only have the morphological marking of the case feature as defined in DATMARK if each preceding case specified word form shows this feature as well. MARLIN is thus applied to each word form individually. If the adjective and the noun, for example, have the marking as demanded in DATMARK, but the determiner appears without it (cf. *mit einig-e gut-en Artikel-n* 'with some good articles'), MARLIN is violated twice since neither the adjective nor the noun fulfil the constraint. It also takes into account the number of case specified word forms preceding another such word form. If a case form has a morphological marking like in DATMARK although several preceding case specified word forms do not have this marking, MARLIN is violated in accordance with the amount of "omitted" case forms. The fact that the noun in the NP *mit einig-e* *gut-e Artikel-n* 'with some good articles', for example, omits the determiner as well as the adjective with regard to the fulfilment of DATMARK runs counter to the principle of linearity twice, so MARLIN is also violated twice in this NP. Basically, MARLIN is only relevant and violable if there are two or more case specified word forms in an NP.

We assume that the aforementioned constraints have the following ranking: CASESPEC >> IDENTPLUR >> DATMARK >> MARLIN. This assumption is explained by the fact that there is a preference for the case specification of the noun as well as for the unambiguous morphological marking of the dative case in plural, particularly in the codified standard language. However, before presenting the OT competitions in detail now, a general note is necessary. The candidates of an OT competition need to have the same structural and particularly the same lexical features, but different morphosyntactic features. Therefore, not all possible examples are equally suitable as candidates. For instance, the lexical material in the list of examples in scheme 1 is too heterogeneous, not only concerning the determiners and the adjectives, but also the nouns and their different word endings in *-e, -el* or *-er*. In all three types of phrases, the problem is solved by means of a focus on NPs with the same lexical material and on a noun ending in *-el* in each type of phrase. This also means that a structure with lexical material that is different from the candidates, but with the same morphosyntactic case features has the same position in the ranking list and thus the same degree of markedness and grammaticality.[10] In addition to that, we define different sets of candidates for separate competitions and we make a comparison between candidate profiles beyond the competitions that they appear in.

type I phrases

As to type I phrases, the emphasis is put on three sets of candidates with and without an attributive element. The three sets of candidates consist of the following lexemes:

(4) Lexemes for the three sets of candidates in the type I phrases:

for the set of candidates I: *Artikel* 'article'
for the set of candidates II: *prima* 'great', *Artikel* 'article'
for the set of candidates III: *80, Artikel* 'article'

---

[10] This argument does not hold good in every case: in the *Gebrauchsstandard* as well as in colloquial German, nouns ending in *-el* in plural, for example, can appear in a dative NP that can formally be interpreted as a singular NP, which violates IDENTPLUR (cf. *guten Artikel_* 'good articles' DAT or 'good article' ACC). However, an NP with the same inflectional suffixes and with a noun ending in *-er* cannot be interpreted as a singular NP, so IDENTPLUR is fulfilled (cf. *netten Leute_* 'nice people' DAT, *guten Kräuter_* 'good herbs DAT').

For the set of candidates I, there is the following table as an overview of the OT competitions of all relevant varieties:[11]

Table 1: case variation in the set of candidates I

candidates	CASESPEC	IDENTPLUR	DATMARK	MARLIN
☞ c_1: (mit) Artikeln				
c_2: (mit) Artikel	*![12]	*		

In table 1, the case specified candidate c_1 is optimal because it does not violate any constraint. The candidate c_2 is not optimal as the head of the NP is case indifferent and the NP cannot be identified unambiguously as a plural NP by the noun *Artikel* 'article'. However, it is exactly because of the case indifference of the noun that c_2 cannot violate DATMARK. In addition to that, none of the candidates violates MARLIN for the following trivial reason: c_1 has only one and c_2 has no case specified word form so the principle of linearity cannot be violated at all. This, by the way, also applies to the sets of candidates II and III.

The overview of all OT competitions for the set of candidates II is shown in table 2:

Table 2: case variation in the set of candidates II

candidates	CASESPEC	IDENTPLUR	DATMARK	MARLIN
☞ c_1: (mit) prima Artikeln				
c_2: (mit) prima Artikel	*!	*		

Also in table 2, no constraints are violated by the case specified candidate c_1. In particular, there is no violation of DATMARK and MARLIN. As the noun is the only case specified word form, these two constraints only refer to the word *Artikeln* 'articles' and are fulfilled in c_1. Thus, c_1 is the optimal candidate. The case indifferent candidate c_2, violating CASESPEC and IDENTPLUR, is not optimal.

---

[11] It shall be mentioned again that all candidates in all OT competitions are NPs and that they are only embedded into a PP to illustrate more clearly their status of being dative plural NPs. Thus, the preposition *mit* 'with' is enclosed in brackets.

[12] For the sake of simplicity, we will mark all violations that are regarded as "fatal" with the exclamation mark, knowing that the violation only means grammatical markedness and not ungrammaticality in some varieties.

Table 3 is an overview of all OT competitions for the set of candidates III:

Table 3: case variation in the set of candidates III

candidates	CASESPEC	IDENTPLUR	DATMARK	MARLIN
☞ c₁: (mit) 80 Artikeln				
c₂: (mit) 80 Artikel	*!			

Table 3 shows the overview of the OT competitions of all relevant varieties for the set of candidates III. The structures of this set of candidates also represent NPs with nouns of measurement (cf. *nach 80 Metern* 'after 80 metres'). It can be seen that the optimal candidate c₁ violates no constraints. The candidate c₂ appears with the cardinal figure adjective *80* und is thus identifiable unambiguously as a plural NP. Even if c₂ does not violate the constraint IDENTPLUR, it still is not optimal.

At this stage, the three sets of candidates can be compared with reference to standard and colloquial German. If the three tables that have been shown represent the OT competitions in codified standard German, c₁ is grammatical, whereas c₂ is ungrammatical in each competition. The optimal candidates in each competition can also be considered grammatical in the *Gebrauchsstandard* as well as in colloquial German. Furthermore, it can be seen that c₂ in table 3, fulfilling IDENTPLUR, has the better constraint profile than the candidates c₂ in table 1 and in table 2. Because of this comparison, it is obvious that the candidate with the better constraint profile is also grammatical, but marked in a variety that is closer to the codified standard language (e. g. the *Gebrauchsstandard*). On the other hand, candidates with a worse constraint profile (cf. *mit Artikel_* 'with articles', *mit prima Artikel_* 'with great articles') are ungrammatical in a variety close to the codified standard language, but they are still grammatical, but marked in a variety far from the standard language.

type II phrases

For the generation of the set of candidates of type II phrases, the lexemes *all* 'all' and *Artikel* 'article' are used. Table 4 summarizes all OT competitions of the standard as well as of the colloquial varieties with such type II phrases:

Table 4: case variation in type II phrases

candidates	CASESPEC	IDENTPLUR	DATMARK	MARLIN
☞ c_1: (mit) allen Artikeln				
c_2: (mit) allen Artikel			*!	
c_3: (mit) alle Artikeln			*!	*
c_4: (mit) alle Artikel			*!*	
c_5: (mit) all Artikel	*!	*		

The candidate c_1 is optimal since it violates no constraint. The candidate c_2 infringes DATMARK for the noun has no suffix that marks the dative case in plural unambiguously. C_2 does not violate MARLIN because of the fact that the distribution of suffixes in c_2 does not violate the principle of linearization. However, MARLIN is contravened by the candidate c_3 since the noun fulfils DATMARK, but the adjective does not, which runs counter to the principle of linearization of this kind of case marking. Because of that, the constraint profile of c_2 is better than the constraint profile of c_3. The candidate c_4, in turn, has a lower position in the ranking list than c_3 because both its case specified word forms violate DATMARK. At the same time, c_4 does not infringe MARLIN because there is no suffix marking the dative case unambiguously in plural. The candidate c_5, which contains a determiner without a suffix, also has to be taken into consideration.

Since there are no determiners and adjectives with grammatical features, but without a suffix in German (cf. Gallmann 1990: 186), the determiner *all* 'all' is case indifferent. Because of that, it cannot transfer the grammatical feature of case to the noun. Also, there is no genuine case specification as the noun *Artikel* 'articles' in the syntagm *mit all_ Artikel_* 'with all articles' appears without a case suffix. Moreover, c_5 cannot be identified unambiguously as a plural NP given the reading of the determiner *all* 'all' as being singular as well as the reading of *Artikel* 'article(s)' as being an uncountable noun. It can be concluded that c_5 violates the constraints CASESPEC and IDENTPLUR and thus has the worst constraint profile of all candidates.

If table 4 represents the codified standard language, the boundary of grammaticality is between c_1 and c_2. C_1 is grammatical, whereas all other candidates are ungrammatical. The farther a variety is away from the codified standard language, the lower its boundary of grammaticality is in the table and the more candidates are acceptable in this variety. Thus, their position in the ranking indicates their degree of markedness. All these results are caused by the constraints and their ranking. It could be said, for instance, that the boundary of grammaticality of the *Gebrauchsstandard* is between the candidates c_2 and c_3. In this case, c_2 is also grammatical, but more marked than c_1. An example from the *Ge-*

Variation in the case system of German – linguistic analysis and optimality theory 187

brauchsstandard with an adjective instead of a determiner, but else with the same structure as c_2 is, for instance *mit extremistischen Inhalte_* 'with extremist contents' in *Tages-Anzeiger Online* (17.11.08).

type III phrases

The candidates of the following OT competitions consist of the lexemes *einig* 'some', *gut* 'good' and *article* 'article'. Table 5 is an overview of the OT competitions of the standard as well as of the colloquial varieties with such type III phrases:

Table 5: case variation in in type III phrases

candidates	CASESPEC	IDENTPLUR	DATMARK	MARLIN
☞ c_1: (mit) einigen guten Artikeln				
c_2: (mit) einigen guten Artikel			*!	
c_3: (mit) einigen gute Artikeln			*!	*
c_4: (mit) einige guten Artikeln			*!	**
c_5: (mit) einigen gute Artikel			*!*	
c_6: (mit) einige guten Artikel			*!*	*
c_7: (mit) einige gute Artikeln			*!*	**
c_8: (mit) einige gute Artikel			*!**	
c_9: (mit) einig gut Artikel	*!	*		

The candidate c_1 is optimal as it fulfils all constraints. Each one of the candidates c_2, c_3, and c_4 infringes DATMARK once because each candidate has one case specified word form without a suffix that would mark the dative case in plural unambiguously. However, c_2, c_3, and c_4 have a higher position in the ranking list than the candidates c_5, c_6, and c_7 since all of them violate DATMARK twice. The positions in the ranking list of c_2, c_3, and c_4 are based on how many times they violate MARLIN. C_2 fulfils MARLIN, c_3 infringes it once – *Artikeln* 'articles' is marked in accordance with DATMARK, but *gute* 'good' is not – and c_4 violates MARLIN even twice. The reason is that *guten* 'good' as well as *Artikeln* 'articles' are marked according to DATMARK, whereas *einige* 'some' is omitted. The situation of the candidates c_5, c_6, and c_7 is similar as the less a candidate violates MARLIN, the better its position is in the ranking list. Even if the candidate c_8 does not infringe MARLIN – there is no single suffix in this NP marking the dative case in plural unambiguously – , it is placed lower than the aforementioned candidates in the ranking list because it violates DATMARK three times. However, c_8 is placed better than c_9, a candidate that has only case indifferent word forms, so CASESPEC is contravened. C_9 also violates IDENTPLUR since the word *einig* with the meaning of 'united' can also belong to an adjectival lexeme and be understood as being singular.[13]

Finally, table 5 is interpreted with reference to standard and colloquial German. If table 5 represents the OT competition in codified standard German, c_1 is grammatical, whereas all other candidates are ungrammatical. The boundary of grammaticality of the *Gebrauchsstandard* seems to be between c_4 and c_5. If, however, table 5 represents a variety that is far from the standard, the boundary of grammaticality might well be between c_8 and c_9.

5.3 Evaluation

The OT competitions presented in the preceding section illustrate three aspects. First of all, they present the phenomena of case variation as variation of case marking in dative plural NPs. Secondly, the competitions show how all these phenomena have to be established in the continuum of grammaticality, grammatical markedness and ungrammaticality. Thirdly, the competitions make it clear that – when it comes to variation of case marking – standard and colloquial German varieties have identical ranking lists of candidates, but different boundaries of grammaticality. Thus, in a more general sense, OT is an ideal instrument to combine the grammarian's view with the perspective of variational linguistics.

We would now like to bring our analysis to a close by returning to the four types of case variation suggested in section 3. How can these typological types of case variation be applied to the three kinds of dative plural noun phrases introduced in sections 5.1 and 5.2? Those structures in type I phrases that were not part of the OT competitions represent two types of case variation. On the one hand, this variation in the codified standard language is construction-based. As case specification by an adjectivally inflected word form is not possible, there can be genuine case specification or genuine case indifference of the head of the NP. This difference in construction makes it possible for the noun to be either case specified and thus to have a case suffix (cf. *in dreißig Metern Höhe*) or to be case indifferent and thus not to have a case suffix (cf. *in dreißig Meter_ Höhe*). Moreover, these two phenomena can be considered a kind of vari-

---

[13] It might seem slightly odd that c_5 in table 4 and c_9 in table 5 have the same constraint profile as e.g. c_2 in tables 1 and 2. This is contrary to the intuition according to which the two candidates mentioned first are more marked grammatically. In order to differentiate the four candidates, a further constraint with a relatively high position in the constraint ranking is necessary, with the function to punish the presence of inflectable adjectival word forms (i.e. determiners and adjectives) that are not inflected. Furthermore, this constraint is necessary to avoid that e.g. in table 5, a possible candidate such as *mit einig_ gut_ Artikeln* 'with some good articles' is not placed very high in the ranking list of the candidates.

ety-based variation between two style levels in codified standard German. The same two types of case variation in type I phrases can be found in varieties which accept an NP that has a genuinely case indifferent head and that is ungrammatical in the codified standard language. In the *Gebrauchsstandard*, for instance, there is construction-based as well as – due to the presence of style levels – variety-based variation between an NP with a genuinely case specified noun with a case suffix (cf. *mit 80 Artikeln* 'with 80 articles') and an NP with a genuinely case indifferent noun without a case suffix (cf. *mit 80 Artikel_* 'with 80 articles').

Within the standard and colloquial varieties, further phenomena of construction-based variation can be found. This is obvious when NPs with adjectivally inflected word forms and thus with case specification and NPs without any adjectivally inflected word forms and with genuine case indifference are compared: in the codified standard language, there is construction-based variation between dative NPs like *nach vielen Monaten* 'after several months' and *ab drei Monate_* 'as from three months'. In colloquial German, this type of variation can be found between such plural NPs as *mit allen Artikeln* 'with all articles' and *mit Artikel_* 'with articles'. The (non-)appearance of case specification and of the inflectional suffix *-n* correlates with the presence of the noun in a specific syntactic construction. The construction-based variation between case specified and case indifferent nouns does not necessarily have to lead to variation of case forms. In the *Gebrauchsstandard*, for example, an NP with a case specified noun without a suffix and an NP with a genuinely case indifferent noun can also be regarded as construction-based variants.

A further basic type of variation, overlying all competitions, is the variation resulting from the different positions of the boundaries of grammaticality of the varieties in the OT ranking lists above. Variety-based variants are phenomena that are above the boundary of grammaticality in one variety, but below that boundary in another variety. C_2 in table 5, for example, is a variety-based variant as this candidate is acceptable in the *Gebrauchsstandard*, but not acceptable in the codified standard language. Also, we assume that variety-based variation is possible *within* one variety. This can be explained as follows: the candidates that are above the boundary of grammaticality and thus grammatical in a variety show different grammatical markedness. Therefore, these candidates are classified as variants on different style levels of a variety.

6. Final remarks

In the preceding sections, the regularities of case marking in German as well as four types of variation were presented. Then, after introducing OT briefly, we analyzed selected types of phrases by means of OT. It was our aim to demonstrate that OT can also be applied to at the interface of standard and colloquial

German. We showed this by focussing on dative plural NPs, where variation of case marking in standard German and in colloquial German can be analyzed in the same way. Thus, grammatical as well as marked and ungrammatical structures can be identified for all varieties, which differ in the fact that their boundaries of grammaticality have different positions in the ranking list. It remains to examine what further phenomena can be analyzed with the constraints presented in this paper and what further constraints need to be defined (cf. e.g. Giger 2008).

It is obvious that not only case variation in dative plural NPs can be analyzed by means of OT. It can also be used to describe other inflectional variations in the present-day language. This concerns, for instance, the construction-based variation of genitive NPs that are inflected or not inflected: under certain conditions, speakers tend towards omitting the genitive suffix -(e)s in strong masculine and neuter nouns (cf. *des Abkommen_/Abkommens* 'of the agreement' GEN, *des Dativ_/des Dativs* 'of the dative' GEN, *Zweifelsfälle-Duden* 2007: 993 f.). Obviously, there is a conflict between a constraint such as "A noun that is part of the strong inflectional paradigm has to carry the genitive suffix -(e)s" and other constraints referring to the fact that the noun belongs to a specific class (e.g. a foreign word) and determining that these nouns do not have the inflectional suffix -(e)s. These constraints can be formalized analogous to the constraints used for the analysis of case variation in dative plural NPs. They are ordered in a specific constraint hierarchy for competitions so the possible candidates can be in competition with each other. One could also try to cover the aspect of plural forms with the suffix -s (cf. *Pizzen* vs. *Pizzas* 'pizzas'), which occur more and more frequently, by means of OT. To do this, the conditions for the presence of a plural suffix -s in the present-day language have to be examined first of all. Wegener (2007: 44 f.) compiled these conditions in her overview of the "Entwicklungen im heutigen Deutsch" ('developments in present-day German'). Moreover, it is also in the area of sentence structuring that variation can be described by means of OT. Müller (1999) exemplifies this by focussing on the order of the immediate constituents of the clause.

All these OT analyses, however, only focus on codified standard German. By contrast, we have developed an optimality-theoretic approach to cases of variation in codified standard German, in the *Gebrauchsstandard* as well as in colloquial German. We hope that there will be more analyses examining the scope of these varieties by means of OT since there is no doubt that this is the area with the most diversity – and thus with the most competitions between the different candidates.

7. Literature

Ammon, Ulrich. 1995. *Die deutsche Sprache in Deutschland, Österreich und der Schweiz. Das Problem der nationalen Varietäten.* Berlin: de Gruyter.

Barbour, Stephen & Patrick Stevenson. 1990. *Variation in German. A critical approach to German sociolinguistics.* Cambridge: Cambridge University Press.

Businger, Martin. 2010. "Optimalitätstheorie". *Syntax. Grundlagen und Theorien. Mit einem Beitrag von Martin Businger* (UTB 3319) by C. Dürscheid, 154-172. 5th edition. Göttingen: Vandenhoeck & Ruprecht.

Di Meola, Claudio. 1998. "Semantisch relevante und semantisch irrelevante Kasusalternation am Beispiel von 'entlang'". *Zeitschrift für Sprachwissenschaft* 17. 204-235.

Duden. 2007. *Richtiges und gutes Deutsch. Wörterbuch der sprachlichen Zweifelsfälle.* 6th edition, completely revised by Peter Eisenberg. Mannheim & Leipzig & Wien & Zürich: Dudenverlag.

Duden. 2009. *Die Grammatik.* 8th edition, revised. Volume 4. Mannheim & Leipzig & Wien & Zürich: Dudenverlag.

Dürscheid, Christa. 2007. "Quo vadis, Casus? Zur Entwicklung der Kasusmarkierung im Deutschen". *Wahlverwandtschaften. Valenzen – Verben – Varietäten. Festschrift für Klaus Welke zum 70. Geburtstag* ed. H. E. H. Lenk & M. Walter, 89-112. Hildesheim & Zürich & New York: Olms.

Dürscheid, Christa & Inga Hefti. 2006. "Syntaktische Merkmale des Schweizer Standarddeutsch. Theoretische und empirische Aspekte". *Schweizer Standarddeutsch. Beiträge zur Varietätenlinguistik* ed. C. Dürscheid & M. Businger, 131-161. Tübingen: Narr.

Gallmann, Peter. 1990. *Kategoriell komplexe Wortformen. Das Zusammenspiel von Morphologie und Syntax bei der Flexion von Nomen und Adjektiv* (Reihe Germanistische Linguistik 108). Tübingen: Niemeyer.

Gallmann, Peter. 1996. "Die Steuerung der Flexion in der DP". *Linguistische Berichte* 164. 283-314.

Giger, Nadio. 2008. *Kasusvariation im schweizerhochdeutschen Standard und Nonstandard – eine optimalitätstheoretische Betrachtung.* Lizentiatsarbeit Universität Zürich, unpublished.

Hentschel, Elke & Harald Weydt. 2003. *Handbuch der deutschen Grammatik.* Berlin: de Gruyter.

Herrgen, Joachim. 2005. "Sprachgeographie und Optimalitätstheorie. Am Beispiel der *t*-Tilgung in Auslaut-Clustern des Deutschen". *Zeitschrift für Dialektologie und Linguistik* 72. 278-317.

Herrgen, Joachim. 2009. "Varietät und Variation in optimalitätstheoretischer Sicht". *Variatio delectat. Empirische Evidenzen und theoretische Passungen sprachlicher Variation. Klaus J. Mattheier zum 65. Geburtstag* (Vario

Lingua 37) ed. P. Gilles, J. Scharloth & E. Ziegler, 105-123. Frankfurt a. M.: Lang.

Jacobs, Joachim. 2007. "Vom (Un-)Sinn der Schreibvarianten". *Zeitschrift für Sprachwissenschaft* 26. 43-80.

Köpcke, Klaus-Michael. 2005. "Die Prinzessin küsst den Prinz – Fehler oder gelebter Sprachwandel?" *Didaktik Deutsch* 17. 67-83.

Müller, Gereon. 1999. "Optimality, markedness and word order". *Linguistics* 37. 777-818.

Müller, Gereon. 2000. *Elemente der optimalitätstheoretischen Syntax.* Tübingen: Stauffenburg.

Wegener, Heide. 1986. "Gibt es im Deutschen ein indirektes Objekt?". *Deutsche Sprache* 14. 12-22.

Wegener, Heide. 2007. "Entwicklungen im heutigen Deutsch – Wird Deutsch einfacher?". *Deutsche Sprache* 35. 35-62.

Zifonun, Gisela. 2003. "Dem Vater sein Hut. Der Charme des Substandards und wie wir ihm gerecht werden". *Deutsche Sprache* 31. 97-126.

Petra Campe (Ghent)

Syntactic variation in German adnominal constructions
An application to the alternatives 'genitive', 'apposition' and 'compound'

1. Introduction

This paper will illustrate the idea that paradigmatic variation, the network of related structures expressing a similar meaning, can be used as a heuristic tool to identify the prototypical semantics of a certain construction. The case study involves syntactic variation between the German adnominal genitive and apposition on the one hand, and between the genitive and compound on the other. On the basis of a small but fairly representative data base, I intend to argue that an important driving force behind this and probably other types of lexico-syntactic variation is conceptual differentiation. In both cases, alternation is possible, yet a systematic confrontation of the constructions shows that it is subject to a number of restrictions.

To express adnominal relations in German a number of alternating constructions are available such as bare morphological cases, in particular the genitive case as in example (1), prepositions (2), and more peripheral constructions such as apposition (3) or compound (4)[1]:

(1) *die dunklen Augen des^{Gen} jungen Arztes* (Ks:311)
    'the eyes of the young doctor'
(2) *die Menschen im^{Prep} Dorf* (Ks:56)
    'the people in the village'
(3) *in Richtung Parlamentspalast^{App}* (Pf:143)
    'in direction parliament palace'
(4) *Ananassaft^{Comp}* (Ks:14)
    'pineapple juice'

Although linguistic literature often mentions this alternation, no preferential norms are stated. Instead only prototypical tendencies towards a certain construction in certain contexts are given (e.g. Duden 1998: 672 or Zifonun et al. 1997: 1981 for the variation genitive – apposition). Though one could interpret these tendencies as norms, no explanation is provided, neither for the norm nor

---
[1] The examples in this paper are mainly excerpted from novels, the full references of which can be found in the bibliography.

for the deviations from the norm (which can be regarded as variation). It is therefore the main goal of this paper to show that the prototypical semantics of each alternating construction can provide an explanation for the fundamental strategy underlying the alternation and variation. Questions such as 'what semantic elements does the speaker wish to focus on?' or 'what does he/she really want to express?' seem to guide the choice for a certain construction. The semantic similarity of the paradigmatic alternatives conversely does allow (peripheral) variation. The present analysis, which is based on empirical data, will consider major tendencies detected in these data as norms, and minor tendencies as instances of variation.

Before I embark on the actual analysis, a brief introduction of theme, goals and methodology of its larger research framework, which focuses on the grammatical coding of adnominal relations in general, is in order. For this research, I started from the morphological genitive case. A long tradition of research into case-marked languages has revealed that cases that were once autonomous often in a later stage of the language coincide with others. Or, when the number remains the same, the semantic-conceptual field that is covered by the individual cases can vary from one stage of the language to the other. During this conceptual reorganisation, the role of morphological cases ('synthetic cases') is often strengthened or even taken over by prepositions ('analytical cases') or other constructions such as apposition or compounding. An illustration of this phenomenon in Modern German is the putative fact that the adnominal genitive construction is gradually giving way to prepositional coding (5, 6), discussed for example by Weier (1968: 239).

(5) a. *sich einer^{Gen} Sache erinnern*
'to remember oneself of something'
b. *sich an^{Prep} eine Sache erinnern*
'to remember (at) something'
(6) a. *die Schönheit Laures^{Gen}*
'the beauty Laure's'
b. *die Schönheit von^{Prep} Laure* (Pf:259)
'the beauty of Laure'

Other linguists, as for instance Brinkmann (1971: 68-69), however still attribute an individual meaning to the genitive, delimiting this case from other adnominal constructions (7):

(7) *der Genitiv [hat] im substantivischen Bereich seinen Platz. Substantive werden miteinander durch den Genitiv verknüpft. Das ist heute die legitime Verwendung des Kasus. Sie grenzt sich allerdings gegen andere sprachliche Möglichkeiten ab, substantivische Begriffe aufeinander zu beziehen (…). Der Wert dieser Möglichkeiten wird (abgesehen vom In-*

halt der beteiligten Substantive) von der Leistung der dabei eingesetzten sprachlichen Gebilde bestimmt (my profiling, P. C.).
'the genitive [has] its own place in the nominal field. Nouns are joined by means of the genitive. That is the present legitimate use of the case. Its use contrasts, however, with other linguistic possibilities to relate nominal concepts to one another (...). The value of these possibilities is (apart from the contents of the nouns) determined by the used linguistic construction'

In order to substantiate Brinkmann's thesis, a systematic confrontation between the genitive and its linguistic alternatives or competitors is required. At a more abstract level, the analysis of these alternatives aims at providing empirical evidence for the basic theoretical assumption, 1) that syntax and therefore also syntactic variation is generally semantically motivated and 2) that the systematic investigation of the paradigmatic alternation potential of a construction is an efficient, even necessary instrument to pinpoint its semantic essence. Previous research illustrated the intimate relationship between conceptualisation and linguistic coding with respect to the genitive and its prepositional alternatives (Campe 1997, 1998). This paper will focus on the more peripheral alternatives of the apposition (chapter 1) and the compound (chapter 2). Only through the delimitation of the differences between the genitive and its competitors, the position of this case in the adnominal field can be fully ascertained.

2. Apposition: exhaustivity versus holisticity

Although the variation between genitive and apposition[2] is more restricted than the one between genitive and prepositions, the genitive does alternate with an apposition: especially the quantitative genitive, as in example (8), and the related genitives of material and of content[3], as in (9):

---

[2] The examples in this chapter illustrate the construction traditionally called 'apposition', more in particular the 'restrictive apposition' ['enge Apposition', e.g. Flämig (1991: 128)] or 'partitive apposition' (e.g. Gallmann 2007: 4), as opposed to 'non-restrictive appositions' of the following kind: 'Herr Mertens, der Koch' ('Mr. Mertens, the cook'). Restrictive or partitive appositions are sometimes more preferably categorised as (separately written) 'compounds' (cf. chapter 2; see Guelpa 1995 for a detailed discussion) or 'juxtapositions' (cf. Joosten & Vermeire 2004: 4). For a crosslinguistic definition of 'compound', see Donalies (2003).

[3] Though closely related to the quantitative genitive, the genitive of material codes a relation between an object and its constituting material (*'einen Geysir braungurgelnden Wassers'* (Ks:374) 'a geyser of brown splashing water') rather than a relation between a mere quantity and its comprising whole: "die Maßeinheit gibt Auskunft darüber, in welcher Form das Gemessene oder Gezählte in Erscheinung tritt: über einen Aggregatzustand, über eine Dimension oder einfach über eine Form" (Eisenberg 1994: 257) ('the mass unit provides information about the formal appearance of the measured or

(8) *in einem Glas Wassers*^{Gen} (Pf:74)/*in einem Glas Wasser*^{App}
     'in a glass of water/in a glass water'
(9) a. *ein Strom heißen Bleis*^{Gen} (Ks:145)/*heißes Blei*^{App} (material)
        'a flow of hot lead/hot lead'
     b. *einen Schwarm kleiner Fische* (Ks:324)/*kleine Fische* (content)
        'a swarm of small fish/small fish'

For this alternation, the basic questions to be answered are: 'are these constructions freely interchangeable or not?'; 'is one construction perhaps more prominent than the other (norm vs. variation)'? and most importantly, 'what is the underlying factor?'.

A quantitative relation can be narrowed down to a relation between two nouns (N1-N2), in cognitive linguistic terms[4], a trajector (TR) and a landmark (LM), where the TR (N1) constitutes a quantified part of the LM (N2). It is essesential for a quantitative relation that the LM is a *multiplex, externally bounded* entity. Figure 1, taken from Talmy (1988: 181), visualises what is meant by the terms 'multiplexity', as opposed to 'uniplexity', and 'bounded' as opposed to 'unbounded'. These categories obviously relate to the traditional opposition between count and mass nouns. A more detailed system of attributes concerning a quantity's disposition is, however, needed for the description of quantitative relations and their grammatical coding. In short, the opposition uniplex/multiplex relates to a quantity's state of articulation into *equivalent* elements. A referent is *uniplex*, when it consists of only one such element, as the small *a* in Figure 1:

---

counted entity: a condition of aggregateness, a dimension or merely a form'). The genitive of content (*zu einem Haufen glühender Äste* (Ks:206) 'to a stack of glowing branches') is the counterpart of the material genitive, relating to a discrete multiplex (*ein Ast – mehrere Äste* 'a/one branch – several branches') rather than a continuous multiplex LM (*Wasser* 'water') (see infra). Paradigmatic alternation potential differentiates these genitives from the quantitative genitive: a paraphrase with the preposition *aus* ('out of') and with an existential verb (e.g. *bilden* 'form/build') is possible. The genitive of content furthermore allows a paraphrase with *mit* (*ein Strauß duftender/mit duftenden Rosen* (Dd 4: 646) 'a bouquet of smelling/with smelling roses'). Both genitives contain a classifying aspect (*Strauß = Rosen; Geysir = Wasser*) and are both mensural and sortal, which is not the case for the quantitative genitive.

[4] Cf. e.g. Langacker (1987). "The notions of trajectory (TR) and landmark (LM) date back to the Gestalt psychology distinction between figure and ground. Foregrounded parts in a scene or in a conceptual domain are called *figure*, and those which are downplayed are termed *ground*. Cognitive linguists like (...) Langacker (1987) have applied these notions to the description of language. This has yielded a parallelism between figure and trajector on the one hand, and between ground and landmark on the other. Thus, the TR is the profiled or highlighted entity, while the LM merely acts as a reference point for the TR. It usually happens that the LM is bigger in size and it gets a relative fixity of location, as opposed to the TR" (Peña Cervel 1998-99:263).

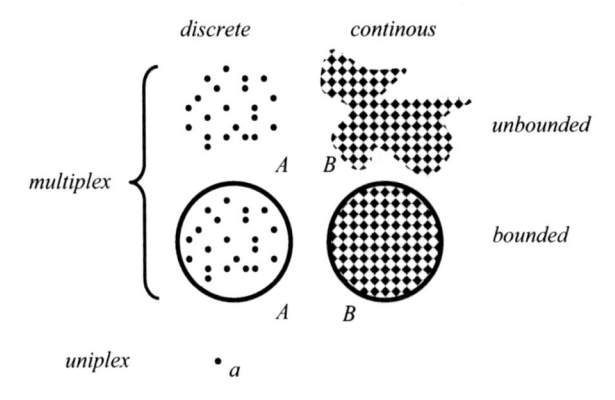

```
                discrete        continous
              ⎧   ·· ·· ·         ░░░░
              ⎪   · · ·         ░░░░░░      unbounded
              ⎪   ·· ·· ·        ░░░░░
   multiplex  ⎨      A       B
              ⎪     ╱· ·╲        ▓▓▓
              ⎪    ( · · )      ▓▓▓▓▓       bounded
              ⎪     ╲· ·╱        ▓▓▓
              ⎩      A             B

   uniplex    • a
```

Figure 1: Multiplexity vs. uniplexity

A person or a chair are examples of uniplex entities. A referent is, however, *multiplex* when it can be divided into several equivalent elements, as for example *water* can be. Many abstract nouns, for example 'friendship' or 'displeasure', correspond to concrete multiplex nouns, as the increase and division of their referents invariably yield a similar kind of predication. The concept of boundedness relates to the question whether the multiplex entity is conceptualised as an individual entity, that is as quantitatively bounded, for example 'this (glass of) water', or as continuing indefinitely and therefore as unbounded, as in 'water'. The boundedness of the entity can be inherent (internal), as in 'group'. Talking about a group implies talking about an inherently limited number of people. On the other hand, an entity can also be bounded externally, as in '*the* water' or '*a glass of* water'. Besides the opposition boundedness/unboundedness, the internal structure of multiplex referents is of importance. The referent is *discrete*, when its composition is conceptualised as having breaks, interruptions, as is the case with 'group' or 'furniture'. Otherwise it is identified as being *continuous*, for example 'water' or 'butter'.

It is essential for a quantitative relation that the LM is a multiplex (continuous or discrete), externally bounded entity, as in examples (10-11). Typically these entities become *referential* through *external bounding* and bounding takes place through quantification, either by means of an (in)definite article or a pronoun, as in example (10) ('*the* women') or by means of a quantitative adnominal construction like the genitive in (11) ('a piece *of*'):

(10) (*die größte*) *der*[Gen] *Frauen und Mädchen* (Ks:16)
     [LM= externally bounded discrete multiplexity]
     '(the tallest of) the women and girls'

(11) (*der Geruch*) *eines Stücks silberbestickten*^{Gen} *Brokats* (Pf:45)
[LM= externally bounded continuous multiplexity]
'(the smell of) a piece of silver-embroidered brocade'

Quantitative relations should be distinguished from partitive relations, as in (12-13), in which the TR constitutes a part, not a quantity of the LM. The difference between a quantitative relation as in (10-11), and a partitive relation, as in (12), in which the LM is a uniplexity, is straightforward. In (13), however, the LM is a multiplexity that is inherently bounded. The TR therefore cannot instantiate the LM: each of the gentlemen is not 'a council', whereas the piece in (11) instantiates the brocade, therefore is itself brocade:

(12) *die dunklen Augen des*^{Gen} *jungen Arztes* (Ks:311)
[LM = uniplexity]
'the dark eyes of the young doctor'

(13) *die stolzen, mächtigen Herren des*^{Gen} *Stadtrats* (Pf:251)
[LM = inherently bounded discrete multiplexity]
'the proud, powerful gentlemen of the city council'

Although the genitives in (8-9/10-11) are traditionally called 'partitive genitives', I prefer the term 'quantitative genitives', to avoid confusion with the genitives in (12-13), which also express a 'part-of'-relation and which I thus call 'partitive genitives'. This semantic difference is supported by the paradigmatic potential of both constructions: whereas the quantitative relation can be paraphrased with an appositive construction (14) quite easily rather than with the preposition 'in', the opposite can be said of the partitive construction in (13), as is illustrated in (15):

(14) a. *ein Stück *in*^{Prep} *besticktem Brokat*
'a piece *in embroidered brocade'
b. *ein Stück bestickter*^{App} *Brokat*
'a piece embroidered brocade'

(15) a. *die Herren im*^{Prep} *Rat*
'the gentlemen in the council'
b. *die Herren *Rat*$^{App.}$
'the gentlemen *council'

Two important properties of the partitive semantics of the genitive are:

1. Its use imposes a stable, static relation between the referents of two entities. This relation is lasting, often permanent. When a dynamic, mutational element is implied, a prepositional phrase has to be used (16).
2. Its use enables conceptualisation of an intrinsic, inherent relation between two entities (17). For instance, a 'top' of something can hardly be conceptualised without referring to the relevant whole which it is a permanent part of.

Because of this intrinsicness, the genitive has to be used and a prepositional phrase is hardly possible:

(16) *die Fahrt *der^{Gen}/in^{Prep} der Stadt*
 'the drive *of/in the city'
(17) *der Gipfel eines^{Gen} 2000 Meter hohen Vulkans* (Pf:152)/*?*auf^{Prep} einem 2000 Meter hohen Vulkan*
 'the top of/*?on a 2000 meter high volcano'

A consequence of these components of stability and intrinsicness of the genitive semantics is for the relation between TR and LM to work holistically and to involve the totality of the LM. On the one hand, this holisticity contrasts with the fragmentary nature of the prepositional relation, which aims at a mere individual localisation of the TR with respect to the LM, as is illustrated in (18). Whereas the genitive encodes the fact that this person visited the whole of South-Africa, i.e. the most important places all over this country, the prepositional construction expresses a visit that was probably limited to one South African region. Similarly, the relation between a rector and his university is a unique one: a university usually has only one rector. Prepositional coding is therefore less likely (19a). If, however, this one university is compared to other universities, the function of rector becomes less unique, which seems to allow a PP (19b). The relation between a professor and a university is, by contrast, not at all unique: his function relates to a part of the university, not to the university as a whole. Consequently, a PP is preferred (19c), unless the relation is narrowed down to a (more or less) unique one, through the use of e.g. a superlative or the adjective 'whole' (19d):

(18) *sein Besuch Südafrikas^{Gen} >< sein Besuch in^{Prep} Südafrika*
 'his visit of South Africa >< his visit in South Africa'
(19) a. *er ist der Rektor der^{Gen}/??an^{Prep} der Universität Gent* (+ Holisticity)
 'he is rector of the/??at the university Ghent'
 b. *er ist Rektor dieser^{Gen}/an^{Prep} dieser Universität* (+/- Holisticity)
 'he is rector of this/at this university'
 c. *er ist Professor ?der^{Gen}/an^{Prep} der Universität Gent* (- Holisticity)
 'he is professor ?of the/at the university Ghent'
 d. *er ist der mächtigste Professor der^{Gen}/?an^{Prep} der ganzen Universität*
 (+ Holisticity)
 'he is the most powerful professor of the/?at the whole university'

On the other hand, the holisticity of the genitive, more particularly of the quantitative genitive, contrasts with the exhaustiveness of the appositive construction. The absence of a determiner for the LM allows the LM to be a nonreferential, ungrounded noun, which relates to a type rather than to an instance. The mass noun *Kilo* in (20) does not elicit a partitive relation, but encodes an individual quantity, which takes its shape from the type of material indicated by the LM. The TR relates to the LM exhaustively and instantiates it. The TR and LM of the genitive construction, however, usually relate to two interdependent entities. The genitive LM has a restricting reference point function with respect to the TR. A dependency relation is expressed, whereas the apposition focuses on an equality relation. This remains the case, when the genitive LM is not determined by an (in)definite article or pronoun, as in (21) (cf. Leys 1998: 10). The alternation between genitive and apposition is the purest in this case.[5] The genitive LM refers to a (subcategory of a) type, as does the appositive LM. Notice, however, the fact that the genitive LM cannot be separated from the TR (dependency relation), whereas the appositive LM can (equality relation) (22a), as well as the fact that the appositive LM has a strong and not a weak ending, which would indicate a dependency relation (22b). For the encoding of the mere quantitative relation in (21) and the material relation in (23), the genitive and the apposition are rather unmarked alternatives, since the semantic aspects of quantification and exhaustivity are in balance. This is not the case, however, for the genitive of content as in (24), which is preferred here, because the unity[6] expressed by the

---

[5] The genitive is morphologically impossible in the case of feminine and plural bare nouns (*ein Kilo *Butter*^{Gen}/*Bohnen^{Gen} 'a kilo *butter/*beans'), so that a (case indifferent) apposition is obligatory (*ein Kilo Butter*^{App}/*Bohnen*^{App}). Genitive and apposition are here in complementary distribution. According to Behaghel (1923-32: 532) this substitution goes back to the 15th century, since when a number of genitives lost the morphological -*s* ending, which led to case syncretism (nominative/accusative). By analogy, singular male and neutral bare nouns prefer the apposition to the genitive (*ein Liter ?Wassers*^{Gen}/*Wasser*^{App} 'a litre ?of water/water'). In the case of an undetermined LM modified by an adjective, the apposition is often preferred as well. Formally, Duden (1985: 463/4) claims that in case of a nominative, accusative or dative TR, the apposition is preferred (*mit 30 Kisten lagerfähigen*^{App} *Äpfeln* 'with 30 boxes non-perishable apples'); the relation between a dative singular TR and a plural LM is however preferably coded by a genitive or a nominative (*der Erlös aus einem Zentner lagerfähiger*-^{Gen}/*lagerfähige*^{Nom} *Äpfel* 'the gains of 50 kg of non-perishable/non-perishable apples') and a genitive TR is preferably combined with a genitive (*der Preis eines Pfundes (selten: Pfund) gekochten*^{Gen} *Schinkens* 'the price of a pound (seldom: pound) of boiled ham'). In linguistic literature it is often claimed that the genitive is preferred in more formal language ("Allerdings tritt, besonders bei Erweiterung des zweiten Gliedes, in gehobener Sprache nicht selten das alte Genitivverhältnis deutlich hervor: (...) *vor einem Glas leidlich trinkbaren Bieres*, (...) *eine Kanne heißen Wassers*" [Guelpa 1995:345-46] 'In formal language however, especially in case of modification of the second constituent, frequently the old genitival relation is clearly more prominent'.) For an overview of the results of a survey of native speaker intuitions and the role of number/gender of the appositional case congruence, see Hentschel (1993).

[6] The function of the TR here is to connect the individual entities of the LM to build a unity. This unification is subjectively enforced by the speaker, who actually organises the referential jumble of the LM mentally through the TR. The conceptual principle underlying this unification is called 'closure' ('Gestaltschließung'). That both aspects

collective TR-noun is opposed to the multiplexity of discrete entities referred to by the LM. For this reason, the partitive semantics seem to prevail over the exhaustivity semantics in this relation:

(20) *ein Kilo Butter^{App} >< ein Kilo dieser^{Gen} Butter >< ein Kilo *diese^{App} Butter*
 'a kilo butter >< a kilo of this butter >< a kilo *this butter'
(21) *auf eigenen kleinen Parzellen Landes^{Gen}* (Pf:221)/*Land^{App}, ein Kilo echter^{Gen}/echte^{App} Butter*
 'on own small plots of land/land; a kilo of real butter/real butter'
(22) a. (*Echte^{App}/*echter^{Gen}*) *Butter habe ich heute schon 2 Kilo verarbeitet.*
 '(real/*of real) butter I have used already 2 kilo today'
 b. *die drei Pfund rote/*roten Äpfel* (Bhatt 1990:56)
 'the three pounds red apples'
(23) *in einer riesigen Sintflut destillierten^{Gen} Wassers* (Pf:159)/*destilliertes^{App} Wasser*
 'in a gigantic flood of distilled water/distilled water'
(24) a. *ein Strauß duftender^{Gen} (seltener) duftende^{App} Rosen* (Dd 4:646)
 'a bouquet of smelling (seldom) smelling roses'
 b. *eine Horde (randalierender^{Gen}) Halbstarker (seltener) (randalierende^{App}) Halbstarke* (ibid.)
 'a horde of (noisy) rowdies (seldom) (noisy) rowdies'

It is noteworthy that the exhaustive quantifiers *alle*, *sämtliche* and *beide*[7] ('all'/ 'both') cannot be used with a genitive, as is shown in (25), because the genitive fundamentally expresses a partitive relation, albeit a holistic one. The genitive always has a reference-limiting effect, as in (26), which is not compatible with

---

(unity/multiplexity) are important is grammatically evident in that a singular or a plural verb can follow the NP: *ein Haufen faulender (...) Orangen lag/lagen auf dem Tisch* (Dd Wtb: 1156) 'a stack of rotting oranges lies/lie on the table'. Inherently bounded multiplex nouns like *Haufen* are traditionally called 'collective nouns'. For a detailed study of collective nouns and relationality (in Dutch), see Joosten & Vermeire (2004).

[7] *Beide* contrasts with 'all', in that it partly has a different syntactic behaviour: "Als pränominales Element links von der lexikalischen Nominaleinheit steht das flektierte bzw. unflektierte ALL- am Anfang der NG, auch wenn andere Determinantien in der NG vorhanden sind (...). ALL- unterscheidet sich in dieser Hinsicht auch von den beiden übrigen sog. Allquantoren, da *beid-* und *jed-* nicht immer in Anfangsstellung der NG vorkommen, z.B. *die/meine beiden; ein jeder* (Schanen 1993: 43) [versus *die allen (*Kinder*) 'the all children']. – As a prenominal element on the left side of the lexical nominal entity, the inflected or noninflected ALL- has its position at the beginning of the NP, even if other determinants are present (...). ALL- differs in this respect from both other so-called all-quantifiers, since *beid-* and *jed-* do not always occur in an initial position: e.g. *die/meine beiden; ein jeder* ('the/my both; each one'). *Sämtlich* behaves as *beid-* and *jed-* (*die sämtlichen Brücken* 'the whole bridges').

the fundamental meaning of exhaustive quantifiers like 'all' or 'both'[8]. The latter only occur in a genitive construction when they are used as determiners of the TR-noun, so that the exhaustivity refers to the TR only, and not to the (partitive) relation between TR and LM (27). Example (28) illustrates the fact that in the case of uniplex LMs exhaustive quantitative relations with 'all' are encoded prepositionally.[9] The opposition between the reference restricting genitive and the non-restrictive, exhaustive apposition is also highlighted by partitive-like constructions as in (29). Since the TR refers to an identified entity, the genitive is not allowed (cf. Bhatt 1990: 151):

---

[8] This does not imply, that a similar construction is impossible in German. In this respect Paul (1959: 294) indicates the following: "Ungehörig wird der Gen. Partitivus verwendet, wo die Quantität des Gen. und des regierenden Wortes sich decken, vgl. *Alle drei seiner Bundesgenossen* Gutzkow, R.8, 206, *fast alle der wohlhabenden Bürger* Tieck 20, 418" 'Inappropriately the Gen. Partitivus is used, when the quantity of the Gen. and of the head noun is equal, cf. *all three of his allies; almost all of the prosperous citizens*'. That in these examples the quantifiers *drei* and *fast* may have elicited the use of the genitive could be of importance. Behaghel (1923: 493) however claims that in earlier stages of the German and especially Gothic languages, the genitive was not unusual in this kind of contexts.

[9] The preposition *an* profiles an extrinsic, exhaustive 'contact'-relation (*eine Rekordmenge an qualitativem Heroin* [GN 27/02/99] 'a record quantity (at) qualitative heroin'), as opposed to the intrinsic partitive relation of the genitive (*eine Rekordmenge qualitativen Heroins* 'a record quantity of qualitative heroin') and the mere exhaustive relation expressed by the apposition (*eine Rekordmenge qualitatives Heroin* 'a record quantity qualitative heroin'). Cf. Campe (1999: 367-69) for details on the abstract use of 'an' and this preposition's variation with the genitive. Interestingly in English the quantifiers 'all' and 'both' can be used appositively – as well as with the genitive-like *of*-construction: *all (the) bridges/all of the bridges; both (the) bridges/both of the bridges*. With respect to the first example, Langacker (1992: 485) argues as follows: "*All* profiles a mass, whose relation to the reference mass is one of *coincidence*, that is, it exhausts the reference mass. Thus for *all* (...) the subpart relation between the masses fails to quality as a proper one – the degree to which the profiled mass is *restricted* vis-à-vis the reference mass is zero". It thus seems that here the German language is more consequent than English (as is Dutch: *al(le)/beide *van^{Gen} de bruggen* >< *al de^{App} – de beide^{App} bruggen*), as it does not allow the genitive construction after exhaustive quantifiers. Not only the Germanic, but also the Romance languages have different perspectives in this respect: whereas Latin allows apposition and genitive (*omnes – uterque homines^{App}/hominum^{Gen}*), French has only the appositive construction (*tous les^{App} ponts; tous ponts^{App} confondus* >< *tous *des$^{\pm Gen}$ ponts*). A similar case is the (im)possibility of genitive/apposition in exhaustive explicative relations in different languages: *die Stadt Köln^{App}/*Kölns^{Gen}* (city = Cologne) >< *the city (of) Cologne, der Monat Mai^{App}/*Mais^{Gen}* >< *the month (of) May*; however *das Wort Einsamkeit^{App}/*der Einsamkeit^{Gen}* ~ *the word loneliness/*of loneliness* >< *la ville (de) Cologne, le mot (de) solitude* (for details on the classifying genitive and its restricted alternation with the appositive construction, cf. infra and Campe 1999: 411-417).

(25) alle/sämtliche/beide *der^{Gen} Brücken; alle/sämtliche/beide Brücken^{App}
'all/all/both *of the bridges; all/all/both bridges'
(26) einige/zwei/mehrere der^{Gen} Brücken >< einige/zwei/mehrere Brücken^{App}
'some/two/several of the bridges >< some/two/several bridges'
(27) a. alle Häuser und Geschäfte des^{Gen} (...) Dorfes (Ks:233)
'all houses and shops of the village'
b. auf sämtlichen Brücken der^{Gen} Stadt Paris (Pf:144)
'on all bridges of the city Paris'
c. zu beiden Seiten des^{Gen} Portals (Pf:196)
'to both sides of the porch'
(28) wie alles *dieses^{Gen} Bootes >< alles an^{Prep} diesem Boot (Ks:126)
'as everything *of this boat >< at this boat'
(29) a. uns heutigen^{App}/*heutiger^{Gen} Menschen (...) leuchtet das sofort ein (Pf:129)
'us contemporary people/*of contemporary people (...) comprehend that immediately'
b. ich alter^{App} Mann/*alten^{Gen} Mannes
'I old man/*of old man'

Another interesting opposition in this respect is the one in (30): although *beide* and *zwei* both refer to 'two' entities, the exhaustive quantifier *beide* can only be used appositively and not with a genitive. The partitive quantifier *zwei* by contrast can only be used with a genitive, since the apposition elicits a semantic change: *zwei Freunde*:

(30) beide *meiner^{Gen}/meine^{App} Freunde >< zwei meiner^{Gen}/*meine^{App} Freunde
'both *of my/both my friends >< two of my/two *my friends'

Whereas the collective, exhaustive semantics of 'all' or 'both' is not compatible with the partitive semantics of the genitive, the genitive is allowed if this exhaustivity is conceptualised in a non-collectivising way. Consider example (31), in which the indefinite pronoun *jeder* (also *jeglicher* or *jedermann* ['each']) refers to an exhaustive class, as do 'all' and 'both'. With this pronoun a group, however, is not conceptualised collectively, but in an individualising way, since one particular individual is introduced as representing the whole group. Figure 2 visualises this opposition between collective and non-collective exhaustivity.

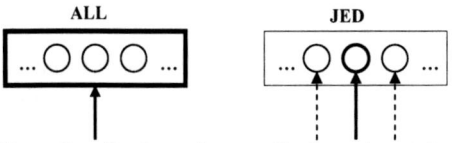

Figure 2: collective and non-collective exhaustivity

In accordance with this individualising conceptualisation the pronoun *jeder* is used with a singular verb and a singular noun in the appositive construction, as is illustrated in (32) and unlike 'all' *jeder* allows a certain variation, which enforces its non-collectivising meaning: *jeder* can also be coded as *ein jeder* or *jeder einzelne* ('each one'/'each individual[ly]') (33):

(31) *jedes der^{Gen} Kinder*
 'each (one) of the children'
(32) *jedes Kind^{App} hat >< alle Kinder^{App} haben das bestätigt*
 'each child has >< all children have affirmed that'
(33) *ein jedes/jedes einzelne der^{Gen} Kinder*
 'each one/every single one of the children'

The quantitative genitive in (31) does not only alternate with the exhaustive apposition in (32), but also with a construction with *unter* (34). In the prototypical spatial use of this preposition (35), its LM is a concept that has a certain expanse and both covers and encompasses the referent of the TR. In example (34), which uses *unter* in a figurative sense, the semantic elements of covering and encompassing are relevant. The search domain of the preposition, which prototypically constitutes a region underneath the LM, is taken here as the interior of a set of entities which comprises the LM. In other words, the *unter*-LM refers to the group, in which the TR is enclosed. Precisely this localising semantic component of 'being enclosed by, in the middle of' distinguishes the prepositional from the genitival use. Note that the semantic aspect of enclosure blocks the use of *unter* in the case of a bipartite or a bipartitely conceptualised LM, as in examples (36-37). An exhaustive apposition is, however, possible:

(34) a. *jedes der^{Gen} Kinder/unter^{Prep} den Kindern*
 'each of the children/under (among) the children'
 b. *der angesehenste der^{Gen} Parfumeure/unter^{Prep} den Parfumeuren*
 (Pf:189; PP) 'the most respected of/under (among) the perfumers'
(35) *eine Bank unter^{Prep} dem Chor* (Pf:198)
 'a bench under(neath) the choir'
(36) *am rechten der^{Gen} beiden Leiterholme* (Ks:17)/*unter^{Prep} den beiden Leiterholmen/am rechten Leiterholm*
 'at the right (one) of (the)/*under (among) (the) both ladder stiles/at the right ladder stile'
(37) *die mittlere der^{Gen} (...) Hütten* (Ks:297)/*unter^{Prep} den (...) Hütten/die mittlere Hütte*
 'the middle of/*under (among) the cabins/the middle cabin'

The semantic component of 'being enclosed by, in the middle of' finally implies a non-uniqueness, which is connected with the concept of inconspicuousness. In (38), the prepositional alternative implies 'just one (fish) of many, nothing important', whereas the meaning of the genitive is merely quantitative. The semantic difference is even clearer if the TR is not a mere quantifier, but the same NP as in the LM (39). The prepositional variant locates a certain type of fish among the many other types of fish; inconspicuousness is expressed. The genitive, however, expresses an intrinsic part/whole-relation and no inconspicuousness, and is therefore hardly possible in this context. Therefore the genitive is possible and even preferred if the opposite, conspicuousness, is expressed, as in (40). This kind of genitive, called the 'intensifying genitive', refers to the prototype, the most important and therefore intrinsic instantiation of the type named in the LM. The prepositional variant (which is less likely here) on the other hand profiles the individual status of this particular important fish, as against other kinds of ordinary fish (40). An appositive construction lacks both connotations (*ein Fisch* ['one fish']):

(38) *einer der*^{Gen} *Fische/unter*^{Prep} *den Fischen*
'one of the fish/under (among) the fish'
(39) ??*ein Fisch der*^{Gen} *Fische* → *einer der*^{Gen} *Fische* >< *ein Fisch unter*^{Prep} *den Fischen* (Ks:56)
'??a fish of the fish → one of the fish >< a fish under (among) the fish'
(40) *der Fisch der*^{Gen} *Fische* >< *der Fisch ?unter*^{Prep} *den Fischen*
'the fish of the fish >< the fish ?under (among) the fish'

The genitives of material and of content are related to the (rather peripheral) classificational genitive, as in (41). A classification relation typically obtains if the referent of the TR hyperonymically predicates the genitive-marked LM, which refers to the 'Geltungsbereich' (categorical membership) of the TR's referent. The NP can alternate with a predicative construction with e.g. *sein* or *bilden* (devocalisation is a characteristic). Since the LM of a genitival classificational relation is typically abstract in nature, the referential difference between e.g. 'devocalisation' and 'the devocalisation' is obviously smaller than between 'butter' and 'this butter'. Unsurprisingly, the appositive paraphrase evokes a smaller semantic change than the quantifying genitive with a definite LM (a kilo butter >< of this butter). Still, both constructions are not always interchangeable, even if variation is possible. In (42) the function of the apposition seems to be limited to the scientific-categorial character of the LM's referent (Hackel 1971: 143). The apposition seems to have a kind of name giving effect (equational, exhaustive relation), whereas the genitive profiles a partitive, holistic relation. In a number of cases, the apposition has a disambiguating effect with respect to the genitive alternative (43):

(41) a. *das Merkmal der^{Gen} Stimmlosigkeit/Stimmlosigkeit^{App}* (Engelen 1990: 5)
'the characteristic of devocalisation/devocalisation'
b. *der Begriff der^{Gen} Gewaltenteilung/Gewaltenteilung^{App}* (ibid.)
'the concept of separation of powers/separation of powers'
(42) a. *vom Gefühl Liebe^{App} gibt es unzählige Beispiele* (Hackel 1971: 143)
'of the feeling love there are countless examples'
b. *die Mutter wurde vom Gefühl *Liebe^{App}/der^{Gen} Liebe überwältigt* (id.: 144)
'the mother was overwhelmed by the feeling *love/of (the) love'
(43) a. *der Hauptfeind des^{Gen} Faschismus* (Hackel 1971: 144)
'the main enemy of fascism' (→ fascism has an enemy >< is an enemy)
b. *der Hauptfeind Faschismus^{App}*
'the main enemy fascism' (→ fascism is an enemy)

Not all classificational genitives can easily be turned into an apposition. In (44a) an appositive paraphrase is hardly possible. At best, a non-restrictive apposition can be used, as in (44b). Instantiated (concrete) genitive LMs can hardly be paraphrased appositively (45). Accordingly, the non-referential *Hund* in the apposition in (46) becomes referential in its genitival counterpart, resulting in ungrammaticality:

(44) a. *die Tugend der^{Gen} Beharrlichkeit/*?Beharrlicheit^{App}*
'the virtue of perseverance/*?perseverance'
b. *diese Tugend, ?Beharrlichkeit^{App}/die Beharrlichkeit, eine lobenswerte Tugend^{App}*
'this virtue, ?perseverance/the perseverance, a praiseworthy virtue'
(45) a. *das helle Dreieck des^{Gen} Buchteingangs* (Ks:30)/*Buchteingang^{App}*
'the bright triangle of the bay-entrance/*bay-entrance'
b. *an dem kleinen farbigen Fleck seines^{Gen} Kopfputzes* (Ks:39)/*Kopfputz^{App}*
'at the small colourful spot of his headdress/*headdress'
(46) *das Wort Hund^{App}/*des Hundes^{Gen}*
'the word dog/*of the dog'

Quantifying and classificational appositions need to be distinguished from those in (47-50). The apposition illustrated in these examples has two subcategories: the explicative (47) and the determinative one (48), both combining a definite TR with a proper name or a generic noun used as proper name. Whereas the former is not interchangeable with a genitive (only an identifying relation is expressed, cf. 47), the latter is. If variation is possible, this is the result of a metonymic extension from an individual partitive reference point function (genitive) to a name-giving function (apposition) (48). This becomes clear in the syntactic behaviour of both constructions. For the examples in (47) a non-restrictive apposition (between commas) is possible (49a), whereas a construction with a qualifying adjective is not (50a). For the examples in (48), by contrast, a non-restrictive apposition is not possible (49b), whereas a construction with a qualifying adjective is (50b). The examples in (51) show how the apposition functions as a name and the genitive as an entity:

(47) a. *die Stadt Köln^{App}/*Kölns^{Gen}*
 'the city Cologne/*of Cologne'
 b. *die Bundeskanzlerin Merkel^{App}/*Merkels^{Gen}*
 'the chancellor Merkel/*of Merkel'
(48) a. *der Flughafen Köln^{App}/Kölns^{Gen}*
 'the airport Cologne/of Cologne'
 b. *die Regierung Merkel^{App}/Merkels^{Gen}*
 'the government Merkel/of Merkel'
 c. *in Richtung Parlamentspalast^{App}/des^{Gen} Parlamentspalastes* (Pf:143)
 'in direction parliament palace/of the parliament palace'
(49) a. *die Bundeskanzlerin Merkel^{App}/Merkel, die Bundeskanzlerin*
 'the chancellor Merkel/Merkel, the chancellor'
 b. *die Regierung Merkel^{App}/*Merkel, die Regierung*
 'the government of Merkel/*Merkel, the government'
(50) a. *die Merkelsche^{Adj} Regierung*
 'the Merkelian government'
 b. *die *Merkelsche^{Adj} Bundeskanzlerin*
 'the *Merkelian chancellor'
(51) a. *der Flughafen Kölns^{Gen} ist typisch für die Stadt >< ?der Flughafen Köln^{App} ist typisch für die Stadt*
 'the airport of Cologne is typical of that city >< ?the airport Cologne is typical of that city'
 b. *der Flughafen Kölns^{Gen} und der Roms^{Gen} (von Rom) >< der Flughafen Köln^{App} und *der Rom^{App}*
 'the airport Cologne and the one of Rome >< the airport Cologne and *the one Rome'

3. Compound: subclassification versus specification

In German linguistic literature, the parallellism between the German genitive and compound has been noted for a long time (e.g. Behaghel 1923-32; Brinkmann 1971; Lauterbach 1993), as is shown in the examples in (52). One of the historic (early Modern High German) basic constructions of the nominal compound[10] is an NP with a preposed genitive attribute, which is illustrated in e.g. Pavlov (2005) (53). A number of compounds has retained the historic genitive

---

[10] as opposed to the so-called 'root compounds' ('Stammkomposita'). For details, see e.g. Wackernagel (1905: 48), De Grauwe (1994), Lühr (2004: 3); Pavlov (2005: 114).

ending -*s* of masculine/neutral nouns, as is shown in (54). By analogy, even feminine nouns can have this *s*-ending (*Muttersvater*):

(52) a. *den Schlüssel des*^{Gen} *Gefängnisses/Gefängnisschlüssel*^{Comp} (Ks:16)
'the key of the prison/the prison key'
b. (*die Tür*) *der Kajüte des*^{Gen} *Eigners/Eigner-Kajüte*^{Comp} (Ks:22)
'(the door of) the cabin of the owner/of the owner cabin'
c. *als hervorragendes Mitglied der*^{Gen} *Crew/Crew-Mitglied*^{Comp} (Ks:143)
'as eminent member of the crew/crew member'
(53) *das reichs regiment; der pfaffen standt; königs kinder* (Pavlov 2005:108)
'the realm^{Gen} regiment; of the priests rank; of king children'
(54) *Gotteshaus; Muttersvater; Namen/Namensliste*
'God's house (church); mother's father; name/name's list'

It is generally known that German is a language that makes ample use of compounds[11]. In this respect, the alternation between a genitive and a compound can also be illustrated by the fact that German compounds are often translated by a 'genitive' (or an equivalent construction) in less 'compound-sensitive' languages, such as Dutch ('van'-PP) (55-56):

(55) a. *das Überstundengeld*^{Comp} (Ms:K-6) → *het geld van het overwerk*
'the overtime money → the money of the overtime'
b. *die Warschauer-Pakt-Staaten*^{Comp} (Ms:K-13) → *de staten van het Warschaupact*
'the Warsaw Pact states → the states of the Warsaw pact'
c. *zum Autogramm-Schreiben*^{Comp} (Ms:K-5) → *voor het zetten van handtekeningen*
'for the autograph writing → for the putting down of autographs'
(56) *Arsenal-Funktionär*^{Comp} (Ms:K-15) → *een functionaris van Arsenal; een Arsenalfunctionaris*^{Comp}
'an asenal-official → an official of Arsenal; an Arsenal-official

Notwithstanding the obvious alternation potential of both constructions, a systematic investigation allows us to detect a number of restrictions.

The first restriction, which is usually the main difference mentioned in literature, is of a referential nature. Only the nuclear noun (TR; *der Ananassaft*) is used referentially in both constructions, whereas the dependent noun (LM) is prototypically referential in genitive (*der Saft der*^{Gen} *Ananas*) and non-referential in compound constructions (*der Ananassaft*). The opposition between definiteness and indefiniteness, which is important for the genitive relation, is therefore irrelevant for compounds. The semantic consequence is the class-restricting effect of the compound-LM: it demarcates a subtype of the main class referred to by the TR. The genitive LM however has a specifying effect and indicates the

---

[11] Cf. e.g. Lauterbach (1993: 172), Lühr (2004: 4), Pavlov (2005: 105).

whole of which the TR constitutes a component. Compounds, therefore, have a tendency towards concept building, genitives towards individualisation (Lauterbach 1993: 183). Or, as Brinkmann (1971: 69; 74-75) puts it:

> "bei einer Zusammensetzung entsteht ein neuer <u>Allgemein</u>begriff (...), geht es um verschiedene <u>Arten</u>, bei genitivischer Fügung um einen <u>bestimmten</u> Platz in der Welt" (my profiling, P.C.) 'in the case of a compound a new general concept emerges (...), different sorts of involved, in the case of a genitive construction a specific place in the world is involved'.

It is not clear how many pineapples went into the pineapple juice in (57), nor does the material of my clothes necessarily have to be clothing material:

(57) *Ananassaft* (Ks:14); *Kleiderstoff*
'pineapple juice; clothes material'

The compound seems to highlight a qualitative element (which *kind* of juice?, which *kind* of material?) that plays only a minor role with respect to the genitive. This case rather serves identification (*which* juice?, *which* material?) through indication of partitivity. The compound indicates partitivity as well as quality[12]. Compare in this respect examples (58-59). (58) illustrates that instantiation seems to correspond with genitives and typification with compounds. Example (59) furthermore illustrates that seemingly similar constructions cannot alternate in certain contexts precisely because of their characteristic properties. With its partitive meaning the genitive in (59a) differs from the compound, which indicates a type (59b). In the case of a 'part' (genitive), the bottle cannot

---

[12] A more peripheral alternative for the genitive, which – like the compound – profiles a qualitative aspect of the relation, is the (referential) adjective (cf. Paul 1959: 284). Compare in this respect the following examples: *die göttliche Kraft* (Ks:23)/*die Kraft Gottes* 'the divine power/the power of god'; *der südlichste Ort des ganzen italienischen Festlands* (Ks:92)/*des ganzen Festlands Italiens* 'the most southern part of the whole Italian mainland/of the whole mainland of Italy'; *die nächste Vorstellung des Grenouillschen Seelentheaters* (Pf:168)/*des Seelentheaters Grenouilles* 'the next performance of the Grenouillian soul theatre/of the soul theatre of Grenouille'. Whereas the genitive focuses on a merely partitive relation, the adjective functions as value concept, attitude (cf. example 52). The classification is conceptualised as an opinion. Compare the following alternation pair: *die französischen Weine/die Weine Frankreichs* 'the French wines/the wines of France'. The adjective evokes the quality label 'expensive', 'luxurious' much more than the genitive construction. Referential adjectives (*königlich*) differ from 'normal' adjectives (*schön*) in a number of ways: they allow neither alternation with a predicative adjective (*der Palast ist *königlich* >< *schön* 'the palace is *royal >< pretty'), nor graduation (*der *königlichere/schönere Palast* 'the more *royal/more pretty palace') or determination by an adverb of degree (*der Palast ist *äußerst königlich/äußerst schön* 'the palace is extremely *royal/pretty'). For details, see Campe (1999: 437-447). For referential vs. predicative adjectives, see e.g. Vendler (1968: 86ff.) For the (negative) value connotation typical of ad hoc compounds in newspaper language, see Peschel (1998: 127).

be 'empty', whereas it can if the 'bottle-*type*' is meant (compound), in which case the adjective 'empty' is preferred to 'full'. The apposition, which profiles exhaustivity, can hardly be combined with the adjective 'empty' (59c). The '*with*'-PP, which encodes a container/contained-relation is finally combined with 'half-empty' or 'half-full' rather than with 'empty' or 'full' (59d):

(58) *der Kopf dieses Hais ist kein typischer Haikopf*^{Comp}/??*dieser Haikopf ist kein typischer Kopf eines*^{Gen} *Hais*
'the head of this shark is no typical sharkhead >< this sharkhead is no typical head of a shark'

(59) a. *eine *leere/volle Flasche dieses*^{Gen} *Whiskys*
'an *empty/full bottle of this whiskey'
b. *eine leere/?volle Whisky-Flasche*^{Comp} (Ks:250)
'an empty/?full whiskey bottle'
c. *eine *?leere/volle Flasche Whisky*^{App}
'an *?empty/full bottle whiskey'
d. *eine *leere/?volle Flasche mit*^{Präp} *Whisky*
'an *empty/?full bottle with whiskey'

In a number of cases, the qualitative aspect of the compound meaning evokes a semantic differentiation that prevents interchangeability of genitive and compound. Though *Brecht-Theater* in (60) can mean 'the theatre of (Bertolt) Brecht' and in that sense can be paraphrased as 'das Theater Brechts/von Brecht', the main interpretation of the NP is 'theatre typical of/in the way of Brecht' and can therefore better be paraphrased with an adjective: 'Brechtian theatre' (60) (see also footnote 12). Compounds with a proper name as TR (60-61) apparently developed fairly recently and are subject to grammaticality discussion. This seems logical in view of the incompatibility of the type status of the LM and the instance status of the proper name as TR of the compound. Nevertheless, examples as those in (61) tend to appear more frequently nowadays, especially in journalistic and scientific German. A certain qualifying component is present in this kind of compounds as well:

(60) *Brecht-Theater* (Rössler 1970:80): *von/in der Art von Brecht (Brechtsches Theater)*
'Brecht theatre: of/in the way of Brecht (Brechtian theatre)'
(61) *zur Tapana-Familie* (Ks:209); *die Popelnik-Affäre* (Ms:K-12)
'to the Tapana family; the Popelnik affair'

Compounds possess a more indefinite meaning as well as a larger pragmatic freedom than the genitive. This freedom is e.g. manifested in the fact that a compound can often hardly be interpreted without the help of (textual) context or of background knowledge of the communication participants. There seems to be a continuum between internally and externally interpretative compounds.[13] The relation between TR and LM of the former can be derived from the obvious combination of the semantics of the individual referents of TR and LM. Prototypical instances are the so called 'relational' or 'inherent' compounds, which usually relate a deverbal or deadjectival noun (TR) to an object (LM), as in (62), or inherent nouns such as kinship terms to the object of this inherency relation, as in (63).

(62) *die Abenteuersteigerung*^{Comp} (Ks:44)/*Steigerung der*^{Gen} *Abenteuer* (die Abenteuer steigern)
'the adventure increasement/increasement of the adventures (to increase the adventures)'

(63) *die Kannibalen-Tochter*^{Comp} (Ks:75)/*die Tochter des*^{Gen} – *eines*^{Gen} – *von*^{Präp} *Kannibalen*
'the cannibals daughter/the daughter of the – a – of cannibal(s)'

So called 'stereotype compounds'[14], illustrated in (64), are less easily interpretable. The *Fabrik* does not imply an inherent relation of the same level of *Tochter* in (63). Still, it does relate to something which is 'fabricated'. *Tod* in *Schnee-Tod* however is not used relationally in example (65), even though it is an inherent noun ('someone dies'). The interpretation of the relation between TR and LM has to be derived from the prototypical meanings of both components: the spatial aspect of *Schnee* leads to the (possible) interpretation 'death in the snow':

(64) *die Gardinenfabrik*^{Comp}/?*Fabrik der*^{Gen} – *von*^{Präp} *Gardinen*
'the curtain factory/factory of the – of curtains'

(65) *Schnee-Tod*^{Comp} (Lauterbach 1993:207)/*Tod *des*^{Gen} *Schnees* – *Tod im*^{Präp} *Schnee*
'snow-death/death *of the snow – death in the snow'

Examples (62)-(65) illustrate the fact that the larger the potential is of the compound to serve as an alternative for the genitive, the more inherent its TR is. The other end of the continuum is built by fully context-based compounds[15], such as the ad-hoc compounds in (66): An *Elefantenkissen* could be a cushion in the form of an elephant, with an elephant print, or bought for the good cause of saving the African elephant. *Bananenheizung* can only really be understood if one is aware of briquets made of banana skins. A genitive alternative is hardly possible here:

---

[13] For details on the interpretation (strategies) of German compounds, see e.g. Lühr (2004: 6ff.).
[14] See e.g. Motsch (1992), Lühr (2004: 10ff.)
[15] Peschel (1998: 125) notes that ad-hoc compounds are more prominent in newspaper language, literary texts and advertisements.

(66) a. *Elefantenkissen*^{Comp} (Nl-1)/*Kissen* *der^{Gen} *Elefanten*
'elephants cushion/cushion of the elephants'
b. *Bananenheizung*^{Comp} (Lauterbach 1993: 203)/*Heizung der^{Gen} *Bananen*
'bananas heating/heating of the bananas'

Genitive and compound also differ at a formal level. The obvious difference of the absence of an article determining the compound LM was already mentioned. Moreover, both constructions do not possess the same combination potential with other sentence constituents. This can be illustrated by means of their potential for modification. In the compound, word formation and syntax overlap – a phenomenon called "Lexemsyntax" in Pavlov (2005: 100). Consequently, the whole unit of TR *and* LM is modified. This is not necessarily the case for the genitive, which is basically a syntactic phenomenon: either the TR or the LM is modified by the PP in (67) or the relative clause in (68). The compactness of the compound also allows a double relation with respect to the TR, which is impossible for the genitive (69):

(67) *die Werftarbeiter*^{Comp} *von Henri Latour* (Ks:17) >< *die Arbeiter der*^{Gen} *Werft von Henri Latour*
'the shipyard workmen of Henri Latour >< the workmen of the shipyard of Henri Latour'
(68) a. *die Sekretärin der*^{Gen} *Direktorin, die ich gestern gesehen habe*
'the secretary of the (female) manager, whom I saw yesterday'
b. *die Direktionssekretärin*^{Comp}, *die ich gestern gesehen habe*
'the executive secretary, whom I saw yesterday'
(69) a. *die starre Killerphysiognomie*^{Comp} *des Raubfisches* (Ks:29)
'the rigid killer physiognomy of the predatory fish'
b. *die starre Physiognomie eines*^{Gen} *Killers* *des Raubfisches
'the rigid physiognomy of a killer *of the predatory fish'

Due to the absence of a referent of the compound LM, modification of the TR or LM individually is basically impossible, although examples can be found sporadically[16] (70), which then seem to corroborate the syntactic part of the compound's 'lexemsyntax-'character:

(70) a. *ein Luftballonakrobat, der den einen aufzublasen beginnt, während der andere eben platzt* (Böll [Pavlov 2005: 112])
'a hot air balloon acrobat, who starts blowing up the one, while the other one bursts'

---

[16] For more examples, see also e.g. Donalies (2003: 87).

b. *auf den großen Hof, der mit (...) den alten geplatzten Matratzenhaufen wirklich nicht sehr einladend aussah* (Fallada [ibid.])
'onto the big court, that with <...> the old burst mattresses pile really didn't look very inviting'
c. *David Wahl legte die braune Jungshand auf die der Schwester* (A. Zweig [ibid.])
'David Wahl put the brown boy's hand onto the one of the sister'

Through the incorporation of the object ('patient') of the deverbal TR in (71), the use of a subjective genitive ('agent') is allowed. Alternatively, an NP with *durch* could be used, which stresses the agentive character of the subject more strongly. A compound with an agentive LM in combination with an object genitive (72) seems to be rare, however. The fact that the patient or theme role is more intrinsically connected with the action expressed by the verb than with the agent-role is reflected iconically in the incorporation of the patient in the compound:

(71) *die Gebührensenkung^{Comp} der Post* (Lauterbach 1993: 197)/*die Senkung der^{Gen} Gebühren durch die Post*
'the rate cutting of the post/the cutting of the rates by the post'
(72) *die Machtübernahme^{Comp} der^{Gen} Nazis/*die Nazi-Übernahme^{Comp} der^{Gen} Macht*
'the power take-over of the Nazis/the Nazi-take-over of the power'

Compounds and genitives also differ as far as intonation is concerned. Whereas the former carry stress on the first part, the latter prototypically emphasise the second part (73). Interestingly, in both cases the dependent LM is emphasised. However, whereas the LM of the compound is a topic at an informative level, the LM of the genitive seems to function as the focus, as is shown in (74): the new information is the 'mouth'. That the mouth of a shark is meant, is known information.[17] Compare in this respect the anaphoric possessive pronoun *seines* in *seines Schädels*. The minimal pair in (75) profiles this change of focus: for the genitive, the 'apposition' is the main focus of attention, for the compound, that is the 'concept'. Example (76) illustrates, how the alternation between genitive and compound can be exploited at textual and stylistic levels[18]. This example also illustrates the condensing, 'language economical' function of the compound vis-à-vis the genitive:

(73) *die Inselbewohner^{Comp} >< die Bewohner der/einer^{Gen} Insel* (Ks:36)
'the island inhabitants >< the inhabitants of the/an island'

---

[17] On an informative level, and also on the level of word order, compounds and preposed genitives seem to show resemblance (see Campe 1999: 199-226).

[18] For details on the textual-stylistic function of the compound, see e.g. Wildgen (1982), Peschel (1998).

(74) *und dann dieser schreckliche, wulstige Halbkreis unterhalb seines Schädels: das Hai<u>maul</u>*^{Comp} *(Ks:29) >< ?das Maul des*^{Gen} <u>Hais</u>
'and then this terrible, thick semicircle underneath his skull: the shark mouth ><?the mouth of the shark'

(75) *der Begriff der*^{Gen} <u>Apposition</u> *(Löbel 1993:152) >< der Appositions<u>begriff</u>*^{Comp} *(ibid.)*
'the concept of the apposition >< the apposition concept'

(76) *in den Eingang der*^{Gen} <u>Bucht</u> *(Ks:28)/auf das helle Dreieck des Bucht<u>eingangs</u>*^{Comp} *(Ks:30)*
'in the entrance of the bay/onto the bright triangle of the bay entrance'

Finally, whereas the semantic relations encoded by the genitive (e.g. partitive, possessive) can also frequently be coded by a compound[19], the opposite is often not the case. Consider the following examples, in which the LM is not nominal (77), no partitive relation (in a general sense) is expressed (78), the LM relates to a prepositionally encoded complement or adverbial adjunct of the deverbal TR (79), or the LM relates to the TR additively[20] (80).

(77) *Nebenbett* (Ks:13) (preposition); *Stau-Schapp* (Ks:17) (verb)
'next-to (additional) bed; store-shelf'

(78) *Hai-Stock* (Ks:23) ('gegen'); *Hammerhai* (Ks:17) ('mit hammerförmigem Kopf')
'shark-stick ('against'); hammer shark ('with hammer shaped head')'

(79) *Studieneinstieg* (Einstieg 'ins' Studium); *Küstenfabrik* (Fabrik 'an' der Küste)
'studies entry (entry into the studies); coast factory (factory 'at' the seaside)'

(80) *alle Tierfreunde des Fuchses* (Freund + Tier)
'all animal friends of the fox (friend + animal)'

4. Conclusion

By investigating the German adnominal genitive and its more peripheral 'competitors', apposition and compound, I have highlighted the methodological importance of the paradigmatic alternation potential in the analysis of syntactic

---

[19] Cf. Vandermeeren (1998: 249): "Komposita, die eine Ganzes-Teil-Struktur aufweisen, können generell mit der Genitivkonstruktion umgeformt werden" 'compounds that have a whole-part structure can generally be transformed to a genitive construction'.

[20] Meant here are the so-called copulative compounds. See e.g. Guelpa (1995: 336-37) for the distinction between (the large category of) determinative N-N-compounds, of which the first constituent generally determines the second, and (the smaller category of) copulative N-N-compounds.

constructions. In this way, individual semantic aspects of the different constructions can more easily be 'pushed to consciousness' (Davidse 1996: 326).

This study has led to the observation that certain semantic-syntactic contexts clearly seem to prefer a genitive as a norm, whereas others induce encoding by means of an apposition or compound.

Whereas variation between genitive and apposition seems rather free in quantitative contexts, a systematic comparison reveals that lexical/semantic, referential and grammatical/syntactic factors seem to restrict it. The genitive prototypically encodes an intrinsic, partitive, *holistic* relation, the apposition by contrast a more extrinsic, quantitative, *exhaustive* relation.

In partitive contexts, variation between genitive and compound also occurs. Notwithstanding the obvious alternation potential of both constructions, the investigation reveals a number of restrictions of a lexical/semantic, referential, textual/stylistic, informative and grammatical/syntactic nature. The compound can be prototypically distinguished from the genitive in that it focuses on an extrinsic, *typifying*, *qualitative* relation rather than on an intrinsic, *individualising*, *merely partitive* relation.

Pinpointing the above semantic aspects led to a better insight into the semantic-syntactic identity of the genitive as assumed by Brinkmann (1971: 68-69), which can thus be paraphrased schematically as an unlocalistic partitive relation between two entities. From this prototypical meaning accompanying aspects such as intrinsicness, holisticness, ... emerge. These aspects, which are absent in or left unprofiled by the genitive alternatives, should, however, not be seen as components of the genitival meaning itself and are, therefore, neither necessarily nor in joint combination instantiated by each individual genitive construction.

These two case studies further illustrate the idea that paradigmatic variation can be used as a heuristic tool to identify the prototypical semantics of a certain construction. Conceptual differentiation is, in other words, an important driving force behind this type of lexico-syntactic variation. In this respect, the semantic identity of an individual construction could be considered as its 'norm'. The semantic similarity of the paradigmatic alternatives conversely does allow (peripheral) variation and sometimes even causes constructions that were once autonomous to coincide in a later stage of the language or the semantic-conceptual field that is covered by the individual constructions to be reorganized.

5. Bibliography

5.1 Primary references

Konsalik, Heinz G. 1996. *Das Riff der roten Haie*. Bergisch Gladbach: Gustav Lübbe (= Ks).

Süskind, Patrick. 1985. *Das Parfum. Die Geschichte eines Mörders*. Zürich: Diogenes (= Pf).
Menasse, Eva. 2003. *Vienna*. Köln: Kiepenheuer & Witsch (= Mn).
Noll, Ingrid. 1996. *Kalt ist der Abendhauch*. Zürich: Diogenes (= Nl).
GermNews. http://www.germnews.de (= GN).

5.2 Secondary references

Behaghel, Otto. 1923-32. *Deutsche Syntax. Eine geschichtliche Darstellung*. Heidelberg: Winter.
Bhatt, Christa. 1990. *Die syntaktische Struktur der Nominalphrase im Deutschen*. Tübingen: Narr.
Brinkmann, Hennig. 1971. *Die deutsche Sprache. Gestalt und Leistung*. Düsseldorf: Schwann.
Campe, Petra. 1997. "Genitives and *von-* Datives in German: A Case of *free* Variation?". *Lexical and Syntactical Constructions and the Construction of Meaning* ed. M. Verspoor, K. D. Lee & E. Sweetser, 165-185. Amsterdam: Benjamins.
Campe, Petra. 1998. "Paradigmatische Variation als linguistisches Instrument, oder wie sich der adnominale Genitiv im Deutschen gegen präpositionale Eindränger hält". *Leuvense Bijdragen* 87. 337-369.
Campe, Petra. 1999. *Der adnominale Genitiv im heutigen Deutsch. Versuch einer kognitiv-linguistischen Analyse des reinen Kasus im Vergleich zu alternativen Konstruktionen*. Unpublished PhD dissertation, Katholieke Universiteit Leuven.
Davidse, Kristin. 1996. "Functional dimensions of the dative in English. *The Dative: Descriptive Studies* ed. W. Van Belle & W. Van Langendonck, 289-338. Amsterdam: Benjamins.
De Grauwe, Luc. 1994. "De plaatsing van het genitiefattribuut en diens ontwikkeling tot compositum, in een aantal oudere continentale bijbelvertalingen vergeleken". *Amsterdamer Beiträge zur älteren Linguistik* 40. 173-182.
Donalies, Elke. 2003. "Hochzeitstorte, laskaprasol, elmas küpe, cow's milk, casa de campo, cigarette-filtre, ricasdueñas .... Was ist eigentlich ein Kompositum?". *Deutsche Sprache* 31. 76-93.
Duden. 1985. *Richtiges und gutes Deutsch* (Duden Band 9). Mannheim: Dudenverlag.
Duden. 1998. *Grammatik der deutschen Gegenwartssprache* (Duden Band 4). Mannheim: Dudenverlag.
Duden. *Das große Wörterbuch der deutschen Sprache*. Mannheim: Dudenverlag.
Eisenberg, Peter. 1994. *Grundriß der deutschen Grammatik*. Stuttgart: Metzler.
Flämig, Walter. 1991. *Grammatik des Deutschen*. Berlin: Akademie Verlag.

Gallmann, Peter. 2007. <http://www2.uni-jena.de/philosophie/germsprach/syn tax/1/doc/skript/Block_I_Skript.pdf.
Guelpa, Patrick. 1995. "Nominalkomposita (N + N) und Apposition im Deutschen". *Sprachwissenschaft* 20.1. 336-350.
Joosten, Frank & Lea Vermeire. 2004. *Collectiva en relationaliteit*. Leuven: Departement Linguïstiek.
Hackel, Werner. 1971. "'Der Begriff der Entfernung' oder 'der Begriff Entfernung'". *Sprachpflege* 7. 143-147.
Hentschel, Elke. 1993. "Flexionsverfall im Deutschen? Die Kasusmarkierung bei partitiven Genitivattributen". *Zeitschrift für germanistische Linguistik* 21.3. 320-333.
Langacker, Ronald W. 1987. *Foundations of cognitive grammar. Volume 1: Theoretical prerequisites*. Stanford: Stanford University Press.
Langacker, Ronald W. 1988. "An overview of cognitive grammar; A view of linguistic semantics; the nature of grammatical valence; A usage-based model". *Topics in cognitive linguistics* ed. B. Rudzka-Ostyn, 3-161. Amsterdam: Benjamins.
Langacker, Ronald W. 1992. "The symbolic nature of cognitive grammar: The meaning of of and of of-periphrasis". *Thirty years of linguistic evolution* ed. M. Pütz, 484-502. Amsterdam: Benjamins.
Lauterbach, Stefan. 1993. *Genitiv, Komposition und Präpositionalattribut – zum System nominaler Relationen im Deutschen*. München: Iudicium.
Leys, Odo. 1998. "Zum Genitivattribut im Deutschen". *Productivity and creativity. Studies in general and descriptive linguistics in honour of E.M. Uhlenbeck* ed. M. Janse, 549-557. Berlin: De Gruyter.
Löbel, Elisabeth. 1993. "Zur Distribution und Abgrenzung von enger Apposition und Attribut". *Studien zur Syntax und Semantik der Nominalgruppe* ed. M. Vuillaume, J.-F. Marillier & I. Behr, 145-166. Tübingen: Narr.
Lühr, Rosemarie. 2004. "Nominalkomposition im Altindischen und Altgriechischen". *Komplexe Wortstrukturen. Komposition, Inkorporation, Polysynthese* ed. E. Nowak, 107-214. Berlin: Technische Universität Berlin – Institut für Sprache und Kommunikation.
Motsch, Wolfgang. 1992. "Wieviel Syntax brauchen Komposita?". *Festschrift für W. Fleischer zum 70. Geburtstag* ed. R. Grosse, G. Lerchner & M. Schröder, 71-78. Frankfurt: Lang.
Paul, Hermann. 1959. *Deutsche Grammatik. Band IV: Syntax*. Halle: Niemeyer.
Pavlov, Vladimir M. 2005. "Zur Entwicklung der substantivischen Zusammensetzung im Frühneuhochdeutschen". *Sprachwandel und Gesellschaftswandel – Wurzeln des heutigen Deutsch* ed. K. J. Mattheier & H. Nitta, 99-117. München: Iudicium.
Peña Cervel, Sandra. 1998-99. "The prepositions *in* and *out* and the trajector-landmark distinction". *RESLA* 13. 261-271.

Peschel, Corinna. 1998. "Von Milliardenjungfern, Luthertötern und Sperminatoren. Zu einer text(sorten)-spezifischen Interpretation von Wortneubildungen". *Zielsprache Deutsch* 3.98. 121-128.

Rössler, Rudolf. 1970. "Beiträge zur funktionalen Sprachlehre (III). Zum Genitiv in der deutschen Sprache der Gegenwart". *Sprachpflege. Zeitschrift für gutes Deutsch* 19. 74-80; 118-121; 163-168.

Schanen, François. 1993. "ALL-: Determinans? Quantor? Identifikator? Totalisator?". *Studien zur Syntax und Semantik der Nominalgruppe* ed. M. Vuillaume, J.-F. Marillier & I. Behr, 41-64. Tübingen: Narr.

Talmy, Leonard. 1988. "The relation of grammar to cognition". *Topics in cognitive linguistics* ed. B. Rudzka-Ostyn, 165-203. Amsterdam: Benjamins.

Vandermeeren, Sonja. 1998. "Semantik deutscher Substantivkomposita mit Verwandtschaftsbezeichnungen". *Deutsche Sprache* 26. 240-255.

Vendler, Theo. 1968. *Adjectives and nominalizations*. The Hague: Mouton.

Wackernagel, Jacob. 1905. *Altindische Grammatik II, 1: Einleitung zur Wortlehre. Nominalkomposition*. Göttingen: Vandenhoeck & Ruprecht.

Weier, Winfried. 1968. "Der Genitiv im heutigen Deutsch". *Muttersprache* 78. 222-235/257-269.

Wildgen, Wolfgang. 1982. "Makroprozesse bei der Verwendung nominaler ad-hoc-Komposita im Deutschen". *Deutsche Sprache* 10. 237-257.

Zifonun, Gisela, Ludger Hoffmann, Bruno Strecker et al. 1997. *Grammatik der deutschen Sprache* (Schriften des Instituts für deutsche Sprache 7). Berlin: de Gruyter.

Joybrato Mukherjee (Giessen)

Corpus-based Insights into Verb-complementational Innovations in Indian English
Cases of Nativised Semantico-structural Analogy

1. Introduction

In the course of British colonisation, the English language was transported to many new territories outside Britain on virtually all continents over the past few centuries. In those colonies in which British settlers remained a tiny fraction of the total population, e.g. India and Nigeria, English never became a dominant native language (as it did, for example, in Australia and North America). Nevertheless, since gaining independence many of these countries have retained the English language both as an official language and as a communicative device for a wide range of communication situations, including education and academia, politics and administration, newspapers and fiction writing. In fact, in many of the former non-settler-dominated colonies, new non-native varieties of English have developed over the past decades, which Kachru (1985a: 211) refers to as "institutionalised second-language varieties".

Fully institutionalised second-language varieties can be viewed as endonormatively stabilised as they have a potential to develop their own norms and standards which are generally accepted as being characteristic features of a "new" English variety. In Schneider's (2003, 2007) evolutionary model of the emergence of New Englishes, endonormative stabilisation is the fourth of five phases:

> "As the English language has been uprooted and relocated throughout colonial and postcolonial history, New Englishes have emerged by undergoing a fundamentally uniform process which can be described as a progression of five characteristic stages: FOUNDATION, EXONORMATIVE STABILIZATION, NATIVIZATION, ENDONORMATIVE STABILIZATION, DIFFERENTIATION." (Schneider 2003: 243)

In Schneider's (2003) model, the foundation phase captures the period at the very beginning of colonising a new territory, in which the English language is transplanted to a new region. Exonormative stabilisation refers to the period in which the English language is used by an increasing number of settlers in the new territory with a clear orientation towards British English standards and norms. In the nativisation period, the English language becomes an integral part of the local linguistic repertoire, and both the settlers' identity and the English language become more and more localised. In the phase of endonormative stabilisation, new local standards and norms emerge, followed by the development of regional variants within the new English variety in the very last phase, i.e. differentiation.

With approximately 35 to 50 million competent speakers, standard Indian English is the largest institutionalised second-language variety of English, in fact the third largest variety worldwide, outnumbered only by American English and British English (in terms of numbers of speakers). As has been discussed in detail elsewhere (cf. Mukherjee 2007), the situation of present-day Indian English is an almost prototypical example of endonormative stabilisation. Table 1 provides a synopsis of the parameters and criteria that Schneider (2003, 2007) sketches out for this phase.

Table 1: Endonormative stabilisation of present-day Indian English: parameters and criteria[1]

Parameter	*Criterion*	+/–
History and politics	Post-independence?	+
	Self-dependence?	+
Identity construction	STL/IDG strands interwoven?	–
	New nation with panethnic identity?	+
Sociolinguistics of contact, use, attitudes	Acceptance of local norms?	+
	Positive attitude to local variety?	+
	Literary creativity?	+
Linguistic developments, structural effects	Stabilisation of a new variety?	+
	Codification (e.g. dictionaries)?	+
	Relative homogeneity of local norms?	+

With regard to all categories, ranging from the historical and political situation to sociolinguistic and linguistic aspects, the plus sign in the right-hand column indicates that the situation today represents a typical case of endonormative stabilisation. The only exception is the fact that in present-day India the settlers (in Schneider's (2003) terminology the "STL strand") and the indigenous population (the "IDG strand") do not represent two threads that are intricately interwoven, with a new identity emerging from the interaction of the two groups. This is because there are hardly any descendants of British settlers left. The so-called Anglo-Indian community only forms a minute fraction of India's total population. As has already been pointed out by Schilk (2006: 280), this criterion is particularly useful for settler-dominated varieties such as Australian English,

---

[1] Cf. Mukherjee 2007.

but seems to be largely irrelevant in the context of non-settler-dominated New Englishes such as Indian English.[2] There is a rich body of literature on the linguistic aspects of endonormative stabilisation in present-day Indian English on virtually all levels of analysis, including the seminal work by Kachru (1983, 2005), the largely intuition-based dictionaries by Nihalani et al. (1979, 2004) and corpus-based studies, e.g. by Shastri (1988, 1992). It should be noted, however, that previous research has tended to focus on the areas of pronunciation (e.g. phoneme replacements), morphology and lexis (e.g. new lexical items), syntactic categories (e.g. use of the progressive), idiom and style (e.g. the frequent use of forms that are marked as archaic in native varieties of English). Apart from some laudable exceptions (cf. e.g. Shastri 1996), structural effects at the lexis-grammar interface have not been analysed on the basis of corpus data until very recently. Olavarría de Ersson and Shaw (2003), Mukherjee and Hoffmann (2006) and Hoffmann and Mukherjee (2007) show that Indian English verb complementation also differs from other varieties not only quantitatively with regard to the frequency and distribution of the verb-complementational patterns of particular verbs (e.g. *give* and its patterns), but also qualitatively in that individual verbs are used in constructions in which they are not admissible in native varieties of English (e.g. *put* in the ditransitive construction). The latter type of deviations from native norms in Indian English can be viewed as truly creative innovations because new forms and structures emerge on grounds of Indian English users' autonomous and L2-internal extension and modification of the lexicogrammatical system of English. In the present paper, I will focus on three kinds of creative innovations in Indian English lexicogrammar: (1) "new" prepositional verbs (e.g. *he ordered for a beer*); (2) "new" ditransitive verbs (e.g. *I put him a question*); (3) "new" light-verb constructions (e.g. *she took rest*). Before I discuss these creative innovations (see section 3), however, the concept of creative autonomy that users of Indian English exert has to be discussed in the context of two other determinants that are relevant to the formation of institutionalised second-language varieties, i.e. the role of interference from local L1s and the persistent influence of the common core shared with other varieties of English (see section 2).

---

[2] Note in this context that there is no unanimous agreement on the extent to which present-day Indian English is an exponent of endonormative stabilisation. While Schilk (2006) and Mukherjee (2007) place special emphasis, albeit to different degrees, on those aspects that are indicative of endonormative stabilisation, Schneider (2007: 165ff.) largely focuses on features that are representative of phase 3, i.e. nativisation.

2. The New English triangle: Indian English between common core, interference and autonomy

Institutionalised second-language varieties should best be viewed as semi-autonomous as they are characterised not only by creative autonomy (resulting, for example, in verb-complementational innovations such as "new" prepositional verbs), but also by interference and the common core. As Indian English is a non-native variety, interference effects are bound to occur, and features from local languages are transferred to Indian English, most notably in the area of pronunciation (leading, for example, to the replacement of phonemes that do not occur in Indian languages by more familiar ones). Also, one should not ignore the fact that in spite of the potential to develop its own norms and the many innovations and deviations from native norms that can indeed be found, present-day Indian English has to a very large extent been shaped by those features that are shared by all varieties of English, i.e. the common core, and that, historically, go back to native varieties of English. For example, the basic word order of Indian English and the inventory of function words such as prepositions have been taken over from the historical input variety, British English, and have remained unaffected by autonomy and interference ever since. Figure 1 provides a visualisation of the three determinants in the form of a triangular model (cf. Mukherjee 2007: 180).

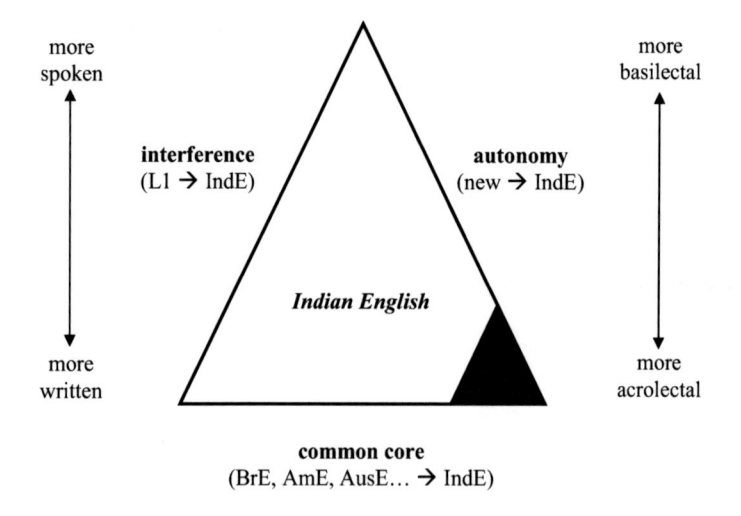

Figure 1: Indian English in the triangle of three determinants: common core, interference and autonomy (adapted from Mukherjee 2007: 180)

Note that the model also captures systematic correlations between the three determinants on the one hand and two gradients of variation within Indian English on the other: (1) the gradient from more spoken to more written styles of Indian English; (2) the gradient from basilectal and pidginised forms of Indian English to acrolectal standard Indian English. The more spoken and basilectal the variant is, the more it is marked by features of interference and/or autonomy and the more remote it is from the common core shared with – and taken over from – native varieties of English. Conversely, the more written and acrolectal the variant is, the more it displays features of the common core and the less it is marked by interference and/or autonomy.

In the present paper, I am concerned with those verb-complementational innovations that occur in acrolectal and written variants of Indian English and that are, thus, generally accepted as localised forms of standard Indian English. Such innovations can be plotted onto the shaded area in the bottom-right hand corner of the triangle in Figure 1.

As will be discussed in section 3, verb-complementational innovations in standard Indian English are usually not accidental results of random deviations from native norms on the part of non-native users of English. Rather, they are based on a rational impetus in general and on analogies that Indian speakers draw betweeen already existing templates in English and potential new forms and structures in particular. In various studies, creative innovations in institutionalised second-language varieties have been traced back to forces of regularisation that are believed to lead to modifications of the morphosyntax of English in areas of "inherent vulnerability in English" (Williams 1987: 166) and at "predetermined breakage points" (Sand 2005: 203): L2 users of English are, thus, licensed to "stretch the system" (Christian Mair, pers. comm.), for example in terms of a mechanism that has been described as "nativised semantico-structural analogy":

> [Nativised semantico-structural analogy is] "a process by means of which non-native speakers of English as a second language are licensed to introduce new forms and structures into the English language because corresponding semantic and formal templates already exist in the English language system." (Mukherjee and Hoffmann 2006: 166f.)

At the level of morphology, for example, South Asian users of English create new lexical items by applying word-formation rules to lexical components to which they are not applied in British English (cf. e.g. Kachru 1983, Baumgardner 1998), e.g. the suffixation with *-ee* and the prefixation with *de-*, leading to new nouns such as *affectee* (i.e. someone who is affected) and new verbs such as *de-friend someone* (i.e. no longer be someone's friend). The fact that corresponding semantic and formal templates already exist in English (e.g. derivative nouns such as *interviewee* and derivative verbs such as *decontrol*) explains that the creative autonomy in extending existing word-formation rules to new lexical items is actually based on a rational approach to – and extension of – the productive patterns inherent in English morphology.[3]

3. Creative innovations in Indian English verb complementation

In the following, I will focus on creative innovations in standard Indian English verb complementation that can be explained by nativised semantico-structural analogy (see section 2). As such verb-complementational innovations usually occur in low frequencies in standard Indian English (with the native forms clearly outnumbering the innovative forms), large corpora of acrolectal variants of Indian English are needed to find authentic examples of creative innovations.

3.1 "New" prepositional verbs

Prepositional verbs are defined by Quirk et al. (1985: 1155) as follows: "A prepositional verb consists of a lexical verb followed by a preposition with which it is semantically and/or syntactically associated". In their usage guide to Indian English, Nihalani et al. (2004) list various prepositional verbs that are acceptable in Indian English but that are not used in British English, a case in point being *discuss about*:[4]

> "*discuss* 'We were discussing about politics.'
> The insertion of the superfluous preposition 'about' after this verb is extremely common wherever English is a second or a foreign language. It is frequently found after the noun, of course, as in 'They had a discussion about transformational grammar', but BS [British Standard English] speakers generally prefer 'They discussed the problem of rising prices'. ('To discuss on' also occurs in IVE [Indian Variants of English].)" (Nihalani et al. 2004: 66)

Such innovative combinations of verbs and prepositions for which usually one-place verbs (e.g. *discuss*) are used in native varieties of English, are not a mar-

---

[3] This said, it should not go unmentioned that an analogy-based explanation of new forms can only offer a diagnostic explanation of the potential reasons that might have led to the innovations at hand; the prognostic power of nativised semantico-structural analogy and its relevance to the psychological reality are open to debate (cf. Hartford 1989: 103).

[4] Note, as Nihalani et al. (2004: 66) point out, that many of the new prepositional verbs such as *discuss about* occur not only in standard Indian English, but also in acrolectal and written variants of many other institutionalised second-language varieties, including for example African Englishes and Singaporean English (cf. Hartford 1989, Nesselhauf 2009). On the one hand, this corroborates the assumption that L1-independent general mechanisms of analogy and regularisation are at work, and, on the other hand, such observations call for comparative studies of second-language varieties of English worldwide (see section 4).

ginal phenomenon in Indian English. Table 2 provides an overview of "new" prepositional verbs in Indian English that are listed in Nihalani et al.'s (2004) usage guide and their frequencies in the Indian component of the International Corpus of English (ICE-India). Like all the other ICE corpora, ICE-India is a representative and balanced 1-million-word corpus of standard Indian English, including 400,000 words from a wide range of written genres and 600,000 words from a wide range of spoken genres (cf. Greenbaum 1996).

Table 2: "New" prepositional verbs in ICE-India

"New" prepositional verb	Occurrences in ICE-India
answer (v.) *to*	1
approach (v.) *to*	2
comprise of	8
demand (v.) *for*	1
discuss about	14
enter into	16
invite for	3
mention (v.) *about*	14
order (v.) *for*	2
request (v.) *for*	6
visit (v.) *to*	2

If we abstract away from the individual "new" prepositional verbs, a uniform pattern of analogy emerges. Generally speaking, the new forms can be viewed as being licensed, as it were, by already existing semantic and formal templates. For example, the emergence of *discuss about* in Indian English can be explained by the existence of the semantically closely related verb *talk about* (= semantic template) and the frequent collocation of the derivative noun *discussion* and the preposition *about* (= formal template). Thus, the processes that lead to the "new" prepositional verbs listed in Table 2 can be viewed as cases of nativised sematico-structural analogy as defined in section 2. In examples (1) to (5), all of which are taken from ICE-India, the semantic and formal templates that form the basis for the analogy that Indian speakers draw are indicated underneath each of the examples.[5]

---

[5] The templates are compatible with – and do not contradict – other, more general and/or cognitive motivations for the emergence of "new" prepositional verbs, e.g. the explicit prepositional marking of the spatial direction in verbs of movement (e.g. *enter X > enter into X*) and the choice of *about* as a universal and the most salient marker of aboutness in prototypical and non-protypical verbs of saying (e.g. *discuss X > discuss about X*), as discussed by Williams (1987) and Hartford (1989) respectively.

(1) *Yeah Yeah uh what manner you people are **approaching to** the higher authorities?* <ICE-India S1A-083>
  ← semantic template: *appeal to* (v.)
  ← formal template: *approach to* (n.)

(2) *... the train will **comprise of** forty vans each with a capacity of nine* <ICE-India S2B-001>
  ← semantic template: *consist of* (v.)
  ← formal template: *be comprised of* (v. pass.)

(3) *... whenever I **enter into** the class They laugh at me* <ICE-India S1A-001>
  ← semantic template: *come into* (v.)
  ← formal template: *entrance into* (n.)

(4) *Now when you **ordered for** the beer did you get the beer?* <ICE-India S1B-061>
  ← semantic template: *ask for* (v.)
  ← formal template: *order for* (n.)

(5) *He has **visited to** the following study areas at respective dates during his fellowship period* <ICE-India W1B-020>
  ← semantic template: *go to* (v.)
  ← formal template: *visit to* (n.)

Given that the "new" prepositional verbs can be traced back to existing templates and explained as the results of L2-internal restructuring processes based on semantic and formal analogies, the question of a possible L1 influence (in the sense of interference), which traditionally plays a major role in research into non-native varieties of English, is perhaps largely irrelevant in this particular context. Additionally, as there are almost 600 indigenous languages spoken in present-day India with even the largest speech community by far, i.e. speakers of Hindi, accounting for only a third of the total population, it is also difficult to identify the influence of any particular L1. In discussing various reasons for the emergence of "new" prepositional verbs of saying such as *discuss about* in Nepali English (a clearly less institutionalised variety than Indian English), Hartford (1989) points out that due to the wide-spread occurrence of such verbs in many other varieties of English world-wide (e.g. in West Africa, Papua New Guinea and Singapore), it is pointless to assume that in each individual variety an L1 influence can be detected:

> "Unless one could show that, for every NNE [non-native English] lect, the relevant L1 categories code these constructions in such a way as to account for the same forms in each lect, then the importance of L1 must be minimal, and incidental where a match does appear." (Hartford 1989: 115)

In fact, it seems more reasonable to view "new" prepositional verbs in Indian English – and other second-language varieties of English – as creative innovations that are caused by L2-internal analogies that L2 speakers of English draw because of the inner logic of the new forms.

3.2 "New" ditransitive verbs

Another very interesting area in which verb-complementational innovations can be observed in Indian English are "new" ditransitive verbs, i.e. verbs that are not admissible in the ditransitive construction in native varieties in general and British English (as the historical input variety) in particular but that are accepted – and used – in the ditransitive construction in standard Indian English. In the ditransitive construction, the verb is complemented with two objects, both of which are realised as noun phrases. As will be shown in the following, "new" ditransitive verbs are also products of the process of nativised semantico-structural analogy (cf. Mukherjee and Hoffmann 2006). Note, however, that in native varieties of English, too, the ditransitive construction can be extended to novel verbs. In example (6), which was already mentioned by Green (1974), the verb *cry*, which is typically used intransitively, occurs in the ditransitive construction. In example (7), the verb *have*, is used in the ditransitive construction, which is usually not admissible in native varieties of English.

(6) **Cry** me a river (Timberlake 2003)
(7) ... she now **had** him a room in the basement ... (Grisham 2002: 25)

The examples show that by combining verbs like *cry* and *have* with the ditransitive construction the lexical meaning of the verbs changes in such a way that it fits the syntactic meaning of the ditransitive construction. From a construction-grammar perspective (cf. Goldberg 1995, 2006), the ditransitive construction is one of the basic argument-structure constructions because it verbalises a basic event type, namely a transfer event. Thus, its meaning can be described as 'X causes Y to receive Z'. As Mukherjee (2005) shows, there is a wide range of 'grammatically institutionalised ditransitive verbs', e.g. *give* and *send*, whose meaning is such that they can be easily 'fused', as it were, with the ditransitive construction. However, there are also many other 'potentially ditransitive verbs' which are usually not used ditransitively and which can be fused with the ditransitive construction only on grounds of specific – and creative – licensing strategies, e.g. metaphorical extension. The meaning of *cry* in example (6), for instance, is metaphorically extended so that it now refers to a transfer event in which a river of tears is transferred from the agent to the recipient (by means of crying).

In Indian English, the ditransitive construction is fused with verbs that are not used ditransitively in British English. Table 3 lists such "new" ditransitive verbs that are attested in the ditransitive construction in ICE-India. Neither do these verbs occur in the ditransitive construction in the British component of ICE (ICE-GB) nor are they rated as fully acceptable in the ditransitive verbs by various British English native-speaker informants.

Table 3: "New" ditransitive verbs in ICE-India[6]

"New" ditransitive verb	Occurrences in the ditransitive construction
convey	2
furnish	1
gift	2
inform	4
present	1
provide	24

In the following examples, the "new" ditransitive verbs listed in Table 3 are illustrated.

(8) *The envoy also **conveyed** the French Prime Minister Mr Rokha's invitation ...* <ICE-India S2B-004>

(9) *Can you **furnish** me Dr. Shastri's address?* <ICE-India W1B-006>

(10) *You **gifted** me two such wonderful hours today* <ICE-India W2F-006>

(11) *I will be very glad if you kindly **inform** me the final and exact schedule of selection committe meetings, ...* <ICE-India W1B-030>

(12) *... and Congress-I ... cannot **present** us a viable government with the help of which it can rule the whole of the country* <ICE-India S1A-005>

(13) *Since they could not be taken back into the army he had asked the State Government to **provide** them other jobs* <ICE-India W2C-001>

As is the case for *cry* in the ditransitive construction, the "new" ditransitives in Indian English can be regarded as being licensed by a creative impetus. Specifically, the underlying mechanism is another case of nativised semantico-structural analogy: Indian English speakers draw an analogy between the meaning of established ditransitive verbs (the most prototypical verb being *give*) and the meaning of the ditransitive construction (= semantic template) as well as the syntactic patterns of the ditransitive construction (= formal template) on the one

---

[6] Note that *provide* is commonly used in the ditransitive construction in American English (cf. Quirk et al, 1985: 1210, Mukherjee 2001: 299). Various American English native-speaker informants also accept *present* in the ditransitive construction.

hand and "new" ditransitive verbs on the other. This process is visualised in Figure 2.

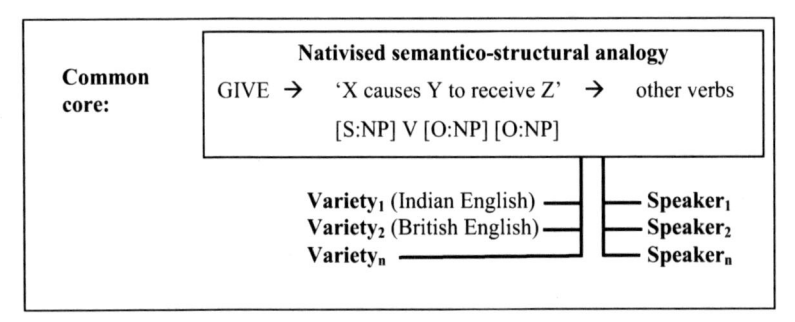

```
Common      Nativised semantico-structural analogy
core:       GIVE  →   'X causes Y to receive Z'   →   other verbs
                      [S:NP] V [O:NP] [O:NP]

                      Variety₁ (Indian English) ──┐  ┌── Speaker₁
                      Variety₂ (British English) ─┤  ├── Speaker₂
                      Varietyₙ ───────────────────┘  └── Speakerₙ
```

Figure 2: Extending the ditransitive construction to novel verbs: a case of nativised semantico-structural analogy (Hoffmann and Mukherjee 2007: 19)

As the case of *cry* in example (6) shows, the extension of the ditransitive construction to novel verbs is a ubiquitous process that is part of the common core of English grammar. Also, as example (7) from Grisham's (2002) novel *The Summons* indicates, the range of verbs used in the ditransitive construction varies not only from variety to variety (e.g. British English vs. Indian English), but also from one individual speaker to another.

The low figures in Table 3 make it clear that many "new" ditransitive verbs occur only rarely even in a 1-million-word corpus like ICE-India. In order to find more authentic instances of both the verbs listed in Table 3 (i.e. more tokens) and other "new" ditransitive verbs (i.e. more types), larger corpora of Indian English are needed. Unfortunately, balanced corpora larger than ICE-India have not yet been compiled – and given the limited resources available for mega-corpus compilation projects, the idea of a very large and representative Indian National Corpus, comparable to the British National Corpus (BNC), will presumably remain wishful thinking for the foreseeable future.

With the advent of the world-wide web, however, it has become possible to compile larger databases by utilising the vast amount of data available on the Internet. In an innovative pilot study, Hoffmann (2007) has sketched out how a homogeneous corpus of the on-line archive of the CNN transcripts can be compiled in a semi-automatic way and how the data can be automatically reformatted in such a way that they can be used as a linguistic corpus. Hoffmann's (2007) 'webpage-to-megacorpus' method has also been used by Mukherjee and Hoffmann (2006) for the compilation of a web-derived corpus with texts from the on-line archive of the Calcutta-based national Indian newspaper *The Statesman*. The web-derived Statesman Corpus includes approximately 31 million words from a wide range of newspaper texts. The four major steps of the compilation procedure are summarised in Figure 3.[7]

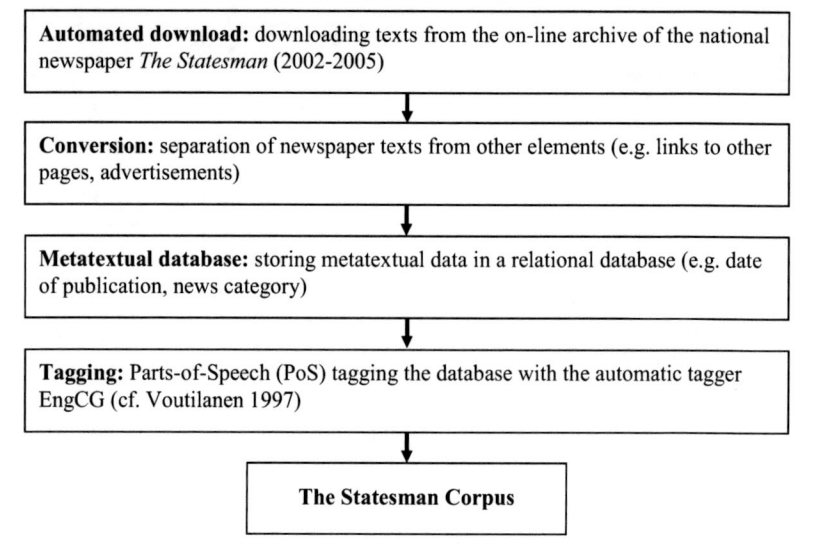

```
┌─────────────────────────────────────────────────────────────────┐
│ Automated download: downloading texts from the on-line archive  │
│ of the national newspaper The Statesman (2002-2005)             │
└─────────────────────────────────────────────────────────────────┘
                                │
                                ▼
┌─────────────────────────────────────────────────────────────────┐
│ Conversion: separation of newspaper texts from other elements   │
│ (e.g. links to other pages, advertisements)                     │
└─────────────────────────────────────────────────────────────────┘
                                │
                                ▼
┌─────────────────────────────────────────────────────────────────┐
│ Metatextual database: storing metatextual data in a relational  │
│ database (e.g. date of publication, news category)              │
└─────────────────────────────────────────────────────────────────┘
                                │
                                ▼
┌─────────────────────────────────────────────────────────────────┐
│ Tagging: Parts-of-Speech (PoS) tagging the database with the    │
│ automatic tagger EngCG (cf. Voutilanen 1997)                    │
└─────────────────────────────────────────────────────────────────┘
                                │
                                ▼
                  ┌──────────────────────────┐
                  │   The Statesman Corpus   │
                  └──────────────────────────┘
```

Figure 3: Compiling the Statesman Corpus: from webpage to mega-corpus

Although the Statesman Corpus is restricted to newspaper language, it provides a particularly valuable database for the description of Standard Indian English for various reasons:

- The database is very large and makes it possible to find low-frequency forms and structures that do not occur in 1-million-word standard corpora of Indian English.
- As it includes acrolectal written English, deviant forms and structures – even if they occur with low frequencies – can be taken to be acceptable innovations and not mistakes committed by speakers with a low level of L2 competence and/or performance errors in on-line speech production.
- Newspaper language is of particular importance in the context of second-language varieties of English as it exerts a much more prominent standardising and normative influence on L2 users of English than is the case in native varieties of English.

---

[7] For more detailed information on the compilation procedure see Mukherjee and Hoffmann (2006) and Hoffmann (2007).

Corpus-based Insights into Verb-complementational Innovations in Indian English 231

The Statesman Corpus provides us with many more instances of "new" ditransitives than ICE-India. This holds true for both types and tokens. As for types, Table 4 lists all the verbs that are attested in the ditransitive construction in the Statesman Corpus at least once.

Table 4: "New" ditransitive verbs in the Statesman Corpus[8]

"New" ditransitive verb	Occurrences in the ditransitive construction
advise	10
brief	1
confer	3
despatch/dispatch	1
explain	2
father	1
gift	26
impart	8
inform	4
intimate	1
notify	1
present	18
print	1
provide	217
put	2
remind	4
rob	4
submit	1
supply	15
threaten	1

In Table 4, those verbs that occur more than five times in the ditransitive construction in the Statesman Corpus are highlighted in boldface. In contradistinction to verbs that are attested only marginally in the ditransitive construction (e.g. *notify, threaten*), these verbs can be viewed as being grammatically institutionalised as ditransitive verbs in Indian English. Given that *provide* and – to a lesser extent – *present* are acceptable in the ditransitive construction in American English (see above) and that *supply* is also sporadically attested ditransitively in British English (cf. Mukherjee 2005: 82; 207), the most interesting cases of the six verbs in boldface, representing genuinely Indian English innovations, are *advise, gift* and *impart*. Some illustrative examples are given in (14) to (16).

---
[8] *Provide* is again included here as a "new" ditransitive because the reference variety is, for historical reasons, British English (see also footnote 5).

(14) *I have **advised** him some technical changes like using both hands while stopping the ball.* <The Statesman 2004-03-26>
(15) *She said she wanted to **gift** him a dream.* <The Statesman 2003-02-17>
(16) *... teachers should study at least five times more than the students to be able to **impart** them the correct knowledge and wisdom.* <The Statesman 2004-11-13>

The ditransitive use of *advise*, *gift* and *impart* is licensed by the process of nativised semantico-structural analogy as depicted in Figure 2. In examples (15) and (16), the similarity in meaning between *give* as the prototypical ditransitive verb with a transfer meaning on the one hand and *gift* and *impart* on the other is straightforwardly clear – in fact, both verbs could easily be replaced by *give*. In example (14), *advise* also refers to a transfer process which has a meaning similar to the ditransitive verb *offer*.

The case of *gift* is particularly interesting not only because it occurs relatively frequently in the ditransitive construction in the Statesman Corpus but also because this example shows that the higher number of tokens of a given verb in a larger corpus makes it possible to describe the meaning extension of a verb more precisely. In particular, it should be noted that *gift*, albeit not an institutionalised ditransitive verb in British English, does sporadically occur in British English but is restricted to the domain of sports commentaries (e.g. *gift the player the ball*). In the 100-million-word BNC, there is only a single occurrence of *gift* outside the sports domain:

(17) *By conceding on the timetable, O'Neill **gifted** the Republicans an important advantage, helping them by drastically curtailing the protracted and damaging interplay of pluralist forces that would have otherwise taken place over the budget.* (BNC:EAY:1342)

Still, this example can be viewed as an extension of the use of *gift* in sports commentaries. In Indian English, however, no such register-specific restrictions seem to apply. *Gift* is used both in sports commentaries, see example (18), and in contexts in which no conceptual or metaphorical links to the domain of sports can be detected, see example (19).[9]

(18) *He was forced to bring down Nabi in the danger zone after **gifting** him the ball ...* <The Statesman 2003-12-12>
(19) *Delay means serious risk of **gifting** Islamabad a talking point* <The Statesman 2002-10-26>

The case of *gift* thus illustrates that Indian English users not only extend the ditransitive construction to novel verbs on grounds of semantico-structural

---

[9] Consider also example (15).

analogies, but that they may also broaden the range of domains in which a given verb is admissible in the ditransitive construction.

The remaining "new" ditransitive verbs in Table 4 also exemplify the process of nativised semantico-structural analogy, although it remains to be seen in the light of the low number of occurrences to what extent their ditransitive use is institutionalised in Indian English. Two illustrative examples are given in (20) and (21).

(20) The employee is also required to *inform* the appointing authority the amount of monthly instalment ... <The Statesman 2004-08-1>
(21) I *put* him a question as to whether he had an auspicious time for ... <The Statesman 2003-08-09>

Even if such uses are considered as *ad-hoc* nonce-formations, they are indicative of the rational impetus that is at the root of the process of nativised semantico-structural analogy: verbs that are semantically related to established ditransitive verbs and therefore relatable to the ditransitive construction with its structure and semantics can be used ditransitively as well. In fact, it seems rather implausible from a merely rational point of view that *inform* (~ *tell*) and *put* (~ *ask*) are not used in the ditransitive construction in present-day British English.

Put and *inform* are interesting cases because they were used ditransitively in earlier stages of British English. Examples (22) and (23) are taken from the online Gutenberg archive (cf. <http://www.gutenberg.org/>). Given that Henry James and Charles Dickens used the verbs ditransitively in their fiction writing, one must assume that the ditransitive construction was admissible for *put* and *inform* in native varieties of English in the 19th and the early 20th century.

(22) He hadn't enquired, he had averted his head, but Chad had *put* him a pair of questions that themselves smoothed the ground. (Henry James: *Ambassadors*)
(23) I have often the satisfaction of hearing the publican, the baker, and sometimes even the parish-clerk, petitioning my housekeeper ... to *inform* him the exact time by Master Humphrey's clock. (Charles Dickens: *Master Humphrey's Clock*)

There is a range of verbs that are attested in the ditransitive construction in earlier stages of native English varieties but that are no longer used ditransitively in native Englishes today, e.g. *address* and *say*. However, as Hoffmann and Mukherjee (2006) show, it is only *put* and *inform* that can be found in the ditransitive construction *both* in a 23.5-million-word web-derived corpus obtained from the Gutenberg archive with texts from the 17th to the 19th century *and* in the Statesman Corpus of present-day Indian English. All the other "new" ditransitives in present-day Indian English listed in Table 4 cannot be traced back to earlier stages of British English so that there is no empirical support for the superstrate retention hypothesis, i.e. the assumption that Indian English speakers have preserved old forms that are no longer used in British English. Rather, most of the "new" ditransitives represent clear cases of creative innovations that are based on an L2-internal, rationally motivated and analogy-driven restructuring of the verb-complementational system of English along the lines of nativised semantico-structural analogy.

3.3 "New" light-verb constructions

In a pilot study based on web-derived corpora, Hoffmann et al. (2007) have shown that light-verb constructions are an area in which L2 speakers of English in Bangladesh, India, Pakistan and Sri Lanka modify existing forms or create new forms. Light-verb constructions are constructions in which a semantically fairly empty ('light') verb and a lexically more specific ('heavy') deverbal noun (e.g. *have a look*) are combined. This construction is semantically equivalent to the use of the simplex root verb (e.g. *look*) from which the deverbal noun in the light-verb construction is derived.[10] For the purpose of the present paper, the focus will be on those light-verb constructions in Indian English:

– that include the most prototypical light verbs *have*, *take* and *give*;
– that include deverbal nouns that are isomorphous with the corresponding simplex verb (e.g. *look* (v.) = *look* (n.) as in *take a look*, but not *argue* (v.) ≠ *argument* (n.) as in *have an argument*);
– that are semantically equivalent with the corresponding simplex verb (e.g. *boost* (v.) = *give a boost*, but not *say* (v.) ≠ *have a say*).

In ICE-India and the Statesman Corpus, many instances of creative innovations in the area of light-verb constructions can be found. Structurally, they can be grouped into the following two categories: (1) light-verb constructions with zero articles and definite articles; (2) light-verb constructions with deviant light verbs or deviant deverbal nouns.

In British and American English, light-verb constructions include an indefinite article before the deverbal noun. In Indian English, however, speakers also at times use the definite article instead, see example (24), or omit the (indefinite) article altogether, see example (25).

---

[10] Light-verb constructions have spawned a vast literature and have been treated under various alternative labels, e.g. "expanded predicates" (cf. Algeo 1995) and "stretched verb constructions" (cf. Allerton 2002). It is beyond the scope of the present paper to discuss in detail the differences between the various approaches and terminologies; suffice it to say that the variability in terminology also reflects a lack of agreement on how to define and demarcate the phenomenon. In the present paper, light-verb constructions will be defined rather narrowly, following Hoffmann et al. (2007).

(24) Now **take the taste** *of uh the potato chips* <ICE-India S1B-021>
(25) *Therefore, madam some changes have been brought by this government ... to* **give boost** *to the infrastructure industry* <ICE-India S1B-052>

Indian English speakers allow for more variation in the prenominal position of a light-verb construction, which is reflected by the variability of (zero) article usage in established verb-noun collocations in English. Note, for example, that the use of the definite article in *get the taste of sth.* in the sense of *taste* (v.) *sth.* is fully acceptable, so that the use of *take the taste* in Indian English seems to be based on a systematic extension of the definite article to light-verb constructions. Also, *give boost to sth.* can be viewed as an analogy-based formation because other, formally equivalent (semi-)idiomatic constructions with *give*, e.g. *give rise to sth.* and *give birth to sth.* do not include a prenominal indefinite article either.

Indian English speakers sometimes also use variants of established light-verb constructions in which the verb-noun collocations are different from the ones that one would expect in native varieties of English. Specifically, this group includes the cases in which either the light verb or the deverbal noun deviates from the preferred choice in British English. Consider examples (26) to (29).

(26) *Now if you* **give a look** *at the figures ...* <ICE-India S1B-040>
(27) *This helps tremendously to* **take a** *deep* **inbreathe** *without any strain...* <ICE-India S2A-055>
(28) *Supporters thronged the airport and the club lawns to* **have a glimpse** *of their Samba star.* <The Statesman 2002-07-05>
(29) *We* **took a glimpse** *of the unit.* <The Statesman 2002-04-19>

In examples (26), the preferred choice in British and American English is the light verb *have* and *take* respectively; *give* is usually not found in this combination with *look* (n.). The rational impetus for this form in Indian English seems to be a general extension of the light verb *give* to new collocates (such as *look*), which is in line with the much higher frequency of *give* in Indian English in general and the formation of new verb-noun-collocations with *give* in Indian English in particular (cf. Mukherjee and Hoffmann 2006).[11] In example (27), the usual deverbal noun in native varieties of English is *breath*.[12] In this particular

---

[11] The verb *give* occurs 1797 times in ICE-India, but only 1064 times in ICE-GB (which also includes 1 million words of spoken and written English from the same genres as ICE-India). In this context, Mukherjee and Hoffmann (2006: 154f.) discuss various examples of new collocations and constructions in which *give* is used in Indian English, e.g. *give a complaint* (~ *make a complaint*) and *give explanation to sth.* (~ *explain sth.*).
[12] In example (27), the deverbal noun *inbreathe* can be viewed as being isomorphous with the corresponding verb *breathe in* under the assumption that the preposition has been prefixed to the verb.

case, the innovation seems to come in at the level of derivational morphology. In examples (28) and (29), Indian English speakers use the deverbal noun *glimpse* in contexts in which native speakers would prefer the deverbal noun *look*. The new light-verb constructions *have a/the/Ø glimpse* and *take a/the/Ø glimpse* are presumbaly motivated by the existing formal template *catch a glimpse* and the semantic templates *have a look* and *take a look*, respectively; here again, we have classic cases of nativised semantico-structural analogy. Note, however, that while *have a/the/Ø glimpse* occurs 60 times in the Statesman Corpus (2.3 instances per million words), the variant *take a/the/Ø glimpse* is only sporadically attested with two occurrences in the entire corpus (0.08 instances per million words). Neither *have a/the/Ø glimpse* nor *take a/the/Ø glimpse* occur in 8.6 million words of British English in the quality newspapers and periodicals of the BNC.

As Hoffmann et al. (2007) compare light-verb constructions in web-derived corpora of various South Asian Englishes, their findings corroborate the assumption that verb-complementational innovations of a similar kind can be found in virtually all second-language varieties of English. Under the assumption that English in Sri Lanka has developed into a second-language variety in its own right (cf. e.g. Herat 2006) and cannot be considered a learner language – as, for example, suggested by Fonseka (2003) –, verb-complementational deviations from the historical input variety of British English in acrolectal written newspaper language in Sri Lanka represent true innovations and candidates for emerging local norms. From this perspective, it does not come as a surprise, for example, that the "new" light verb-constructions *have a/the/Ø glimpse* and *take a/the/Ø glimpse* also occur in a 26-million word corpus of Sri Lankan newspaper English, albeit sporadically (0.65 instances and 0.11 instances per million words respectively). It thus seems that similar processes of analogy-based restructurings of the verb-complementational system, allowing for new patterns to emerge, are at work in different L2 varieties of English.[13]

The low frequencies of occurrence for "new" light-verb constructions such as *have a/the/Ø glimpse* and *take a/the/Ø glimpse* even in very large web-derived corpora highlight the limits of 1-million-word standard corpora of L2 varieties of English such as ICE-India. In fact, many creative verb-complementational innovations, which by their very nature are low-frequency phenomena, do not even occur in ICE-India and would go unnoticed if much larger corpora were not compiled and consulted. For example, while *have a/the/Ø glimpse* occurs three times in ICE-India, the variant *take a/the/Ø glimpse* does not. The existence of the latter variant, however, is particularly interesting because it may imply that in present-day Indian English, both the preferred form in British Eng-

---

[13] Alternatively, one might also argue that some of the new forms in Sri Lankan English are due to an 'epicentral' influence exerted by the largest and most dominant South Asian variety by far, i.e. Indian English, on much smaller neighbouring anglophone speech communities (cf. Mukherjee 2008).

lish (*have a look*) and the preferred form in American English (*take a look*) can serve as input into the process of nativised semantico-structural analogy. In a wider setting, it is high time that after 60 years of Indian independence from Britain, the focus in research into Indian English be shifted from a comparison with the historical input variety and be broadened to comparative studies of all major varieties of English in general and American English as the overwhelmingly largest variety in particular.

4. Concluding remarks

The present paper has provided an overview of verb-complementational innovations in Indian English with regard to prepositional verbs, ditransitive verbs and light-verb constructions. The innovative forms and structures have been shown to be based on a rational impetus, which makes Indian English users of English draw analogies between existing formal and semantic templates in English on the one hand and the newly emerging forms on the other: this process can be defined as nativised semantico-structural analogy.

At a methodological level, the present case studies have shown that standard-size 1-million-word corpora of Indian English are often too small to present authentic instances of creative innovations, which by defintion are low-frequency phenomena. It is thus necessary to complement the analysis of standard-size corpora with the compilation and analysis of larger databases. The world-wide web in general and the on-line archives of Indian English newspapers in particular lend themselves to the creation of web-derived corpora of standard written Indian English, representing a very significant part of acrolectal variants of present-day Indian English.

What lies ahead is a systematic and more comprehensive account of all areas in which creative innovations in Indian English verb complementation – and in other lexicogrammatical domains (e.g. collocations, cf. Schilk 2006) – can be found. It would also be interesting to compare the findings for Indian English with other second-language varieties of English in South Asia and elsewhere in order to identify shared innovations in L2 Englishes worldwide. For example, "new" prepositional verbs such as *discuss about* are not restricted to Indian English but seem to be ubiquitous (cf. Hartford 1989: 115) and seem to reflect general innovative processes in L2 speakers' usage; more research is needed in order to capture such verb-complementational 'Angloversals' – a term that Sand (2005) uses for shared morphosyntactic features of contact varieties of English.

Many of the morphosyntactic features shared by contact Englishes worldwide can also be found in learner Englishes. Twenty years ago, Williams (1987, 1989) suggested approaching second-language varieties of English from the perspective of second-language acquisition (SLA) theory, given that individual interlanguages and institutionalised second-language varieties share many language acquisition phenomena and many formal features. Unfortunately, this plea has been largely ignored over the past two decades, probably also because linguists interested in L2 varieties did not want to describe L2 Englishes in terms of learner Englishes in general and error analysis in particular. With the advent of various ICE corpora of L2 varieties and learner corpora like the International Corpus of Learner English (ICLE), however, an integrated and comparative approach to second-language varieties and learner Englishes is not only compelling and useful, but also empirically feasible on a large scale (cf. e.g. Nesselhauf 2009, Mukherjee and Hundt forthcoming).

While this is a welcome development from a descriptive perspective, a word of caution is necessary. Specifically, it needs to be stressed that SLA concepts for the description of interlanguages will need to be adapted to the fundamentally different contexts of usage of institutionalised second-language varieties such as Indian English. With regard to the verb-complementational innovations discussed in the present paper, for example, processes of nativised semantico-structural analogy should not be viewed as overgeneralisations in the sense of overextensions of rules leading to deviations from a certain norm that will have to be ironed out at some later point of the acquisition process. Rather, in the context of institutionalised second-language varieties, in which L2 users are licensed to develop their own local norms, verb-complementational innovations are best seen to be exponents of a 'creative idiomaticity' (cf. Prodromou 2007) on the part of competent L2 users of acrolectal variants of Indian English.[14] That is to say, although we may find the same forms and structures in endonormatively stabilised L2 varieties of English and in interlanguages based on teaching and learning as a foreign language, the underlying processes are inherently and fundamentally different: while Indian English users shape their own variety of English by bringing in creative innovations, e.g. in the area of verb complementation, foreign language learners are bound to orient themselves towards exonormative standards set by speakers outside their own speech community. Therefore, I strongly recommend that the distinction between 'norm-developing' L2 speakers and 'norm-dependent' foreign-language learners of English (cf. Kachru 1985b) be upheld in future research.

---

[14] Note, however, that Prodromou (2007) applies the concept of 'creative idiomaticity' to users of English as a lingua franca (ELF). In my view, however, ELF is an epiphenomenon which is based on the output of a wide range of very different groups of speakers, including L2 speakers of English, who also use the English language for many purposes within their own speech communities (e.g. Indian English speakers), and foreign-language learners of English (e.g. English learners in Germany).

5. References

Algeo, J. 1995. "Having a look at the expanded predicate". *The Verb in Contemporary English: Theory and Description*, ed. B. Aarts & C.F. Meyer, 203-217. Cambridge: Cambridge University Press.
Allerton, D. J. 2002. *Stretched Verb Constructions in English*. London: Routledge.
Baumgardner, R.J. 1998. "Word-formation in Pakistani English". *English World-Wide* 19(2). 205-246.
Fonseka, G. E. A. 2003. "Sri Lankan English: exploding the fallacy". Paper presented at the 9th International Conference on Sri Lankan Studies, Matara, 28-30 November 2003.
Goldberg, A. E. 1995. *Constructions: A Construction Grammar Approach to Argument Structure*. Chicago, IL: University of Chicago Press.
Goldberg, A. E. 2006. *Constructions at Work: The Nature of Generalization in Language*. Oxford: Oxford University Press.
Green, G. 1974. *Semantics and Syntactic Regularity*. Bloomington, IN: Indiana University Press.
Greenbaum, S., ed. 1996. *Comparing English Worldwide: The International Corpus of English*. Oxford: Clarendon.
Grisham, J. 2002. *The Summons*. New York: Doubleday (Random House).
Hartford, B. S. 1989. "Prototype effects in non-native English: object-coding in verbs of saying". *World Englishes* 8(2). 97-117.
Herat, M. 2006. "Substitute *one* in Sri Lankan English". *Leeds Working Papers in Linguistics* 11, <http://www.leeds.ac.uk/linguistics/WPL/ WPL11.html>.
Hoffmann, S. 2007. "From web-page to mega-corpus: the CNN transcripts". *Corpus Linguistics and the Web*, ed. M. Hundt, N. Nesselhauf & C. Biewer. Amsterdam: Rodopi. 69-85.
Hoffmann, S., M. Hundt & J. Mukherjee. 2007. "Indian English – an emerging epicentre? Insights from web-derived corpora of South Asian Englishes". Paper presented at the 28th ICAME Conference, Stratford-upon-Avon, 23-27 May 2007.
Hoffmann, S. & J. Mukherjee. 2007. "Ditransitive verbs in Indian English and British English: a corpus-linguistic study". *Arbeiten aus Anglistik und Amerikanistik* 32, 5-24.
Kachru, B. B. 1983. *The Indianization of English: The English Language in India*. Delhi: Oxford University Press.
Kachru, B. B. 1985a. "Institutionalized second-language varieties". *The English Language today* ed. S. Greenbaum, 211-226. Oxford: Pergamon.
Kachru, B. B. 1985b. "Standards, codification and sociolinguistic realism: the English language in the outer circle". *English in the World: Teaching and*

Learning the Language and Literatures ed. R. Quirk & H. G. Widdowson. Cambridge: Cambridge University Press. 11-30.

Kachru, B. B. 2005. *Asian Englishes: Beyond the Canon*. Hong Kong: Hong Kong University Press.

Mukherjee, J. 2001. "Principles of pattern selection: a corpus-based case study". *Journal of English Linguistics* 29. 295-314.

Mukherjee, J. 2005. *English Ditransitive Verbs: Aspects of Theory, Description and a Usage-Based Model*. Amsterdam: Rodopi.

Mukherjee, J. 2007. "Steady states in the evolution of New Englishes: present-day Indian English as an equilibrium". *Journal of English Linguistics* 35(2). 157-187.

Mukherjee, J. 2008. "Sri Lankan English: evolutionary status and epicentral influence from Indian English". *Anglistentag 2007 Münster: Proceedings* ed. K. Stierstorfer, 359-368. Trier: WVT.

Mukherjee, J. and S. Hoffmann (2006): "Describing verb-complementational profiles of New Englishes: a pilot study of Indian English". *English World-Wide* 27(2). 147-173.

Mukherjee, J. & M. Hundt (forthcoming): *Exploring Second-language Varieties of English and Learner Englishes: Bridging a Paradigm Gap*. Amsterdam: Benjamins.

Nesselhauf, Nadja. 2009. "Co-selection phenomena across New Englishes: parallels (and differences) to foreign learner varieties". *English World-Wide* 30(1). 1-26.

Nihalani, P., R. K. Tongue & P. Hosali. 1979. *Indian and British English: A Handbook of Usage and Pronunciation*. Delhi: Oxford University Press.

Nihalani, P., R. K. Tongue, P. Hosali & J. Crowther. 2004. *Indian and British English: A Handbook of Usage and Pronunciation*. Second Edition. Delhi: Oxford University Press.

Olavarría de Ersson, E. O. & P. Shaw. 2003. "Verb complementation patterns in Indian standard English". *English World-Wide* 24(2). 137-161.

Prodromou, L. 2007. "Bumping into creative idiomaticity". *English Today* 23(1). 14-25.

Quirk, R., S. Greenbaum, G. Leech & J. Svartvik. 1985. *A Comprehensive Grammar of the English Language*. London: Longman.

Sand, A. 2005. *Angloversals? Shared Morpho-syntactic Features in Contact Varieties of English*. Freiburg: Habilitationsschrift.

Schilk, M. 2006. "Collocations in Indian English: a corpus-based sample analysis". *Anglia* 124(2). 276-316.

Schneider, E. W. 2003. "The dynamics of new Englishes: from identity construction to dialect birth". *Language* 79(2). 233-281.

Schneider, E. W. 2007. *Postcolonial English: Varieties around the World*. Cambridge: Cambridge University Press.

Shastri, S. V. 1988. "The Kolhapur corpus of Indian English and work done on its basis so far". *ICAME Journal* 12. 15-26.

Shastri, S. V. 1992. "Opaque and transparent features of Indian English". *New Directions in English Language Corpora: Methodology, Results, Software Developments*, ed. G. Leitner, 263-275. Berlin: Mouton de Gruyter.

Timberlake, J. 2003. *Justified*. CD. Sony BMG.

Voutilainen, A. 1997: "The EngCG-2 Tagger in Outline", <http://www.ling.helsinki.fi/~avoutila/cg/doc/engcg2-outline/engcg2-outline.html>.

Williams, J. 1987. "Non-native varieties of English: a special case of language acquisition". *English World-Wide* 8(2). 161-199.

Williams, J. 1989. "Language acquisition, language contact and nativized varieties of English". *RELC Journal* 20(1). 39-67.

Reinhard Goltz (Bremen)

Norms and Variation in the Process of Modernizing and Vitalizing the Low German Regional Language

> *When I was born you know I couldn't speak and go*
> *my mother worked each day and she learned me to say*
> *mother and father and son sister and uncle have fun*
> *and she learned me to say life is so hard each day*
> The Lords, Poor Boy (1966)

1. Introduction

Low German, spoken in the northern part of Germany, exists in a number of distinct varieties. A main feature of this regional language is the lack of a linguistic norm, both in pronunciation and in spelling, covering the whole language area. The status of a regional language implies that a High German standard, as well as a North German vernacular,[1] accompanies this language and has done so for the last four hundred years. With High German taking the role of a standard there has been little need to improve a norm-constructing process. To an ever increasing extent this situation of a clear distinction between a standardized High German and a Low German language, rich in varieties, has changed.

At the moment Low German, as well as the language situation in Northern Germany,[2] appears to be changing dramatically, and that for a number of reasons, all heading in different directions:

1. As Low German is an endangered language, only being transmitted from one generation to the next to a small degree, people use it in fewer situations. For many people the language has been restricted to a number of key words and

---

[1] There is indeed no fixed set of items defining a Northern German vernacular. Traditionally this variety was described as "Hochdeutsch auf niederdeutschem Substrat" ('High German on a Low German basis'). The Variantenwörterbuch (Ammon et al. 2004) distinguishes for Germany between six larger areas, among them "D-nordost" and "D-nordwest" which are subsumed under the term "D-nord". Further it is stated that between these areas of regional variety there are "Unterschiede im Wortschatz, in der Aussprache und teilweise sogar in der Grammatik [...]. Diese Unterschiede, vor allem die der Aussprache, sind größtenteils bedingt durch die zugrunde liegenden Dialekte" (2004: XLVII) ('differences in the vocabulary, in the pronunciation and partly even in the grammar. Most to these differences, especially those concerning pronunciation, are determined by dialects').

[2] Schröder & Elmentaler (2009) approach the same subject from a different point of view in the project "Sprachvariation in Norddeutschland (SiN)".

sayings. No doubt, for many speakers of Low German the ability to handle the linguistic systems has decreased.
2. This is the main reason why the influence of High German has increased strongly over the last 60 years.
3. In certain cultural fields, such as literature and theatre, and media fields, such as radio and television, the necessity to leave the local dialect has fostered the spread of supra-regional elements within the Low German community.
4. There is a tendency, which is particularly apparent with Low German writers who are especially aware of their language, to avoid Low German items related to High German and therefore use 'distant forms', seemingly the better Low German forms.

There are two clear trends: transferring elements from High German into Low German and deliberately choosing 'distant forms'.

Changes on the different levels of the linguistic system can be registered: phonology, morphology, syntax, lexic, phraseology and text. It is not unusual for languages in close contact that they have an impact on each other. All speakers of Low German also use Standard German, and most of them use Standard German much more than Low German. Stellmacher deduces from this situation of diglossia that there is an influence on the Low German grammar,

> "weil der Sprecher eben an mehreren Sprachformen (…) teilhat, und zwar Sprachformen mit unterschiedlich gestalteten phonetisch-phonologischen Grammatiken." (Stellmacher 1990: 147) 'because the speaker participates in several varieties, namely varieties of which the phonetical-phonological grammars are formed in different ways.'

And he suggests that the intensity of the influence depends on the linguistic consciousness of the speakers, ranking lexical or grammatical features:

> "Es scheint, daß die standardsprachliche Beeinflussung dort am nachhaltigsten ist, wo es im Sprecherbewußtsein um nicht sprachprägende sprachliche Einheiten geht." (Stellmacher 1990: 147). 'It seems as if the influences from the standard language were most effective in such fields, which are not language forming linguistic unities, according to the consciousness of the speakers.'

The data collected for this survey are by no means representative as there have not been any larger linguistic studies recently.[3] Strictly speaking these data are not valid, especially as there are no indications as to the frequency of the phenomena, to their determination according to factors like age, regional or social background. Deviations of what could be called a Low German norm were registered, but it is uncertain whether they are indicative of processes of change, showing clear directions, or whether there is a great deal of uncertainty when

---

[3] This report is based mainly on a lecture given in 2007; recently first results of the project "Sprache in Norddeutschland" (SiN) and other smaller surveys have been published, cf. Schröder & Elmentaler (2009), Elmentaler (2008), (2009a), (2009b).

using Low German so that different forms can be used parallel. They could be seen as suggesting a process of language attrition, with the loss of patterns of a language within a bilingual situation. At least the large number of phenomena and examples demonstrate that they cannot be taken as single mistakes, but that they illustrate the direction the parts and the structure of the Low German language are heading.

The examples were taken from the Low German news bulletins, broadcast each working day from the major radio stations in Bremen and Hamburg, with the audio media having been a motor of language modernisation during the last decades. From this sample such features were incorporated that show perceptible deviations to an expected standard. Other results and patterns were elicited from experimental tests, used in courses on linguistic acceptability, which I held together with Peter Nissen in Schleswig-Holstein between 2000 and 2007. Both sources are characterized by a process of transforming Standard German texts into appropriate Low German forms.

With the increasing influence of the standard language, the Low German system is gradually losing its stability. In 2007 the number of Low German speakers has decreased to half of the number of 1984.[4] Furthermore, the number of those who declare that they can understand Low German well or very well is three times as high as those of the speakers. This situation indicates the acceleration in the process of language adaptation.

2. Constructing a norm for Low German and changing linguistic features

Due to a long process of language suppression, marginalization many speakers of Low German believe that their language is inferior and that it is not ruled by any grammatical structures.[5] The idea that Low German has got anything to do with grammar does not particularly imply to the systematic construction of the language and its items. But in fact hardly anybody within the last 400 year actually did mention norms, and the lack of a process of norm-development is evident. Low German has not developed any kind of standard, which is obviously typical not only for Low German, but also for other regional languages in Europe.[6] As a language, which had only been spoken and not used either in government or administration, Low German had been taught naturally, i.e. it was

---

[4] Cf. Stellmacher (1987) and Möller (2008); although the data are based on different samples, and therefore cannot be compared in a strict sense, they do indicate a distinct trend.

[5] Up to now there has only been one attempt to write a general grammar covering all the Low German language areas (except the East Low German dialects in the area of the former German Democratic Republic): Niederdeutsche Grammatik (1998).

[6] Cf. Goltz (2009).

passed from one generation to the next, which means that there has been no education system which could have supported language abilities as well as language awareness. The Low German Grammar of 1998 literally expresses its role as one between constructing a norm and strengthening the independence of the language.[7]

This might be the dominant impression when looking at Low German and the place of this language in society. But there has been a cultural side of the language for some 150 years, and therefore a more differentiated approach to the language is needed. Concerning the writing of Low German, there have been a number of attempts to find and to set up a trans-regional standard.[8] And not only the activities of mass media like radio and television have raised the discussion about a standardization of spoken Low German in the middle of the 20th century.

When talking about norms, most of the confident speakers of Low German can certainly indicate which forms fit their local system, and which do not. But on the other hand they do know that there is a large variety of dialect and sub-dialect forms in Low German. Thus speakers do know their local forms, but with no standard at hand, they also know that many other forms might be possible. According to this kind of local and regional co-existence of linguistic features, the number of varieties does not include socially determined patterns or historical elements.

At the beginning of the 21st century Low German is hardly ever found as a first language. This refers both to what is ideally called the mother tongue as well as to the role the language plays as a means of everyday communication. For many people in Northern Germany, Low German has become a second language, with Standard German being used as the first one. For more than 400 years there has been a history of contact between Low and High German: two closely related languages, both being involved in a process of giving and taking, but with a much stronger High German influence on Low German than the other way round. The last 400 years of language history in Northern Germany can be described as a process of adapting Low German to High German.

---

[7] Cf. Niederdeutsche Grammatik (1998: 22): "Obwohl die Grammatik keine Normierung des Niederdeutschen beabsichtigt, kann sie gleichwohl in diese Richtung wirken. Eine derartige Wirkung wird von den Verfassern in Kauf genommen, sofern sie die Eigenständigkeit des Niederdeutschen stabilisiert." ('Although the grammar does not intend to construct a norm for Low German, it might as well result in such a norm. The authors accept such an effect, as long as it strengthens the independence of the Low German language.')

[8] Cf. Kellner (2002). Still highly influential are the spelling rules by Johannes Saß. The traditional Saß concept from the mid 1950's has recently been extended by adding modern words to the dictionary which might not be found in reality, but which were constructed using patterns taken from neighbouring languages, such as Dutch or Danish. In the area of East Frisia spelling rules were published for this particular dialect area in the late 1980's. These rules have been followed strictly up to now.

Elements of transfer[9] can clearly be seen on the morphological resp. on the morphosyntactic level. Especially when themes of topical interest are involved, in spontaneously spoken language one can make out many syntactical and lexical features that show influences from the standard.[10] For a long time the phonologic seemed to be stable, but new studies show that also here changes are affecting the Low German system. There is a distinct trend from old *s* + *l, m, n, p, t* and *w* (e.g. *slapen, smieten, snacken, spelen, stuken, swümmen*) to new ʃ + *l, m, n, p, t* and *w* (*schlapen, schmieten, schnacken, schpelen, schtuken, schwümmen*).[11] This change takes place in two ways: the few peripheral areas in which ʃ + *l, m, n, p, t* and *w* has been part of the system for a long time[12] influence the neighbouring areas; and frequently used words which have become part of the North German vernacular, tend to use the High German matrix, e.g. *snacken* was the normal Low German form, when it was transferred into the North German vernacular, it was changed to *schnacken*, and this word found its way back into the Low German lexicon.[13] Although there are no surveys with respect to the

---

[9] Cf. Hansen-Jaax (1995). – Schröder (2004: 35-97, especially paragraph: Integration hochdeutscher Elemente in das Niederdeutsche, 76-79).

[10] Elmentaler (2008) lists a number of examples, comparing Low German answers to High German input forms, using Wenker sentences of the 1879/80 exploration and new enquiries made in 2006. He finds three different cases: a) the increase of variety (e.g. old *Buddel* – new *Buddel, Flasch*), b) replacement of forms (e.g. old *wovähl* – new *wievill*), c) decrease of variety (e.g. old *vundaag, hüüt* – new *hüüt*).

[11] Mensing (1927-35, VI: 271) mentions that "*sch* heute unter hochd. Einfluß vielfach an Stelle des alten *s* getreten [ist]" ('in many cases *sch* has replaced the old *s* under High German influence'). For him this phenomenon is connected more with the age of the speakers that with the region they come from. For the presence Stellmacher (2005: 171) notes for the area of the Unterweser a change towards the Standard German form: "Zu verändern scheint sich auch das Bild von anlautendem *sm-* zu *šm-*. [...] Gleiches gilt für das Verhältnis von *s* vor *t/p*." ('The occurance of *sm-* seems to be changing to *šm-*. [...] The same goes for *s* in front of *t/p*'.)

[12] This goes for example for Schleswigsch. Jensen (2007: I) surprisingly points out for the Schleswig area that few old speakers still have *s* + *p* or *t*; but the normal forms are *schp* and *scht*; in the case of *schl, schm, schn* and *schw* there is no alternative mentioned for this region. For Northern Frisia Jensen (2009: II, § 8) notes that the pronunciation of the *s* is "uneinheitlich" ('heterogeneous'): "Auch hier wirkt sich der hochdeutsche Einfluss mit der Aussprache des *s* als *sch* aus. Am deutlichsten gehalten hat sich das *s* auf den Inseln, aber auch auf dem Festland hat das *sch* noch längst nicht so sehr Einzug gehalten wie einige Kilometer weiter östlich, wo bei diesen Buchstabenkombinationen fast durchgängig *sch* gesprochen wird." ('Here also the High German influence by articulating the *s* as *sch* can be seen. Most distinctly the *s* is still present on the islands, but also on the main land the *sch* is by far not as strong as some kilometres to the East, where these combinations of consonants are generally pronounced *sch*.')

[13] Duden. Rechtschreibung (1996: 658) mentions: "**schnacken** (*nordd. für* plaudern); Platt –"; this entry was only slightly changed for the 24th ed. (2006: 900): "**schnacken** (*nordd. für* plaudern); 'Platt schnacken'"; in both cases the noun *Schnack* is mentioned in spe-

s/sch-change covering the whole Low German language area, the old *s*-forms are still in use in many places, and it seems untimely, when it is announced that they "in größeren Teilen des niederdeutschen Kernraums bereits als veraltet gelten müssen".[14]

It seems that the Standard German system is taking over the role of the matrix, giving out the models for the processes of change. This also means that the Low German language system has lost its vitality to a high degree. By taking over patterns from Standard German, the loss of traditional forms is being accelerated. Should this development continue in a linear way, the stock of linguistic patterns of Low German will fade into a variety close to a North German vernacular. But language change will certainly not follow a strict line. One of the reasons is that, besides the pressure coming from High German, there are continuing efforts to expand the structural and functional range of Low German. Especially the media have worked in this direction for several decades.

It is not clear in which way the fact that Low German is merely a nonstandard language affects the process of change. Günter Rohdenburg, a scholar of English philology, has described the variety of forms in different parts of the language system, and he has concentrated on morphosyntactic elements. He classes Low German among dialect systems, and points out that they are more natural and closed within their own borderlines than standard languages: "Universale Prinzipien können sich vermutlich deshalb in dialektalen Systemen eher und deutlicher entfalten, weil diese von normativen Zwängen weitgehend frei geblieben sind."[15] On the other hand, normative compulsion certainly produces stability within the linguistic system. With this stability lacking, and in addition with strong influences from a typologically closely related language, it might only be a small step from language change to language attrition.

In this report, taken from practical language experience, I shall concentrate on morphosyntactical and lexical phenomena. Besides that, Standard German influence is evident in syntax, especially when looking at the conjunctions used to initiate subordinate clauses. In phraseology most patterns chosen follow Standard German patterns, and even in phonology we find the tendency towards a linguistic re-arrangement.

---

cial articles. The Variantenwörterbuch (Ammon et al. 2004: 678) lists *schnacken* and *Schnack* as well, but it adds a cross reference to *Klugschnacker(in)*. Hennig & Meier (1956-2006, IV: 373) mention under the main entry *snacken*: "vereinzelt *schnacken*" ('sporadically *schnacken*').

[14] Elmentaler (2008: 72) ('in larger parts of the Low German core area have to be considered to be archaic').

[15] Rohdenburg (2004: 116) ('Universal priciples can probably develop easier and more distinct within dialect systems as there has been a minimum of normative restraints on them').

3. Morphosyntactic categories

Morphosyntactic elements are morphological items carrying our syntactical functions. In everyday speech these elements are not being mentioned as carefully as for example phonological or lexical ones. Therefore these elements are good indicators of language stability. Every sentence has a certain number of morphosyntactic elements, thus the competent handling needs a solid set of forms known from experience. When using such elements the speaker has to be aware of the construction of the whole sentence. With many speakers Low German seems to be used in phrases, language structure is relatively stable within short sentences. As the production of longer texts is generally unusual these days, one can expect a strong influence on the Low German system from standard patterns.

Although there is no overall standard, there are regional traditions in using certain forms and avoiding others. It is evident that regional varieties can serve the same function. With regards to the appearance of unexpected forms, it is generally not easy to decide whether these are the appropriate regional forms, accepted parallel forms, or constructions from outside the traditional Low German system, using patterns adapted from Standard German or other languages.

3.1 Plurals of Nouns

The lack of a supra-regional standard in Low German[16] is responsible for the fact that the dialects have preserved a large variety of plural forms, recorded in the regional dictionaries. For *Appel* one can find *Appel, Appeln, Appels, Äppel, Äppels*, and for Westphalia also *Appele* and *Äppele* are mentioned. This coexistence might cause uncertainties among the speakers when they come upon words which are not used very often. On the other hand many Low German plurals follow Standard German patterns (Low German *Book*, Pl. *Böker* corresponds with Standard German *Buch*, Pl. *Bücher*, using the pattern Umlaut + -*er*). But again, we find examples of avoiding such forms. Speakers following this avoiding strategy tend to use *s*-plurals as alternative patterns. These *s*-plurals appear much more frequently in Low German than in Standard German, where they are restricted to a number of foreign words. Thus the use of *s*-plurals may be a regarded an element to constitute distant forms. With speakers not very proficient with this language one can also realize that they tend to use English patterns when speaking a language different from Standard German. The *s*-plural could also be read as an influence from English patterns.[17]

---

[16] Cf. Niederdeutsche Grammatik (1998: 146-150).
[17] Jensen (2009: 2.1) notes that the distant forms *Fruunslüüd* and *Mannslüüd* are much more unusual that *Fruuns* and *Männer*, the first one using the *s*-plural, the other one using the Standard German pattern.

(1) *För de Ämters gellt...* (expected form: *Ämter*)[18]
    'For the administration it was decided...'
    (HG: Für die Behörden wurde festgelegt...)
(2) *De Schools blievt dicht.* (expected form: *Scholen*)[19]
    'The schools are being kept closed.'
    (HG: Die Schulen bleiben geschlossen.)

3.2 Adjective Inflection

Adjective inflection is a field which cannot be described properly for the whole Low German language area. At the moment it is very hard to say whether a certain form follows a regional Low German tradition, or whether there is supraregional Low German influence, or influence from a regional vernacular or from Standard German. Stellmacher noted at the end of the 20th century: "Dabei herrscht eine ziemliche Regellosigkeit."[20] As a result we find a multiplicity of forms, e.g. for the strong declination of the singular nominative masculine there can be at least four varieties:[21]

Table 1: Variety in Adjective Declination

Masc. Nom. Sing.	en *dick* Kopp
	en *dicke* Kopp
	en *dicken* Kopp
	en *dicker* Kopp

For all four forms it is possible to postulate analogies so that all are supported in different ways: the form without a declination mark (*dick*) corresponds to neuter forms in the same position for (*en ool Book*) and also with English constructions; according to the Niederdeutsche Grammatik the *e*-ending is most frequent (*dicke*) and therefore it serves as a standard. This form corresponds to the weak declination in the same position (*de dicke Kopp*) and to the feminine form in the

---

[18] For *Amt* neither Mensing (1927-1935) nor Hennig & Meier (1956-2006) mention plural forms. The predominance of singular forms might cause this uncertainty.
[19] Mensing (1927-1935) mentions *Scholen* within the sentences indicating the phrasal use of the word; in Hennig & Meier (1956-2006) "Plural *-(e)n*" is part of the grammatical information.
[20] Stellmacher (1990: 163) ('In fact, the use of the patterns is rather accidental').
[21] Cf. Niederdeutsche Grammatik (1998: 191f.); Lindow mentions as Low German standard *dicken*, cf. Wolfgang Lindow (3rd ed.: 273); for Schleswig and North Frisia *dicke* is mentioned as normal, cf. Jensen (2007: 3.3.1) and (2009: 3.3.1); in the Probstei it is *dicken*, cf. Graf (2007: 3.3.1).

same position (*en ole Kann*); the *en*-ending corresponds to the non-nominative position (*He hett en dicken Kopp*) and illustrates the tendency to use a system with one homogeneous form for all cases; and the *er*-form finally refers to the Standard German pattern (*ein dicker Kopf*).

Table 2: Adjective Declination

			strong declination	weak declination
Masc.	Sing.	Nom.	*dicke Foot*	*de dicke Foot*
		Non-Nom.	*dicken Foot*	*den dicken Foot*
	Plur.	Nom.	*dicke Fööt*	*de dicken Fööt*
		Non-Nom.	*dicke Fööt*	*de dicken Fööt*
Fem.	Sing.	Nom.	*ole Straat*	*de ole Straat*
		Non-Nom.	*ole Straat*	*de ole Straat*
	Plur.	Nom.	*ole Straten*	*de olen Straten*
		Non-Nom.	*ole Straten*	*de olen Straten*
Neutr.	Sing.	Nom.	*witt Huus*	*dat witte Huus*
		Non-Nom.	*witt Huus*	*dat witte Huus*
	Plur.	Nom.	*witte Hüüs*	*de witten Hüüs*
		Non-Nom.	*witte Hüüs*	*de witten Hüüs*

Obviously in former times there has been a platform giving these forms a particular regional background. But this platform seems to be fading so that the whole range can be found within the same area. And it is not clear whether people consider the use of this variety to be a deviation hurting the system or as sign for flexibility, which could even be seen in a positive way. But the deviations from the expected forms indicate the instability of the adjective inflection.[22]

The strongest influence certainly comes from Standard German. This is obvious in the case of translating news texts from Standard German into Low German, especially when words are effected which are not part of the traditional lexicon. Although it is not impossible that the *-en*-endings in the strong declina-

---

[22] The instability can also be seen when looking at the strong declination of the neuter in singular nominative: The Niederdeutsche Grammatik (1998: 191f.) has *en ool Book* as the main form, but *ool/olet* is also mentioned. For Schleswigsch the same forms are presented, cf. Jensen (2007: 3.3); for North Frisia Jensen (2009: 3.3) mentions the type *ole Book* as normal, on the other hand "das *-t* im Singular Neutrum wird nur einmal genannt" ('the *-t* in singular neuter is only mentioned once'). Lindow (3rd ed.) also mentions *oles*, a form that seems to be influenced by Standard German but which is in common use in several Low German dialect areas.

tion are influenced by the non-nominative singular forms or the plural forms of the weak declination, it is more likely that they were affected by Standard German patterns using the ending -*en* for the strong declination in plural:

(3) (LG trad.) ... *mit radikaal-islaamsche Taliban-Rebellen...*
'... with radical islamistic taliban rebels...'
(HG: ... mit radikal-islamisch**en** Taliban-Rebellen...)
(LG transfer: ...mit radikaal-islaamsch**en** Taliban-Rebellen...)

In other cases even the inflection of a complex phrase, consisting of adjective and noun, is affected.

(4) (LG) *In swore Fäll mutt ... betahlt warrn.*
'In severe cases there has to be paid...'
(HG: In schwer**en** Fäll**en** ist ... zu zahlen.)
(LG transfer: In swor**en** Fäll**en** mutt ... betahlt warrn.)

3.3 Verb Inflection

A special kind of language change can be seen when looking at the verb inflection. It is typical for a number of Low German verbs that their vowels in the present tense 2nd and 3rd person singular are shortend, e.g. *schrieven: ik schriev, du schrifft, he schrifft, wi schrievt*; this phenomenon can be accompanied by an umlaut, e.g. *lopen: ik loop, du löppst, he löppt, wi loopt*. The following consonant is also affected, usually voiced ones are changed into voiceless ones (*schrieven – du schriffst*); voiceless consonants are usually not shifted (*lopen – du löppst*), but there are exceptions (*söken – du söchst*).

The texts of the radio news show that the clear restriction of the short vowels to the position of two singular forms is fading:

(5) ..., *dat 50.000 junge Lüüd en Lehrsteed söcht.* (expected form: söökt)
'..., that 50.000 adolescents are looking for an apprenticeship contract position.'
(HG: ..., dass 50.000 Jugendliche einen Ausbildungsplatz suchen.)

One can only speculate about the reasons for this change from the expected *söökt* to *söcht*. It looks as though the form of the 3rd person plural is constructed under the influence of the 3rd person singular. There is a clear distribution in Standard German: *sie sucht* (sg.) and *sie suchen* (pl.). This pattern has not been drawn into the Low German system yet, although there are areas with *en*- plurals (East Frisia, Schleswig, Mecklenburg-Vorpommern). On the other hand the differentiation by vowel shift is a pattern that does exist in Standard German, but which occurs less frequently than in Low German (e.g. *werfen: ich werfe, du wirfst; laufen: ich laufe, du läufst*). Trying to look for parallel structures might be responsible for the fact that those Low German verbs are especially affected where the Standard German equivalents do not show any kind of vowel shift. It is interesting to note that in all cases found so far it is the singular form that is transferred into the plural system, and not vice-versa. This might be due to the higher frequency in everyday speech, with sentences like *Wat söchst du dor?* as guidelines. In this special case the choice of *söcht* instead of *söökt* might be supported by the spelling with *ch* which is closer to the Standard German pattern.

The Low German verbs *stahn, gahn, slaan* and *doon* produce a special kind of vowel shift in the present tense forms of the 2nd and 3rd person singular: *steihst/steiht, geihst/geiht, sleist/sleit* and *deist/deit*. There is some provisional indication that also in these cases the singular pattern can be taken over into the plural system:

(6) *Lüüd, de nich smöökt,* **steiht** *in Neddersassen ünner beter Schuul.* (expected form: staht)
'Non-smokers in Lower Saxony are protected in a better way.'
(HG: Nichtraucher stehen in Niedersachsen unter besserem Schutz.)

A special feature of Low German is the use of constructions with the verb *doon* where *doon* takes the position of a modal verb, carrying the grammatical information, and the second verb is in the infinitive. The use of such forms is generally restricted to verbs in subordinate clauses (LG: *Ik weet, dat he kamen deit*, HG: *Ich weiß, dass er kommt*; Engl.: 'I know that he comes'); and in certain main clause positions the stress is put on the verb (LG: *Verköpen do ik nix*, HG: *Ich verkaufe nichts*, Engl.: 'I don't sell anything'). The use is also optional (*Ik weet, dat he kamen deit* stands parallel to *Ik weet, dat he kummt*). We have little knowledge about the frequency with which simple verb constructions and verb-*doon*-constructions occur in every day spoken language or in written texts. There seem to be two tendencies that can be described: As there is no support by Standard German structures *doon* as a modal verb is decreasing. On the other hand, in primarily written texts, and in translated texts such as the radio news, verb-*doon*-constructions are becoming more and more popular, because they indicate a clear distance between Low German and Standard German, taken as a sign for the independence of Low German: "Die sog. *tun*-Umschreibung wird als eine deutliche Eigenheit des Nd. angesehen."[23]

(7) a. *De Mann, de dat Kind bisiet bringen dee...*
(7) b. (alternatively) *De Mann, de dat Kind bisiet bröcht hett...*
'The man who killed the child ...'
(HG: Der Mann, der das Kind ermordete ...)

---

[23] Stellmacher (1990: 173f.) ('the so called *doon*-periphrasis is esteemed a distinct peculiarity of Low German').

3.4 Female Forms of Nouns

For the marking of female forms of nouns Low German uses several patterns. Most frequent is certainly the use of the suffix *-in* which is also used in Standard German. According to the natural gender the masculine *Lehrer* can be turned into a female *Lehrerin*. Another pattern seems to have lost strength, especially as it is not backed by Standard German pattern: the suffix *-sch(e)* can still be found in a number of lexicalized forms such as *Kööksch* (HG: *Köchin*, Engl.: 'female cook') or *Neihersch* (HG: *Näherin*, Engl.: 'sempstress'). This pattern is being strengthened, although there are dialect areas in which *-sch(e)* is considered pejorative. Especially with new words from the fields of politics and administration this old pattern has found its way back into the language system. Thus the *Richtersch* stands besides the *Gesundheitsministersch* and the *Fernsehansegersch*.

(8) *Bundeskanzlersch Merkel kümmt vundaag mit den französöschen Ministerpräsident tohoop.*
'Today Chancellor Merkel meets the French Minister President.'
(HG: Bundeskanzlerin Merkel trifft sich heute mit dem französischen Ministerpräsidenten.)

4. Vocabulary

It is typical for Low German that under the general roof of the language there are many differences from one area to another. A great number of these lexical differences have been described in extensive projects, e.g. "Der Deutsche Sprachatlas" and "Der Deutsche Wortatlas", now in digitally presented in the DIWA project. The map '*sprechen*' for instance indicates geographical areas for *snacken, praten, küren, spreken* and *reden* which are partly clearly determined and partly merge with each other.[24] With regard to processes of changing it seems that, at least at this stage, these forms are stable. The differences are being kept, each word indicating a certain area. One could have expected that the North Lower Saxon form (*snacken*) as the one of the largest areas and the strongest appearance in cultural contexts and in the media, would have ousted the other ones, but there are no hints of such a change. Other traditional differences, indicating strong Standard German influence on the phonetic structure in certain areas, such as the one between *Week* and *Woch* for 'week' or the one between *Kark* and *Kirch* for 'church', also seem to be unaffected.

It is to be expected that new lexical items more than traditional ones tend to be loan words, in the particular case of Low German at the beginning of the 21st century taken from Standard German or English. Only a few typical cases will

---

[24] Unfortunately the map in König (2007: 176) lists the standardized form *schnacken*.

be discussed here. Before that the focus shall be put on functional words. More than transmitting meaning, these are responsible for the organization of the parts of speech involved. Thus changes within the field of functional words indicate traces of a different, and in a way more general and decisive kind of structural change within the language than the processes connected with finding words to express meaning.

4.1 Functional Words

Linguistic research on Low German usually points out regional differences. This is especially true for lexical and morphosyntactic items. But research has hitherto only taken little interest in the processes of change and within this field the organisation of items within sentences and texts has been considered to be marginal. The following collection can only give a first indication of ongoing processes.

4.1.1 The Definite Article

The linguistic elements used to form the definite article show that the Low German system is placed structurally between the Standard German system, differentiating form according to case and gender, and the one article-form generally used in English.

From here we find two different tendencies in Low German. Taking a historical point of view the general tendency certainly leads away from analytic markings and to synthetic ones. On the other hand a strict orientation according to standard forms causes, at least in spoken language which is based upon the standard, a stronger differentiation of the system of forms.

The first tendency can be seen in the northern most areas of Low German, in Schleswig. Here the system is approaching the general article form. People use *de* here in the object case of the masculine, instead of *den* as in most other Low German areas. Braak noted: "In der schleswigschen Mundart sind der dritte und vierte Fall vom ersten verdrängt und mit ihm zusammengefallen."[25] He ascribes this phenomenon to influences from Danish and Frisian language patterns.[26] Such an attribution does not match the fact that in East Frisian *de* is used for all cases of the masculine.[27]

Only three decades later Stellmacher describes the appearance of such forms as a part of a dynamic process, which is only partly restricted by geographical

---

[25] Braak (1956: 29). ('In the dialect of Schleswig the third and the fourth case have been replaced by the first one and have coincided with it.'). Also cf. Jensen (2007: 3.1) and (2009: 3.1).
[26] cf. Braak (1956: 30).
[27] A look at the East Frisian magazin "Diesel" proves that all masculine cases are expresses only by *de*. On the other hand, *dat* is used for neuter singular in all cases.

items: "Die Tendenz zur Monoflexion bei den Mask. wird aber immer stärker."[28] Table 3 shows the 'normal' Northern Lower Saxon system[29] and Table 4 the simplified Schleswigsch system.[30]

Table 3: Definite article in Northern Lower Saxon

LG (N. Lower Saxon)		masc.	fem.	neutr.
Sing.	Nom.	*de* [də]	*de* [də]	*dat* [dat]
	Dat.	*den* [dɛn]	*de* [də]	*dat* [dat]
	Acc.	*den* [dɛn]	*de* [də]	*dat* [dat]
Plur.		*de* [də]		

Table 4: Definite article in Schleswigsch

LG (NF)		masc.	fem.	neutr.
Sing.	Nom.	*de* [də]	*de* [də]	*dat* [dat]
	Dat.	***de*** [də] (9)	*de* [də]	*dat* [dat]
	Acc.	***de*** [də] (10)	*de* [də]	*dat* [dat]
Plur.		*de* [də]		

Table 4 shows that the gender distinction in the object case (*den* m., *de* f., *dat* n.) is no longer complete, as *de* can be masculine or feminine. The definite articles of male and female forms have been parallelized.

(9) *Dat höört **de** Mann to.*
 'That belongs to the man.'
 (HG: Das gehört dem Mann.)
(10) *Ik seh **de** Mann.*
 'I see the man.'
 (HG: Ich sehe den Mann.)

---

[28] Stellmacher (1990: 160) ('the tendency in masculine to mono-flexion is growing stronger').
[29] Cf. Niederdeutsche Grammatik (1998: 151).
[30] The table does not mention the genitive forms because these are produced synthetically in Low German and therefore underlie different rules.

With *den*-forms being extinguished from the system, the pressure on the three dat-positions left obviously increases. Only the singular neuter forms keep *dat*, all the others are covered by *de*. And there are signs of further changes.[31] At least with modern words for which the gender appears to be doubtful, maybe involving questions of the natural gender or analogue constructions, there is a tendency to use *de* even for neuter. Table 5 shows this pattern used in the declination of *Baby*:

Table 5: Definite article in Schleswigsch (tendency)

LG (NF)		masc.	fem.	neutr.
Sing.	Nom.	*de* [də]	*de* [də]	***de*** [də] (11)
	Dat.	*de* [də]	*de* [də]	***de*** [də] (12)
	Acc.	*de* [də]	*de* [də]	***de*** [də] (13)
Plur.		*de* [də]		

(11) ***De** Baby liggt in de Wagen.*
 'The baby is lying in the pram.'
 (HG: Das Baby liegt im Wagen.)
(12) *He schenkt **de** Baby de Ball.*
 'He gives the ball to the baby.'
 (HG: Er schenkt dem Baby den Ball.)
(13) *Se wickelt **de** Baby.*
 'She changes the baby's nappies.'
 (HG: Sie wickelt das Baby.)

Standard German shows a much more differentiated system of definite articles. Compared to Low German the relations between words in Standard German rely strongly on the article (Table 6):

---

[31] Cf. Jensen (2007: 3.1) and Jensen (2009: 3.1), where the neuter *dat*-forms are mentioned as the ones regionally expected, but a special explanation says: "Umgangssprachlich wird relativ oft im Neutrum auch der Artikel *de* statt *dat* verwendet." ('In the vernacular the article *de* instead of *dat* is used relatively often'.)

Table 6: Definite article in Standard German

Standard German		masc.	fem.	neutr.
Sing.	Nom.	*der* [deːɐ]	*die* [diː]	*das* [das]
	Dat.	*dem* [deːm]	*der* [deːɐ]	*dem* [deːm]
	Acc.	*den* [deːn]	*die* [diː]	*das* [das]
Plur.		*die* / *den* / *die*		

Table 7: Definite article in Low German (transfer from Standard German)

LG (Standard transfer)		masc.	fem.	neutr.
Sing.	Nom.	*de* [də]	*de* [də]	*dat* [dat]
	Dat.	*den* [dɛn]	*de* [də]	***den*** [dɛn] (14)
	Acc.	*den* [dɛn]	*de* [də]	*dat* [dat]
Plur.		*de* / ***den*** [dɛn] / *de* (15)		

With Standard German acting as a sort of structure guide for new developments in Low German, there is on the other hand a tendency to follow the more differentiated article structure. Most Low German speakers will consider the forms mentioned here false or defective. Nevertheless they do occur, and they obviously follow certain rules. The outstanding patterns are those that are affected: dat. sing. with the neuter (Standard German *dem*) and dat. pl. (Standard German *den*). Phonologically these new *den*-forms have been adapted to the Low German system: we find [dɛn], and not the Standard forms [deːm] resp. [deːn].

(14) *En Gootachten, in den seggt warrt...*
'An expertise in which is noted ...'
(HG: Ein Gutachten, in dem es heißt ...)

(15) *Se warrt mit den Bundesdagsfraktschonen snacken.*
'She will talk to the fractions of the Bundestag.'
(HG: Sie wird Unterredungen mit den Bundestagsfraktionen führen.)

4.1.2 Demonstrative Adjectives

Morphosyntactic elements indicating the inflection of complex noun phrases show a large range of regional varieties in Low German. Topical data in this field have not been elicited and sorted yet. That is why I shall concentrate on the demonstrative adjectives and on the case of the following Standard German patterns:

Table 8: System of demonstrative adjectives: Low German and Standard German

LG (N Lower Saxon)		masc.	fem.	neutr.
	Nom.	düsse	düsse	düt
Sing.	Dat.	düssen	düsse	düt
	Acc.	düssen	düsse	düt

Standard German		masc.	fem.	neutr.
	Nom.	dieser	diese	dieses
Sing.	Dat.	diesem	dieser	diesem
	Acc.	diesen	diese	dieses

Table 9: Low German System of demonstrative adjectives (transfer from Standard German)

LG (Standard transfer)		masc.	fem.	neutr.
	Nom.	düsse	düsse	düt
Sing.	Dat.	düssen	düsse	**düssen** (16)
	Acc.	düssen	düsse	düt

(16) *Noch in düssen Johr ...* (expected form: in düt Johr/düt Johr)
  'Still this year ...'
  (HG: Noch in diesem Jahr ...)

As with the articles, the *-m*-endings have not found their way into the system yet. But the influence from Standard German is obvious: *diesem* is possible for dat. sing. masculine as well as for neuter forms, this parallelization has been taken over into the Low German system. It should also be mentioned that the phonetical structure of *düssen* comes quite close to *diesen*, and that the appropriate

Low German form does not need a preposition. In Standard German both, *in diesem Jahr* and *dieses Jahr*, can be used alternatively.

4.1.3 Interrogatives

Interrogatives are frequently needed in everyday speech where they have the function of drawing the listener's attention to the essence of the following sentence and at the same time requesting an answer.[32] From this particular role of the interrogatives one might expect a strong influence from Standard German into Low German. At this point it would be interesting to see how the Low German system reacts in such cases where Standard German offers more than one option, e.g. for 'why': *wieso*, *weshalb*, *warum*. On the other hand there seems to be a strong regional tie with the Low German interrogatives so that one can expect a set of regionally distributed forms which might be strong enough to resist the influence deriving from Standard German.

At the beginning of the 20th century irritation first arose about the use of the Low German interrogatives *wokeen* and *wonehm* as documented in an article dealing with these words used as relative pronouns introducing relative clauses.[33] Whereas the linguists (Wisser and Mensing) maintained that *de* covers this function in traditional Low German, the poet (Ortlepp) stated clearly:

> "Daß diese Formen vom Hochdeutsch beeinflußt sind, mag zugegeben werden, aber ich will doch schreiben, wie die Leute jetzt sprechen, nicht, wie sie eigentlich sprechen sollten." 'That these forms have been influenced by High German, may be admitted; anyway, I want to write the way the people speak now-a-days, not the way they should speak.'

This part on the interrogatives is based on a questionnaire, filled in by competent speakers of Low German[34]. As only 14 participants took part, the numbers are by no means representative. Ten short questions had to be translated from Standard German to Low German, initiated by the primary interrogatives *was*, *wann*, *wie*, *wo*; there were *wer*-questions in all four cases of the singular (that is: *wer*, *wessen*, *wem* and *wen*); finally there were two questions with the compound interrogatives *wofür* and *womit*.

---

[32] Cf. Appel (2007: 204-207).
[33] Cf. Wisser et al. (1919).
[34] Cf. course „Plattdüütsch schrieven", organized by the Schleswig-Holsteinische Heimatbund, October 2005 in Rendsburg.

Survey of the results:[35]

- "*wann*" [*wanehr*; SL: *wann*] – *wann* (8), *wannehr* (2), *wennehr* (2), *woneem* (1), *to wat för'n Tiet* (1)
- "*was*" [*wat*] – *wat* (14)
- "*wie*" [*wodat*; SL: *wie/wo*] – *wie* (3), *woneem* (2), *wonehr* (2), *wodennig* (2), *woans* (1), *wo* (1), *wieans* (1), *wosük* (1), *op wat för'n Oort* (1)
- "*wo*" [*wo(r)/woneem*] – *wo* (8), *wor* (3), *woneem* (3)
- "*wer*" [*wokeen/welkeen/keen/wer/wen/wem*; EaFr: *well/wat för een*; Pr: *wer*] – *wokeen* (5), *wer* (4), *keen* (1), *woneem* (1), *wo* (1), *woll* (1), *wecker* (1)
- "*wessen*" [*well(s), wem sien/wems*; EaFr: *wells/well sien*; SL: *wessen/wer sien*; Pr: *wem sien*] – *wokeen sien* (7), *wen sien* (3), *wers* (1), *woneem sien* (1), *wat vun* (1), *wecke sien* (1)
- "*wem*" [*wem*; EaFr: *well*] – *wokeen* (7), *wo* (2), *wer* (2), *wecken* (1), *woneem* (1), *wat vun een* (1)
- "*wen*" [*wen*, EaFr: *well*] – *wokeen* (5), *wat vun een* (3), *woneem* (2), *wer* (1), *wen* (1), *welkeen* (1), *wecken* (1)
- "*wofür*" [*woto/worför*] – *woto* (7), *woför* (5), *to wat* (1), *för wat* (1)
- "*womit*" [*wo(r)mit*] – *womit* (7), *mit wat* (4), *wodennig* (1), *wosüük* (1), *woans* (1)

Some results in detail:

1. The only reliable and stable form is *wat* for '*was*'.
2. All the other interrogatives show a large range of varieties which cannot be explained by regional diversification alone. Most of the participants came from Schleswig-Holstein, one from Mecklenburg. The fact that 14 people name 6 different forms as an average, with 9 forms as a maximum, must be considered a clear sign of uncertainty when using interrogatives. The multiplicity of the offerings indicates that there is hardly any idea of standard forms. One has the impression of individual patterns more than of patterns taken from the language system.
3. In all instances, except for the forms of declination of '*wer*' in the object cases (*wessen, wem, wen*), there are larger groups of patterns which are identical in form with Standard German forms or closely related to these: *wer* (4), *wie* (3), *wann* (8), *wo* (8), *womit* (7), *wat* (13) and *woför* (5).
4. Established Low German forms which differ distinctly from Standard German patterns are mentioned, but can hardly ever reach the majority: *wokeen/keen* (5/1), *woans/wodennig* (1/2), *wannehr* (2), *woneem* (3).

---

[35] The forms are written in a normative spelling so that only those forms are indicated which show structural differences; in brackets: the forms expected according to the Niederdeutsche Grammatik (1998) and in the case of the East Frisian forms according to Buurman (1962-1975); in round brackets: the number of the times mentioned.

5. Several times phrases consisting of more than one word are being offered. This result is an effect of the process of de-lexicalization: *op wat för'n Oort* (1, '*wie*'), *to wat för'n Tiet* (1, '*wann*'), *wat vun een* (1, '*wem*'; 1, '*wen*'), *för wat* (1, '*wofür*'), *to wat* (1, '*wofür*'), *mit wat* (3, '*womit*').
6. Obviously the use of *woneem* can be extremely flexible. It has to be pointed out that different people used this word. According to dictionaries and the grammar, *woneem* has its place in the system corresponding to the Standard German '*wo*'. Expectedly *woneem* is mentioned 3 times in its traditional place. But it is astonishing that *woneem* is also mentioned for: '*wie*' (3), '*wann*' (1), '*wer*' (1), '*wessen*' (1), '*wem*' (1) and '*wen*' (1). According to these answers, *woneem* is not suitable only for '*was*', '*wofür*' and '*womit*'. It seems that this word has to a certain degree gained a position which could be described as a 'general interrogative'. Obviously *woneem*, not being supported by Standard German patterns, has lost its clearly defined place within the system. Following this course, *woneem* will be eliminated from the Low German system in the long run. But again, we can also see a development heading in another direction: sticking to such forms which do not follow Standard German patterns, and deliberately using forms considered as 'typical Low German'– no matter whether they do actually fit or not.

4.1.4 Personal Pronouns

A number of transfer processes from Standard German patterns to the Low German system affect highly frequently used elements of speech. By looking for analogies even grammatical markings which identify certain forms are being surrendered. An example taken from the personal pronouns might illustrate this. Most frequent are these forms:

Table 10: Personal Pronouns

		Singular	Plural
1st person	Nom.	*ik*	*wi*
	Non-Nom.	*mi*	*uns*
2nd person	Nom.	*du*	*ji*
	Non-Nom.	*di*	*ju*
3rd person	Nom.	*he, se, dat*	*se*
	Non-Nom.	*em*, **ehr**, *dat*	**jem**

Generally speaking High German patterns are likely to influence those Low German forms which are supported by similarities to standard forms. Thus a tendency of instability within the field of the personal pronouns can be expected for the 3rd pers., sing., fem., non-nom. (*ehr*, HG *sie*, Engl. *her*), the 2nd pers. pl. nom. (*ji*, HG *ihr*, Engl. *you*), the 2nd pers. pl. non-nom. (*ju*, HG *euch*, Engl. *you*) and the 3rd pers., pl., non-nom. (*jem*, HG *sie*, Engl. *them*). In fact for the position of 2nd pers. pl. there are no signs of change. The results are much different when looking at the forms of the 3rd pers. In Low German we traditionally find a clear distinction between nominative (*se* for sing. and pl.) and non-nominative (with sing. fem. *ehr* and pl. *jem*). Standard German uses *sie* in all these positions. With *se* already existing within the Low German pattern there is a tendency to use this pronoun in all positions where Standard German uses *sie*: "An die Stelle des Nicht-Nom. der 3. Pers. Sing. Fem. (*ehr*) und der 3. Pers. Pl. (*jem*) tritt zunehmend die Form *se*."[36]

(17) a. Sing. Fem.: *Ik heff ehr sehn.*
b. *Ik heff se sehn.*
'I have seen her/saw her.'
(HG: Ich habe **sie** gesehen.)
(18) a. Pl.: *Ik heff jem sehn.*
b. *Ik heff se sehn.*
'I have seen them/saw them.'
(HG: Ich habe **sie** gesehen.)

Written Low German texts from the last decades show this phenomenon of following the Standard *se*-form in non-nominative positions increasingly. It seems to be inevitable that the items used in instable positions are taken from the existing Low German vocabulary. The result therefore has a Low German outfit.

This process of change can be observed in different Low German areas in differently intensity, but it is not a regional feature in the first place. During the time of transmission, two forms can coexist. Once the system has become instable, different features can get involved and even new grammatical determinations might be established. The present-day situation in the Probstei is characterized as follows: "Im Objektfall steht hier ursprünglich nur das Pronomen *ehr*.

---

[36] Niederdeutsche Grammatik (1998: 155) ('the positions of non-nom. 3rd pers. sing. fem. (*ehr*) and of 3rd pers. pl. (*jem*) is being increasingly taken over by *se*'). A similar situation is described for Schleswigsch: "Im Objektfall grundsätzlich *se*, Singular früher grundsätzlich *ehr*, heute unter dem Einfluß des Hochdeutschen gelegentlich auch *se*", cf. Jensen (2007: 4.1.1) ('In the object case generally *ehr*, today under the influence of High German occasionally also *se*'). Lindow (3rd ed.: 272) does not mention *se* in the singular non-nominative position, but this certainly does not reflect the real language situation, but a certain idea of a Low German standard that is not affected by Standard German.

Doch die Probsteier unterscheiden an dieser Stelle zunehmend Dativ (*ehr*) und Akkusativ (*se*)."[37]

4.1.5 Indefinite Pronouns

Due to the aspect of the distant form, the indefinite pronoun *keeneen* is more popular than *nüms*. With this support *keeneen* has even widened its functional range. Until recently *keeneen* was only used for persons, with the meaning 'no one'. According to this function we find sentences like this:

(19) *Keeneen hett em sehn.*
 'Nobody has seen him/saw him.'
 (HG: Niemand hat ihn gesehen.)

New is the use of *keeneen* as the intensifying form of *keen*. This special kind of functional widening is being supported by the fact that *keeneen* is obviously understood as an analogue form to *nienich*, which describes a stronger *nie*. Now *keeneen* can even accompany nouns. The intensifying form carries the meaning 'none at all':

(20) *Keeneen Auto weer op de Straat.*
 'In the street there was no car at all.'
 (HG: Überhaupt kein Auto war auf der Straße.)

4.1.6 Prepositions

For a long time purists have been complaining about the fact that the use of prepositions in Low German increasingly follows Standard German models. There is certainly a set of prepositions which are used similarly in both lan-

---

[37] Graf (2007: 4.1.1) ('In the object case originally there was only the pronoun *ehr*. But people in the Probstein increasingly distinguish between dative (*ehr*), and accusative (*se*)'. Mensing (1927-1935, 1: 1060f.) mentions this differentiation between dative and accusative as well, he writes about *ehr*: "Dativ des geschlechtlichen Pronomens der dritten Person: *ik heff er dat seggt*. Die Form dringt aber auch in den Akkusativ (für *se*): *ik heff er drapen* "habe sie getroffen", und ebenso für *se* in den Akkus. und (seltener) den Dativ des Plurals" (Dative of the personal pronoun of the third person: *ik heff er dat seggt*. But the form also infiltrates the accusative (for *se*): *ik heff er drapen* "have met her", and also for *se* in the accusative and (more rarely) the dative of the plural'). Under the key word *se* Mensing(1927-35, 4: 443) writes: "Nom. des persönlichen Fürworts der dritten Person im Pural aller Geschlechter; Dat. u. Akkus. dazu *er*; seltener noch im Akkus. *se*. Zuweilen wird unterschieden: *ik heff se sehn* für den Plural (lat. eos, eas, ea) und *ik heff er sehn* für den Singular des Femininums (lat. eam)" ('Nominative of the personal pronoun of the third person of all genders; dative and accusative also *er*; more rarely also in the accusative *se*. Sometimes there is a distinction: *ik heff se sehn* for the plural (lat. eos, eas, ea) and *ik heff er sehn* for the singular of the feminine gender (lat. eam)').

guages, such as the local prepositions *an, bi, in, üm* or *ut* (HG: *an, bei, in, um, aus*). Other traditional prepositions now compete with Standard German patterns, e.g. in the Probstei[38] *binnen* and *buten* (HG: *innerhalb, außerhalb*; Engl.: 'inside, outside') were marked 'more rarely' than *innerhalb* and *unterhalb*, for Schleswigsch[39] both forms are mentioned parallel. – Besides these new forms we also find forms which have changed their range:

> "Den nd. Präpositionen und Adverbien wird überhaupt eine größere Bedeutungsvielfalt als den hochdeutschen nachgesagt, vor allem auch eine von der Standardsprache teilweise verschiedene. Das erklärt sich aus dem stärker analytisch geprägten Sprachbau des Nd." (Stellmacher 1990: 182) 'The Low German prepositions and adverbs are generally supposed to have a larger rage of meaning than the High German ones, especially it is said that the meaning is partly different from the one in Standard Language. This might be educed from the more analytic structure of the Low German language.'

The change from traditional *na* to new *to* clearly shows the influence of Standard German:

(21) a. (LG trad.) *Ik gah na'n Koopmann.*
 b. (LG transfer) *Ik gah to'n Koopmann.*
 'I go to the merchant.'
 (HG: Ich gehe zum Kaufmann.]

This change has not been documented yet. The Niederdeutsche Grammatik states for *na*: "Der Gebrauch dieser Präposition unterscheidet sich erheblich vom Gebrauch der entsprechenden Präposition im Hochdeutschen."[40] Here the difference is pointed out, but this position would seem to indicate a decisively prescriptive grammatical concept.

Among the local prepositions the use of *mank* (HG: *zwischen*; Engl.: 'amongst') and *twüschen* (HG: *zwischen*; Engl.: 'between') also indicates changes. Mensing saw a clear distinction: "*twischen* unterscheidet sich von *mank* dadurch, daß es nur gebraucht wird, wenn es sich um 2 Personen oder Parteien handelt."[41] Perhaps the explicitly mentioned number '2' is slightly irritating – what Mensing is referring to is the difference between countables and uncountables. What we learn from his remark is that at least in the traditional system there has been a clear distribution between both prepositions, quite similar to the functions of the English forms *among* and *between*.[42] Standard German does not

---

[38] Cf. Graf (2007: 6.0).
[39] Cf. Jensen (2007: 6.0).
[40] Niederdeutsche Grammatik (1998: 224) ('The use of this preposition differs considerably from the use of this preposition in High German').
[41] Mensing (1927-35, 3: 585) ('*twischen* differs from *mank* in such a way that it is only used when 2 persons or parties are involved.').
[42] The Niederdeutsche Grammatik (1998) does not make this opposition clear, but the articles *mank/middenmank* (223f.) and *twischen* (224f.) describe the difference.

have any kind of differentiation like this, as *zwischen* serves both functions. The model of the Standard German pattern now allows a widening of the range of *twüschen* and therefore sentences such as:

(22) *Dor is brunen Zucker **twüschen** den witten.*
'There is brown sugar amongst the white one.'
(HG: Es befindet sich brauner Zucker zwischen dem weißen.)

The latest grammatical descriptions *So schnacken wi twischen Flensburg un Schleswig, So snackt wi in de Probstee* and *So snacken wi in Nordfreesland* indicate an alternative use of *twischen* and *mang*.[43] Obviously both forms can serve both functions. In constellations like this we find one trend following the Standard German solutions (here *twüschen*), and another trend that emphasises the distant forms. In this sense *mank* is a much better indicator of Low German than *twüschen*, and slogans like this are not surprising:

(23) *Platt mank Bookdeckels*
'Platt between book covers'
(HG: Platt zwischen Buchdeckeln)

4.1.7 Split Pronominal Adverbs

Pronominal adverbs are used as pro-forms for prepositional phrases. The splitting of pronominal adverbs, announced as preposition stranding, with the adverb in the prefield and the preposition left behind, occur in a number of German dialects, but they are certainly supposed to be typical for Low German.[44] Forms indicating preposition stranding are found in the Northern German colloquial language (*Da halt ich nichts von* or *Da halt ich nichts davon* instead of Standard German *Davon halte ich nichts*). Low German dictionaries as well as the Niederdeutsche Grammatik mention the non-separated forms as a lexical unit, whereas the splitting is a result of organizing the parts within phrases or sentences: "Adverbien, die von Pronomen abstammen und mit Präpositionen verbunden sind, werden im Nd. wie dem älteren Hochdeutschen als eine trennbare Wortart behandelt und demgemäß im Satz verwendet."[45] It must be pointed out that the use of the splitting of pronominal adverbs is optional, although this construction is preferred. But generally both constructions are accepted.[46]

---

[43] Jensen (2007: 6.0) and Graf (2007: 6.0).
[44] Fleischer (2002) discusses this phenomenon for a greater number of German dialects.
[45] Stellmacher (1990: 183) ('In Low German as well as in older High German adverbs that derive from pronouns and connected with prepositions, are used as a separable part of speech, and thus they are used within the sentence').
[46] Cf. Niederdeutsche Grammatik (1998: 205): "Die Distanzstellung ist nicht obligatorisch. Nebeneinander können auftreten 'Dar *ekelt mi* vör.' und '*Mi ekelt* darvör.'" ('the distant position is not compulsory. 'Dar *ekelt mi* vör.' and '*Mi ekelt* darvör.' can

Having this in mind we constructed a test to find out, whether there is a difference between the actual use and the acceptance of split pronominal adverbs. Within a course we asked 26 speakers of Low German first to translate a sentence (*Ich habe mir mehr davon versprochen*) into Low German, and secondly we asked the same people to tick off the options on another paper and to decide between the evaluative categories 'good', 'all right' and 'not all right'.

Table 11: Use of adverbs when translating "*davon*" in "*Ich habe mir nichts davon versprochen*" into Low German

dorvun	17
dor ... vun	3
others	6

Obviously most of the speakers stick to the pattern of the source language. Only 3 out of 26 actually used the split construction, although *dorvun* and *dor ... vun* are accepted at almost the same rate, as Table 12 shows.

Table 12: Acceptance of solutions when translating "*davon*"

	good	all right	not all right	no answer
dorvun	14	8	2	2
dor ... vun	13	11	2	–

4.2 Lexical Words

There are several fields where Low German has found its place in the media, and in this field the language has to serve a wider functional range, for instance when it has to transport the latest world news. In contexts like this the traditional vocabulary cannot offer sufficient lexical items to transmit the proper meaning. At least within Low German as a language of the media there is a great need to introduce new elements.[47] Within the last ten years Low German vocabulary ex-

---

occur side by side.') In the syntax chapter the same phenomenon is mentioned again, (1998: 281): "Pronominaladverbien als Adverbialbestimmung werden jedoch häufig in ihre beiden Bestandteile getrennt." ('Pronominal adverbs used as adverbial adjuncts are often separated into two parts.')

[47] Cf. Möhn/Goltz (1999).

pansion has been accompanied along two lines: the first one is committed to the idea of documentation[48], whereas the second one stresses the character of language planning, and thus vocabulary items are being offered which were constructed and may never have occurred in real speech before.[49]

There is no doubt that the greatest amount of change within the Low German language takes place within the field of vocabulary. This is true for every day language as well as for media language. In this report only three special phenomena will be mentioned, all of which result from the strong influence of Standard German patterns on the Low German language.

In a great number of cases, especially in the news, Low German has to deal with words that do not appear in any dictionary. The treatment of such words gives an idea of the strategies of vocabulary expansion used. *Streik, Extremisten* and *Terroristen* are taken from the field of present-day society and politics. The use of these words is certainly not restricted to the media, but they are not mentioned in any of the traditional Low German dictionaries. This circumstance might be the reason for the fact that competent speakers find different solutions. A number of them choose a foreign word and integrate it into the Low German phonology, in fact '*Streik*' remains *Streik* (Engl. 'strike'), '*Extremisten*' remains *Extremisten* (Engl.: 'extremists') and '*Terroristen*' remains *Terroristen* (Engl.: 'terrorists'). Other examples are: *Investitschoon, Oppositschoon, Aktschoon, Konkurrenz, Examen, Garantie, Kandidaat, Prozess*.

But there is also a tendency to revitalize old parts of the traditional vocabulary or to paraphrase these words. In the news we find *Lawai* for '*Streik*', *lilleke Lüüd* for '*Extremisten*' and *verdüllte Lüüd* for '*Terroristen*'. *Lawai* was used in the context of an uprising of dyke workers in 1765 in East Frisia. Now, within the context of international social and political news, this word gets a topical meaning, and its regional range is broadened as well. Paraphrasing is a popular way of avoiding words which look or sound like Standard German. *Lilleke Lüüd*[50] as well as *verdüllte Lüüd*[51] use *Lüüd* '*Leute*' as an appropriate basic noun which is preceded by an adjective. In both cases adjectives were chosen which are only used at the North Western edge of the Low German language area, in East Frisia and in the Emsland. Thus in a way they are free for a new semantic charging. The only question is whether the listeners of the radio news actually comprehend the meaning that was originally intended. This certainly remains a

---

[48] The Institut für niederdeutsche Sprache produces such a list under the title „inslex" on its internet presentation: http://www.ins-bremen.de.
[49] Cf. Sass (2002).
[50] The word *lelk* is listed by: Byl/Brückmann (1992: 76): "lelk (Adj.) böse, boshaft, gehässig, gemein; häßlich, scheußlich; schlecht, schlimm; unartig, ungezogen".
[51] The regional dictionary by Byl/Brückmann (1992: 151) says: "verdüllt (Adj.) verteufelt, verdammt (auch Interj.); sehr böse, erzürnt, rasend".

problem until the listeners have got used to the special use of these constructions and recognize their character as a term.

There is a second way of indicating that a chosen Low German word is definitely different from any word in Standard German. This strategy is a sort of 'sound shift in reverse'. In such cases historical processes of sound shift, such as the shift of certain consonants or the diphthongisation of long vowels, is implemented now. From such an ahistorical point of view and searching for analogies, the *ei* in *Streik* could generally be shifted into *ee* (cf. HG *Kleid* – LG *Kleed*) or *ie* (cf. HG *mein* – LG *mien*). Because of the higher frequency of the *ie*-solution this is the pattern adopted in a form like *Striek*. From this noun it is possible to derive the verbs *strieken* or *bestrieken*:

(24) *De Striek vun de ... löppt hüüt wieder.*
'The strike of the ... is being continued today.'
(HG: Der Streik der ... wird heute fortgesetzt.)
(25) *De Bedriev bi de Bahn warrt bestriekt.*
'The railway workers are on strike.'
(HG: Der Bahnbetrieb wird bestreikt.)

This speaker accepts a collision with the existing verb *strieken* which is used similar to Standard German *streichen*[52]. That this particular kind of avoiding words structurally identical with Standard German is not an exception, show words like *Kries* (derived from HG *(Land-)Kreis*), *Gesett* (derived from HG *Gesetz*), *Insatt* (derived from HG *(Militär-)Einsatz*) or *tosättlich* (derived from HG *zusätzlich*).

A second field of vocabulary where changes can be recognized can be described as a synonymous situation in which one of the items is supported by a Standard German form and the other one not. In the 1920's Mensing noted for *Heven*: "Das Wort ... wird fast nur noch in bestimmten Wendungen und Reimen gebraucht. Schriftsteller (bes. Groth) ziehen es dem unter hd. Einfluß vordringenden *Himmel* vor."[53] Some fifty years later *Heven* had almost died out, at least as part of spoken language. But Mensing also points out that literature brought this word back into the language, or more precisely: written language. This shows that the medium of writing can be an important factor for language stabilization. In the meantime the distant form *Heven* has found its place within the weather news vocabulary. And in this context even the adjective *hevenschattig* can be found for the Standard German *bedeckt*.

---

[52] In fact the collision is not very strong in the past tense, as *strieken* 'streichen' is a strong verb, so that sentence (25) would ask for *bestreken*.
[53] Mensing (1927-1935, 2: 686) ('The word ... is mostly restricted to certain phrases and rhymes. Writers (esp. Groth) prefer it to *Himmel* which expands under High German influence').

Lexical alternatives often occur in such cases where distant forms were used traditionally but which were then superposed by a form close to the standard. This is the case of the opposition *vundaag* vs. *hüüt*, at least in those areas where *vundaag* was used.[54] Here again *hüüt* as the form close to the standard is the word most frequently used in spontaneous spoken language, whereas *vundaag* is on its way to dominate the written language, especially in the context of the media and culture.[55] In this new role *vundaag* even spreads across the traditional lexical isoglosses and is being used within the traditional *hüüt* area.[56] The finding of a distant form is obviously a strong motive for many speakers – or better: writers – of Low German.[57] This motive leads to a productive use of a number of old lexical items. Similar processes can be expected for the pairs like *faken* vs. *oft*, *daal* vs. *rünner*, *verleden* vs. *letzt*, *hinner* vs. *achter* and *gries* vs. *grau*.

A third phenomenon is the replacement of traditional and distant vocabulary by forms which are supported by Standard German. The following example shows that this process of shifting might use an intermediate stage in which elements of the noun phrase can be affected:

(26) a. *Dat Schapp steiht an de Wand.*
 b. ***De** Schapp steiht an de Wand.*
 c. ***De** Schrank steiht an de Wand.*
 'The cupboard stands against the wall.'
 (HG: Der Schank steht an der Wand.)

With the Standard German matrix (*Schrank*, masculine) first the gender of the traditional word is changed.[58] In a second step the noun itself is replaced.

---

[54] Cf. map '*heute*' in König (2007: 182f).

[55] Mensing wrote in the 1920ies about the relationship between *hüüt* and *vundaag*: hüüt „tritt in den Städten und bei dem jüngeren Geschlecht auf dem Lande immer mehr an die Stelle des alten plattd. *vundaag*", Mensing (1927-1935, II: 975) ('in the cities and among the younger generation in the country it replaces more and more the old Low German *vundaag*'). Elmentaler (2008: 71) shows that at least in Rieseby (Schleswig-Flensburg) the parallel use of *vundaag* and *hüüt* can not longer be found, only *hüüt* is left here.

[56] Stellmacher (2005: 171) finds that the traditional distinction between word areas is fading. He describes that the river Weser no longer is a strict isogloss between the westerly *Himmel* and the easterly *Heven*.

[57] In modern literature Stellmacher (2005: 171) even found *hüütvandags*. The fact that this new form was created shows that the system is instable, or to take it from the positive side: the system has become more flexible.

[58] Henning Meier (1956-2006, V: 51) documents the alternative genders: "n., auch m.". Mensing (1927-1935, 4: 292), written some 70 years earlier, only knows the neuter for *Schapp*.

5. Results and New Tasks

The examples show that processes of shifting can be described on the different linguistic levels of present-day Low German. Changes show up at different stages, from the first vague indication to fully conventionalized features. This also goes for syntactical constructions[59] which have not been described in this report, but tests have been made for example about the construction of Low German subordinate clauses under the influence of Standard German. In this way every critical view on the elements and the structure of present-day Low German is a sort of test of its vitality. Other fields could be focussed upon, such as the stability of the apocope-isogloss, the stability of Low German using a unity form for the plural inflexion in the present tense of verbs, the isogloss showing this unity plural inflection (*-t* vs. *-en*),[60] the isogloss marking the opposition between *wesen* und *sien*.[61]

The change is evident. We do, however, have to decide whether the system is affected or whether we are dealing with the punctual integration of items from Standard German. With respect to the vocabulary Stellmacher points out the difference between a shift within the system and lexical adoption.[62]

The data could be read as the result of normal processes of language change. However, the great number of grammatical fields involved points in another direction, and that is a kind of language attrition. The great number of changes indicate that the structure of Low German is severely endangered. The evidence of the examples might be limited by the fact that the strong influences from Standard German patterns are partly a result of a translating situation based on written sources.

Nevertheless the fact that many unexpected forms are used, also forms that differ from the patterns given by traditional grammars, is a clear indication of the uncertainty of many speakers of Low German when using this language. But

---

[59] Cf. Appel (2007).
[60] According to the Niederdeutsche Grammatik (1998: 65), this change is already taking place within the cities: „In einigen Stadtmundarten (z. B. Hamburg) gleicht sich die Bildung des Plurals im Präsens dem standarddeutschen Muster an. / wi hal-en / ji haal-t / se hal-en". ('In several city dialects (e.g. Hamburg) the forming of the plurals in the present tense equals the Standard German forms. / wi hal-en / ji haal-t / se hal-en'.)
[61] Mensing (1927-35, 5: 599) noted for Schleswig-Holstein: Formen von *wesen* "beginnen aber vor der zum Hochd. stimmenden Form *sien* zurückzuweichen, die in der Osthälfte von Holst. und in den Städten die beiden alten Formen oft schon völlig verdrängt hat" ('are beginning to lose ground against *sien*, which is coherent with the High German form and have replaced both of the old forms often completely in the Eastern part of Holstein and in the cities'). The Niederdeutsche Grammatik (1998: cf. 96-98) does not register this opposition.
[62] Cf. Stellmacher (2005: 171).

as long as we do not know what amount of change a language can cope with, we can only speculate about the intensity of the danger for the language.

One can expect that the stability of the forms depends strongly on the age, and also on the presence of Low German within the region. There is certainly a lack of linguistic awareness and there is certainly a lack of stable speakers of Low German. The same applies especially for the media, for radio and television, as well as for the theatres: among many of those protagonists the use of Low German is at least defective.

Generally there are two directions in the development of Low German. A strong impulse to copy patterns known from Standard German, accompanied by a weaker impulse to cling to distant forms. This clinging to elements that are not supported by Standard German occurs principally in written texts, and generally they seem to be well received among the Low German language community.

Up to now there has been only little linguistic research on the changes within the structure of the Low German language. There is no greater data corpus. Low German is on the way to becoming a shadow language of Standard German, restricted merely to a Standard German system, augmented by a set of sound shift elements and elements that also have their place within the Northern German vernacular. Linguistic research is necessary to register processes of attrition and processes that strengthen vitality. But linguistic research is also necessary in the name of language planning and finding ways to reduce the strong pressure from Standard German and to give Low German a future as a language with its own typical structure.

6. Literature

Ammon, Ulrich, Hans Bickel & Jakob Ebner. 2004. *Variantenwörterbuch des Deutschen. Die Standardsprache in Österreich, der Schweiz und Deutschland sowie in Liechtenstein, Luxemburg, Ostbelgien und Südtirol*. Berlin: de Gruyter.

Appel, Heinz-Wilfried. 2007. *Untersuchungen zur Syntax niederdeutscher Dialekte. Forschungsüberblick, Methodik und Ergebnisse einer Korpusanalyse*. Frankfurt: Lang.

Braak, Ivo. 1956. *Niederdeutsch in Schleswig-Holstein. Wegweiser für die Lehrerfortbildung. 2. Halbjahr 1956, Heft 2* ed. the Kultusministerium des Landes Schleswig-Holstein. Kiel: Hirt.

Buurman, Otto. (1962-1975). *Hochdeutsch-plattdeutsches Wörterbuch. Auf der Grundlage ostfriesischer Mundart*. Neumünster: Wachholtz.

Byl, Jürgen & Elke Brückmann. 1992. *Ostfriesisches Wörterbuch. Plattdeutsch/ Hochdeutsch – Oostfreesk Woordenbook. Plattdütsk/Hoogdütsk*. Leer: Schuster.

Duden. [21]1996. *Die deutsche Rechtschreibung. Auf der Grundlage der neuen amtlichen Rechtschreibregeln*. Mannheim: Duden.

Duden. ²⁴2006. *Die deutsche Rechtschreibung. Auf der Grundlage der neuen amtlichen Rechtschreibregeln.* Mannheim: Duden.
Elmentaler, Michael. 2008. "Varietätendynamik in Norddeutschland". *Sociolinguistica* 22: Dialektsoziologie. 66-86.
Elmentaler, Michael. 2009a. "Hochdeutsch und Platt – zwei ungleiche Nachbarn". *Deutsch und seine Nachbarn* ed. M. Elmentaler, 31-45. Frankfurt/M.: Lang.
Elmentaler, Michael. 2009b. "Modernes Niedersächsisch. Dialektwandel im nordniederdeutschen Raum". *Low Saxon dialects across borders – Niedersächsische Dialekte über Grenzen hinweg* ed. A. N. Lenz, C. Gooskens & S. Reker, 339-365. Stuttgart: Steiner.
Fleischer, Jürg. 2002. *Die Syntax von Pronominaladverbien in den Dialekten des Deutschen: eine Untersuchung zu Preposition Stranding und verwandten Phänomenen* (Zeitschrift für Dialektologie und Linguistik, Beihefte 123). Stuttgart & Wiesbaden: Steiner.
Graf, Jan. 2007. *So snackt wi in de Probstee.* Passade: Plaggenhauer.
Goltz, Reinhard. 2009. "Niederdeutsch: vom wenig einheitlichen Profil einer bedrohten Regionalsprache". *Neben Deutsch. Die autochthonen Minderheiten- und Regionalsprachen Deutschlands* ed. C. Stolz, 59-86. Bochum: Universitätsverlag Dr. N. Brockmeyer.
Hansen-Jaax, Dörte. 1995. *Transfer bei Diglossie. Synchrone Sprachkontaktphänomene im Niederdeutschen.* Hamburg: Dr. Kovac.
Hennig, Beate & Jürgen Meier, eds. 1956-2006. *Hamburgisches Wörterbuch.* Neumünster: Wachholtz.
Jensen, Annemarie. 2007. *So schnacken wi twischen Flensburg un Schleswig.* Krummbek: Plaggenhauer.
Jensen, Annemarie. 2009. *So snacken wi in Nordfreesland.* Buxtehude: Plaggenhauer.
Kellner, Birgit. 2002. *Zwischen Anlehnung und Abgrenzung: orthographische Vereinheitlichung als Problem im Niederdeutschen.* Heidelberg: Winter.
König, Werner. 2007. *dtv-Atlas Deutsche Sprache.* München: dtv.
Lindow, Wolfgang. 1984. *Plattdeutsch-hochdeutsches Wörterbuch.* Leer: Schuster.
Lindow, Wolfgang, Dieter Möhn, Hermann Niebaum, Dieter Stellmacher, Hans Taubken & Jan Wirrer. 1998. *Niederdeutsche Grammatik.* Leer: Schuster.
Mensing, Otto. 1927-1935. Schleswig-Holsteinisches Wörterbuch. Vol. 1-5. Neumünster: Wachholtz.
Möhn, Dieter & Reinhard Goltz. 1999. "Zur Aktualität des plattdeutschen Wortschatzes. Eine Vitalitätsprüfung am Beispiel von Nachrichtensendungen". *Jahrbuch des Vereins für niederdeutsche Sprachforschung* 122. 67-90.
Möller, Frerk. 2008. *Plattdeutsch im 21. Jahrhundert. Bestandsaufnahme und Perspektiven. Mit einem Aufsatz von Michael Windzio.* Leer: Schuster.

Niederdeutsche Grammatik 1998 = Lindow et al. 1998.

Rohdenburg, Günter. 2004. "Grammatische Parallelen zwischen niederdeutschen Mundarten und Nichtstandardvarietäten im Englischen aus typologischer Sicht". *Jahrbuch des Vereins für niederdeutsche Sprachforschung* 127. 85-122.

Saß, Johannes. 2002. *Kleines Plattdeutsches Wörterbuch.* Neumünster: Wachholtz.

Schröder, Ingrid. 2004. "Niederdeutsch in der Gegenwart: Sprachgebiet – Grammatisches – Binnendifferenzierung". *Niederdeutsche Sprache und Literatur der Gegenwart* (= Germanistische Linguistik 175-176) ed. D. Stellmacher, 35-99. Hildesheim: Olms.

Schröder, Ingrid & Michael Elmentaler. 2009. "Sprachvariation in Norddeutschland (SiN)". *Jahrbuch des Vereins für niederdeutsche Sprachforschung* 132. 41-68.

Stellmacher, Dieter. 1987. *Wer spricht Platt? Zur Lage des Niederdeutschen heute. Eine kurzgefaßte Bestandsaufnahme.* Leer: Schuster.

Stellmacher, Dieter. 1990. *Niederdeutsche Sprache. Eine Einführung.* Frankfurt: Lang.

Stellmacher, Dieter. 2005. "Das Niederdeutsche an der Unterweser". *Jahrbuch des Vereins für niederdeutsche Sprachforschung* 125. 163-174.

Wisser, Wilhelm, Otto Mensing & O. Ortlepp. 1919. "Wokeen, wonehm". *Quickborn* 13. 11-12.

Claudia Maria Riehl (Köln)

Norm and variation in language minority settings

1. Introduction

1.1 General observations

In discussions on norms and variations, minorities represent an exceedingly interesting subject. This applies particularly to non-local minorities which are minorities in one setting but are part of a majority elsewhere. One of the largest examples of this type of group are German-speaking minorities who use German as their first language but belong to a nation with a different official first language.[1] When looking at the question of norms in this particular context, the concept of pluricentric languages introduced by Kloss (1978), appears to be a helpful model (cf. Clyne 1992: 1). A pluricentric language is a language with various interacting centers, where each center codifies its own national norms. The relationship between national varieties is dynamic and interactive since they are affected by mutual influences. However, the actual differences are not significant, in most cases. In addition, pluricentricity is, for the most part, asymmetrical. National varieties of more dominant nations are traditionally more prestigious (cf. Clyne 1995: 21). Ammon (1995) also differentiates between *Vollzentren* (full centers), *Halbzentren* (semi-centers) and *Subzentren* (sub-centers). Full centers represent language communities that have developed codices (dictionaries, spelling and pronunciation guides, grammars), e.g. Germany, Austria and Switzerland, whereas semi-centers have no own codices at their disposal – only models (model speakers/writers and model texts). They constitute regional communities in different-speaking nations, e.g. Luxembourg, South Tyrol and East Belgium. These groups have established conventions that might differ from the standard varieties used in the full centers. Sub-centers, on the other hand, are regional communities who employ variants of a codified standard.[2]

Ammon (1995: 391) claims, however, that transitions and gradations between full centers and semi-centers have to be considered. This holds true especially for areas where German enjoys official language status, e.g. South Tyrol

---
[1] Prominent groups are so-called border minorities such as South Tyrol, Alsace and East Belgium (cf. Riehl 2008).
[2] As Ammon (1995: 101ff.) points out, subcenters often share features with half or even full centers (e.g. Bavarian dialects in Germany share features with Austrian German or Swiss Standard German).

and East Belgium. Because it is used as an official language, a certain degree of codification or conventionalism is required. If a language is used as an official language, specialist or technical literature and even belles-lettres are published in this idiom. In consequence, there is a broader range of model texts on one hand and of norm authorities on the other.[3] In this case, a conventionalized but not codified norm of a regional (endogenous) standard emerges, which coexists with substandard varieties used in the same region, e.g. dialectal varieties in South Tyrol. As a result, when discussing norms, a variety spectrum has to be considered that comprises a written and spoken norm of a specific language.

In comparison, it is more difficult to define language norms in areas where the minority language is only used as a spoken variety. In this case, the language has no official status and the possibility of developing specific variants of a local standard is much more restricted. If the community refers to a written variety of German, the exogenous standard of Germany (or Austria) functions as an official norm. But, usually German dialects spoken in the respective community are enclosed by a genetically unrelated language (e.g. French in Alsace).[4] In this context, not only do the convergence of different dialects come into play (cf. Rosenberg 2003) but also various instances of transfer from the respective majority languages (cf. Thomason/Kaufmann 1988). This is especially true for German varieties in South Eastern and Eastern Europe, as well as for language islands in South and North America and Australia (Riehl 2010).

The present article examines some grammatical features that emerge in German-speaking minorities and describes the development of the German language in these particular language contact situations. Based on these findings, the different problems that emerge in defining subsistent norms in minority speech communities will be discussed.

1.2 Corpus and definitions

The analysis includes a wide range of different German-speaking communities all over the world, both language enclaves (see Riehl 2010) and border minorities. The border minorities taken into consideration are South Tyrol and East Belgium. The analysis is based on data collected by the author between 1992 and 1996 (see Riehl 2001). The language enclaves are comprised of German-speaking communities in Middle and Eastern European countries investigated in a project by Eichinger, Riehl and others (cf. Eichinger/Plewnia/Riehl 2008). They are supplemented by data on Australian German published by Clyne (1994) and on Pennsylvania German (published in Fuller 2001, Huffines 1994,

---

[3] Norm authorities are, among others, proof-readers, model speakers and language experts (cf. Ammon 1995: 78ff.) and Hundt (in this volume).

[4] In this case the dialects are considered as so-called *Dachlose Außenmundarten* (Kloss 1977).

Louden 1994). Namibia plays an exceptional role: Here German functions as a co-official language in addition to English and Afrikaans. Data on Namibian German had been collected by the author in 1999 and are unpublished yet.

Since the use of the minority language differs greatly between various communities, different levels of norms have to be taken into account:

1. Grammatical norms in a narrower sense, such as typological features concerning word order, semantic categories (tense, aspect, mode), case-marking etc. These types of norms are usually codified in grammars and infringements of these norms are generally sanctioned.
2. Stylistic norms: Certain grammatical features and collocations may vary according to the register in use. These norms are not necessarily codified but based on conventions and recommendations conveyed in school books, style guides and by language authorities.
3 Communicative-pragmatic norms: Grammatical features such as word order may vary in spoken and written utterances. In spoken conversations word order often follows pragmatic rules, e.g. extra-position in German (see 2.1.1).

The latter two types can be subsumed under the term 'norms of usage' (*Sprachgebrauchsnormen*) as opposed to 'norms of the system' (*Sprachsystemnormen*), i.e. grammatical norms in a narrower sense.[5]

2. Grammatical changes

As Ammon points out in his 1995 publication, regional variation in the lexicon is very frequent since lexical items differ according to the diversity of natural environments and national institutions. E.g.: *Pad* (afr. = 'dirt road') is a typical natural phenomenon in Namibia, *carabinieri* (ital. = 'Italian military police') a term specific for the Italian administration. Both realities do not exist in other German-speaking areas. As a result, the terms are "borrowed" by the regional German variety. In comparison to lexical differences, it is much more complicated to assess variation in syntax and morphology. One major problem is that, in general, grammatical changes observable in German-speaking minority settings are compared to the German standard. However, especially in the domain of syntax, certain features do not necessarily infringe on the norms of the language system, but on stylistic or communicative-pragmatic norms (cf. 2.1.1).

---

[5] For an exhaustive discussion of the notion of norm see Dovalil (2006: 27ff.).

2.1 Syntactic developments

2.1.1 Gradual Removal of the Sentence Brace

A distinctive phenomenon of German syntax is the so-called *Satzklammer* ('sentence brace'). This particular construction is marked by the finite part and the infinite parts of the verb framing or encapsulating other components of the clause (e.g. *du* hast *gestern das Haus geputzt,* lit. '*you* have *yesterday the house* cleaned'). However, the brace construction is not compulsory in all contexts. In spoken language, components are often placed after the infinite verb part (so-called 'extra-position'). Extra-position primarily has a communicative-pragmatic function. Complex, semantically important or rhematic components can be placed at the end of a clause. Eisenberg (2004: 402) therefore suggests differentiating between grammatically and stylistically motivated extra-position. Extra-position is grammaticalised for adverbial and complement clauses and infinitive constructions with *zu*. The line between grammatically and stylistically motivated extra-position, however, is difficult to draw, as the latter follows a norm of usage (*Sprachgebrauchsnorm*). That is why many examples in written corpora of East Belgian and Namibia German do not infringe on a grammatical norm, although they are stylistically marked:[6]

(1) a. *Die 7 Zwerge werden numeriert **durch Zahlen***
   [instead of: *Die 7 Zwerge werden durch Zahlen nummeriert*]
   'The 7 dwarfs are counted by numbers' (East Belgian German)
  b. *Schade war [...], daß es sehr unruhig war **im Saal***
   [instead of: *Schade war [...], daß es sehr unruhig im Saal war*]
   'It was a pity that there was a lot of noise in the hall' (Namibian German)

Since similar examples are quite frequent in written texts from both speech communities, these patterns may be considered part of a regional norm of language usage (for a discussion see Riehl 2001 and below section 5).

The remainder of this article will focus on oral utterances that not only infringe on stylistic norms, but also on language system norms. According to Eisenberg (2004:402) extra-position infringes on the grammatical norm of standard German when a pronominal object is postponed (2a). This also holds for direct thematic objects (2b,c):[7]

---

[6] For examples from East Belgium see Riehl (2001), the Namibia data is unpublished.
[7] For the following examples from Eastern European varieties of German see the respective articles in Eichinger/Plewnia/Riehl (2008).

(2) a. *Dort hawen wir Arbeitstage verdient **uns***
[instead of: *Dort hawen wir uns Arbeitstage verdient*]
'There we deserved working days (for ourselves)' (Russian German)
b. *... die Kinder haben kaufen können **Möbel***
[instead of: *... die Kinder haben Möbel kaufen können*]
'The children were able to buy furniture' (Ukrainan German)
c. *Keiner hatte gehabt **nur ein Rad***
[instead of: *keiner hatte nur ein Rad gehabt*]
'Nobody owned only one bicycle' (Polish German)

Another instance of non-conformant use is the extra-position of an infinitive within multiple verb groups, cf.:

(3) a. *Dann hat sie die Maschin* (= Auto) *hingestellt, **sind wir gegangen essen***
[instead of: *Dann hat sie die Maschin hingestellt, sind wir essen gegangen*]
'Then she parked her car, and we went to eat' (Russian German)
b. *[…] dass ich die verschiedene Sprachen **kann sprechen***
[instead of: *dass ich die verschiedenen Sprachen sprechen kann*]
'[…] that I'm able to speak different languages' (Australian German, unpublished data)

Examples such as 3b) illustrate another typical phenomenon that emerges as a result of extra-position, i.e. the proximity of the discontinuous constituents auxiliary and participle:

(4) a. *Am besten **hat gesprochen** die Ältst*
[instead of: *Am besten hat die Älteste gesprochen*]
'The oldest one spoke best'
b. *Ohren **haben gehört** etwas*
[instead of: (*Die*) *Ohren haben etwas gehört*]
'(My) ears have heard something' (Russian German)

As mentioned above, the brace construction is typical for German. So it appears that its gradual deconstruction is induced by the respective contact languages which do not have this differentiation. Another explanation may be that the brace construction is not a stable grammatical feature, because it contradicts a cognitive principle, i.e. the principle of proximity identified by Givón (1990: 970f.). He states that "entities that are closer together functionally, conceptually, or cognitively, will be placed closer together at the code level, i.e. temporally or spatially."

According to Givón, there is a general tendency to keep grammatical operators near their operands. This principle is also evident in the fact that the relative proximity of grammatical morphemes to the root indicates conceptual scope relations. Thus, the examples listed under number (1)-(4) correspond better to the *proximity principle* than expressions that follow the codified norm.

2.1.2 Gradual Removal of the Verb-Last-Position

Another characteristic of German is the determination of main and subordinate clauses by the position of the verb: Whereas in main clauses the finite verb is placed in the second position, in subordinate clauses it is at the end, e.g. *Tom geht nach der Schule nach Hause* (main clause) vs. *Ich weiß, dass Tom nach der Schule nach Hause geht* (subordinate clause). This differentiation is gradually removed in language contact situations, thus generalizing the verb second position for all kinds of affirmative sentences. The beginning of this development can be observed in indirect questions:

(5) a. *Musst du fragen, wo kriegst du das*
    [instead of: *Musst du fragen, wo du das kriegst*]
    'You have to ask, where you can get this' (Namibian German)
    b. *Wissen Sie, weshalb schrieb ich?*
    [instead of: *Wissen Sie, weshalb ich schrieb*]
    'Do you know, why I wrote' (Russian German)

In speech communities who have frequent contact with the surrounding language, all types of subordinate clauses display instances of verb second generalization (in Clyne's corpus of Australian German 45 % of all subordinate clauses follow the verb second pattern, cf. Clyne 1994: 114):

(6) a. *Vorher schon, **weil ich hab** gelernt auf Kaufmann*
    [instead of: *..., weil ich auf Kaufmann gelernt habe*]
    'Even before this, because I have been trained to be a businessman' (Ukrainian German)
    b. *das hilft für den Kindern vielleicht noch, die Fremdsprachen viel besser zu behalten oder erlernen, **dass sie können** die deutsche Sprache*
    [instead of: *..., dass sie die deutsche Sprache können*]
    'That might help children to learn and retain foreign languages, so that they know the German language' (Hungarian German)
    c) *und **wenn ma sind** in Geschäft kommen*
    [instead of: *und wann wir ins Geschäft gekommen sind*]
    'and when we entered the shop' (Czech German)

One explanation of the gradual removal of the verb-last-position is that bilingual speakers attempt to reduce syntactic complexity. Additionally, differences in word order between main and subordinate clauses do not exist in the respective contact language (such as Russian, Czech, Hungarian etc.). Consequently, by reducing the varieties of word order types it is possible to diminish the mental overload caused by managing two language systems (see Clyne 2003: 202ff.).

2.2 Morphological Developments

2.2.1 Removal of Nominal Inflexion and Case Syncretism

In minority settings where German has official or co-official status, e.g. in Namibia, the case system of the language is still retained. Morphological change is only noticeable in the dative singular of so-called weak nouns, ending in *e*. Here the flexiv has been removed, cf.:

(7) a. *Er hieß Albers mit Nachname*
[instead of: *Er hieß Albers mit Nachname**n***]
'His surname was Albers' (Namibia)
b. *Sie geben es dem Löwe*
[instead of: *Sie geben es dem Löwe**n***]
'They give it to the lion' (Namibia)[8]

In German-speaking language enclaves who do not use Standard German on a daily basis, case merger of dative and accusative is a widespread phenomenon. Despite variation due to the age of the speakers and contact with Standard German, reduction processes follow a clear path, starting with feminine nouns and the plural forms of nouns in noun groups containing definite articles, especially after prepositions. As a result, the indefinite articles, as well as masculine and neutral gender are affected. This development is fostered by the fact that many dialects which are spoken in minority settings show similar examples of case merger. Nevertheless, case merger appears in all speech communities, irrespective of the type of dialect in use, cf.:

(8) a. *Ich hab bei einer Bekannte geschlafen hier in **die** Stadt*
[instead of: *Ich hab bei einer Bekannten geschlafen hier in **der** Stadt*]
'I spent the night at a friend's house here in town' (Romanian German)
b. [*Wo sprechen Sie am meisten Deutsch?*] *Nur **in die** Kirche **mit meine** Kameradinnen*
[instead of: *Nur in der Kirche mit meinen Kameradinnen*]
'[Where do you speak German most often?] Only in the church with my friends' (Ukrainian German)

---

[8] This tendency can also be observed recently on the German mainland.

c. ... ***von die*** *zwanzig Kilo noch Hälfte – dann waren mir **bei die** Bauern arbeit*
[instead of: *von den zwanzig Kilo noch die Hälfte – dann waren wir bei den Bauern arbeiten*]
'a half of twenty kilograms – then we were working at the farmers' (Czech German)

To illustrate this development, the following section will provide evidence from a case study on Russian German.

2.2.2 Evidence from a Case Study

The case study is based on a sample of eight interviews of second generation speakers, each about one hour in length. The participants were all born between 1932 and 1942.[9] Although it is rather small, the corpus is used to illustrate, via quantitative data, the result of the qualitative analysis of the entire data base (as described in 2.1). There was no single instance of dative case marker in the feminine or plural of noun groups in the analyzed corpus. Three speakers used the feminine dative article *der* on a single occasion, i.e. in the collocation *in der Schule* – which can be interpreted as an instance of idiomatic usage.

However, case merger in the masculine (and neuter) gender is not as consistent. Here, 65 % of the occurrences show accusative forms, cf.:

(9) *Mei Vadder hat auch viel gewusst von Regime,* **den** *Stalin un alles* [instead of: *dem*]
'My father also knew a lot about the regime, (the) Stalin and everything'

In 10% of the occurrences the contracted form of the preposition *in* and the definitive article *dem* [= im] is employed, mostly with reference to time: *im Monad, im zweiunddreißigsten (Jahr)*.[10]

At the same time, the dative is still retained in possessive-constructions, replacing the attributive genitive. In this case, the dative marks the possessum and is followed by the possessive pronoun and the possessor: *der Mutter ihr Haus* (lit. 'the mother her house' = mother's house'), cf.:

(10) a. *dem ersten Mann sein Sohn* lit. the first husband (dat.) his son [= the son of the first husband]
b. *meiner Tochter ihren Sohn* lit. my daughter (dat.) her son [= the son of my daughter]

---

[9] For a more detailed description see Berend/Riehl (2008).
[10] However, we have to consider cases with a zero case marker. These cases emerge, when the article is dropped under the influence of the Russian language system, cf. *in Institut, an Fluss, von Regime*.

Half of the speakers employ the dative marking with possessive pronouns, but alternate with accusative forms:

(11) *Da sind sie gange bei unsere Gewohnung, ja? Andere Sonntag gehen se bei ihrer Gewohnung*
'Then they went to our (nom./acc.) home, you know? The other Sunday they went to her (dat.) home'

In contrast, the inflexion of the pronominal system is still intact and used by all speakers. However, this observation doesn't hold true for other minority varieties, e.g. Pennsylvania German. Instances of case merger within the pronominal system are quite common her, cf.:

(12) a. *ich hab sie geschder gholfe* (*'Ich hab sie gestern geholfen'*) [instead of: *ich hab ihnen gestern geholfen*]
'I helped them yesterday' (Pennsylvanian German, Fuller 2001:359)
b. *fer was schwetzt er net zu sie* (*'Für was schwätzt er nicht zu sie'*) [instead of: *Für was schwätzt er nicht zu ihr*]
'why doesn't he talk to her?' (Pennsylvanian German, Huffines 1994: 51)
c. *ich helf ihn bluge* (*'Ich helf ihm pflügen'*) [instead of: *ich helf ihm pflügen*]
'I help him plough' (Pennsylvanian German, Louden 1994: 84)

Thus, evidence from my case study and from other studies on language enclaves confirms that there is a gradual dispersion of case reduction. Apparently personal pronouns are more resistant to merger as nouns or pronouns in attributive positions (possessive and demonstrative pronouns). The reason is that case-marking inflectional morphemes are more prone to merger than full listed items (Rosenberg 2003: 309). Whereas nouns, possessive pronouns and demonstrative pronouns are stored in decomposition, personal pronouns are full listed. Another explanation might be that they are often composed of suppletive forms (consisting of different lexical stems, *es, er* vs. *ihm, ihn*) (Rosenberg 2003: 293). Additionally, the comparatively high retention of case in the pronominal system may be motivated by frequency and the degree of animacy of the participants (cf. Rosenberg 2005).

The frequency argument also holds true for Zürrer's data on Walser German (see Zürrer 1999). In this variety, the frequency of nouns has a central impact on whether the dative form is still in use or not. Highly frequent lexemes such as *töchter* ('daughter'), *wetta* ('sister'), *muma* ('aunt') were used with dative-endings to a much higher extent than other nouns (ibd.: 200).

Case merger may also be considered a result of internal language change. As dative/accusative syncretism emerges in a number of dialects of Modern German, some of the developments in the minority varieties could have been influenced by the dialect substrate. However, it has to be taken into account that the respective minority settings reflect different stages of development. Minorities who use standard German as a language of instruction (Namibia, East-Belgian, Romania) find themselves at the beginning of the development, showing merely loss of dative marking with weak nouns (ex. 7). In speech communities that do not use a standard variety of German, case syncretism in noun groups (mainly displayed by the definite or indefinite article) is very frequent. In the end, dative and accusative merger also affects the pronominal system, as illustrated by the development in Pennsylvania German. In the latter case, this process can be also interpreted as an instance of convergence towards the contact language (English) which does not differentiate between dative and accusative pronouns either.[11]

3. Possible Explanations for Grammatical Change

As illustrated in the previous section, most of the phenomena are examples of simplification and acceleration of internal language developments leading to changes in the grammatical system of German-speaking minorities. This process is, among others, motivated by the lack of external norms (mainly norms of a written language) that could decelerate internal developments of a language system (such as case merger in German). On the other hand, acceleration of typological developments occurs in accordance with inherent developmental tendencies.

As Michael Clyne (1991: 179) points out, there is evidence from studies of immigrant bilingualism that the speech of bilinguals will diverge from that of monolinguals in the heartland of the immigrant language not only because of the effects of the dominant language but also because, in the relative isolation of the immigrant situation, changes in accordance with the dominant typology of the language are accelerated. Additionally, language change can be caused by cognitive principles (proximity, language economy). Whereas the grammatical device of the brace construction in German infringes on the principle of proximity (see above, p. 273), i.e. the general tendency to keep grammatical operators near their operands, the over-generalisation of V2-word-order and the gradual removal of the V-last-order in subordinate clauses follow the principle of economy. Here, simplification and reduction of mental load might play a similar role as typological convergence towards the contact language (cf. Gilbert/Fuller 2003, Rosenberg 2003).

---

[11] For a similar development in Texas German cf. Boas (forthc.); for a discussion of the impact of language contact on language change see Heine/Kuteva (2005).

4. Are there Minority Norms?

As described in the preceding sections, there are remarkable similarities in the development of German in language contact settings all over the world. The question that arises in this context is, whether particular features are given the status of grammatical norms in the respective speech communities or not. As mentioned above, it is possible to establish a norm where a written variety exists (by way of model texts). This holds true for minority settings where German is used as official language or language of schooling. In this situation, the variety can be considered an instance of 'regional German' that differs only slightly from the standard used in one of the full centers. In addition to this written version, a spoken variety of German (a dialect or regional koiné) used in the community follows its own subsistent norms.

Since norms and variants of norms are only established where codification takes place or where the ways of speaking are highly conventional, it is much more difficult to define norms in speech communities that only use a spoken variety of the language. The question emerges of how to describe varieties such as *Russlanddeutsch* ('Russian German') or *Ungarndeutsch* ('Hungarian German'). Both are spoken varieties with a high degree of internal variation. The following observations may illustrate the difficult nature of this issue:

1. There is a high instability between different generations within the respective speech communities. In a test carried out by Zürrer (1999) on the use of dative plural marking in Walser German, it became apparent that case reduction is highly dependent on the age of the speakers. Whereas younger generations do not inflect almost 85 % of the possible forms, older generation speakers use almost 83 % of the inflexions in the correct way.
2. Variation also occurs in the language use of the same speaker. The Russian German speaker KS, for instance, uses the standard form of the participle of the verb *sprechen* ('to speak'), i.e. *gesprochen,* in one setting and the deviant form *gesprecht* some instances later:

    (13) a. *Zu Hause? Wie die Muddr noch äh an Leben war, habn mer* **gsproch(n)** *alles zu Deutsch*
    'At home? When mother still was alive, we always spoke German
    b. *wann sekrety ze byli* ['*wir hatten ja Geheimnisse*'] [...] *habn mer alles auf Russisch* **gesprecht***, dass sie net versteht*
    'When we had secrets, we spoke always in Russian, so that she wouldn't understand'

3. The difference between competence and performance is much higher than in majority settings which is illustrated in Zürrer's test (1999: 196ff.): Middle and older generation participants are often uncertain of particular features and

frequently correct themselves. One participant, who did not inflect any of the dative forms in the test, changed all of the forms correctly after being asked about it. This case underlines the importance of metalinguistic knowledge and language awareness in a discussion of norms (see Riehl 2005).
4. In contrast to indigenous minorities, German-speaking minorities have a standard variety at their disposal (i.e. the exogenous standard of Germany) which can be learned as a second language. In this case, it has to be taken into account that interlanguage effects might occur. Most of the speakers will acquire Standard German only to a certain extent and, as a result, will use learner varieties at different levels. Even speakers of the oldest generation who had instruction in German at school, display transfer phenomena from standard German into their regional variety – especially when they use it in a formal context (for a detailed discussion cf. Berend/Riehl 2008).
5. In many minority settings only a small number of speakers can be regarded as language experts. Consequently, there are almost no language authorities that could serve as model speakers.[12]

5. Evidence for Subsistent Norms

There are various ways to track subsistent norms or conventions within minority groups. One possibility is grammatical tests as used by Zürrer (1999). In this case, participants have to reflect on different possibilities and decide on a particular grammatical option. They have to access their linguistic competence in order to choose the form consistent with the grammatical norm. Another method is grammatical judgement tasks. In comparison to the first test, these tasks demonstrate different possibilities (norm consistent and non consistent variants) and the participants have to decide on the right item (by means of introspection). However, in this case, a passive knowledge of the exogenous standard – transfered in church services, television, or in language courses – cannot be excluded. Consequently, the answers given by the participants might not reflect the actual norm of usage in the respective community.

To cope with this problem other methods, such as the analysis of performance data, are required. One criteria for defining a regional norm is the frequency of use. Thus, in a case where almost no participants use a particular form (e.g. dative case marker), it can be assumed that this feature does not exist in the active repertoire of the speech community – although speakers would choose it in a grammatical judgement test. A corpus that contains data of natural spoken language may also contain sanctions pronounced by other speakers[13] as well as

---

[12] That is why, in many cases, visitors from Germany are considered language experts and are asked about the correctness of particular features.
[13] For a discussion of the impact of sanctions on a definition of norms see Hundt (in this volume).

self-corrections. But taking into account the problems discussed in section 4, it still remains rather problematic to obtain reliable evidence of what can be termed a 'norm' in this kind of setting.

6. Conclusion

Many speech communities that use German as a minority language display interesting common features of internal language change, but in different stages of development. However, it is difficult to define norms, especially when the community does not use an official written code of the language. In order to address conventions, variations among generations, individual speakers and transfer phenomena from the exogenous standard have to be taken into account. So it appears to be rather problematic to differentiate between conventional options and individual variations.

7. References

Ammon, Ulrich. 1995. *Die deutsche Sprache in Deutschland, Österreich und der Schweiz. Das Problem der nationalen Varietäten*. Berlin & New York: de Gruyter.

Berend, Nina. 1998. *Sprachliche Anpassung. Eine soziolinguistisch-dialektologische Untersuchung zum Rußlanddeutschen*. Tübingen: Narr.

Berend, Nina & Claudia Maria Riehl. 2008. "Russland". *Handbuch der deutschen Sprachminderheiten in Mittel- und Osteuropa* ed. L. M. Eichinger, A. Plewnia & C. M. Riehl, 17-58. Tübingen: Narr.

Berend, Nina & Klaus Jürgen Mattheier, eds. 1994. *Sprachinselforschung. Eine Gedenkschrift für Hugo Jedig*. Frankfurt: Lang.

Boas, Christian B. 2009. *The life and death of Texas German*. Durham.

Born, Renate. 2003. "Regression, convergence, internal development: The loss of the dative case in German-American dialects". *German Language Varieties Worldwide: Internal and External Perspectives* ed. W. D. Keel & K. J. Mattheier, 151-164. Frankfurt: Lang.

Clyne, Michael. 1991. *Community Languages: The Australian Experience*. Cambridge: University Press.

Clyne, Michael. 1992. "Pluricentric languages – Introduction". *Pluricentric Languages: Differing Norms in Different Nations* ed. M. Clyne, 1-9. Berlin & New York: de Gruyter.

Clyne, Michael. 1994. "What can we learn from Sprachinseln? Some observations on 'Australian German'". *Sprachinselforschung. Eine Gedenkschrift für Hugo Jedig* ed. N. Berend & K. J. Mattheier, 105-121. Frankfurt: Lang.

Clyne, Michael. 1995. *The German Language in a Changing Europe*. Cambridge: University Press.

Clyne, Michael. 2003. *Dynamics of Language Contact. English and Immigrant Languages.* Cambridge: University Press.

Dovalil, Vít. 2006. *Sprachnormenwandel im geschriebenen Deutsch an der Schwelle zum 21. Jahrhundert. Die Entwicklung in ausgesuchten Bereichen der Grammatik.* Frankfurt: Lang.

Eichinger, Ludwig M., Albrecht Plewnia & Claudia Maria Riehl, eds. 2008. *Handbuch der deutschen Sprachminderheiten in Mittel- und Osteuropa.* Tübingen: Narr.

Eisenberg, Peter. 2004. *Grundriß der deutschen Grammatik. Vol. 2: Der Satz.* Stuttgart & Weimar: Metzler.

Gilbert, Glenn & Janet Fuller. 2003. "The linguistic atlas of Texas German revisited". *German Language Varieties Worldwide: Internal and External Perspectives* ed. W. D. Keel & K. J. Mattheier, 165-176. Frankfurt: Lang.

Givón, Talmy. 1990. *Syntax: A Functional-Typological Introduction. Vol. II.* Amsterdam & Philadelphia: John Benjamins.

Heine, Bernd & Tania Kuteva. 2005. *Language Contact and Grammatical Change.* Cambridge: University Press.

Keel, William D. & Klaus J. Mattheier, eds. 2003. *German Language Varieties Worldwide: Internal and External Perspectives.* Frankfurt: Lang.

Kloss, Heinz. 1977. "Über einige Terminologie-Probleme der interlingualen Soziolinguistik". *Deutsche Sprache* 5. 224-237.

Louden, Mark L. 1994. "Syntactic change in multilingual speech islands". *Sprachinselforschung. Eine Gedenkschrift für Hugo Jedig* ed. N. Berend & K. J. Mattheier, 73-91. Frankfurt: Lang.

Riehl, Claudia M. 2009. *Sprachkontaktforschung. Eine Einführung.* 2nd revised ed. Tübingen: Narr.

Riehl, Claudia M. 2005. "Code-switching in bilinguals: impacts of mental processes and language awareness". *Proceedings of the 4th International Symposium on Bilingualism* ed. J. Cohen et al., 1945-1957. Somerville, MA: Cascadilla Press.

Riehl, Claudia M. 2008. "German-Romance language contact and language conflict in Italy, France and Belgium". *Multilingual Europe: Reflections on Language and Identity* ed. J. Warren & H. Benbow, 129-148. Cambridge: Cambridge Scholar Press.

Riehl, Claudia M. 2010. "Discontinous language spaces (Sprachinseln)". *Language and Space. An International Handbook of Linguistic Variation, Vol. 1* ed. P. Auer & J. E. Schmid, 332-354. Berlin & New York: de Gruyter.

Rosenberg, Peter. 2003. "Comparative speech island research: some results from studies in Russia and Brazil". *German Language Varieties Worldwide: Internal and External Perspectives* ed. W. D. Keel & K. J. Mattheier, 199-238. Frankfurt: Lang.

Rosenberg, Peter. 2005. "Dialect convergence in the German language islands (Sprachinseln)". *Dialect Change: Convergence and Divergence in European Languages* ed. P. Auer, P. Kerswill & F. Hinskens F., 221-235. Cambridge: University Press.

Thomason, Sarah G. & Terrence Kaufman. 1988. *Language Contact, Creolization, and Genetic Linguistics.* Berkeley, Los Angeles & Oxford: University of California Press.

Zürrer, Peter. 1999. *Sprachinseldialekte. Walserdeutsch im Aosta-Tal (Italien).* Aarau, Frankfurt & Salzburg: Sauerländer.

VarioLingua
Nonstandard – Standard – Substandard

Band 1 Klaus J. Mattheier / Edgar Radtke (Hrsg.): Standardisierung und Destandardisierung europäischer Nationalsprachen. 1997.

Band 2 Evelyn Ziegler: Sprachgebrauch – Sprachvariation – Sprachwissen. Eine Familienfallstudie. 1996.

Band 3 Göz Kaufmann: Varietätendynamik in Sprachkontaktsituationen. Attitüden und Sprachverhalten rußlanddeutscher Mennoniten in Mexiko und den USA. 1997.

Band 4 Rolf Kailuweit: Vom EIGENEN SPRECHEN. Eine Geschichte der spanisch-katalanischen Diglossie in Katalonien (1759-1859). 1997.

Band 5 Arno Scholz: Neo-standard e variazione diafasica nella canzone italiana degli anni Novanta. 1998.

Band 6 Jannis K. Androutsopoulos: Deutsche Jugendsprache. Untersuchungen zu ihren Strukturen und Funktionen. 1998.

Band 7 Jannis K. Androutsopoulos / Arno Scholz (Hrsg.): Jugendsprache – langue des jeunes – youth language. Linguistische und soziolinguistische Perspektiven. 1998.

Band 8 Verena Krus-Bühler: Strukturen des Wortschwunds in Lincolnshire: *Real-time* und *Apparent-time*. 1999.

Band 9 Michael Schreiber: Textgrammatik – Gesprochene Sprache – Sprachvergleich. Proformen im gesprochenen Französischen und Deutschen. 1999.

Band 10 Szilvia Deminger / Thorsten Fögen / Joachim Scharloth / Simone Zwickl (Hrsg.): Einstellungsforschung in der Soziolinguistik und Nachbardisziplinen – Studies in Language Attitudes. 2000.

Band 11 Francesca Sboarina: Il lessico medico nel *Dioscoride* di Pietro Andrea Mattioli. 2000.

Band 12 Klaus Mattheier (ed.): Dialect and Migration in a Changing Europe. 2000.

Band 13 Christian Timm: Das dreigliedrige Allokutionssystem des Italienischen in Neapel. 2001.

Band 14 Anne Cammenga-Waller: Substandard im Deutschen und Französischen. Lexikologische Studien zur zeitgenössischen Konsumliteratur. 2002.

Band 15 Thomas Krefeld (ed.): Spazio vissuto e dinamica linguistica. Varietà meridionali in Italia e in situazione de extraterritorialità. 2002.

Band 16 Pietro Maturi: Dialetti e substandardizzazione nel Sannio Beneventano. 2002.

Band 17 Christiane Wössner: *Qua parlón fa noantri!* Spracherhalt und ethnische Identität in Chipilo - einer Sprachinsel des Veneto in Mexiko. 2002.

Band 18 Jannis K. Androutsopoulos / Evelyn Ziegler (Hrsg.): „Standardfragen". Soziolinguistische Perspektiven auf Sprachgeschichte, Sprachkontakt und Sprachvariation. 2003.

Band 19 Christel Schlindwein: *...je ne me lasse point de te lire.* Zur Sprachgeschichte des Alltags in französischen Briefen in Deutschland (1792–1813). 2003.

Band 20 Alexandra N. Lenz / Edgar Radtke / Simone Zwickl (Hrsg.): Variation im Raum. Variation and Space. 2004.

Band 21 Szilvia Deminger: Spracherhalt und Sprachverlust in einer Sprachinselsituation. Sprache und Identität bei der deutschen Minderheit in Ungarn. 2004.

Band 22 Dirk Deissler: Die entnazifizierte Sprache. Sprachpolitik und Sprachregelung in der Besatzungszeit. 2., korrigierte und ergänzte Auflage. 2006.

Band 23   Alexandra N. Lenz / Klaus J. Mattheier (Hrsg.): Varietäten – Theorie und Empirie. 2005.

Band 24   Danielle A. V. Löw-Wiebach: Language Attitudes and Language Use in Pitmedde (Aberdeenshire). 2005.

Band 25   Claudia Bluhm-Faust: Die Pädagogisierung der deutschen Standardsprache im 19. Jahrhundert am Beispiel Badens. 2005.

Band 26   Rembert Eufe: *Sta lengua ha un privilegio tanto grando.* Status und Gebrauch des Venezianischen in der Republik Venedig. 2006.

Band 27   Nina Berend / Elisabeth Knipf-Komlósi (Hrsg.): Sprachinselwelten – The World of Language Islands. Entwicklung und Beschreibung der deutschen Sprachinseln am Anfang des 21. Jahrhunderts.The Developmental Stages and the Description of German Language Islands at the Beginning of the 21st Century. 2006.

Band 28   Winifred V. Davies / Nils Langer: The Making of Bad Language. Lay Linguistic Stigmatisations in German: Past und Present. 2006.

Band 29   Christian H. Münch: Sprachpolitik und gesellschaftliche Alphabetisierung. Zur Entwicklung der Schreibkompetenz in Katalonien seit 1975. 2006.

Band 30   Janet Spreckels: *Britneys, Fritten, Gangschta und wir:* Identitätskonstitution in einer Mädchengruppe. Eine ethnographisch-gesprächsanalytische Untersuchung. 2006.

Band 31   Isolde Opielka: *Residencia tomada a los jueces de apelación, por Alonso de Zuazo, Hispaniola, 1517.* Partielle kommentierte Edition, diskurstraditionelle und grapho-phonologische Aspekte. 2008.

Band 32   Brigitte E. Lambert: Family Language Transmission. Actors, Issues, Outcomes. 2008.

Band 33   Doris Schüpbach: Shared Languages, Shared Identities, Shared Stories. A Qualitative Study of Life Stories by Immigrants from German-speaking Switzerland in Australia. 2008.

Band 34   Annalisa Buonocore: Varietà dialettali microareali della Costiera Amalfitana. 2009.

Band 35   Ellen Rötterink: Parler scout en réunion. Analyse du style communicatif d'un groupe de jeunes. 2009.

Band 36   Jo-anne Hughson: Diversity and Changing Values in Address. Spanish Address Pronoun Usage in an Intercultural Immigrant Context. 2009.

Band 37   Peter Gilles / Joachim Scharloth / Evelyn Ziegler (Hrsg.): Variatio delectat. Empirische Evidenzen und theoretische Passungen sprachlicher Variationen. Herausgegeben von Peter Gilles, Joachim Scharloth und Evelyn Ziegler für Klaus J. Mattheier zum 65. Geburtstag. 2010.

Band 38   Csilla Anna Szabó: Language shift und Code-mixing. Deutsch-ungarisch-rumänischer Sprachkontakt in einer dörflichen Gemeinde in Nordwestrumänien. 2010.

Band 39   Till Stellino: Kommunikations- und Sachwandel in der süditalienischen Weinproduktion. Eine Neukonzeption von *Wörter und Sachen.* 2010.

Band 40   Alexandra N. Lenz / Albrecht Plewnia (eds.): Grammar between Norm and Variation. 2010.

www.peterlang.de

Przemysław Tajsner

Aspects of the Grammar of Focus
A Minimalist View

Frankfurt am Main, Berlin, Bern, Bruxelles, New York, Oxford, Wien, 2008.
393 pp., num. graph.
Polish Studies in English Language and Literature. Edited by Jacek Fisiak. Vol. 24
ISBN 978-3-631-57955-8 · pb. € 56.50*

The book examines the aspects of focus within the recent minimalist paradigm. Focus is viewed here as a grammar's response to the requirements of the systems external to (narrowly defined) language. Thus, the properties of focus are explored at the two interfaces: syntax-phonology and syntax-semantics. The book surveys some recent views on the interface and left-periphery status of focus. With respect to the semantics of focus, the book argues for its tripartite division into: information, non-exhaustive identification, and exhaustive identification. It further contains a proposal of the phase-based derivation of sentences featuring focus in English, and finally, offers an account of Polish, in which focus interestingly correlates with the phenomenon of scrambling.

Contents: Focus · The Minimalist Program · Syntax · Grammar · Nuclear Stress · Syntax-phonology Interface · Syntax-semantics Interface · Left-periphery · Topic · Phases · Derivation by Phases · Scrambling · Spell Out · Cleft Sentences · Emphatic Stress · Probe-goal · Agree · Interface Condition · Last Resort · Feature Checking · Tropicalization · Functional Heads · Information Structure

Frankfurt am Main · Berlin · Bern · Bruxelles · New York · Oxford · Wien
Distribution: Verlag Peter Lang AG
Moosstr. 1, CH-2542 Pieterlen
Telefax 0041 (0)32/376 17 27

*The €-price includes German tax rate
Prices are subject to change without notice
Homepage http://www.peterlang.de